Ethnicity and
Populist Mobilization

Ethnicity and Populist Mobilization

Political Parties, Citizens and Democracy in South India

NARENDRA SUBRAMANIAN

OXFORD
UNIVERSITY PRESS

OXFORD

UNIVERSITY PRESS

YMCA Library Building, Jai Singh Road, New Delhi 110001

Oxford University Press is a department of the University of Oxford. It furthers the
University's objective of excellence in research, scholarship, and education
by publishing worldwide in

Oxford   New York
Auckland   Bangkok   Buenos Aires   Cape Town   Chennai
Dar es Salaam   Delhi   Hong Kong   Istanbul   Karachi   Kolkata
Kuala Lumpur   Madrid   Melbourne   Mexico City   Mumbai   Nairobi
São Paulo   Shanghai   Singapore   Taipei   Tokyo   Toronto
and an associated company in Berlin

Oxford is a registered trade mark of Oxford University Press
in the UK and in certain other countries

Published in India
By Oxford University Press, New Delhi

© Narendra Subramanian 1999

The moral rights of the author have been asserted
Database right Oxford University Press (maker)
First published 1999
Oxford India Paperbacks 1999
Second impression 2002

ISBN 0 19 565223 1

Typeset in Garamond TTF
By Excellent Typesetters, Pitampura, Delhi 110034
Printed in India at Rashtriya Printers, Delhi 110032
and published by Manzar Khan, Oxford University Press
YMCA Library Building, Jai Singh Road, New Delhi 110001

In Memory of
P. Venkatarama Das (1906–96)
and for Mini

Contents

Contents

Tables

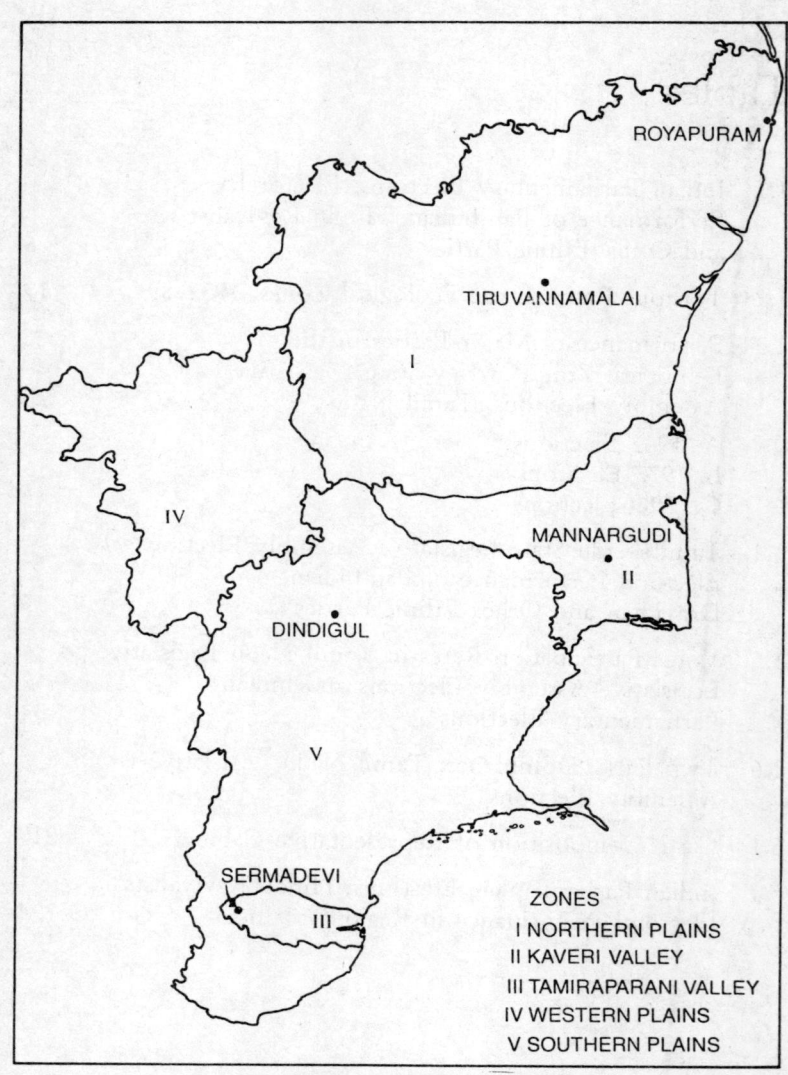

ROYAPURAM

TIRUVANNAMALAI

I

IV

MANNARGUDI

II

DINDIGUL

V

SERMADEVI

III

ZONES

I NORTHERN PLAINS
II KAVERI VALLEY
III TAMIRAPARANI VALLEY
IV WESTERN PLAINS
V SOUTHERN PLAINS

MAP : TAMIL NADU

Abbreviations

ADMK	Anna Dravida Munnetra Kazhagam (Anna's Party for the Progress of Dravidam)
AITUC	All India Trade Union Congress
BJP	Bharatiya Janata Party (Indian People's Party)
Congress	Indian National Congress
CPI	Communist Party of India
CPI (M)	Communist Party of India (Marxist)
DK	Dravidar Kazhagam (Party of the Dravidians)
DMK	Dravida Munnetra Kazhagam (Party for the Progress of Dravidam)
INTUC	Indian National Trade Union Congress
LPF	Thozhilaalar Munnetra Kazhagam (Federation for the Progress of Labour)
MDMK	Marumalarchchi Dravida Munnetra Kazhagam (Revitalized Party for the Progress of Dravidam)
PMK	Paattaali Makkal Katchi (Party of the Toiling People)
RSS	Rashtriya Swayamsevak Sangh (National Service Society)
VHP	Vishwa Hindu Parishad (World Hindu Council)

Acknowledgements

This book grew out of a doctoral dissertation I completed at the Department of Political Science at MIT. I was fortunate to receive support and encouragement from many during the various phases of this project.

The field work was supported by the American Institute of Indian Studies, the American Council of Learned Societies and the Social Science Research Council. Grants from the American Council of Learned Societies and the Social Science Research Council, the MacArthur Foundation in association with the Centre for International Studies at MIT, the Augustana College Research Fund and the McGill Faculty Research Grants Committee helped me while I wrote my dissertation and later reworked it.

The Centre for the Study of Developing Societies, Delhi, and the Madras Institute of Development Studies granted me affiliation during my field work. I was given permission to use the libraries of the Anna Arivaalayam, the Periyar Thidal, the University of Madras, the Madras Institute of Development Studies, *The Hindu*, *The Indian Express* and the Tamil Nadu state archives in Madras; the Institute for World Affairs library and the Nehru Memorial Library in Delhi; the Library of Congress and the Van Pelt Library at the University of Pennsylvania, in the United States; and the India Office Library and the University of London library in the United Kingdom. The Centre for International Studies at MIT, Augustana College and McGill University afforded me congenial settings to work on my manuscript at different stages.

The project was deeply influenced by the sharp criticism and helpful suggestions from the members of my dissertation committee—Myron Weiner, David Washbrook, Josh Cohen and Jonathan Fox. David Washbrook and James Manor encouraged me to undertake a study of South Indian politics. Stanley Tambiah and Harbans Mukhia extended their warm encouragement and practical help in my efforts to convert my dissertation into the book. Amrita Basu, Tarini Bedi, Michael Brecher, Vince Brown, Roger Karapin, Minakshi Menon, Phil Oxhorn, John Rogers,

Ajantha Subramanian, Sonia Verma, Crawford Young, Maren Zerrifi and anonymous referees offered many valuable comments on drafts of the manuscript.

For helping me gain access to documents and interviewees, I am particularly indebted to Sathyavani Muthu, Murasoli Maran, C. Subramaniam, J. C. D. Prabhakaran, K. Nagaimugan, K. Veeramani, S. Guhan, D. K. Oza, M. Balasubramaniam, A. Pannerselvam, K. Anguswami, B. Valarmathi, T. Govindarajan, B. Neelakantan, Aa. Subramaniam, A. Natarajan and the late N. D. Sundaravadivelu. I am grateful to many friends and relatives for their help with practical aspects of my field work—S. C. Govindarajan, K. S. Ranganathan, V. Vasanthi Devi, P. V. Das, Ajantha Subramanian, K. S. Subramanian, L. M. Sakthivel, Renu Addlakha, K. Nagaraj, A. Nityanandam, K. S. Santhanakrishnan, K. Chandru, A. Vidyasagar, Jayaprakash, Mushtaq, Sundar, N. Karuppannan, Swaminathan, Pirai. Arivazhagan, Nadanam, Srinivasan and Chinnaraj; and to others for their warm hospitality— my late grandparents, V. Janaki Das and P. V. Das, Deepti Mehrotra, Praveen Kumar, K. S. Rajagopal Mudaliar, K. Santhanakrishnan, Sanjay Pradhan and P. T. Venugopal. Many interviewees were generous with their time, sometimes at considerable inconvenience.

My research assistants—Indhumathi Ravishankar, T. N. Gopalan, Tarini Bedi, B. Ramesh, V. Bhashyam, S. Shankarraj, Paula Bub, Billy Gathings and Kate Goodrich—helped make the study what it is. M. Shankar helped me take my first steps in Lotus and D-Base. Jane Tiedge patiently typed parts of the manuscript. Tarini Bedi helped me bring it all together at the end. Special thanks are due to Nitasha Devasar and Anupama Arora for overseeing the production of the book and giving it the last lick of paint.

I met Minakshi Menon while I did my field work and she has been my very best friend since then. Mini's support, understanding, patience, and personal and intellectual company sustained me through this study. Spooky, a more recent housemate, has also been there for me, though more silently.

Preface

I suspect this book is both timely and untimely. It is timely because it concerns ongoing ethnic upheaval and points to responses that could direct a politics of the kindred towards building communities of difference. It is untimely as it highlights a somewhat unnoticed case in which the politics of blood did not lead to rivers of blood, contrary to the predominant trend.

The restriction of violent ethnic conflict has typically been attributed to the crafting of institutions appropriate for conflict management by far-sighted statesmen, or the emergence of such institutions because ethnic leaders locked in combat found them to be of mutual benefit. It is such solutions that most scholars and policy makers continue to seek to ethnic conflict, with diminishing success. This book points to other ways in which ethnic conflict has been curtailed. It shows that an active citizenry and flexible leaders may urge the very institutions formed to promote a politics of the kindred towards some tolerance of difference.

My work does not place me squarely within any of the fuzzily bounded theoretical/methodological camps that dominate political science, the trade I am licensed to practise. I draw from different theoretical traditions and disciplines to explain specific changes in South Indian politics and advance more general arguments about factors shaping mass politics. Although I march without a flag, I briefly indicate here some theoretical traditions I draw on or depart from, and my personal links to the story that follows.

Historical institutionalism has drawn the attention of political scientists to institutional changes over long time spans, which is a major concern of this book. However, very few scholars in this tradition have offered compelling accounts of how the norms which govern institutions are shaped and changed. I have drawn from historical anthropology to understand the formation and reconstruction of norms, and how this shapes the strategic orientations of institutions and the varied outlook of their members.

Rational choice theory claims to explore the micro-foundations of political action. I pursue this aim by departing from the way

rational choice theory has been practised by most of its proponents. Not only did I study the bases of individual motivations
through micro-level ethnography, I take individuals embedded in
particular social contexts as my units of analysis. I thereby explain
strategic interaction without resort to game theory. Ethnography,
which I embraced just as it was getting marginalized within
anthropology, helped me provide thick descriptions of mass
mentalities and offered many insights into policy implementation
and coalition formation. It helped me link local-level decisions and
actions to macro-level institutional, discursive and policy changes.

I draw two lessons from interpretive social theory, which aid
my explanatory project. First, as explanation requires an empathic
understanding of the meaning context of action, students of mass
politics need to feel the diverse passions that drive it, although
without completely sharing them. Second, as scholars are inevitably engaged with what they study (disengagement being merely a
form of engagement one may choose), objectivity requires recognizing and acknowledging one's modes of engagement, and choosing and changing them consciously. Both these considerations have
taken me back to features of Weberian sociology marginalized until
recently in the social sciences.

The reflexive turn in anthropology and cultural studies has led
many of its proponents to abandon a concern with explanation.
The recognition that many features of society, including patterns
of knowledge generation, are constructed through the interplay of
imagination and power has increased, rather than diminished, my
interest in explaining the ways in which these aspects of the social
universe are crafted. Interpretation is important to understanding
the interactions between social context and subjectivity—of both
social actors and observers. However, I remain convinced that
explanation is necessary for us to appreciate the formation of the
social contexts we study and to assess the scope for changes in these
contexts. Moreover, explanation is crucial if we are to draw lessons
from our study of particular social contexts that can orient us as
scholars and citizens in these as well as other contexts. As Weber
showed, scholars can provide explanations even without stepping
entirely outside the hermeneutic circle enveloping them and their
objects of knowledge.

Some political scientists assume that the close study of particular
contexts can only lead to atheoretical and idiographic narratives.

However, studies of this kind have for long helped generate theories when their findings were placed in a comparative context. In this study, I formulate theories of mass politics by placing the detailed empirical analysis of a case in a comparative perspective. Such detailed analysis, which is generally not feasible in single-authored studies encompassing many cases, is crucial to make theoretical abstractions come alive and capture the texture of a rapidly changing world.

Although the need for theory-driven research has acquired the sanctity of common sense in political science, one too often finds pre-existing theories driving the research, rather than research yielding the theories. If we have theoretical ambitions, we should make theory while we tell stories, not just fine-tune already formed theoretical orientations. We need to adopt flexible research designs, open not just to the falsification of hypotheses, but to the ongoing generation of new ones if we find that we not only anticipated the wrong answers, but also asked the wrong questions. My use of ethnography and textual interpretation to supplement methods more commonly employed in political science has helped me in this regard, as has my reliance on diverse theoretical influences.

I view the explanations I provide primarily as contributions to comparative political sociology and have crafted them accordingly. But, they may be read otherwise (e.g. as empirical social theory, materialist social/cultural history, misguided anthropology), especially as I engage diverse bodies of literature. Besides, I inevitably speak in many voices in this book because of two kinds of tensions: between my training in Western social science, now globalized, and my engagement in studying the 'non-Western' society in which I was born and raised; and between my analytical bent and my fondness for story-telling.

My explanations are not only a result of recovering and synthesizing elements of existing theories. I attempted to maintain a peripheral vision for what lay outside the frames of these theories, and refocused my sights periodically on important questions I glimpsed on the margins. This required an understanding of how features of my personal and professional socialization shaped the questions I asked and the answers I anticipated. In the course of my research, I came to understand better how my self-presentations as a diasporic Indian (but culturally rooted Tamil) and declassed intellectual of colour influenced my position as a scholar and the responses of those I studied. Understanding brought with it some personal change, which required overcoming much internal resistance, and changes in my scholarly postures.

As what we are and what we become influence our work, the arguments we advance are better if we clarify our relationship with our work, partly because they thereby become easier to criticize. It is only by doing so that we can break fully with a past in which colonizers, presumed to be detached observers, arrogated to themselves the power to speak of colonized societies. The acknowledgement of the scholar's links to the society studied is especially pertinent in this case as my life has been closely entwined with the story I tell here, which is therefore my story in more ways than one. I indicate how early life experiences and people important in my life have linked me to the story I tell, of the Dravidian parties of south India. This is another modest step towards claiming for everyone the ability to speak of India's multi-faceted present.

The Dravidian movement has for almost a century been closely connected with many features of life in Tamil Nadu, where I spent my first fourteen years and to which I returned periodically thereafter. However, the caste origins of my parents defies the implacable antagonism which the early Dravidianists proclaimed between Brahmins and other Tamils—my father is a Brahmin and my mother a 'non-Brahmin', i.e. descended from two intermediate mercantile/artisanal castes. Nevertheless, Dravidianist appeals to caste and language influenced the outlook and experience of some members of my family. My maternal great grandfathers were associated with the non-Brahmin movement which arose in the late colonial period. One, V. Chakkarai Chettiar, was an important 'non-Brahmin' public figure (trade unionist, theologian, city politician) at a time when Brahmins dominated many public spheres, a participant in some non-Brahmin conferences and a friend of E. V. Ramaswami Naicker (popularly called Periar), the first major Dravidianist leader. The other, Ponnuswami Naidu, was a district-level leader of the Justice Party, an early Dravidianist organization. While my great grandfathers died before I was born, my kinship with them influenced how some interviewees saw me. Others saw me as a Brahmin despite my 'non-Brahmin' upbringing, confirming my sense, already sharpened by diasporic living, that identities are socially constructed.

The outlook of my maternal grandfather, P. Venkatarama Das (to whom the book is dedicated), gave me an early feeling for the cultural soil on which Dravidianism grew. My grandfather was a member of the Congress party (henceforth Congress), but shared the staunch anti-Brahminism of the early Dravidianists. He often related tales of 'Brahmin arrogance and atrocities', quoted poems critical of Brahmins and frequently recounted a chance he had to meet Periar. The Dravidianist patriarch evidently appreciated my grandfather's commitment to overcoming caste barriers, shown in his promotion of inter-caste marriages within his family. My grandfather also felt a strong attachment to the Tamil language and its literature, which fed Dravidianism too. Invocations of Murugan, whom Tamil revivalists glorify as the 'god of the Tamils', were among his favourite lullabies, with which he lulled me and other children to sleep. He was nevertheless not averse to Periar's atheism.

While conceiving the social world in terms of essentialized ethnic categories, my grandfather engaged very closely across ethnic boundaries. People were to him 'Muslims', 'Naidus', 'Chettiars', yet equally friends. More significantly, he married a woman of a different caste and religion, and warmly accepted a Brahmin as his son-in-law despite his anti-Brahminism. I have grown to find my grandfather's world, where ethnicity played a role in harmonious interaction, in grave peril. Knowing him helped me appreciate the rich texture of this world and contributed to my urge to defend its defensible features. This appreciation and this urge are crucial motivations behind this study. It was therefore only apt that my grandfather's home town be one of my local cases, and that he helped me greatly in my research there. To my regret, he did not live to see this book published.

My father, K. S. Subramanian, too had a feel for popular culture and politics, although he became sufficiently westernized to be somewhat distant from the soil of Dravidianism. Despite being a Brahmin, growing up poor and rising through education helped him empathize with the emergent petty intelligentsia that flocked to the Dravidianist banner as he attained adulthood. His accounts of inter-caste relations in the stratified Tamiraparani valley, where he lived as a child, helped me understand non-Brahminist outrage.

My personal experiences also contributed to my understanding of Dravidianism's offshoots. The *Dravida Munnetra Kazhagam*

(DMK) supplanting Congress from power in Tamil Nadu is my earliest political memory. The dismay of most adults in my family at the DMK's victory, partly because a great uncle was a major Congress leader, made for a stark contrast with the joyous celebration I saw on the streets. This discordance stimulated my interest in understanding ethnic and populist politics, whose spirit was so foreign to the culturally vacuous brand of secularism then popular among the professional élite, including my parents.

Soon after the DMK assumed power, I happened to meet Sathyavani Muthu, who was then the DMK's most important woman leader as well as its most prominent scheduled caste (untouchable) leader, when her daughter's family moved into a house we were vacating. I learnt that Sathyavani Muthu's son-in-law was named Ravana Das, a most unusual name as Ravana is the chief villain in standard versions of the Hindu epic, the Ramayana. As the background to his naming was explained to me, I came to know of the Dravidianist reading of the Ramayana as a fable of the Aryan invasion of southern India. This inversion, according to which Ravana was the righteous defender of the indigenous Dravidian community rather than an evil abductor of other men's wives, seemed unlike any of my parents' straight modernist narratives and made me feel that there was more to the DMK than I had been told. Thrilled to hear of the circumstances under which we had met much earlier, Sathyavani Muthu extended me considerable help during my field work.

When I was about eleven, a major split arose in the DMK, with the expulsion of the popular film star, M. G. Ramachandran (MGR). The new party he formed, the *Anna Dravida Munnetra Kazhagam* (ADMK), contested its first by-election in my grandfather's home town of Dindigul, where I then lived. I attended many of the public meetings of the election campaign and sensed the surge in the ADMK's popularity and the DMK's decline. Although I was attracted by neither MGR's films nor the social outlook associated with them, I was moved by the popular sympathy MGR evoked. I saw how far removed Congress was from the popular pulse, as some of its orators thought they had a chance to win this election, in which the party fared miserably.

Periar died in his nineties later that year and my grandfather hung up a portrait of his in his room, in a gesture through which Tamils show their respect for deities, deceased family members and political leaders. I noticed that no other portraits adorned the walls of the room. This surprised me as my grandfather had been an active Congress member and wore *khadi* (homespun cloth) in true Gandhian fashion. This experience evoked my interest in the deep significance Periar and non-Brahminism had for many Tamils, independent of party allegiances.

The year I spent at my grandparents' house has a bearing on this study in yet another way. I had been educated until then in schools in which English was the medium of instruction and Tamil given limited significance. So deep is the colonial legacy that students are prohibited from speaking any Indian language other than during language classes in such schools. The time I spent in Dindigul in the mid-1970s helped me improve my formal Tamil and brought me in close contact with Tamil revivalism, particularly in the person of my Tamil teacher, *Pulavar* Ramaswami. The facility which I then began to acquire in the formal Tamil of public discourse was renewed by my exchanges with enthusiastic and eloquent Dravidianist activists in the course of my research.

I have barely acknowledged contact with female relatives so far. This absence, partly a reflection of women's marginality in public life, is nevertheless peculiar as my mother, V. Vasanthi Devi, has been a somewhat prominent advocate of women's rights, ethnic harmony and improvements in higher education. My mother has been distant from popular cultural fora, Dravidianism's crucible. I suspect this distance arose partly because Dravidianism was often articulated in aggressive masculine tones, the belligerence of which *sometimes* turned inward in acts of self-immolation, although it *rarely* turned outward in the form of massive violence towards others. My wife, Minakshi Menon (to whom this book is also dedicated), helped me see this and much more.

Notions of protecting a 'community of mothers' have been among the ADMK's central appeals, women were among the ADMK's core supporters and a woman, J. Jayalalitha, became the party's leader after its initial leader died. My position as a man hampered my appreciation of the ADMK's gendered appeals and support base, partly because it restricted my ability to interview women and discuss their sentiments. The sexual persona MGR assumed in his films helped him attract women, and men too. But, it is not easy for a male stranger to raise such issues with women in India. Perhaps the problem was that I remained a stranger to most of the women I interviewed, while to some of the men I almost became a friend after hours of conversation over tea, snacks or meals. As my ethnic and class identities are both ambiguous and fluid, I found ways around various delicate problems with male interviewees. I could not switch wavelengths as readily to hear women's voices, partly because my gender identity is more fixed, both because of and despite myself, and resorted too often to inferring women's sentiments from their actions.

A well-meaning historian once said that he aimed to give the voiceless a voice. I have no such pretensions, for the 'voiceless' already have voices. The subaltern speaks. The problem is: can we hear her? We need to tune our ears to hear other voices, but be aware that when we depict what we hear the best we can do is to speak in our own voices. In the ambiguous tones in which Western social science and post-colonial ambition engage with each other in the succeeding pages, I fancy that at moments I found my voice.

As a work of social science, this book adopts a type of narrative which some may consider particularly inadequate to tell the story of the Dravidian parties. So much were cinema, theatre, novels and short stories the stuff of Dravidianist politics that perhaps it is such media that can best capture Dravidianism's characteristic features. The idea of fiction as a mirror for Dravidianist politics occurred to me when I was told how Annadurai, the DMK's founding leader, frequently wore make-up and acted in plays during the DMK's early years. I visualized an image of the leader getting make-up applied in a thatched hut, his face turned towards a viewer or photographer who has caught him by surprise. This image felt like the inspiration for a novel or a film, and others like it conjured up by field work roam my imagination. But, as I have chosen to make theory while telling stories, this is the work I offer you.

Montreal
December 1997

Note: Proper names are Romanized as they tend to be in Indian English and Tamil expressions transliterated to convey the standard pronunciation. All translations are mine.

I

Introduction

ETHNICITY, CONFLICT AND PLURALISM

Ethnic political forces have grown almost throughout the world over the last two decades, often inducing violent conflict, threatening the integrity of nation-states, and causing the erosion of pluralism and democracy. Concern about these trends has motivated considerable research into the construction of social identities and the determination of the strategies of ethnic movements and parties. These studies provide abundant evidence that currently salient social identities and ethnic cleavages, and the notions of cultural tradition upheld by ethnic mobilizers are of recent manufacture, not deeply rooted in history. Many of them show that states have promoted particular visions of ethnic and national traditions[1] and shaped the incentives of ethnic mobilizers through constitutional design and social policy.[2] Other studies have traced ways in which the formation of centralized states, the colonial encounters that often accompanied this process, and the emergence of 'print capitalism' encouraged the formation of sharply bounded ethno-national groups.[3]

Not only have state formation and state policy been considered crucial in shaping ethnic identities and ethnic political strategies, but many scholars have also seen the promotion by states of compacts between ethnic élites to share power, ration resources and regulate conflict as the key to maintaining stability and democracy in culturally diverse societies. Scholars and publicists have extolled the accommodative capacity of the consociational arrangements seen in Lebanon, Belgium and Switzerland, the federal systems which exist or once existed in the former Soviet

---

[1] See Anderson's (1983) discussion of 'official nationalism', Laitin's (1986) notion of hegemonic states and Pandey's (1990) analysis of colonial historiography.

[2] See Horowitz (1985), Banton (1983), and Laitin (1992).

[3] See Hobsbawm & Ranger (1983), Anderson (1983) and Dirks (1992).

Union and Yugoslavia, Canada and India, and the preferential policies instituted in the United States and Malaysia.[4]

However, such institutions collapsed in different ways in Cyprus, Lebanon, Czechoslovakia, Yugoslavia and the Soviet Union, suffered erosion in India, provoked strong opposition in Canada, and have been beset with much uncertainty since they were reinstated in Lebanon. They have endured only in countries like Belgium and Switzerland where ethnic tensions were relatively weak before they were established, or in those like Malaysia where political competition has been abridged and the political dominance of the ethnic majority enshrined. This shows that state-crafted accommodative institutions do not ensure the maintenance of pluralism in contexts of growing ethnic mobilization. This is because the incentives for moderation that such institutions offer ethnic mobilizers rarely produce substantive and enduring commitments to tolerance even if they do influence their tactics. Mobilizers who once accepted such institutions may challenge them when faced with new pressures and opportunities or be replaced by emergent counter-élites which launch such challenges.

If accommodative institutions have led to different outcomes, this has not been mainly due to the nature of the ethnic compacts which led to their emergence or the visions that inspired the states which sponsored these compacts, but to changing interactions between political mobilizers and society. This urges one to consider how the trajectories of ethnic politics are shaped not just by state-ethnic élite interactions but also by the ways in which ethnic parties and movements transact with different social groups amidst ongoing social change. While drawing valuable lessons from state-centred approaches to explaining political change, whose proponents called for 'bringing the state back in',[5] I signal my departure from them with the slogan 'bring society back in'.

I use the term ethnicity to refer to communities based on a kinship imagined to exist by virtue of shared cultural bonds of different kinds—language, religion, race, tribe, caste, sect, etc. This is a broader use of the term than that adopted by some scholars, who distinguish ethnic groups from religious and racial ones. I

[4] See Lijphart (1977, 1996), Horowitz (1985), Connor (1984), Brass (1991) and Sowell (1990).

[5] Rueschemeyer, Evans & Skocpol (1985).

prefer the broader usage as religious and racial bonds are often bases on which groups imagine themselves to share 'blood ties', histories and destinies, much as other groups do on the basis of language, tribe or caste ties, and with similar effects. As with conceptions of linguistic or tribal groups, the boundaries of religious and racial groups and the norms said to characterize these groups are constructed in varying ways, having varying implications for relations within these groups and between group members and others. Further, conflicts over varying constructions of identity follow broadly similar patterns in cases of racial identity (e.g. visions of African-American identity propagated by du Bois and Garvey, King and Malcolm X), religious identity (e.g. modernist and revivalist articulations of Muslim identity), linguistic identity (e.g. pan-Indian and Tamil separatist notions of Tamil identity) and tribal identity (e.g. conceptions of Zulu identity upheld by the followers of the African National Congress [ANC] and the Inkatha).

Shared cultural features do not constitute ethnicity unless they are bases on which community is imagined, and ethnic boundaries shift with the way they are imagined. Political mobilization plays a crucial role in the formation of imagined communities. It did in influencing Serbs, Croats and Bosnian Muslims to regard themselves as distinct communities despite sharing the Serbo-Croat language, just as it did in inducing many Hindus and Muslims to consider themselves members of distinct communities while sharing the dialects of the Indo-Gangetic plain, and in urging Bangladeshis, predominantly Muslim, to see themselves as distinct from their fellow Muslims in today's Pakistan.[6]

I use the term *social pluralism* to refer to the existence of many active associations significantly autonomous of the state and of one another. It does not exclusively denote ethnic diversity, although social pluralism would enable citizens to affirm ethnic difference. The adjective 'social' is added to distinguish this concept from that of *organizational pluralism*, introduced in Chapter II. Where the distinction is not crucial, I refer to social pluralism as just pluralism. I define democracy somewhat minimally to denote polities with universal adult franchise, the regular conduct of free elections, the control by popular representatives over public

---

[6] Banks (1996) explores the intellectual history of the notion of ethnicity and many variants of this notion.

decision-making and respect for civil rights. 'Pluralist democracy' denotes a democratic polity characterized by social pluralism.[7]

Although I define democracy in terms of somewhat minimal conditions, I value the ideals motivating more ambitious conceptions of democracy (e.g. to denote polities equally responsive to all the preferences of all its citizens). Indeed, mobilization impelled by such ambitious visions is necessary to ensure the maintenance of basic democratic institutions. I nevertheless opt for the minimal definition as I value the conditions included in it, and even these conditions have proven difficult to realize and sustain. More ambitious visions of democracy are, however, indispensable guides for judgement and action.[8]

India was, until recently, considered a signal success case in the containment of ethnic conflict and the preservation of tolerance and democracy amidst cultural diversity. India's success in this regard has been attributed to the state defining itself as secular, thereby rejecting the claims of religious groups to political rights; its adoption of federalism, with states formed along lines of language use; its threats to repress secession; and its introduction of preferential quotas for groups (largely castes) deemed underprivileged.[9] The success of these policies helped pan-Indian parties—i.e. parties giving all the ethnic groups inhabiting India an equal role in their visions of political community—dominate Indian politics through the first three post-colonial decades.

However, pluralism and democracy have been abridged and accommodative institutions weakened in India over the last two decades. The national government suppressed democracy briefly in the mid-1970s and has resorted more readily to repression since then, especially in border regions where armed secessionist movements have arisen and have continued despite the repression. Further, religious revivalism has grown rapidly, leading to periodic religious riots through much of the country. This is part of a broader trend of the growth of forces presenting ethnic alternatives to pan-Indian nationalism. The share of such parties, which I call ethnic parties, in the popular vote has increased from under

[7] I draw these definitions from Schmitter (1992), Schmitter & Karl (1991) and Dahl (1982).

[8] Chapters II and VII elaborate on this.

[9] See Brass (1991: 111–219, 300–48) and Weiner (1989: 21–37, 77–95).

15 per cent in the first three post-colonial elections to a little over a third in the elections of the 1990s (see Table 1.1). The electoral support of pan-Indian parties has commensurately declined, especially since the late 1980s. While only one Indian state was ruled by an ethnic party until the mid-1960s, ethnic parties have ruled sixteen of India's twenty-six states at different points since then, in many cases for significant periods.[10]

Secessionist violence and state repression, which have been most widespread in Punjab and Kashmir in northern India, have curbed pluralism and the regular conduct of free elections. Yet, ethnic militancy appeared at one point to have been successfully accommodated in these states. Kashmir was incorporated into the Indian union in 1947 through an agreement with the major Kashmiri leaders which accorded this state a special status. The Indian government also created a separate state in 1966 for the speakers of the Punjabi language, of whom the Sikhs form the majority, in response to an agitation led by the Akali Dal, the major Sikh party. Nevertheless, these measures proved inadequate to restrain secessionist militancy by the 1980s.[11]

The state of Tamil Nadu, in southern India, has witnessed contrasting outcomes, which this book explores in detail. The success of ethnic mobilizers has provoked little violent conflict in this state, and has even promoted the growth of political participation and autonomous associational activity, and aided the representation of emergent groups. Further, the success of appeals to identities based mainly on language and caste has inhibited the

---

[10] Jammu & Kashmir was the sole state ruled by an ethnic party until the mid-1960s. Since then, ethnic parties have ruled Tamil Nadu, Andhra Pradesh, Punjab, Assam, Nagaland, Mizoram, Goa, Uttar Pradesh, Madhya Pradesh, Maharashtra, Gujarat, Rajasthan, Himachal Pradesh, Sikkim and Delhi, in addition to Jammu & Kashmir. Electoral results only understate the increased appeal of ethnic alternatives to pan-Indianism.

[11] Discontent grew among Kashmiri Muslims and Sikhs partly because the central government failed to implement crucial aspects of bargains made with ethnic leaders—the conduct of a plebiscite to determine Kashmir's eventual status (independent, part of India, or part of Pakistan) and the transfer of some regions to Punjab. However, secessionist militancy did not erupt in either case (especially Kashmir) until well after the government had reneged on its commitments. See Ganguly (1997), Thomas (1992), Brass (1991: 111–237) and Oberoi (1994).

TABLE 1.1 Indian Parliamentary Elections

Electoral Performance of Pan-Indian, Hindu Revivalist and Other Ethnic Parties[a]

Share of Valid Vote (percentage-wise)

Party	Election year										
	1952	1957	1962	1967	1971	1977[c]	1980[d]	1984	1989	1991	1996
Congress[b]	45.0	47.8	44.7	40.8	43.7	34.5	42.7	48.1	39.5	36.4	28.5
Other Pan-Indian	22.1	23.0	29.7	28.2	32.0	–	–	26.3	30.8	26.5	25.9
Pan-Indian Parties	67.1	70.7	74.5	69.0	75.7	–	–	74.4	70.3	62.9	54.4
Hindu Revivalist Parties	5.9	7.2	7.7	9.4	7.4	–	–	7.5	11.6	21.0	21.4
Other Ethnic	5.6	4.2	6.6	7.8	7.0	8.1	6.5	10.0	12.9	12.6	13.5
Ethnic Parties	11.6	11.3	14.3	17.1	14.4	–	–	17.5	24.5	33.6	34.9

Notes:

(a) Singh & Bose (1984), Brass (1990: 70), Election Commission (1990: 6–12; 1992: 8–16), National Informatics Centre (1996).

(b) Congress denotes the Indian National Congress for 1952–69, Congress (R) in 1971 and 1977, and Congress (I) thereafter.

(c) The main Hindu revivalist party, the Bharatiya Jan Sangh, merged with some Congress offshoots to form the Janata party in 1977 and remained part of this party until after the 1980 elections. The Bharatiya Jan Sangh polled about as many votes as all other ethnic parties combined from 1957 to 1971, the Janata party won in 1977 and was the second strongest party in 1980. So, it is difficult to distinguish the share of the pan-Indian parties from that of the Hindu revivalists for 1977 and 1980.

(d) See footnote c.

growth of religious revivalism. When religious riots engulfed many parts of India at different points over the last decade, the violence has been most limited in Tamil Nadu.

Politicized ethnicity was expressed in a more benign manner in Tamil Nadu although the Indian government did not accommodate ethnic demands in this case any more than it did in the Sikh and Kashmiri ones. The national government rejected the demands of the ethnic parties of Tamil Nadu for secession, and subsequently for increased autonomy for state governments. Its concessions on national language policy failed to satisfy Tamil nationalist sentiments, a discontent that was expressed in major language agitations. It dismissed state governments led by ethnic parties whose terms in office had not expired four times in Tamil Nadu (1976, 1980, 1988, 1991), and twice ruled the state directly for some time to promote the prospects of the party ruling the country (1976–7, 1988–9). While the national government was no less resistant to the demands of the Sikh and Kashmiri Muslim leaders at different points, tolerance and stability were preserved in Tamil Nadu and not in Punjab and Kashmir due to the different ways in which the relevant ethnic parties engaged with society.

The Dravidian movement in Tamil Nadu began during the 1910s by raising militant demands for secession and virulently opposed the upper Brahmin caste with appeals which to some extent resembled those of Nazi anti-Semitism. It however took a populist turn which made it primarily a vehicle of emergent groups rather than of ethnic chauvinism.[12] This book considers the manner in which parties derived from this movement after India's decolonization transacted with emergent social groups to attain sustained electoral success, while strengthening pluralist democracy in certain respects. This case study of the containment of ethnic conflict as a result of party-society transactions makes for a contrast with the more widely discussed instances of states managing ethnic conflict. It also departs from the predominant focus of the recent literature on cases of violent ethnic conflict, which is inadequate to clarify how politicized ethnicity may be reconciled with pluralist democracy.

[12] For earlier accounts of the movement, see Barnett (1976), Irschick (1969) and Hardgrave (1979).

ETHNICITY AND POPULISM

Ethnic appeals have in many cases been intertwined with populist notions of a 'common people', distinguished from a privileged élite. In such cases, the ethnic group being mobilized is loosely identified with a plebeian community, and the élite being opposed is deemed alien. The ideologues of such movements associate the authentic values of the ethnic community with vaguely specified plebeian groups. The cohesion provided by the appeal to common cultural features is reinforced by the outrage evoked by allusions to exclusion from spheres of privilege.

I use the term populism to characterize movements, parties and regimes which articulate notions of a 'people', defined by special norms rooted in its history. The popular community, said to have limited access to various spheres of privilege, is distinguished from the élite, considered dominant in these spheres and taken to embody alternative cultural traditions.[13] A wide range of social categories may be used to define the plastic boundaries between the 'people' and the 'élite'. As the two groups are said to have distinct mores, ethnic categories are particularly suitable for the definition of the popular community, as are indicators of class, status and social marginality. Populist ideologues have distinguished the 'people' from the 'élite' with reference to pigmentation, language and dialect use, types of occupation (associated with more or less prestige), levels of education, patterns of worship, dietary habits, etc.

The concept of populism is analytically useful if applied (only) to cases in which distinctions between a popular community and an élite significantly shape mobilizing strategy, mass response, the composition of support, the structure of movement organizations, and policies promised or adopted. Populist organizations direct their appeals towards groups of intermediate and lower status, and inspire these groups to enter formal politics in opposition to groups and organizations which enjoy greater esteem and power. They draw much of their support, activist corps, and sometimes even ideologues and leaders from intermediate and lower classes and status groups, whose culture imbues the movement. They are closely linked to social networks among such groups, or form such

---

[13] This definition is drawn primarily from Shils (1972) and Laclau (1977). Also see Lyrintzis (1987).

networks if they were absent earlier. Populist regimes face pressure to deliver in some way on their promises to increase the entitlements of emergent groups, and retain support only if they do so.[14] A wide range of ideologies and policies may be taken to represent emergent groups, and populists have drawn on diverse ideological sources (such as socialist, liberal, nationalist, ethnic, fascist).[15]

The tendency of ethnic and populist appeals to reinforce each other fruitfully has attracted little focused attention, although it dates back to the turn of the century. Bulgaria's Agrarian Union equated the peasantry with the popular community and regarded urban groups as foreigners.[16] The Peronists in Argentina, the *Sanchezcerristas* and the *Alianza Popular Revolucionaria Americana* (APRA) in Peru, all three of which primarily mobilized urban-working classes, as well as the peasant revolutionaries of Mexico and their proclaimed successors in the ruling *Partido Nacional Revolucionario* (PNR, later renamed PRI) used *mestizo* motifs in appealing to lower status groups.[17] Anti-colonial nationalists like Gandhi and Sekou Toure employed populist rhetorical strategies in calling for a return to presumed pre-colonial institutions which they deemed more authentic than the liberal modernizing aims of the professional élites of their countries.[18] A combination of populist and ethnic features has been seen more recently in the experiences of Sinhala Buddhist revivalism in Sri Lanka and the Pan-Hellenic Socialist Movement (PASOK) in Greece, and less systematically in the politics of Indira Gandhi in India, Zulfiquar Ali Bhutto in Pakistan, Mujib-ur-Rehman in Bangladesh, and Fujimori in Peru.[19]

---

[14] Note that entitlements are different from property rights. See Sen (1984).

[15] Political forces using 'populist' idioms do not conform to this type if their message does not motivate significant support (e.g. the Russian Narodnaya Volya, Haiti's Francois Duvalier). Nor do regimes whose welfare programmes disregard fiscal constraints if such policies are not systematically legitimized with reference to a populist ideology. Loose usage of the term 'populism' has gained it academic disrepute.

[16] Bell (1977).

[17] See James (1988), Coniff (1982), Chang-Rodriguez & Hellman 1988) and Stein (1980).

[18] See Gandhi (1946) and Jackson & Rosberg (1982).

[19] See Tambiah (1992), Lyrintzis (1983, 1987), Jalal (1995) and Roberts (1995).

The interplay of ethnic and populist appeals has had widely divergent effects on levels of social conflict and the vigour of pluralist democracy. While the anti-élite aspect of populist appeals heightened ethnic antagonisms in some movements, the populist reference to plebeian norms tempered ethnic hostilities in others. In Sri Lanka, the assertion of ethnic pride by Sinhala-Buddhist revivalists was made more strident by the sense that it represented outlooks marginalized by European colonial rule. The energies of newly mobilized groups were primarily directed towards establishing the primacy of Sinhala speakers and the Buddhist religion, and attacking ethnic minorities when they resisted these efforts. The growth of Sinhala Buddhist revivalism led to changes in Sri Lanka's language policy, preferential recruitment of Sinhalese to government employment, the alteration of the constitution along revivalist lines, the growth of ethnic extremism among the minority Tamils, an ongoing civil war and the weakening of democracy.[20]

Contrary to Sinhala Buddhist revivalism, the Dravidian parties of south India shifted their emphasis from policing ethnic boundaries to revaluing plebeian culture. Rather than inspiring attacks against ethnic out-groups, the articulation of ethnic appeals within a populist discourse led Dravidianist regimes to focus on the creation of entitlements for emergent groups. This book considers the conditions under which populism tempers the potential of ethnicity to generate conflict, and enables the maintenance of pluralist democracy.

POPULISM, PLURALISM AND DEMOCRACY

The role that populism has at times played as an ally of stability, pluralism and democracy is surprising for its appeals to a homogeneous popular community and its anti-élite character could have provoked social conflict just as much as ethnic antagonisms have done. It is at odds with the received view of populism, as is the

[20] See Tambiah (1986, 1992). The growth of ethnic extremism has been partially reversed over the past few years by the military defeat of the *Janatha Vimukthi Peramuna* (JVP), the weakening of the Liberation Tigers of Tamil Eelam (LTTE) and the election in 1994 of a President initially committed to pluralism, Chandrika Kumaratunga. However, as Kumaratunga has so far been unable to accommodate or suppress the LTTE, the civil war continues.

very contemporary salience of populism. The received view is based on studies of movements among East European peasants and American farmers in the nineteenth and early twentieth centuries, and urban lower and intermediate classes in Latin America until the 1950s. It assumes that populism finds support primarily among atomized and ill-differentiated groups in mass societies, which seek in populism means to defend old norms in the face of the abrupt disruptions wrought by an emergent capitalism. Such accounts claim that there is a natural fit between notions of a homogeneous popular community and the fuzzy cleavages within mass society, and between the looseness of populist organizations and their poorly organized supporters. They argue that further industrialization would yield better organized social classes, which would find populist appeals too inchoate. So, many took populism to be extinct by the late 1960s.[21]

These studies argue that the disinclination of populists to organize supporters or undertake major property redistribution necessarily causes the demise of populist regimes. While such regimes manage to distribute patronage through periods of high economic growth, it is claimed that their rule leads to leaner times as populists have no strategies for economic growth. When this happens, populists cannot satisfy mass expectations without redistributing property, but are unable to do so as supporters are not sufficiently mobilized to counter the likely resistance of the dominant classes.[22] So, populists lose support or are overthrown through coups enjoying the support of the dominant strata, as Bulgaria's Agrarian Union and Argentina's Peronist regimes did.

Further, these studies argue that the focus on a homogeneous community and a charismatic leader would lead populists to undermine pluralism, thus eroding the basis for democracy. The

---

[21] These accounts were influenced by Durkheim's notion of *anomie* and Marx's discussion of the fate of the peasantry. Although Durkheim did not assume that a shift would necessarily occur from mass society to civil society, his work was appropriated in such a teleological fashion by Parsons and by much of the literature on populism. See Hofstadter (1955), Kornhauser (1959) and Germani (1978).

[22] The land reforms passed in Mexico under Lazaro Cardenas are a minor exception.

authoritarian inclinations of many populists like Vargas, Peron and the APRA are cited in support of this view.[23]

Later accounts have challenged some aspects of the above interpretation of earlier populisms.[24] Moreover, many contemporary developments are at odds with the earlier view. Populist appeals have had renewed salience in a range of semi-industrialized countries with well articulated civil societies. Besides earlier cited examples (Sinhala revivalism, Indira Gandhi, Bhutto, Mujib, PASOK, Fujimori), leaders with populist features such as Echeverria in Mexico, Garcia in Peru, Menem in Argentina, and Brizola and Collor in Brazil have been popular in recent times. Such leaders have drawn substantial support from socially rooted and upwardly mobile groups, which have found sustained appeal in their piecemeal reforms. The Congress party (henceforth Congress) under Indira Gandhi and her successors, and Greece's PASOK have especially retained both substantial support and populist features for significant periods. While Sri Lanka's SLFP and the Pakistan People's Party had weaker populist features and sustained broad support, Brizola, a more full-blown populist, had more limited but durable support until recently.[25]

Even the current global wave of neo-liberal economic reform has not rendered populism unviable. Regimes implementing such reforms, such as Fujimori's in Peru, Collor's in Brazil and the Indian governments of the 1990s, have simultaneously adopted compensatory welfare schemes targeting some lower class groups affected by the reforms. Control over these schemes has given them means to retain some support among these groups and present themselves as champions of the common people.[26]

Further, populism has coexisted with democracy throughout the PASOK's rule in Greece (1981–5; 1989 onwards) and part of

[23] Vargas led an authoritarian regime in the interwar period, Peron participated in one in the 1940s, and the APRA supported another in the 1960s. Peron also repressed opponents after coming to power through free elections in 1946. See Coniff (1982).

[24] See Goodwyn (1976) regarding American populism; and Madsen & Snow (1991) and Kenworthy (1973) on Peronism.

[25] Basurto (1982), di Tella (1990), McClintock (1989), de la Torre (1992).

[26] See Roberts (1995).

Indira Gandhi's rule in India (especially 1969-75).[27] Populists returned to the limelight when military dictatorships were periodically replaced by democratic rule in Argentina (1973-6; 1989 onwards) and Peru (1985 onwards). In many of these cases, populism has emerged and, to varying degrees, endured under conditions of low economic growth. In those cases where populism coexisted with democracy, the limited redistribution of entitlements, which is central to populist agendas, helped contain the discontent of highly mobilized populations in the face of low growth without extensive property redistribution. This book advances an understanding of populism which accounts for its scattered yet sustained appeal in semi-industrialized societies, sometimes amidst economic malaise, and the role it played in some cases as an ally of pluralist democracy.

THE PROBLEM

This study poses the following questions: (1) *How can pluralist democracy be preserved under conditions of high ethnic mobilization when accommodative compacts between states and ethnic élites prove inadequate to the task?* (2) *Under what conditions does populism temper the potential of ethnicity to provoke disintegrative social conflict, and instead promote pluralist democracy?* (3) *When is populism likely to attain sustained success in semi-industrialized societies and aid the representation of emergent social groups?* In answering these questions, it addresses the literature on three themes: ethnicity, mass politics and the foundations of democracy.

THE SCOPE

The book discusses the formation of, and changes in, the social coalitions of ethnic parties. It examines how mobilization shapes mass political sentiments, partisan subcultures and voter alignments. This helps explain changes in long-standing patterns of partisanship, as the motivations that initially underlie voter alignments often influence changes in voting patterns when new political forces emerge. Drawing on Barth's analysis of patterns of

[27] Indira Gandhi assumed clear populist features from about 1969 onwards, but dismantled democracy briefly from 1975 to 1977. After she returned to power in 1980, the populist aspects of her rule were attenuated.

social organization, I use the notion of transactions to capture the reciprocal nature of party-society interactions, which involve the exchange of material and symbolic rewards.[28] While the reciprocal features of party-society interactions may reproduce existing political alignments, they also indicate the conditions under which social groups may transfer their allegiances to new political forces engaging in different types of exchanges with their supporters. This book explores the changes successive mobilizing waves have introduced in clientelist transactions. Not only is the concern with changing social coalitions and subcultures unusual in studies of ethnic politics, which largely ignore these matters due to their emphasis on state-party interactions, it also differs from the largely static nature of studies of partisanship and clientelism.[29]

This study examines the relationship between the appeals of ethnic mobilizers and the motivations which impel mass support, a question which has attracted inadequate attention.[30] This relationship is often indirect because social groups tend to interpret political appeals in terms relevant to their life situation. I show that such processes of mass appropriation of the appeals of political élites are central to the formation of partisan subcultures, which in turn influences the directions of future mobilization. The book outlines the social identities posited by competing mobilizers, changes in these identities over time, and the reasons why specific social groups were attracted to particular definitions of identity. Increased attention is thereby paid to the role of movement supporters in identity construction, contrary to the predominant focus on élite initiatives.[31] I trace the myriad ways in which

[28] See Barth (1981).

[29] Unlike Lipset & Rokkan's (1967) classic discussion of partisanship, the more historically and sociologically rich accounts in Key (1949) and Barnes (1977) provided clues to understand recent changes. Contrary to Schmidt et al. (1977) and Eisenstadt & Lemarchand (1981), Fox (1994) is sensitive to changes in clientelism. Accounts comparable to Weiner (1962, 1967) have not appeared of recent clientelism in India.

[30] The extensive literature on ethnic stereotypes does not systematically explore the interaction between attitudes and ethnic mobilization. See Horowitz (1985: 141–9, 445–9), Tajfel (1982), Billig (1976).

[31] Even Laitin (1986), among the few political scientists to study mass conceptions of identity closely, accords the masses a largely passive role in identity formation.

emergent groups conceived of themselves as citizens as they were incorporated into an expanding public sphere through successive waves of political mobilization, and the impact which the process of incorporation had on the prospects for pluralist democracy.[32] In so doing, the book presents a comprehensive analysis of the relations between social change, party competition, political culture, associational life and regime characteristics.

THE STUDY

The book discusses the mobilization of emergent groups through the use of ethnic and populist appeals in a manner which provoked limited social conflict and promoted pluralist democracy. It considers the growth and rule of parties derived from the Dravidian movement in the South Indian state of Tamil Nadu, a case ideal for a consideration of the primary questions posed here. The Dravidian movement is among Asia's oldest and most durable ethno-national movements. The path it followed is the most significant Asian example of the sustained containment of the destabilizing potential of ethnicity. The Dravidian parties adopted moderate strategies primarily because of leaders' changing perceptions regarding social responses to their appeals, rather than because the state effectively accommodated ethnic demands. The experience of the Dravidian parties is thus a good example of the 'party-society route' to the containment of ethnic conflict.

The history of the Dravidian parties also reveals the most systematic and durable populist features to be seen in the semi-industrialized world. Their experience has involved the sustained interplay of populist and ethnic appeals in the incorporation of emergent groups. These parties grew within semi-industrialized Asia's most stable democracy and invigorated democratic institutions in their area of strength, Tamil Nadu, among the more urbanized and industrialized regions in India.[33] Therefore, the

---

[32] Collier & Collier (1991) provide an impressive comparative account along these lines, which however pays limited attention to parties and social identities.

[33] Tamil Nadu is India's most densely urbanized state, with the second highest level of urbanization (33 per cent compared with 23.3 per cent in the country as a whole). Maharashtra, the only more urbanized state (35 per cent), has a less evenly distributed urban population. Tamil Nadu occupied the

Dravidianist case exhibits all the surprising aspects of the relationship between some contemporary populist forces and pluralist democracy.

Located in India's south-eastern corner, Tamil Nadu is inhabited by about sixty million people, comparable in this regard with countries like France, Italy, Turkey and Thailand.[34] The Dravidian movement has been a significant political force here since World War I. It claimed to represent speakers of the Tamil language, perhaps all South Indians, other than those of the Brahmin caste. It considered this imprecisely defined group the descendants of a Dravidian race, distinct from the Aryans from whom North Indians and South Indian Brahmins were said to have both descended. The movement upheld the culture of the intermediate Hindu castes of Tamil Nadu and promoted revivalist visions of a Tamil national community centred around the norms of these groups. This was the focus of the first mass organization to emerge from the movement, the Self Respect Association, later renamed the *Dravidar Kazhagam* (DK—Party of the Dravidians).[35] The DK highlighted this focus with a call to reject religion, especially Brahminical Hinduism, which it regarded as the foundation of caste-based inequalities.

Until India attained independence in 1947, the Dravidian movement played second fiddle to Congress, which spearheaded India's anti-colonial movement. The Dravidian parties were the first ethnic forces to outdo and marginalize Congress in an Indian state. The Dravida Munnetra Kazhagam (DMK—Party for the Progress of Dravidam), an offshoot of the DK, emerged as the strongest

---

second or third rung among the Indian states in level of industrialization in the 1950s and 1960s when the Dravidian parties grew—although its relative position has since declined. Even now, Tamil Nadu is the most evenly industrialized state, with all but two districts having over five major industrial units. Capitalist agriculture also flourishes in many parts of Tamil Nadu. See Muthiah (1987: 20–1, 201, 211), MIDS (1988: 191).

[34] Department of Statistics (1994); MIDS (1988: 7).

[35] Strictly speaking, the Self Respect Association, begun between 1925 and 1927, merged with a more élite-oriented Dravidianist organization, the Justice Party, in 1938. The Justice Party, in turn, was renamed the DK in 1944. As the original Justice Party was virtually moribund by the time the Self Respect Association joined it, the Self Respect Association and the DK were in effect the same organization, led by the same individual.

alternative to Congress in the 1960s and assumed power in the state in 1967. A decade of DMK rule was followed by another decade with its offshoot, the Anna Dravida Munnetra Kazhagam (ADMK—Anna's Party for the Progress of Dravidam), in power. These two parties, which continue to dominate Tamil politics, have influenced the development of civic life and introduced significant changes in public policy. The focus of the book is Dravidianist mobilization and policy from the birth of the DMK in 1949 to the death of the ADMK's initial leader in 1987. The Dravidian parties' experience before and after this time period is therefore discussed in less detail.

This work explains the success of the Dravidian parties, the strategic course they followed, and their impact. It outlines the parties' changing appeals and support, linking them to both their methods of mobilization and policies. The pertinent data were gathered from movement and non-partisan newspapers and journals; speeches, political tracts, and literary and film productions of political leaders and publicists; government reports; census reports and district gazetteers; results of parliamentary, state assembly and local body elections; and over a hundred élite interviews. Party competition was studied intensively in five state legislative assembly constituencies, whose populations currently range between 250,000 and 450,000, through interviews (about sixty to a hundred per constituency) with local leaders and activists of parties and associations.

THE LAY OF THE LAND: THE CASES

The five constituencies chosen for intensive study represent different socio-economic characteristics; levels of political participation, competition and relative party strength; and timing of initial Dravidianist growth. The rise to dominance of the Dravidian parties involved three steps—the rise of the DMK as the main challenger to Congress in the late 1950s and early 1960s; the DMK supplanting Congress from power in 1967; and the marginalization of Congress and its offshoots after the formation of the ADMK in 1972. The CPI was Congress's main opponent after decolonization, but the DMK overtook it through the late 1950s and early 1960s. The choice of constituencies was influenced by the need to account for Dravidianist growth through these three stages.

Successive waves of political mobilization in Tamil Nadu, which shaped durable subcultures and voter alignments, were concentrated in particular socio-ecological zones. So, variations in the electoral strength of parties and the depth of their subcultures are closely related to the boundaries of these zones. Ecology is closely linked to social structure in predominantly agrarian societies as the assurance of water supply influences crop and settlement patterns, the distribution of cultivable land and class relations. It specifically influenced the caste composition of the population and caste relations in India. As rivers were the primary source of water for crops till the nineteenth century and migration to rural areas relatively low over the last century during which well irrigation increased, the social structure of the river valleys became quite different from that of regions where agriculture depended on rainfall until recently. The river valleys have highly stratified societies with greater population density, and the landed upper castes, untouchables (called the scheduled castes, henceforth SCs) and landless agricultural labour account for a higher proportion of the population. Brahminical norms have had greater social influence and more repression was used to control agricultural labour. In the plains and uplands, on the other hand, the intermediate castes and classes are numerically and socially stronger and have had a longer history of autonomous mobilization.[36]

Of Tamil Nadu's four major river systems, only the social structure of the Kaveri and Tamiraparani valleys conforms to the valley ideal type because water was regularly available there, unlike in the Palar and Vaigai valleys. (As I use ecotype as a shorthand reference to social structure, I refer hereafter only to the Kaveri and Tamiraparani valleys as 'valleys'.) The rest of Tamil Nadu is divided into three regions—the northern, western and southern plains.[37] (Map I indicates the location of the five zones).

Political parties mobilized most intensively in the late colonial period in the areas of flourishing agriculture—the Kaveri and the Tamiraparani valleys; and the western plains, parts of which had considerable well irrigation by then. Congress and the Indian nationalist movement enjoyed significant support in these regions,

[36] See Béteille (1974: 26, 144–5 & *passim*), Baker (1984: 24–5 & *passim*).

[37] Parts of these regions are more appropriately termed uplands, but I call them plains for easy reference as the social structure of the uplands resembles that of the plains. These zones are delineated in Baker (1984: 15, 25–56, 85–97), Stein (1980: 15, 25–9) and Gough (1989: 67–80, 91–104).

the CPI mainly in the valleys and in industrial centres in other regions, and the DK in the Kaveri valley and some commercial towns elsewhere. The Kaveri valley was thus the most intensely mobilized, with a high degree of political competition, and has remained so since. Table 1.2 shows, for instance, that electoral participation has been consistently highest there. Party mobilization was more limited through the late colonial period in much of the northern and southern plains (especially the former), although independent associations were quite active.[38]

TABLE 1.2   Turnout Rates in the Ecological Zones, 1952–89

Year	North	Kaveri	Parani	South	South*	West	Total
1952	53.25	60.64	56.74	55.88	57.22	60.29	55.85
1957	44.84	55.08	48.43	52.10	53.25	51.91	49.33
1962	68.39	76.69	73.06	70.49	70.20	72.50	70.65
1967	75.28	82.25	77.41	76.61	76.04	75.44	76.59
1971	70.82	78.82	74.24	71.37	70.60	69.25	71.84
1977	60.28	73.23	62.44	61.03	61.06	61.67	61.56
1980	64.66	73.80	66.84	63.81	63.52	63.80	65.41
1984	72.52	79.45	73.73	72.83	71.60	73.45	73.56
1989	65.87	75.15	71.92	70.67	69.56	72.54	69.28

Note: *Deep South.

Congress had the deepest subcultures through the 1950s and 1960s in regions intensively mobilized earlier. Although it dominated elections in the southern plains too, its subcultures were shallower there. It faced greatest electoral competition and had the least social presence in the northern plains. The DMK grew most rapidly through the late 1950s and early 1960s in the northern plains (particularly the north-east), taking advantage of the relatively limited strength of Congress. It also built a deep subculture in the Kaveri valley, although its electoral strength was limited there by the enduring strength of older parties. The communists had significant electoral strength till the 1970s in the two valleys, especially the Kaveri valley, but declined in the industrial centres. The DK remained an important force after the emergence of the DMK only in the Kaveri valley, and has declined there too since the late 1950s.

[38] Congress enjoyed early strength in parts of the southern plains adjacent to the Tamiraparani valley.

The DMK gained support in all regions through the late 1960s and early 1970s, but its social presence remained strongest in its old areas of strength, the northern plains and the Kaveri valley. Congress declined throughout the state during this phase, most rapidly in its pocket of historic weakness, the northern plains.

The ADMK performed best from the 1970s onwards in the Tamiraparani valley and the southern and western plains, i.e. in old Congress strongholds other than the always hotly contested Kaveri valley. The DMK retained greatest support in its early bases, the Kaveri valley and northern plains. Congress also retained most residual support where it had built deeper subcultures—in the valleys and western plains. The communists had by then declined even in their old bastions. (Table 1.3 shows zone-wise party performance in key elections.)

TABLE 1.3   Performance of Major Parties in the Ecological Zones in Key State Legislative Assembly Elections, Tamil Nadu

Table 1.3A: 1962 Elections

I Northern Plains[a]

Electorate	7,895,543	
Valid Votes Polled	5,206,834	
Seats	90	

Party	Votes Polled (%)	Cont. Vote Share (%)[b]	S.C.[c]	S.W.[d]
Congress	43.81	43.81	90	47
DMK	35.56	41.87	75	38
CPI	2.05	16.13	12	0
Swatantra	5.60	14.05	37	3

Notes:

(a) Madras city, the districts of Chengalpattu, North Arcot, South Arcot (excluding Chidambaram), Salem and Dharmapuri, and northern portion of Tiruchirapalli district (Perambalur, Vengalam, Ariyalur, Jayankondam, T. Palur, Varahur and Andimadam constituencies). Here and in subsequent footnotes indicating the boundaries of the ecological zones, I refer to districts as they were configured from 1971 to 1977.

(b) Denotes given party's votes polled as per cent of valid votes polled in the constituencies it contested.

(c) Seats contested.

(d) Seats won.

II Kaveri Valley[c]

Electorate	2,361,896
Valid Votes Polled	1,747,649
Seats	27

Party	Votes Polled (%)	Cont. Vote Share (%)	S.C.	S.W.
Congress	47.26	47.26	27	20
DMK	28.78	39.36	20	5
CPI	15.17	26.85	15	2
Swatantra	3.45	9.64	9	0

III Tamiraparani Valley[f]

Electorate	282,207
Valid Votes Polled	200,208
Seats	3

Party	Votes Polled (%)	Cont. Vote Share (%)	S.C.	S.W.
Congress	40.85	40.85	3	3
DMK	14.95	23.06	2	0
CPI	10.09	29.81	1	0
Swatantra	19.52	19.52	3	0

IV Western Plains[g]

Electorate	2,228,736
Valid Votes Polled	1,509,857
Seats	23

Party	Votes Polled (%)	Cont. Vote Share (%)	S.C.	S.W.
Congress	48.66	48.66	23	22
DMK	16.25	20.60	18	0
CPI	15.24	21.28	16	0
Swatantra	6.47	17.24	10	0

(e) Thanjavur district, Chidambaram (in South Arcot district), and central portions of Tiruchirapalli district (Lalgudi, Manachanallur, Srirangam, Kulithalai, Musiri, Uppiliapuram, Tiruchi I & II (S. & N.) and Tiruverambur constituencies).

(f) Ambasamudram, Cheranmahadevi, Tirunelveli, Palayamcottai and Srivaikuntam constituencies (Tirunelveli district).

(g) Coimbatore and Nilgiris districts.

V Southern Plains[h]

Electorate   5,907,054
Valid Votes Polled   4,011,718
Seats   63

Party	Votes Polled (%)	Cont. Vote Share (%)	S.C.	S.W.
Congress	48.00	48.00	63	47
DMK	20.09	44.97	23	7
CPI	9.13	22.34	24	0
Swatantra	12.59	21.19	35	3

Va. 'Deep South'[i]

Electorate   3,374,281
Valid Votes Polled   2,356,403
Seats   37

Party	Votes Polled (%)	Cont. Vote Share (%)	S.C.	S.W.
Congress	49.37	49.37	37	32
DMK	8.24	25.40	12	1
CPI	8.26	22.78	14	0
Swatantra	18.12	26.17	25	0

Table 1.3B: 1977 Elections

I Northern Plains

Electorate   12,479,759
Valid Votes Polled   7,466,913
Seats   104

Party	Votes Polled (%)	Cont. Vote Share (%)	S.C.	S.W.
ADMK	32.98	28.43	94	59
ADMK Front	35.63	35.63	104	63
DMK	27.88	28.43	103	31
Congress-I	13.57	15.76	90	8
Congress Front	14.27	15.13	98	8
Janata	18.72	18.72	104	3

(h) Madurai, Pudukottai, Ramanathapuram and Kanyakumari districts, portions of Tirunelveli district not included in (III) and portions of Tiruchirapalli district not included in (I) and (II).

(i) Ramanathapuram, Tirunelveli and Kanyakumari districts.

II Kaveri Valley

Electorate	3,237,614
Valid Votes Polled	2,268,359
Seats	29

Party	Votes Polled (%)	Cont. Vote Share (%)	S.C.	S.W.
ADMK	23.82	31.72	22	8
ADMK Front	30.94	30.94	29	9
DMK	33.78	33.78	29	14
Congress-I	20.88	25.70	24	4
Congress Front	26.26	26.26	29	6
Janata	10.30	10.30	29	0

III Tamiraparani Valley

Electorate	542,195
Valid Votes Polled	332,844
Seats	5

Party	Votes Polled (%)	Cont. Vote Share (%)	S.C.	S.W.
ADMK	29.53	36.85	4	4
ADMK Front	36.54	36.54	5	5
DMK	13.43	16.76	4	0
Congress-I	21.22	26.48	4	0
Congress Front	27.70	27.70	5	0
Janata	15.34	15.34	5	0

IV Western Plains

Electorate	3,416,575
Valid Votes Polled	2,065,182
Seats	28

Party	Votes Polled (%)	Cont. Vote Share (%)	S.C.	S.W.
ADMK	31.38	35.41	25	22
ADMK Front	34.71	34.71	28	24
DMK	22.79	22.79	28	2
Congress-I	17.00	22.98	21	2
Congress Front	22.00	22.50	27	2
Janata	18.35	18.35	28	0

V Southern Plains

Electorate   8,232,027
Valid Votes Polled   4,974,848
Seats   68

Party	Votes Polled (%)	Cont. Vote Share (%)	S.C.	S.W.
ADMK	31.09	37.95	57	38
ADMK Front	35.35	37.37	66	43
DMK	18.11	19.44	63	1
DMK Front	18.51	19.36	65	1
Congress	21.90	27.76	55	13
Congress Front	25.69	26.78	66	16
Janata	16.46	16.72	66	7
Others	—	—	—	1

Table 1.3C: 1989 Elections

I Northern Plains

Electorate   15,923,515
Valid Votes Polled   10,249,699
Seats   104

Party	Votes Polled (%)	Cont. Vote Shate (%)	S.C.	S.W.
ADMK-JL[j]	21.31	23.99	93	9
ADMK-JL Front	23.23	23.23	104	10
ADMK-JR	8.93	11.25	82	0
ADMK-JR Front	10.92	10.92	104	0
DMK	36.68	42.00	91	78
DMK Front	41.05	41.05	104	88
Congress	18.20	18.82	100	3
Congress Front	18.75	18.75	104	4
Others	—	—	—	2

II Kaveri Valley

Electorate   4,122,412
Valid Votes Polled   3,043,952
Seats   29

Party	Votes Polled (%)	Cont. Vote Share (%)	S.C.	S.W.
ADMK-JL	20.93	24.23	26	3
ADMK-JL Front	24.86	24.86	29	4

Contd.

(j) ADMK (Jayalalitha), one of the two ADMK factions, 1988–9; the other ADMK faction of the period, the ADMK (Janaki), is referred to as ADMK-JR.

Contd.

Party	Votes Polled (%)	Cont. Vote Share (%)	S.C.	S.W.
ADMK-JR	7.10	8.55	24	0
ADMK-JR Front	9.18	9.18	29	0
DMK	34.05	40.06	25	19
DMK Front	40.44	40.44	29	23
Congress	19.74	22.85	25	2
Congress Front	21.97	21.97	29	2

III Tamiraparani Valley

Electorate	679,884
Valid Votes Polled	480,817
Seats	5

Party	Votes Polled (%)	Cont. Vote Share (%)	S.C.	S.W.
ADMK-JL	18.70	18.70	5	0
ADMK-JL Front	18.70	18.70	5	0
ADMK-JR	16.87	20.85	4	1
ADMK-JR Front	18.07	18.07	5	1
DMK	25.70	31.76	4	2
DMK Front	30.56	30.56	5	2
Congress	23.44	29.51	4	2
Congress Front	30.01	30.01	5	2

IV Western Plains

Electorate	4,391,244
Valid Votes Polled	3,117,947
Seats	28

Party	Votes Polled (%)	Cont. Vote Share (%)	S.C.	S.W.
ADMK-JL	23.84	29.84	23	9
ADMK-JL Front	28.06	28.06	28	10
ADMK-JR	9.66	12.01	22	0
ADMK-JR Front	10.66	10.66	28	0
DMK	27.98	42.24	22	11
DMK Front	35.71	35.71	28	14
Congress	18.59	22.48	24	4
Congress Front	20.90	20.90	28	4

V Southern Plains

Electorate	10,076,212			
Valid Votes Polled	6,996,735			
Seats	66 (Elections were not held in 2 constituencies)			

Party	Votes Polled (%)	Cont. Vote Share (%)	S.C.	S.W.
ADMK-JL	21.82	25.44	55	6
ADMK-JL Front	24.51	24.51	66	8
ADMK-JR	8.99	12.75	46	0
ADMK-JR Front	12.01	12.01	66	0
DMK	30.52	34.34	58	40
DMK Front	34.26	34.26	66	44
Congress	23.97	25.56	62	14
Congress Front	25.01	25.01	66	14

Table 1.3C: 1989 Elections—Counterfactual Scenarios[k]

I Northern Plains

Front	Votes Polled (%)	S.C.	S.W.
ADMK Front	34.15	104	34
DMK Front	41.05	104	67
Congress Front	18.75	104	2
Others	—	—	1

II Kaveri Valley

Front	Votes Polled (%)	S.C.	S.W.
ADMK Front	34.04	29	10
DMK Front	40.44	29	17
Congress Front	21.97	29	2

III Tamiraparani Valley

Front	Votes Polled (%)	S.C.	S.W.
ADMK Front	36.77	5	2
DMK Front	30.56	5	2
Congress Front	30.01	5	1

(k) This indicates the situation as it might have been had the ADMK been a united party, by adding the votes gained by the two ADMK factions. This understates the likely strength of a united ADMK, yet indicates the areas of relative strength of the key parties.

IV Western Plains

Front	Votes Polled (%)	S.C.	S.W.
ADMK Front	38.73	28	19
DMK Front	35.71	28	7
Congress Front	20.90	28	2

V Southern Plains

Front	Votes Polled (%)	S.C.	S.W.
ADMK Front	36.52	66	40
DMK Front	34.26	66	20
Congress Front	25.01	66	6

The Cases

Of the five state assembly constituencies closely studied, two are in the northern plains, one metropolitan (Royapuram in northern Madras city) and one semi-rural (Tiruvannamalai); one constituency is in the Kaveri valley (semi-rural: Mannargudi), one in the sourthern plains (a medium-sized town, Dindigul, and its rural hinterland), and one in the Tamiraparani valley (primarily rural: Sermadevi, also called Cheranmahadevi). Map I indicates the location of these constituencies. As constituency boundaries were redrawn over the years, I include within my purview all areas that were part of each of these constituencies at some point after decolonization. All subsequent allusions by name to the five case constituencies are not just to the relevant town, but to the whole region the constituency comprised at any point (e.g. 'Mannargudi' refers not just to Mannargudi town).[39]

[39] For my purposes, the five constituencies include the following areas: (1) Royapuram—Royapuram, Old Washermanpet and Kasimedu: (2) Tiruvannamalai—Tiruvannamalai town, Tiruvannamalai and Kilpennathur panchayat unions, and the old Tandrambattu *firka* in eastern Chengam *taluk*; (3) Mannargudi—Mannargudi town and Mannargudi, Kottur and Nidamangalam panchayat unions; (4) Dindigul—Dindigul town and Dindigul panchayat union; (5) Sermadevi—Sermadevi and Pappakudi panchayat unions and a part of Kadayam panchayat union. The administrative sub-divisions in descending order of size are: state, district, taluk, firka (until 1960)/panchayat union (after 1960)/municipality and panchayat. A panchayat includes a small town, village or group of adjacent villages; a panchayat union includes a

The constituencies intensively studied represent the political experience of the zones in which they are located. Mannargudi witnessed Congress growth from the 1930s and DK and communist growth from the 1940s. The DMK grew from the late 1950s onwards in pockets of former DK strength—larger villages in western and northern Mannargudi. However, Congress and the communists retained significant support—Congress in Mannargudi town (which was at the forefront of anti-colonial agitation in 1942) and western Mannargudi, and the communists in eastern Mannargudi, where they first began mobilizing Tamil agricultural workers and peasants.[40] The strength of older parties hindered ADMK growth, which was insignificant until the party assumed power.[41]

Royapuram and Tiruvannamalai are pockets of early and sustained DMK strength, where the party has performed well since it began to contest elections in 1957. Tiruvannamalai provided two of the DMK's fifteen legislators and one of its two parliamentarians in the 1957 elections.[42] The meeting announcing the DMK's formation was held at Royapuram, where the party headquarters were also located for long, reflecting the intensity of local support for the party. The DMK has been the strongest force in both Royapuram and Tiruvannamalai in most elections since 1957.[43] While Royapuram is an instance of early DMK growth in industrializing areas, Tiruvannamalai reflects early party growth in some

---

number of panchayats; a taluk includes a few panchayat unions and/or municipalities; and a district comprises a few taluks. Royapuram constituency was called Washermanpet until 1971. Sermadevi, a separate electoral constituency during the first elections of 1952, was divided among the constituencies of Ambasamudram and Kadayam for the 1957 and 1962 polls, and reemerged on the electoral map thereafter.

[40] Society is sharply polarized in eastern Mannargudi, part of the old Kaveri delta, and less so in the western part, where canal irrigation was introduced only during British rule. See Baliga (1971: 112–18); Veerayyan (1980) and Bouton (1985).

[41] The ADMK won the constituency only when allied with Congress in 1984 and 1991.

[42] It was then a double-member constituency.

[43] The DMK has won in Royapuram in every election since 1967, except in 1991 when it suffered its worst defeat in the state. The Tiruvannamalai assembly seat switched hands between the DMK and Congress from 1957 to

regions of growing commercial agriculture. Dindigul and Sermadevi saw early Congress dominance and later ADMK dominance. These constituencies, the former predominantly urban and the latter largely rural, are among the few assembly constituencies of Tamil Nadu in which the DMK has never won.[44]

The cases represent not only different phases of Dravidianist growth, but also different levels of strength and rates of decline of the pan-Indian parties. While Congress remained strong even after the ADMK's birth in Mannargudi, Sermadevi and, to an extent, Tiruvannamalai, it declined earlier in Dindigul and Royapuram. Further, early Congress support rested on different foundations in these constituencies. It was based on the formation of deep subcultures in Mannargudi and Sermadevi (and Congress faced significant competition only in the former constituency). In contrast, Congress gained support primarily through patronage distribution and the social influence of notables in Dindigul, Tiruvannamalai and Royapuram.

The cases also vary in the degree and duration of communist support—high and sustained in Mannargudi (based on peasant mobilization); early and durable, but limited to semi-industrial workers in Dindigul; initially high (among industrial workers), but not durable in Royapuram; moderate in Sermadevi (due to activity in industrial and peasant unions in neighbouring areas); and insignificant all along in Tiruvannamalai. The socialists also enjoyed some support in Sermadevi until the mid-1950s, but most of them joined Congress after that.

1967, and the DMK or its ally has won the seat in most elections since then (except in 1984 and 1991, when Congress and the ADMK were allied with each other).

[44] The DMK has never won in 23 of the state's assembly constituencies. This accurately reflects the DMK's weakness in Sermadevi, but is slightly misleading regarding Dindigul where the DMK's ally, the Communist Party of India-Marxist (CPI-M) won the constituency in 1967 and 1989 based primarily on the DMK's support. Neither the DMK nor its ally has ever won in only five of Tamil Nadu's constituencies, among which are Ambasamudram and Kadayam, which border Sermadevi, but not Sermadevi itself. The total number of state assembly constituencies in Tamil Nadu was 151 in 1952 (in just the areas which later constituted Tamil Nadu; there were 309 in all of Madras Presidency, within which the Tamil-speaking areas were contained until 1953); 167 in 1957; 206 in 1962; and 234 from 1967 onwards.

THE SPECIFICITY OF TAMIL POLITICS AND SOCIETY

Tamil Nadu best exemplifies the distinctive features of south Indian society. The Dravidian movement was influenced by the distinctive language, caste structure and religious practices of Tamil Nadu, and the changes the Dravidian parties introduced in Tamil society shaped the peculiarities of the state's political culture. Ten interrelated aspects of Tamil politics are notable in the Indian context. While some of these features are found exclusively in Tamil Nadu, others emerged in some other parts of India too. Yet others appeared early and in a pronounced form in Tamil Nadu, and assumed significance later elsewhere in India.

First, demands for secession arose early in Tamil Nadu. These demands were initially voiced in 1938 by the South Indian Liberal Federation (called the Justice Party), a Dravidianist organization of the late colonial period. Unlike similar demands which emerged in Kashmir and Nagaland on the eve of Indian independence, the Dravidianist demand for secession did not generate much support. Although the major Dravidian parties abandoned their demand for secession in the 1960s, a sense of cultural distinctness remains politically relevant.

Second, party competition became regionalized in Tamil Nadu earlier (from the early 1960s) and more fully than in other Indian states. As in Jammu and Kashmir and Punjab, the divergence began due to the growth of an ethnic party which was regional in its ambit. This party, the DMK, was the second ethnic party to come to power in an Indian state, in 1967.[45] While such ethnic forces grew in other parts of India also, they dominated party politics in Tamil Nadu alone. The growth of the ADMK in the 1970s marginalized pan-Indian parties in the state.

Third, 'non-Brahminism', a term used to refer to the politicization of the notion of a community of 'non-Brahmins' (those other than Brahmins), became a major aspect of Tamil politics. While

[45] The National Conference, based primarily among Kashmiri Muslims, came to power in Jammu & Kashmir after decolonization, but was suppressed from the early 1950s to the mid-1970s because it was suspected of harbouring secessionist ambitions. The Akali Dal, based among the Sikhs in Punjab, came to power in the state in 1967, at the same time that the DMK assumed power in Tamil Nadu. However, the Akali Dal was part of a coalition government, while the DMK had an absolute majority in the legislature.

non-Brahminist notions arose even earlier in Maharashtra, those who promoted them were incorporated into the pan-Indian parties by the 1930s. It is only in Tamil Nadu that non-Brahminism gave rise to a distinct set of political parties of enduring strength, the Dravidian parties.

Fourth, associations of the intermediate and lower castes have been strong for an especially long period in Tamil Nadu, at least since the 1880s. Only in Kerala has their history been comparably long. The current strength of caste associations is also particularly high in Tamil Nadu, being comparably high in Kerala and somewhat lower in Andhra Pradesh, Karnataka and Bihar. The Dravidian parties were the first to associate themselves closely with the demands of the intermediate castes.

Fifth, the state has had the longest history of caste-based preferential policies, and these quotas are most extensive in Tamil Nadu today. While the colonial state introduced preferential treatment for the lower castes in 1885, as much as 69 per cent of the seats in colleges and government jobs have been set aside for the intermediate and lower castes since 1980. The demand for such quotas was a crucial issue which precipitated the formation of the first mass Dravidianist organization, the Self Respect Association. The pressure of the Dravidian parties was among the factors that urged post-colonial Congress regimes to introduce intermediate caste quotas in the state. The Dravidianists substantially increased the scope of these quotas after they assumed power.

Sixth, while mobilization around language and caste has been strong, other visions of community, especially those centred around religion, have been particularly weak. Specifically, Hindu revivalism, a major force in contemporary Indian politics, is nowhere weaker than in Tamil Nadu although Hindus account for as much as 89 per cent of the state's population. Table 1.4 shows that Hindu revivalist parties polled less than 0.3 per cent of the popular vote in every state assembly election except the last one of 1996. Notions of a community of farmers, which have inspired mobilization by political parties in some other parts of India, have influenced the growth of interest groups but not political parties in Tamil Nadu. The rise to dominance of the Dravidian parties, associated with appeals to caste and language, has crucially inhibited the growth of other visions of community.

Seventh, voter participation rates are particularly high, and have been significantly higher than the Indian average since the early 1960s. While turnout rates have ranged between 61.6 per cent and 76.6 per cent in this period in Tamil Nadu, the range throughout India has been 55.3 per cent to 61.3 per cent (see Table 1.5). The higher rates are closely connected with the growth of the DMK. Turnout rates were not appreciably higher in Tamil Nadu than at the national level in the 1950s when Congress dominated both national and state politics. As the DMK's share of the vote increased from 12.8 per cent to 40.6 per cent between 1957 and 1967, the turnout rate increased from 49.3 per cent to 76.6 per cent and has remained relatively high thereafter.

Eighth, electoral politics has been dominated by two parties since the early 1960s, the DMK and Congress from 1962 to 1971, and the DMK and the ADMK since 1972. The two dominant parties polled over 60 per cent of the popular vote in all but two elections since 1962 (see Table 1.6), and probably commanded the support of over 70 per cent of the electorate through this period.[46] The share of the vote polled by the two largest parties declined when DMK-Congress dominance gave way to DMK-ADMK dominance after the ADMK was formed. This is partly because the third party, Congress (I), has had some independent electoral strength through this period, but also because it drew more votes by allying itself with one of the Dravidian parties in 1980, 1984, 1991 and 1996. Congress offshoots like the Janata Dal and the *Tamil Maanila Congress* (TMC—the Tamil State Congress) have similarly benefited from alliances with the Dravidianists. Opinion polls and the results of general elections and by-elections during which Congress was not allied with a Dravidian party suggest that the DMK and the ADMK commanded the support of well over 70 per cent of the electorate through the 1980s. This figure has declined slightly since 1989 due to the emergence of two new parties, the *Paattaali Makkal Katchi* (PMK—Party of Toiling People) and the *Marumalarchchi Dravida Munnetra Kazhagam* (MDMK—Revitalized Party for the Progress of Dravidam), which have drawn their support primarily from former DMK voters.

[46] The two exceptions are the 1977 elections, the last time Congress offshoots retained significant strength, and the 1989 elections, during which the ADMK was temporarily split.

TABLE 1.4 Tamil Nadu State Legislative Assembly Elections
Electoral Performance of Pan-Indian, Dravidian and Other Ethnic Parties
Share of Valid Vote (percentage-wise)

Party	1952	1957	1962	1967	1971	1977	1980	1984	1989	1991	1996
Congress	35.0	45.3	46.1	41.4	—	17.5	20.5	16.5	20.2	15.4	5.7
Other Pan-Indian Parties	31.7	15.8	17.5	12.6	43.1	22.4	10.9	9.7	9.5	6.1	14.1
Pan-Indian Parties	66.7	61.2	63.7	54.0	43.1	39.9	31.4	26.1	29.7	21.5	19.8
DMK	—	12.8	27.1	40.6	48.6	24.9	22.5	29.5	32.4	22.5	42.1
ADMK	—	—	—	—	—	30.4	38.8	37.1	30.7[a]	44.4	21.5
Hindu Revivalists	0.2	0.0	0.1	0.2	0.1	0.0	0.1	0.0	0.0	0.0	1.8
Other Ethnic Parties	8.6	1.4	3.8	0.2	1.7	0.3	0.4	0.4	1.0	7.3	9.5
Ethnic Parties	8.8	14.2	31.0	41.0	50.4	55.6	61.8	67.0	64.1	74.2	74.9

Note: (a) This figure represents the sum of the votes polled by the two ADMK factions in the 1989 elections.

TABLE 1.5   Voter Participation Rates in Tamil Nadu State Legislative
Assembly Elections and Indian Parliamentary Elections*
(percentage-wise)

Year	India	Tamil Nadu
1952	45.7	55.9
1957	47.7	49.3
1962	55.4	70.7
1967	61.3	76.6
1971	55.3	71.8
1977	60.5	61.6
1980	56.9	65.4
1984	64.1	73.6
1989	62.0	69.3
1991	56.7	63.8
1996	—	66.9

Source: *Drawn or compiled from P. Brass (1994: 104); Tamil Nadu Election Commission data disks; Tamil Nadu Legislative Assembly Secretariat (1992: xii–xvi); Press Information Bureau (1996).

TABLE 1.6 Two Party Dominance: Tamil Nadu Legislative
Assembly Elections

Year	Two Largest Parties' Share of Valid Vote (percentage-wise)
1952	48.0
1957	58.1
1962	73.2
1967	82.0
1971	83.6
1977	55.3
1980	61.3
1984	66.6
1989	57.9
1991	67.0
1996	63.6

Ninth, political parties are fairly strong and enjoy considerable stability in support. Voter participation levels have been comparable to those of Tamil Nadu only in other states with similarly strong parties, durable voter alignments, and two-party or two-front dominant electoral systems. Kerala, Punjab and Haryana have exhibited equally high turnout rates throughout the post-colonial period: Maharashtra and Andhra Pradesh did so until the communists declined in the 1960s; and West Bengal and Tripura have done so since the communists become major contenders in the 1960s.[47]

Tenth, civic life has been vigorous. A wide range of associations have been active throughout the century, many of which grew while the Dravidian parties did. Tamil Nadu was the first state to witness the growth of strong farmers' associations and is among the states where cultural societies are most active. Political parties and some associations frequently hold well attended meetings and rallies. Non-electoral political participation peaked during important agitations over language, agricultural and preferential policies.

The course the Dravidian parties followed shaped these specific features of Tamil politics. So the study's explanation of the success and impact of these parties helps one understand Tamil Nadu's political distinctiveness.

Cultural Specificity: Language and Caste

The language and caste structure of Tamil Nadu are very different from those of the Indo-Gangetic valley, which has come to be regarded as India's political heartland in this century. Among the major Dravidian languages of south India, Tamil is most different in syntax and vocabulary from north Indian languages, specifically Sanskrit, the classical language of the Hindu literati, and Hindi, the politically dominant language of post-colonial India. This was conducive to Dravidianist mobilization with reference to language-based identity, particularly when the national government attempted to adopt Hindi as its sole language of official communication in the first two post-colonial decades.

The social reality of caste, which corresponds exactly to scriptural definitions nowhere, is closer to these definitions in the Indo-Gangetic valley, the heartland of classical Hinduism. It diverges from scriptural definitions more in north-eastern and southern India (especially Tamil Nadu and Kerala), where Sanskritic Hinduism arrived relatively late and led to the incorporation of previously existing kin, clan and lineage groups within a caste structure. Two Indian categories correspond to the Portugo-English term

[47] See Singh & Bose (1984: 33, 56, 70, 87, 111, 135, 159).

'caste'—*varna*, a five-fold scriptural categorization; and *jati*, referring to a large number of endogamous or hypergamous groups
expected to follow rules for interaction that vary across region. Jatis
are largely subsumed under the five varna rubrics in north India,
but were not in pre-colonial Tamil Nadu.[48] Indeed, varna was of
limited relevance and there was considerable status fluidity in Tamil
Nadu before the onset of the British rule. The interpretation of
society in terms of scripture and legalization of caste in terms of
varna during colonial rule militated against such status fluidity and
introduced considerable social tensions which enabled Dravidianism's
emergence.[49] Status fluidity has increased after decolonization,
aided partly by the growth of the Dravidian parties.

Organization of the Study

The exposition is organized as follows. Chapter II introduces
crucial concepts and outlines the main arguments. Chapter III
discusses major elements of early Dravidianism and the features of
late colonial society which helped such notions become popular.
Chapter IV, V and VI pertain to the empirical focus of the study,
Dravidianist mobilization from 1947 to 1987. Chapter IV traces
the emergence of the DMK as the major challenger to Congress
from 1949 to 1963. Chapter V explores the DMK's rise to power
and loss of power between 1963 and 1976. Chapter VI discusses
the emergence of an autonomous subculture associated with a
popular film star within the DMK fold, the emergence and growth
of the ADMK based on this subculture from 1972 to 1977 and the
policies the ADMK pursued when it ruled from 1977 to 1988. It
also mentions important subsequent changes in Tamil Nadu's
politics. Chapter VII places the consequences of ethnic mobilization in Tamil Nadu in a comparative context, and draws lessons
from the study for invigorating pluralist democracy in India and
in other regions experiencing considerable ethnic mobilization.

[48] Four varnas are defined in terms of origin myths and occupational
characteristics—*Brahmins* (priests), *Kshatriyas* (kings/warriors), *Vaishyas* (traders) and *Shudras* (manual workers). A fifth group, the untouchables, are
deemed to have no varna. So the varna framework is strictly speaking four-
fold, with a fifth liminal category.

[49] Zvelebil (1973) and Ryerson (1988) discuss the Tamil variant of Hindu
belief and practice. Derrett (1963: 1–31) explores the influence of scripture on
Indian colonial law.

II
Arguments

This book explains the sustained popularity of the Dravidian parties; and accounts for the consequences of Dravidianist success and rule, such as the containment of social conflict, the enrichment of civic life, and the introduction of policies and modes of distribution of patronage giving emergent groups greater representation. In the process, it sheds light on the success of other ethnic and populist forces in semi-industrialized societies, and the factors which influence the impact such forces, as well as other mass parties and movements, have on pluralist democracy.

The central argument of the study is that pluralism within influential political organizations aids social pluralism.[1] *Organizational pluralism* denotes the extent of autonomy and flexibility characterizing both relations within an organization (a movement or party) and transactions between the organization and society. It refers to features of both intra-party and party-society relations as political organizations are rooted in society and their characteristic features are formed and changed through interaction with society.

The processes of mobilization which helped the rise of ethnic parties in Tamil Nadu led to the emergence of a largely inclusive political arena because of the parties' organizational pluralism. The early Dravidianists deployed appeals which could have impaired social pluralism. However, due to the internal pluralism which emerged within the Dravidian parties, these appeals were reconfigured in ways that restricted ethnic violence and contained ethnic animosities. Rather than promoting intolerance, the dominance of the Dravidian parties facilitated the greater representation of emergent groups and the reconstruction of public culture, incorporating the norms of these groups. The intolerant potential of some non-ethnic political forces was also contained because internal pluralism emerged within these organizations (e.g., the Eurocommunist parties and India's parliamentary communist parties).[2]

[1] Phil Oxhorn's generous comments helped me amplify this argument.
[2] I elaborate on this claim in the next section.

Although organizational pluralism promotes social pluralism, social pluralism does not preclude the growth of non-pluralistic parties and movements. Hindu and Sinhala revivalist organizations, for instance, initially grew in pluralistic societies. Social pluralism may remain strong even with the growth of some non-pluralistic organizations if these organizations compete openly with strong and autonomous organizations. This has been the case in western Europe despite the recent growth of xenophobic forces. Besides, some organizations with limited internal pluralism may find incentives to negotiate within a largely pluralistic social framework (e.g. some major partners in corporatist and consociational arrangements). Social pluralism is impaired, however, if organizations lacking internal pluralism become very influential and consequently marginalize more pluralistic forces, as happened in some regions of Hindu, Sikh and Sinhala revivalist strength. Furthermore, pluralistic organizations may emerge in regions with limited social pluralism and aid the growth of social pluralism. This was the case with various citizens' groups which emerged in South America and the Philippines under authoritarian rule, contributed to the overthrow of authoritarianism, and subsequently helped ensure some respect for civil rights in new democracies for over a decade. History is not destiny in the growth of civic life.[3]

Thus, the emergence of organizational pluralism is not necessarily linked to pre-existing levels of social pluralism. Indeed, no conditions can be specified that are both necessary and sufficient for the emergence of organizational pluralism. While the emergence of organizational pluralism aids social pluralism, the causal chain extends no further back. *The emergence of organizational pluralism within influential political organizations alone explains the emergence and maintenance of social pluralism.* Specifically, it explains why some political forces which began with a clear exclusionary potential later promoted social pluralism.

My argument that the emergence of organizational pluralism cannot be traced to other conditions does not, however, imply a prescription for inaction. On the contrary, it indicates that the manner in which citizens intervene in ongoing processes of mobilization can make all the difference to the growth of organizational pluralism, and thus of social pluralism. It highlights the

---

[3] Putnam (1993) offers a different view, which provides no suggestions for promoting pluralism in regions where it is weak.

scope that citizens who value pluralist democracy have to intervene in ongoing mobilization to urge political organizations towards greater internal pluralism and to oppose forces which attack social pluralism. The concluding chapter elaborates on this theme.

ORGANIZATIONAL PLURALISM

Organizational pluralism consists of three components—*leadership flexibility, cadre autonomy* and *supporter autonomy*. Leadership flexibility refers to the extent to which leaders modify their goals and strategies in light of the outlook and interests of support groups and non-supporters they wish to court, as well as local patterns of contention. Flexibility aids social pluralism only if it extends to longer term strategy and goals, rather than being merely tactical. Thus, only strategic flexibility is a component of organizational pluralism; tactical flexibility is not. Tactical flexibility involves appealing to different groups in idioms suitable to attract them or even changing the way a party presents itself to everyone according to its leaders' perception of the general mood without correspondingly altering the party's ultimate goals. This usually does not significantly increase the power that activists or supporters oriented to the new idioms enjoy within the party or change the policies the party is likely to implement if it comes to power.

For instance, the BJP has presented itself alternately as being intent on establishing Hindu hegemony in India, even at the expense of the civil rights of religious minorities, or as aiming to strengthen political institutions by resorting to moderate cultural nationalism. However, it has been closely linked all along with more overtly Hindu nationalist non-electoral organizations and directed appeals and incited violence against Muslims. It has also attempted of late to attract groups from which it has historically drawn limited support by adopting some of their demands or idioms (e.g. supporting caste quotas to attract intermediate and lower castes, claiming eastern Indian religious and political figures as forebears) without giving these groups significant representation in its leadership. The extent of its support for caste quotas has varied depending on calculations regarding maximizing support and some of its local leaders have supported agitations against the quotas. Tactical flexibility was clearly only meant to augment support, and was less effective in this regard because many saw it as a sign of the BJP's opportunism rather than of long-term changes in the party's strategy and goals. Crucially, it did not change the party's tendency to promote intolerance and violence, especially towards Muslims.[4]

In contrast with the BJP, the flexibility of the Dravidian parties extended beyond tactics to ultimate goals, and therefore reinforced social pluralism. The DK virulently opposed Brahmins and Brahminical Hinduism, and both the DK and the DMK demanded secession until the early 1960s. Although these had been central features of these organizations, the DMK and the ADMK abandoned both the emphasis on anti-Brahminism and the demand for secession. Indeed, the ADMK was renamed the All India Anna Dravida Munnetra Kazhagam (AIADMK) in 1976 to stress its acceptance of pan-Indian nationalism (though people continued to refer to it informally as the ADMK), and has been led by a Brahmin (J. Jayalalitha) over the last decade. The DMK formed alliances with pan-Indian parties from the late 1960s onwards, as did the ADMK after it was formed in 1972. It has been part of a front of pan-Indian and ethnic parties (the National Front, later renamed the United Front) since the late 1980s. This front, which formed minority national governments in 1989–90 and 1996–8, argues that the national government should accommodate ethnic forces more and impose its will less on state governments, to help maintain India's territorial integrity and reinforce social pluralism. Some of the United Front government's policies were in tune with this stance.

The strategic flexibility displayed by the leaders of the DMK and the ADMK requires an openness to learning from both past failures and successes. The DMK's early (and many later) leaders began their political careers within the DK, whose leader, E. V. Ramaswami Naicker (popularly called *Periar*—Respected Elder), not only harped on ethnic divisions, but also highlighted his atheism through heretical gestures, opposed decolonization, and rejected electoral politics and the use of cultural fora. As they saw that such a strategy limited the DK's growth among the intermediate castes and classes, otherwise likely to be attracted to the party's call for their greater inclusion, they initiated a change in strategy and goals when they formed the DMK in 1949, a decision that was reinforced by the DMK's rapid growth.

---

[4] See Jaffrelot (1996) and Basu et al. (1993).

The leaders of the Eurocommunist parties and India's parliamentary communist parties similarly changed strategy and goals in response to experience. They saw that their ambition of capturing state power through revolutionary means was unlikely to succeed in their respective countries after World War II. They felt so because of the repressive capacities of the relevant states, the ability and willingness of the United States to support existing regimes against revolutionary opponents, widespread anticipation that life chances would improve after the defeat of fascism and the end of the war (in Western Europe) and decolonization (in India), the partial fulfilment of these expectations and the consequent disinclination of broad sections of the population to support revolutionary ventures. Further, they found that many who desired greater socio-economic equality were uncomfortable with the prospect of collectivization. This led to the abandonment of Leninist strategies, explicitly on the part of the Eurocommunists and implicitly by the CPI and its main parliamentary offshoot, the Communist Party of India–Marxist (CPI-M). The acceptance by these parties of electoral competition and representative institutions, and their adoption of a more flexible attitude towards private property were important in building social pluralism in their regions of strength.[5]

The different trajectory of the communist parties which came to power in Eastern Europe and elsewhere highlights the centrality of learning in leadership flexibility. As these parties suppressed open political competition after they came to power, their hold on power was insulated from popular opinion for a long time. This meant that leaders had less need to be concerned about declining support and to reflect on the reasons for this trend. So, they did not initiate changes to address this problem.

Leadership flexibility does not ensure that a political organization will promote social pluralism as the changes leaders introduce may not be conducive to pluralism. The limited success of some communist parties, for instance, led some factions (e.g. Maoist and Fidelist tendencies) to adopt more vanguardist approaches, much

[5] See Mohan Ram (1969), Sengupta (1980) and Blackmer & Tarrow (1975). Although fundamental changes in property rights are conceivably compatible with social pluralism, a vanguardist willingness to overcome resistance to such changes through repression or dictatorship is not.

as many ethnic militants concluded from the failures of parliamentary ethnic leaders that armed militancy was needed (e.g. ethnic militias in Lebanon and Sri Lanka).[6] Besides, leaders who introduce changes conducive to pluralism will have limited effect unless they gain significant support and build a cadre base. Cadre and supporter autonomy make it likely that leaders get critical feedback regarding their strategy and goals, in the light of which they may alter them, and that new leaders who initiate changes in strategy and goals might gain support. I discuss these components of organizational pluralism, in turn.

Cadre autonomy denotes the autonomy which an organization's formal constituent units (local party units), informal constituent units (party factions) and affiliated units (party-affiliated associations) enjoy from the leadership. I take cadre autonomy to exist if the calls of leaders on some crucial issues are disregarded, alternative commands are issued by members of constituent or affiliated units, and obeyed by significant numbers who are loyal to them or share their outlook. Even if party members usually follow the commands of party leaders, their refusal to do so at crucial junctures suggests that they critically assess the positions of leaders on a variety of issues.

What matters is whether constituent and affiliated units make some independent decisions, not whether organizational rules provide for their doing so. If these units fail to exercise formally recognized decision-making rights, their members will not gain the habit of critically assessing the positions of leaders. Conversely,

---

[6] Armed militancy may sometimes aid social pluralism (e.g. if it leads to the overthrow of intransigent and repressive regimes or forces them to become more accommodative), but did not have this effect in these cases. It did aid social pluralism in South Africa, where the use of armed force by the ANC and its allies was among the pressures which forced the apartheid regime to negotiate a transition to democracy, in response to which the ANC became more accommodative (thereby exhibiting its strategic flexibility). The military gains of the communist New People's Army and the secessionist Moro National Liberation Front weakened Marcos' authoritarian regime in the Philippines. This was among the reasons which prompted the regime towards political liberalization in the mid-1980s. Although the Philippine communists failed to alter their strategy in response to the liberalization and subsequent democratization, this opening led to a transition to democracy and greater social pluralism as forces other than the communists assumed power when the Marcos dictatorship fell.

cadre autonomy may emerge within parties whose formal structure is hierarchical either because the socialization of activists outside the party (such as within independent associations, schools and colleges and kin groups) enables this or because the leaders are unable to exercise control over constituent and affiliated units. The latter is likely if communication links between leaders and cadre are weak (e.g. under conditions of war or dictatorship) or if leaders obviously lack the incentive to discipline cadre who differ from the party line on some issues while remaining loyal to the party.

The CPI and the CPI-M had the hierarchical structure of democratic centralist parties. Nevertheless, dissent and debate were possible on crucial issues, and this proved important in initiating critical shifts. For instance, major differences arose within the CPI at the time of decolonization over the significance of Indian independence, the likely time-frame for revolution and a strategy of armed struggle. The faction which dismissed decolonization as illusory initially won the internal debate and initiated a phase of armed confrontation with the Indian government. However, the other factions remained strong, and reverses in the battlefield and evidence of popular enthusiasm for electoral democracy gained them sufficient cadre support to reorient strategy in the early 1950s. Indeed, many earlier proponents of armed militancy changed their minds and accepted the new strategy in response to experience.

Cadre autonomy and leadership flexibility increased within these parties through the subsequent decades during which they contested elections, largely used legally acceptable methods and came to power at different points in three states. Leaders tolerated considerable differences in outlook and sometimes even in action on some issues. For instance, plans to build a dam which would have hastened the destruction of a rain forest in Kerala, a communist stronghold, evoked such intense and divergent feelings that CPI-M leaders permitted a party-affiliated association engaged in popular science education to spearhead a successful agitation against the dam.[7] Moreover, significant differences arose in 1996 among party leaders over participation in the United Front Government, and were openly aired. Changes in organizational

[7] Zachariah & Sooryamoorthy (1994).

culture and intense confrontation with armed revolutionary off-shoots from the late 1960s to the mid-1970s reinforced the CPI and the CPI-M's acceptance of electoral politics and private property though party programmes claim these were temporary commitments.

The ascent of the Dravidian parties was accompanied by the growth of formal and informal intermediate associations, such as debating fora, literary societies, reading rooms, film fan clubs and what I call talk shops—public spaces (often small shops) where people regularly gather to gossip, discuss social issues, read newspapers and journals, and read them out aloud to others. Although these associations were formally or informally affiliated with the party, they enjoyed considerable autonomy. Most members of the DK's youth wing developed a vision that was different in many respects from that of the DK leadership through the 1940s. For instance, they articulated ethnic appeals within a populist discourse, and saw considerable advantages in decolonization and electoral participation. The fan clubs of the popular film star, M. G. Ramachandran (popularly called MGR), were similarly autonomous of the leaders of the DMK, with which these clubs were affiliated from the late 1950s until 1972. They focused far more on promises to offer protection to the poor than on demands to change language policy or to expand caste quotas.

Constituent and affiliated units are more likely to be able to disregard leaders on crucial issues if their positions on these questions enjoy the backing of many party supporters. Otherwise, party leaders are likely to expel the dissidents or dare them to split the party, thereby forcing them to fall in line or reducing them to an insignificant splinter. So, supporter autonomy is needed to augment the tendency of leadership flexibility and cadre autonomy to promote social pluralism. *Supporter autonomy* alludes to the scope supporters have to appropriate party appeals in ways different from the explicit appeals and preferred programmes of leaders. Its presence is reflected in actions supporters undertake within and outside the party fold and is best detected using the methods of political anthropology as well as those of organizational sociology. Supporters show their autonomy by using the party banner in ways not clearly authorized by leaders and by pursuing some demands through associations unaffiliated with the party.

Socially capable groups are best able to appropriate party or movement appeals in ways that suit their concerns. 'Social capability' refers to the material resources, social skills and links at a group's disposal. It may be contrasted with atomization and *anomie*, as a socially capable group is rooted in a network of social relations and a recognized framework of norms. A group might be socially capable even if it does not enjoy high economic or social status if there are social institutions which enable group members to pool their resources and coordinate their actions. Small traders or small peasants bound by strong caste organizations, unionized agricultural workers or slum dwellers bound by strong kin and caste ties are examples. The social capability of such groups can help them defy more powerful groups to realize some of their ends, even if the former groups accept the dominance of the latter in other respects.

Groups which were socially capable but culturally distinct from the gentry were the mainstay of early Dravidianist social coalitions, and were best able to appropriate party appeals for their ends. Of the DK and the DMK's early core supporters, the small shopkeeper, the small farmer and the artisan took the party's critique of the patterns of patronage distribution prevalent in the early postcolonial period to represent the interests of small property; the new white collar worker found in the demands for expanded access a voice for the emergent vernacular intelligentsia of intermediate caste origin; while the Muslim found in the criticism of aspects of Hinduism such as the caste system and polytheism an acceptance into the political community on more equal terms than many versions of Indian nationalism offered him. The ways such groups saw their parties influenced how they oriented the activities of local party units over which they exercised influence. Party leaders encouraged a degree of supporter autonomy by emphasizing such concerns of these groups in the appeals they directed at them.[8]

Groups with little social capability were less successful in reshaping movement appeals. Thus, some SCs attempted without success to adopt the Dravidian label around the turn of the century.[9] However, some lower class groups were able to orient

[8] This was particularly true of appeals directed at the Muslims. See especially Ramaswami Naicker (1947).

[9] The European missionaries who initially articulated Dravidianist notions in the nineteenth century applied the Dravidian label to both the SCs and

the local initiatives of the Dravidian parties if they were somewhat organized. For instance, artisanal fishermen used the ADMK banner in local struggles with trawler owners without the authorization of party leaders, as did urban squatters to deter police bulldozers.

The presence of a range of socially capable groups is thus a necessary condition for the emergence of supporter autonomy, but a somewhat trivial one as it is present in much of the world today. Besides, it does not ensure the emergence of either supporter autonomy or the other aspects of organizational pluralism.

Dravidian party supporters participated extensively in independent associations. This tendency was greater as caste associations and industrial and agricultural unions were active before Dravidianist growth, and party leaders paid little attention to the formation of corporate organizations until they came to power.[10] Even after the DMK and the ADMK formed industrial unions which accepted state tutelage, some of their supporters remained members of more militant unions. Dravidianist supporters also joined agitations led by independent caste associations and farmers' associations under Dravidianist rule, forcing reluctant concessions from the government. Some independent associations colonized spaces within Dravidian party subcultures, such as some talk shops, making them loci of dissidence within the party.[11] As supporters could challenge Dravidianist regimes when they felt their interests were threatened, some accountability persisted under Dravidianist dominance.

---

the intermediate castes. Some SC intellectuals adopted this label as a term of dignified self-reference and published a journal called *Dravidan* in the 1890s and 1900s. But, organizations dominated by the intermediate and upper non-Brahmin castes laid exclusive claim to the label from the 1910s onwards and relegated the SCs to the periphery of the Dravidian fold. While the SCs are called *adi-Dravidar* (the original Dravidians), the supposed 'original Dravidians' are in effect deemed peripheral Dravidians, much as indigenous Americans are.

[10] In this regard, the Dravidianist experience was akin to that of the populist parties of Colombia and Uruguay, and contrary to that of the 'labour populist' forces in Argentina and Peru. See Collier & Collier (1991).

[11] The Vanniar caste association did so within the DMK subculture in the 1980s, before a new party was formed from this nucleus.

CAUSES OF DRAVIDIANIST SUCCESS

Populism and Ethnicity

It was the populist features of the Dravidian parties which brought them sustained electoral success. The parties' ethnic notions and the charisma of their leaders were effective mainly insofar as they reinforced the parties' populism. The populist nature of Dravidianist mobilization and policy was crucial to two outcomes: the DMK outdoing Congress and the communists by the 1960s; and the DMK and the ADMK marginalizing Congress and other pan-Indian parties by the 1970s.

The Dravidian parties' populist approach to mobilization attracted groups with limited access to the state while Congress dominated Tamil Nadu politics (until the mid-1960s). Of the Dravidianists' main competitors, Congress built support on thin foundations—large-scale industrialization, pan-Indian nationalism and the aggregation of already organized interests. The communists were identified primarily with the propertyless, who form the minority of the population.[12] Dravidian populism successfully addressed the intermediate and lower strata marginal to these strategies, and thus built more inclusive subcultures.

I use the term 'stratum' to allude to the overlap between class and status group. Caste position plays a significant role in defining status in South Asia.[13] Thus, 'intermediate strata' refers to those of both middle caste and middle class position (white collar labour and small to middling property holders). 'Lower strata' refers to

[12] Many from the lower classes had links to property, for instance through tenancy, or were of intermediate caste status. Such groups did not flock towards the communists.

[13] Weber's (1958) identification of caste with status group in India is valid in some respects, but not in others. While the five broad caste categories (varnas) of the normative Hindu social classification provide a first approximation of status, the far more numerous endogamous sub-categories (jatis) enable greater precision. However, the status accorded a given varna or jati is sensitive to local variations in social power and practice. Only in its local significance does caste define status, and it is only in this respect that caste contributes to the notion of stratification used here. See Srinivas (1962), Ludden (1985) and Dirks (1987). While caste is a part of the normative Hindu social order, it also influences social interactions among other religious groups in South Asia.

those from the lower castes, especially the SCs, who own little or no property. The ambiguous location in this stratification scheme of individuals whose class position is incongruent with their caste status does not pose a problem for three reasons. First, there is substantial overlap between class and caste position. Second, sections of castes tend to experience upward or downward mobility together, influenced by similar social changes. So, an individual whose class position is incongruent with the scripturally imputed status of his caste would be part of a similarly situated group, which is his stratum. Third, these social categories are used to explain group responses to political appeals, rather than individual behaviour. There are broad similarities in the outlook of lower middle class Brahmins, SC white collar workers or professionals from mercantile castes.

Groups with some social capability, but limited political influence, provided considerable support to the DMK from the outset. Dravidianist recruitment absorbed the pre-existing social networks amongst these groups, and extended them to include hitherto passive strata. This made the Dravidian parties more cohesive and better linked to society than Congress and the communists were. Other contemporary populist parties, notably the Greek PASOK, the Sri Lankan SLFP and the Peruvian APRA, have also gained extensive support from socially capable intermediate strata.

A range of socially capable intermediate and lower strata played at most subordinate political roles until recently in semi-industrialized societies. Such strata were unable to convert their social capability into political influence because they had been dissociated from the initial formation of centralized states, lacked social skills like education required to play major roles in new political arenas, or belonged to ethnic minorities. These groups, which account for a significant chunk of the population in many semi-industrialized societies, have an affinity with populist notions of an excluded 'people'. Populism offers them means to change the rules of the game so that their material resources and social links can gain them greater social esteem and increased contact with the state. Liberal and socialist appeals often fail to attract these groups, as they offer them no comparable ready route to these ends in the foreseeable future.

Populist and ethnic notions enable the formation of coalitions among groups subject to partial political exclusion. The rhetorical subsumption of these diverse groups under the homogeneous rubric of a popular or ethnic community enables the formation of cohesive coalitions which bridge the interests of these groups. Liberal and socialist appeals are unable to serve this function as effectively as they often address such groups as discrete interest groups; and their programmes, usually more definitely specified than those of populists, make the tensions among these groups' interests more evident. Besides, ethnic and populist conceptions of community are typically closer to the culture of plebeian groups than those posited by liberals and socialists. So, ethnic and populist forces have vanquished liberal and socialist ones in many semi-industrialized countries. The social capabilities of significant sections of the intermediate and lower strata of these regions have strengthened the populist organizations which have emerged among these groups, rather than inhibiting the growth of these organizations.

The Dravidian parties' ethnic notions generated widespread support primarily because they were articulated within a populist discourse. Language and caste categories were evocative because they were used to define a community of the 'people'. Tamil identity, for instance, gained much of its appeal not because it was defined in opposition to other language groups, but because it was associated with plebeian groups, primarily the Tamil speaking intermediate strata, and their social mores. Its thrust was more anti-élite than anti-alien. The Dravidianist politicization of the Tamil identity was aimed against élites in three ways: it associated Tamil identity with non-Sanskritic cultural traditions, strongest among the intermediate and lower castes; it represented the outlook of groups more fluent in Tamil than in English; and it meant opposition to the political élites governing India, who wished to introduce Hindi as the sole national language.

The early Dravidianist definition of Brahmins as alien to Tamil/Dravidian society heightened oppositon to Brahmin dominance in various public spheres, but did not promote a popular perception of the Tamil Brahmin as alien to Tamil society. It influenced the development of the standard Tamil which came into popular usage with the spread of literacy and the printed word through the century. This new standard Tamil drew primarily from the dialects of non-Brahmin castes although Brahmins had been among the culture bearers in pre-colonial society and had dominated early colonial education. But, the periodic calls of the early Dravidianists to expel Brahmins from Tamil Nadu were neither backed by concerted mobilization toward this end nor taken seriously by most movement supporters and society. Despite the success of Dravidian parties in later decades, non-Brahmins did not come to consider local Brahmins alien intruders. At most, Brahmins were taken to have distinct cultural practices to which they tenaciously hung, to be Tamils of a peculiar stripe, to be regarded with suspicion and envy. Thus, the anti-Brahminism of Tamil Nadu was not anti-alien in its thrust.

The following four outcomes clarify that the populist features of Dravidianist ideology were more significant than its ethnic features in generating popular support. First, the cleavages of support between the two major parties of the 1960s, the DMK and Congress, conformed more to the lines of status and occupation than to ethnic boundaries. Second, the ADMK outdid the DMK in the 1970s and 1980s, despite adopting a less militant approach on language and caste demands. It was able to do so because it presented a populist rhetorical and policy package which had broader appeal than that of the DMK, and addressed the range of its populist promises more effectively when it assumed power. Third, MGR, the initial leader of the ADMK, was of non-Tamil origin, a fact which the DMK leaders tried to use to whip up nativist sentiments when the ADMK split from the DMK in 1972. This evoked little response even among core DMK supporters as MGR's career as an immensely popular film star made him a Tamil cultural hero in the popular eye. Besides, DMK leaders had systematically cultivated MGR's appeal until recently, and used it to elicit the votes of fans. Fourth, after MGR's demise in 1987, the ADMK regrouped after a brief internal split under the leadership of Jayalalitha, who had acted alongside MGR in films, and is both a Brahmin and of non-Tamil origin. The origins of the ADMK's leaders beyond the pale of core early definitions of Dravidian ethnicity (Tamil speaking Hindus of intermediate caste status) has not inhibited popular support for the ADMK as these leaders were part of Tamil Nadu's popular culture.[14] Clearly, the

[14] MGR was a non-Brahmin Malayali and thus within the scope of the broader definition of the Dravidian as a non-Brahmin south Indian. But, this was not the definition which took root at a popular level. Jayalalitha's Brahmin origins leave her more clearly beyond the pale.

popular impact of Dravidianist ethnic appeals was to revalue plebeian cultural norms rather than to focus political sentiments on blood ties. This makes for a marked contrast with the sharpening of ethnic boundaries and the widespread violence against out-groups caused by ethnic mobilizers in many parts of the world, such as the former Yugoslavia, Rwanda, Burundi and Sri Lanka.

The ethnic elements in Dravidianist discourse, however, built a sense of ideological coherence, which cemented activist loyalty and enabled party durability through lean times (e.g. the DMK through 1976–89 and 1991–6, when it was out of power).

After populist mobilization propelled the Dravidian parties to power, populist policies enabled these parties to retain support. Although populist promises tend to be vague, supporters expect leaders to live up to the spirit of these promises in some way. The Dravidianists maintained support to the extent that they addressed the expectations their appeals aroused. After the DMK initially assumed power in 1967, it maintained and augmented its support by increasing access for emergent groups (e.g., by increasing the quotas for the BCs and SCs in education and government jobs), and by increasing food subsidies and introducing dry laws. However, it ceased to meet the expectations of many supporters as it abandoned the food subsidies and the dry laws by the early 1970s. So, it lost support to the ADMK which revived some unfulfilled populist promises. The ADMK regime satisfied the expectations of its core supporters more consistently through the 1970s and 1980s and so retained the support that brought it to power for a longer duration than the DMK did.

Populism and Charisma

Although many studies of populism point to a charismatic leader as a typical feature of populist organizations, none clarify the precise link between populism and charisma. While the five major leaders of mass Dravidianist parties had charismatic links with their followers, their charisma was rooted in their ability to present themselves as exemplars of the kind of populist outlook promoted by their parties.

Two crucial splits arose within movement organizations, whose consequences clarify the primacy of populism over charisma as a basis for the support the Dravidianists enjoyed. The first split arose in 1949, in opposition to the authoritarian style, marital plans and patrimonial inclinations of Periar, the DK's leader, which were considered out of tune with movement ideology.[15] The DMK, which was born as a result of that split, also suffered a split in 1972, when MGR left the party, criticizing the rampant corruption in the party and the abandonment of some of the party's populist promises. Both these major splits arose when the spirit of the party's populist outlook appeared to have been violated, and in both cases, the new party became more popular than the old one. The movement's populist notions could thus act at times as a counterweight to the leader's control over the party. Splits within movement organizations were significant only when the new group controlled sufficient organizational resources and could command significant loyalty within the movement subculture. Other attempts to split Dravidian parties failed for want of such strength.[16]

The DMK split once again in 1994, partly in response to the leader's efforts to promote his politically inexperienced son as his successor. The newest Dravidianist party, the MDMK, has made some inroads into the DMK's cadre and, to a lesser extent, its support base.[17] If the MDMK were to grow further, this would reinforce my argument that populism has enjoyed priority over charisma in ensuring Dravidianist mobilizing success.

The susceptibility of the Dravidian parties to splits, albeit only in special circumstances, stands in marked contrast to the experience of most populist parties. Those who attempted to outflank Peronism on working class demands met with little success, for

[15] Periar, who was then in his seventies, married a much younger woman, a common practice which he had himself frequently decried earlier. Many of his supporters found this, and his designation of his wife as his political successor, unacceptable.

[16] This distinguishes my view from theories of norm-oriented movements, which suggest that the norms advanced by such movements are readily available for appropriation by competitors. See Smelser (1962) and Barnett (1976).

[17] The MDMK gained just 5.7 per cent of the popular vote in the 1996 state assembly elections. However, opinion polls and the results of by-elections conducted between 1994 and 1996 suggest that the MDMK was the first choice of other voters too, who tactically voted for the DMK in 1996 to ensure the ADMK's defeat.

instance. The peculiar experience of the Dravidian parties shows that the populist nature of these parties imbued their subcultures in a manner which transcended their leaders' charisma.

SOCIAL STRUCTURE, PARTISANSHIP AND THE DIRECTIONS OF MASS POLITICS

Stratification and Mass Politics

The nature of social stratification, solidarity and state-society links play important roles in my explanation of Dravidianist success, as outlined in the earlier section. Indeed, such variables are crucial to explaining the growth of many recent ethnic and populist parties, for these forces emerged in well-formed civil societies and spawned durable subcultures. The interaction of three factors influences voter attitudes and alignments when parties establish themselves in pluralistic societies: social structure (stratum); prior solidarity (cleavages along which subcultures formed and contention occurred earlier); and ongoing competition among competing political forces. I use the term the 'social matrix of contention' to allude to these three factors, in their interaction.

My account differs from the way in which various scholars relate social structure to the manner of entry of emergent groups into politics. Some correlate the trajectories of peasant action with the structure of rural society—either highly stratified societies with strong social controls, typically found in areas with extensive riverine irrigation, or relatively equal peasant societies with looser social controls, typically found in drier regions.[18] While I derive my ideal-types of rural society (valleys and plains) from the peasant studies literature, party politics in Tamil Nadu does not exhibit one-to-one links between social structure and patterns of political action. Although the social profiles of Tamil Nadu's different plains regions are broadly similar, the DMK achieved early and durable strength in the northern plains, but remained weak for long in the southern and western plains. Similarly, it achieved significant early strength in one of Tamil Nadu's main river valleys, the Kaveri valley, but not in the other, the Tamiraparani valley.

Voter alignments do not merely reflect patterns of stratification as political strategies mediate the influence of social structure on

[18] See Scott (1976) and Paige (1975).

mass political action.[19] For instance, the power of the intermediate castes of the Tamil plains enabled them to forge strong social networks through the centuries; while similar caste groups were subject to the economic and cultural dominance of the landed upper castes in the valleys.[20] These pre-existing intermediate caste networks were available in the plains as a resource for the DMK, which was primarily oriented towards the intermediate strata. The DMK achieved early and durable success in the northern plains because it integrated these networks into its subculture there, unlike in the southern and western plains.[21] It succeeded in doing so in the northern plains both because other parties were weaker there before its emergence, and because it adopted local strategies conducive to building a broad coalition encompassing the intermediate and some of the lower strata. The DMK failed to do so in the southern plains because the Congress subculture was strong prior to the DMK's emergence, and it tried to compensate for its early weakness by associating itself too closely and exclusively with a particular caste cluster, the Mukkulathor.[22]

Some scholars have explained the different ways in which mass politics was shaped in Latin America and the Balkans with reference to the relative social power and political strategies of classes contending for dominance at the point of mass entry into politics. Mouzelis claims that mass incorporation takes a populist path if the landowning oligarchy and the urban middle classes are of approximately equal strength. If both classes are strong, the middle classes use populist appeals to mobilize the urban working classes in opposition to the oligarchy. If both classes are weak, freeholder peasants have the autonomy to launch their own populist project. When there is significant inequality between the power of the oligarchy and that of the urban middle classes, Mouzelis contends, the masses take a non-populist route into

[19] Wolf (1969) and Migdal (1974) are among the studies of peasant politics which pay attention to political strategies.

[20] See Stein (1980) and Ludden (1985).

[21] Perry (1980) presents a similar argument about the reliance of Chinese communists on secret societies.

[22] 'Mukkulathor' is a term of recent provenance meaning 'those of the three clans/castes'. It refers to three related caste groups, the Kallar, the Maravar and the Ahamudaiyar. See Dumont (1986).

politics.[23] The populist Dravidian parties gained substantial support in both urban and rural areas in a society with a declining landed gentry and a strong and growing urban middle class. This case clearly eludes Mouzelis' theoretical net, devised purely from variables of social structure.[24]

Collier & Collier argue that the nature of the political relations between the oligarchy and the urban middle class, collaboration or conflict, determines the extent and nature of mass mobilization. If the two classes collaborate in a project of gradual reform, the masses are mobilized in a limited and controlled manner. If the oligarchy resists reform, the middle classes mobilize labour to a greater degree in favour of reform, often using populist appeals.[25] The middle classes of Tamil Nadu, both urban and rural, became divided over the first three post-colonial decades in their allegiance to alternative reform projects, associated with Congress and the Dravidianists. So, populist success cannot be attributed to a single political strategy pursued by the middle classes, as the Colliers would suggest.

In regions with strong parties having multi-class bases, the major political strategies followed are often more closely associated with these parties than with particular classes, though segments of different classes contribute to shaping these strategies. The Congress project, especially in its Tamil variant, resembled the Colliers' collaborationist route to a degree. The fraction of the middle classes most intimately linked with colonial knowledge (Western education) and colonial privilege (the upper reaches of the professions) was the primary author of this project. It sometimes adopted the idioms of the declining oligarchy (the landowning upper castes), in which many of its members had their origins.[26] This

[23] Mouzelis (1986).

[24] Besides, Greece, which Mouzelis cites as his case with a strong middle class and a weak landowning class, appears to be an instance of non-populist mass politics only because Mouzelis' analysis does not extend to the last two decades.

[25] Collier & Collier (1991: 748 & *passim*).

[26] The Congress government's land reforms were too extensive and the old landed élites too weak (unless they had found sources of power other than land control) by the early post-colonial decades for the Congress project to conform closely to the Colliers' collaborationist model, based on the Latin American experience in the early decades of the century.

fraction of the Tamil middle class retained its leadership over the Congress project until the 1960s, even while the party's social base expanded.

Dravidianism primarily contested the political dominance of this fraction of the Tamil middle class. It struck at the already declining social power of the old oligarchy only secondarily, if at all. Led by the fraction of the middle classes less closely linked to colonial and early post-colonial state institutions (the petty intelligentsia and those of middling agrarian and mercantile wealth), this project employed the rustic idiom, non-Sanskritic and non-Anglicized, of these groups. This idiom was used to weave notions of a popular ethnic community in which emergent strata found the promise of political representation. The Dravidianist project succeeded because the masses it mobilized found ways to participate in shaping it in ways that represented their interests, however imperfectly.

This book explains Dravidianist success and its consequences with reference to the alternative ways in which competing political parties transacted with society and the different ways in which social groups appropriated competing appeals. It suggests that such analyses of political mobilization, from 'above' and 'below', hold the key to understanding the formation of political allegiances, regimes and their agendas. In Tamil Nadu, the complex processes by which parties 'went to the people' led to the stable incorporation of the masses, arrayed behind competing populist parties, into a democratic political order.[27] Plebeian idioms became ubiquitous, associational life became strong, and people gained a sense of political efficacy, although only limited socio-economic reforms were introduced.

Theorizing Mass Politics

The manner in which I plot the relationship between the appeals of political élites and the mass responses they evoke provides the basis for my departure from the 'collective behaviour' approach to analysing mass politics. Proponents of this approach deduce from the totalizing nature of populist ideologies that populism

---

[27] 'Going to the people' was the watchword of the early Russian populists, but the complex strategies required for success in this ambition were discovered only by later and more successful populists elsewhere.

erodes social pluralism, and from the tendency of ethnic mobilizers to draw somewhat sharp ethnic boundaries that ethnic movements are likely to provoke social conflict. In so doing, they assume that the growth of movements involves the diffusion of movement ideology, which detaches supporters from prior beliefs and links which are at odds with movement ideology. Smelser, a major proponent of the collective behaviour approach, argued that groups whose social position is incongruous with their status aspirations promote movements to change certain social norms or basically transform society's value orientations. The growth of norm-oriented movement leads to the greater acceptance of the norms they promote. Value-oriented movements rarely change social values completely, but their success introduces changes in norms along the lines suggested by their value orientations.[28]

Following the collective behaviour approach, Kornhauser and Germani argued that the growth of populism leads to the imposition of the uniform standards populism upholds, eroding social pluralism. They accorded the social position of groups a significant role in the emergence of ideologies, but not in shaping the movements and parties that espouse these ideologies. This seemed particularly justified in the analysis of populism, which was said to grow among atomized groups not rooted in prior routines which might influence their response to mobilizing appeals.[29]

The significance I accord status incongruence in the emergence of Dravidianist notions is compatible with collective behaviour theory. Various non-Brahmin groups with a limited experience of Western education were galled by the contrast between their social power, albeit limited in some cases, and their marginal position in state-society interactions in the late colonial period. This incongruence was the social basis for the emergence of non-Brahminism, but does not explain the success of the Dravidian parties as non-Brahminist notions were adopted by Congress and other parties too. Besides, non-Brahmin indignation need not have been voiced through notions of a popular community, especially in view of the social eminence of some non-Brahmin groups and the conflicts of interest among non-Brahmins. If non-Brahmin grievances had not been given a populist form, they would most probably have been

---

[28] See Smelser (1962).
[29] Kornhauser (1959), Germani (1978).

fully accommodated within Congress, which gave non-Brahmins increasing prominence and addressed some non-Brahminist demands after the 1920s. This was the outcome in the western Indian state of Maharashtra where non-Brahminist notions appeared even earlier than in Tamil Nadu, but were not articulated within a populist discourse binding strong organizations.[30]

Unlike the collective behaviour school, I take the resources at the disposal of organizations, the capabilities of social groups, prior solidarity and pre-given normative frameworks to mediate the impact of populist and ethnic appeals on mass response and political action. The first two factors are central to the approach of the resource mobilization school, which charts movement and party growth primarily with regard to the resources these organizations accumulate. While rightly emphasizing resources and capabilities, this school ignores the significance of mobilizing appeals and the meaning they acquire for supporters.[31]

The changing structure of society and emergent beliefs exercise a mutual influence on each other. Thus, the context of late colonial and early post-colonial Tamil Nadu proved conducive to the emergence of the crucial elements of Dravidianist ideology, non-Brahminism and Tamil nationalism. Publicists, ideologues and political organizations typically weave such emerging beliefs into political ideologies. Ethnic and populist movements and parties appropriate prevalent beliefs and reconfigure them into discourses about the special character of the people.

Prior solidarity and pre-given normative frameworks influence the meaning supporters attach to political appeals, and thus the images of self and society that loosely bind movements and parties. The loose structure of populist discourse lends itself to diverse interpretations, particularly by socially capable supporters. The meaning such supporters find in the appeals of a pluralistic party influences the party's local strategies and the responses of other groups. As propertied intermediate castes made Dravidianism their vehicle in the northern plains, the interests of these groups became central to local DMK strategy. This alienated most propertyless SCs against whom the intermediate castes were frequently pitted even before the emergence of parties. The SCs were not alienated

---

[30] See O'Hanlon (1985), Omvedt (1976).
[31] See Zald & McCarthy (1987), Tilly (1978).

from the DMK to a comparable extent in the Kaveri valley, where many intermediate caste groups occupied a marginal social position and could make common cause with the SCs in opposing ritual exclusion.

Even if some groups are stably aligned with particular parties or movements, these groups may undertake other forms of collective action. This is particularly likely among supporters of pluralistic parties who are already accustomed to acting on definite conceptions of interest. Such groups may, however, justify their autonomous activities in terms of party ideology. Party growth tends to broaden the social networks linking supporters and widen their ideational horizons. The social capacities of supporters are augmented in the process and a sharper focus given to prior inchoate notions of interest. The increase in the material and normative resources at the disposal of supporters is likely to change some of their actions, even those undertaken in pursuit of preconceived interests. For instance, the intermediate castes of the Tamil plains, which augmented their power and prestige in other ways earlier, used the DMK's accession to power to gain control over credit cooperatives and temple trustee boards.

Such partially autonomous mass appropriation of political appeals, common in pluralistic organizations, constrains regimes these organizations lead to respond to expectations not set solely by the explicit promises of leaders. The book clarifies how resources, capabilities, forms of organization, patterns of solidarity and normative frameworks, both pre-given and emergent, influence the impact of political appeals on collective action and the policy agenda. It thereby shows how totalizing appeals concerning a popular ethnic community may be appropriated to maintain pluralist democracy.

THE IMPACT OF DRAVIDIANIST SUCCESS AND RULE

The leaders and ideologues of the DMK and the ADMK constructed their notions of community in ways that helped blunt the intolerant potential of ethnic and populist appeals. Although they asserted the homogeneity and deep historical roots of the Dravidian community, they deployed notions of political community composed of many partially overlapping layers. Contrary to claims that ethno-national forces define identities around a central cultural symbol, no single attribute was the primary marker of membership in the Dravidian community, whose boundaries were drawn according to the context.[32] The DMK and the ADMK defined these boundaries with reference to categories of status and power, as well as ethnic categories, and this influenced the visions of community which took root in society as these parties grew. Tamil speaking intermediate Hindu castes lay at the core of the DK's vision of political community. But, the strategies of the DMK and the ADMK enabled the incorporation of other groups, even those like Brahmins who were clearly beyond the pale in the early Dravidianist vision. Other groups outside the core of the DK's vision, like the SCs, even found somewhat greater representation with the growth of the Dravidian parties. While the homogeneous aspects of the later Dravidianist notions of community provided organizational cohesion, the layered ones facilitated flexibility in strategy and goals. As community boundaries were sketched in different ways, the Dravidian parties demonized no group in a sustained way.

Such layered notions of community emerged and were flexibly deployed to include most inhabitants of Tamil Nadu in the course of the Dravidian movement's history. The DK virulently opposed Brahmins, Brahminical Hinduism and north Indians in the late colonial period. The Dravidianists did not undertake significant attacks against these groups even then, and movement leaders maintained friendly social contacts with members of these groups.[33] This might however have changed if the DK had gained more widespread support. The DMK, formed in 1949, abandoned calls for drastic action against Brahmins and its anti-north Indian appeals only highlighted opposition to the central government, pan-Indian nationalism and Congress.[34] The DMK's militant language agitations of the 1960s involved extensive confrontation with the police,

[32] See Brass (1991: 20–1, 62–3); Fishman (1988: 39–51); Meinecke (1970: 9–22). The community was not defined in terms of loyalty to a state either, especially after the DMK abandoned secessionism.

[33] For instance, Periar was a good friend of a major Brahmin Congress leader, choosing to consult only him when he contemplated marriage at an advanced age. He engaged Brahmin lawyers and rented out many of the houses he owned to Brahmin tenants.

[34] North Indian merchants in Madras city, who opposed the DMK through the first two decades of its existence and contributed funds to Congress election campaigns during this period, found over a generation that the DMK had not

but not attacks against the non-Tamil speaking inhabitants of Tamil Nadu. After the major language agitations ended in the late 1960s and the ADMK was formed in 1972, appeals to language and caste diminished further in significance, confrontation with the central government declined and Dravidianism moved towards a conciliatory embrace with pan-Indian nationalism. Ethnic mobilization built a largely inclusive political arena mainly because of the *organizational pluralism* which characterized the Dravidian parties.

From Organizational Pluralism to Social Pluralism

Pluralism within influential political organizations aids social pluralism because the tolerance of significant differences within these organizations often fosters in members a tolerance of differences in society; and the ongoing negotiation of intra-organizational differences often builds an institutional culture open to negotiation and compromise with other political forces. Whether this happens depends on the extent to which leaders and activists differ in their preferences regarding strategy and goals, and the extent of differences in the social background and personal culture of leaders, members and core supporters. Significant differences arose within the Dravidian parties regarding visions of the political community and attitudes towards the colonial and post-colonial Indian states. As the DMK grew, its cadre and social bases became diversified in terms of caste, class, region, mother tongue and religious affiliation. The formation of the ADMK led Dravidianists into further new social niches. As a result, party leaders became willing to negotiate with pan-Indian parties and some pan-Indianist leaders whom they had earlier considered arch-enemies, and the Dravidianist agenda was extended beyond changing social relations in Tamil Nadu to changing the structure of Indian federalism.

The three aspects of organizational pluralism tend to reinforce one another. Thus, organizational pluralism often tends to maintain itself once it emerges, and promotes social pluralism that much more effectively. For instance, Dravidianist supporters had greater autonomy as they were socially capable and were involved in independent associations and had somewhat formed notions of

---

hurt their interests. So much so, they gave the DMK campaign funds, not only when it was in power in the 1970s, but also when it was in the opposition in the 1980s and 1990s.

interest even before they had cast their lot with these parties. This urged party leaders to give party-affiliated associations more autonomy as a means to gain them more support, as well as to tolerate the participation of party activists and supporters in independent associations. Further, it helped the emergence of factions associated with dissident interpretations of movement ideology, which were the nuclei of the later born Dravidian parties, the DMK and the ADMK. The combination of cadre and supporter autonomy empowered leaders inclined to be flexible and helped them outdo less flexible ones, a process crucial in the emergence and growth of the DMK. It also constrained leaders to remain somewhat flexible to retain support.

Organizational pluralism aided the emergence of two strong Dravidian parties associated with different versions of the Dravidianist agenda by the 1970s. As different social groups felt an affinity with the two variants of Dravidian populism, the two parties carved out different, though partly overlapping, social niches for themselves. This ensured sustained party competition and programmatic contestation even while the Dravidian parties together commanded over 60 per cent of the popular vote through the last two decades. The pluralism of the Dravidian parties ensured that their electoral dominance did not translate into commensurate control over society. Even while the DMK or the ADMK ruled, both supporters of the ruling party and others could pursue demands somewhat independently and challenge some of the state government's policies. As the Dravidian parties knit emergent groups more closely into their subcultures than the pan-Indian parties had, they linked these groups more closely to representative institutions.[35]

Although the Dravidian parties grew within a state rather than a separate country, their coexistence with stability and pluralist democracy was a result of the paths they took rather than of factors operating throughout India. The persistence of democracy in much of India and the Indian state's strategy for accommodating ethnic demands failed to ensure stability, respect for civil rights and the regular conduct of free elections in regions like Kashmir and

---

[35] Pan-Indian parties incorporated emergent groups more successfully in regions where they mobilized these groups intensively, e.g. Congress in Gujarat and the communists in Kerala.

Punjab. Congress, which ruled India through much of the three decades of Dravidianist rule in Tamil Nadu, was less internally pluralistic and less oriented to social pluralism than the Dravidian parties through much of this period. Further, Congress-led governments often failed to restrain the intolerant actions of forces like the Hindu revivalists.

Moreover, Dravidian party leaders initiated the crucial steps conducive to social pluralism due to their perceptions of public opinion in Tamil Nadu, rather than because of the Indian state's threat of punitive action. For instance, the DMK leaders had decided in private to abandon their demand for secession a few years before the Indian government's ban on secessionists holding political office forced them to go public with this decision. Similarly, it was electoral incentives and the need to present themselves as responsible future rulers, rather than actions of the Indian government, which prompted DMK and ADMK leaders to alter Dravidianist appeals to include groups outside the core of early visions of the Dravidian community.

The sustained presence of a democratic regime in India was however necessary for Dravidianism to have the benign effects it did in Tamil Nadu. During the 'emergency' of the mid-1970s, only Congress and its minor allies were free to mobilize openly and the Dravidian parties were unable to organize effectively underground.[36] If India had taken a sustained authoritarian turn then or later, social pluralism would undoubtedly have suffered long-term damage throughout the country. Conversely, the strength of social pluralism was an impediment to maintaining authoritarianism, for it was among the reasons that urged Indira Gandhi to call elections in pursuit of democratic relegitimation in 1977, and helped the Janata party defeat Congress in these elections and reinstate democracy.

INTERNAL PLURALISM: ITS BOUNDS AND BLESSINGS

The Bounds of Internal Pluralism

The Dravidianists and reformist communists belong to a broader family of movements and parties whose ideologies—ethnic, vanguardist, etc.—lent them the potential to impair social pluralism,

---

[36] The DMK opposed the emergency, but the ADMK did not.

but which promoted social pluralism nevertheless due to the emergence of internal pluralism. The trajectories of these forces strongly confirms the tendency of organizational pluralism to promote social pluralism. Internal pluralism has so deeply affected the socialization of leaders, cadre and core supporters in these cases that these parties are unlikely to seriously undermine social pluralism as long as there are no major changes in the nature of the Indian polity.

Such internally pluralistic parties with potentially exclusionary ideological origins are distinguishable from catch-all parties as they retain elements of continuity with their ideological past. Reformist communists continue to seek greater socio-economic equality, for instance by seeking to restrict erosion in the living standards of the lower classes in the face of neo-liberal economic reform, and present these efforts as steps towards building a socialist alternative to the existing social order. The Indian variants present themselves as genuine popular nationalists, much as their forebears did. The Dravidian parties emphasize the culture of the intermediate and lower castes, resist the introduction of Hindi as India's sole official language and present these positions of theirs as part of an authentic Dravidianist politics.

The sentiments of cadre and supporters are such that leaders need to maintain elements of continuity with movement history to ensure continued support. The links of these parties with their ideological origins provides a sense of coherence essential for the formation of partisan subcultures and constrains cadre autonomy. Members of the subculture have an imprecise yet strong sense of the party's role in society, which is taken to constrain the scope of their legitimate activities. Activists who stray beyond these bounds risk losing their links to the subculture. Dissident factions or party offshoots justify their dissent in relation to aspects of movement ideology, and gain support within the subculture only if they effectively do so. So, such parties do not split often. These limits to cadre autonomy help maintain such organizations and their bounded internal pluralism.

The focus of the Dravidian parties on promoting upward social mobility, and the interests of groups occupying the apex of party subcultures placed definite limits on the extent of cadre and supporter autonomy. While demands could arise for increased entitlements to wage goods and jobs, attempts at basic changes in property rights were not permissible within the Dravidianist fold. If Dravidianist supporters were allowed to participate in unions affiliated with the reformist communist parties, this was partly because these parties had over time moderated their ambitions of substantially redistributing property. Despite these changes in the orientations of the reformist communist parties, Dravidianist regimes acted to curtail the strength of communist and other militant unions as leaders were wary of the ultimate visions impelling the activities of these unions. The DMK introduced minor land reforms in the first years of its rule and Dravidianist dominance of the public sphere inhibited concerted mobilization for further land reform. Although the Dravidian parties promoted social pluralism, their dominance restricted the policy agenda. While the interests of emergent groups gained increased representation, constructions of their interests which challenged the basic structure of property rights were ruled out.

Even some of the restrictions which Dravidianist success placed on the policy agenda contributed to the stabilization of representative democracy in a highly mobilized social terrain. Direct challenges to the interests of the dominant classes often provoke authoritarian responses from these groups and sections of the armed forces (e.g. Chile of the early 1970s). The success of the Dravidianists, rather than revolutionary communists, restricted such challenges in Tamil Nadu and precluded an authoritarian backlash. This was because the Dravidian parties restricted the *type* of demands emerging from society even while demands proliferated, as they do in contexts of high mobilization.

Populism, Clientelism and Bounded Autonomy

Populist policies were crucial in keeping the Dravidian parties in power because promises regarding the distribution of tangible benefits to key support groups were crucial to mobilization, and shaped the expectations of supporters. The material and symbolic exchanges between the Dravidian parties and their supporters had clientelistic features. The clients with whom mass parties transact are best regarded as groups rather than as individuals because parties direct patronage to key support groups and usually attempt to monitor continuity in support at a group, not an individual level.[37] Groups have an incentive to become clients of parties if they lack the power to effectively pursue crucial needs of theirs independently and the state has considerable resources at its disposal.[38] Parties and regimes show an affinity towards clientelism if the promise of ready benefits appears likely to attract a significant clientele and they are able to discern whether significant sections of groups which promise them their support do indeed support them. The preconditions of clientelism were present in post-colonial Tamil Nadu, as in many other semi-industrialized societies—the state had influence or control over a wide range of economic activities, the lower and intermediate strata enjoyed limited access to policy-making other than through party channels, and the precarious economic position of these groups made them eager for immediate benefits. Further, some parties developed strong social roots, and electoral practices enabled them to gauge their sources of electoral support with some accuracy.[39] Besides,

[37] Traditional clientelism, on the contrary, is best conceived as involving exchanges between individuals. Mass parties may also derive support on a 'neo-traditional' basis, by incorporating traditional clientelist links into their support structures, but this is not their specific function.

[38] Groups that are clients of parties may simultaneously mobilize outside the party framework.

[39] While the ballot is secret, votes have been counted by the polling booth (rather than the constituency) in many post-colonial elections. Voters from a village or two, or a couple of urban wards, typically fewer than 2,000 individuals, are assigned to a polling booth. Party representatives are intimately aware of the social composition of the population voting in their booth and note the approximate numbers and social background (caste/class) of those who vote at different points in the day. The social background of voters is either known to activists (especially in rural areas) or gleaned from attire, dialect, manner, etc. Contrary to official rules, poll officials often empty ballot boxes 'carefully' before counting so that votes are counted approximately in the order in which they were cast. The parties' election agents are given updates of the party-wise vote breakdown for the booth as the counting proceeds, as well as the final tally. When correlated with notes about the groups which voted at different points, these figures give activists a fairly accurate picture of the sources of support for the major parties. Such practices enable parties to assess the efficacy of their clientelist strategies and helped me gain a fine-grained picture of partisanship through interviews with activists.

gestures demonstrating partisan loyalties became common even when elections were not being held.[40] The major parties of the state have helped reproduce such conditions and thus the social base for their clientelist strategies.

As client groups gain benefits in return for pledging their support to particular parties, voicing their demands in terms acceptable to these parties, and abjuring modes of mobilization that would be considered signs of disloyalty, they lose part of their autonomy. Clientelist strategies typically distribute benefits and empower supporters only to an extent compatible with their continued dependence on patronage, thus enabling the reproduction of clientelism. Regimes that distribute more substantial benefits which put poorer groups 'on their own feet' and those which pursue development strategies conceived independently of their capacity to generate support are not clientelist. Crucial Dravidianist policies, such as the backward caste quotas and free lunches, were clientelist as they targeted specific groups which gave the ruling party their support in return or were being courted by the ruling party as clients. Further, a person's position within the DMK subculture definitely enhanced his chances of benefiting from the caste quotas while the DMK was in power. While access to the free lunches instituted by the ADMK regime did not depend on one's partisan loyalties, these lunches made the biggest difference to the lower strata and women, which were the ADMK's most significant support groups. Other important policies of the Dravidianist regimes were also clientelistic.

The clients' loss of autonomy is far from total. Bargaining, implicit or explicit, plays a role in determining the terms of the clientelist exchange, especially in conditions of high political participation and intense political competition, such as have existed in India since the 1960s.[41] The implicit price of a vote varies with the capabilities of potential client groups and the number of viable

---

[40] Examples include wearing a *thundu* (a towel which Tamil men drape over their shoulders) with the party colours, hoisting party flags in urban slums and rural hamlets, inviting leaders to conduct party meetings in the locality, extolling film star politicians, and committing suicide to protest against particular policies or demonstrate grief over the demise or feared demise of popular politicians.

[41] See Eisenstadt & Lemarchand (1981: 39–42).

parties competing for the support of these groups.[42] Elements of the clientelist exchange such as the nature of the benefits extended and the implicit duration of the clientelist contract are open to bargaining. In some cases, client groups extend their support in just one election in return for specific benefits, sometimes as meagre as small amounts of food, liquor or money. In other cases, they extend their loyalty over long periods, and the loyalty is contingent only on the party or regime giving some unspecified benefits to some individuals in the group. Other individuals stay on the boat, seeing in the disbursed benefits evidence that the party helps people like them and hoping that their turn will come next.

The former type of exchange, where short-term loyalty is exchanged for insubstantial benefits, was common in Tamil Nadu during the period of Congress dominance in the 1950s, and declined in significance with Dravidianist growth. Such exchanges often worked because the one-shot benefits were reinforced by the party's association with a traditional patron, and many of the rural poor did not believe that the ballot was indeed secret. The latter belief was rational because of the pervasive influence of local notables over nominally impartial institutions. Besides, Congress and state institutions were closely interwined at this point, and it was Congress which benefited most from such exchanges. As part of their effort to break the Congress 'vote banks' during the 1962 elections, DMK activists focused on assuring poor people that they would ensure the secrecy of the ballot.[43]

The latter type of exchange between parties and clients, where both the duration of loyalty and the extent of benefits are greater, has been more common since the 1960s, and has been associated with the Dravidian parties which have grown through this period. As a result, whole families or kin groups have often stayed loyal to a Dravidian party for a generation or longer. Dravidianist transactions with society also had non-clientelist features.

---

[42] For instance, parties tend to spend more during election campaigns in constituencies with intense competition and less in constituencies reserved for the SCs and STs, where the social capabilities of the electorate are generally lower.

[43] Parties continue to distribute food, liquor or money prior to elections, but people rarely feel obliged to vote for the party from which they accept these goods.

Populist and Bureaucratic Clientelism

Dravidianist regimes were more effective than their Congress predecessors in enabling stable governance amidst dense associational activity. This difference was due to the different kinds of clientelist methods these parties employed, which were also important factors in the very success of the Dravidian parties at the expense of Congress. In the first two post-colonial decades, during which Congress ruled Tamil Nadu and most Indian states, the predominant pattern of clientelism throughout India was bureaucratic; whereas during the three decades of Dravidianist rule in Tamil Nadu and in other parts of India since the late 1960s it was populist.[44] The two types of clientelism have so far not been systematically compared.

Populist clientelism differs from bureaucratic clientelism in the kinds of policies adopted, the reach of the clientelist networks through which patronage is disbursed, and the claims with reference to which policies are legitimized. Populist regimes focus government spending on projects whose benefits become quickly available for the satisfaction of mass needs. Bureaucratic clientelist regimes are guided by long-term development strategies, which they consider appropriate for generating support as they are inattentive to mass eagerness to share in the benefits of development as soon as possible. Populist clientelism channels patronage through the extensive social networks of party subcultures, both to supporters and to others from the intermediate and lower strata whose support it hopes to attract. Bureaucratic clientelism involves the distribution of patronage by state officials and local party bosses, often through social élites. While populist clientelism extends patronage more directly to plebeian groups, bureaucratic clientelism is more often parasitic on traditional clientelist bonds.

Populists systematically legitimize their policies with reference to the claims of representing the little folk that impel their mobilization. Bureaucratic clientelism more often adopts an official discourse of development and nation-building, to which the social profile of distribution of benefits is not central. Populist parties are cohesive, as they are bound by adherence to a particular kind of populist outlook. Their supporters see in the wide

[44] Chubb (1982) and Weiner (1967) discuss bureaucratic clientelism. Mouzelis (1986) and Coniff (1982) discuss populist clientelism.

distribution of benefits to plebeian groups evidence of the parties' distinctive populist character. Bureaucratic clientelist parties are often not cohesive, as the trajectories of their factions are determined by party bosses whose loyalty to the party depends on the success they achieve in factional battles. People give credit for the benefits they receive, and thus their support, directly to the ruling party under populist rule. It is local bosses who gain such credit in bureaucratic clientelist regimes, and so the ruling party is unable to ensure as easily that the patronage it distributes does lead to increased support.

Populist clientelism is better attuned to gaining the support and maintaining the loyalty of emergent groups in contexts of high political participation and associational activity. The differences in the kind of clientelist transactions in which the Dravidian parties and Congress predominantly engaged helped the former parties outdo the latter in Tamil Nadu. The limited capacity of bureaucratic clientelism to incorporate a highly mobilized public was a crucial reason which urged Congress and some of its offshoots to assume populist features in different parts of India from late 1960s onwards. However, these parties did not do so effectively in Tamil Nadu. Moreover, they did not incorporate emergent ethnic sentiments effectively, and so became marginalized.

Congress, unlike the DMK, became less internally pluralistic when it made its populist turn outside Tamil Nadu. While the Janata party and Janata Dal were more internally pluralistic than Congress, they lacked the cohesion of the Dravidian parties. So, in regions where Congress and its centrist offshoots were electorally strong, populism only aided the maintenance of a weakened representative democracy (and failed to achieve even that during the 'emergency' of the mid-1970s when democratic rule was suspended throughout India), was often intolerant of autonomous initiative, and led to some amount of political fragmentation rather than to sustained programmatic contestation and improved accountablility.[45] The different consequences of populism in Tamil Nadu, on the one hand, and in parts of northern and western India, on the other, clarify that it is the organizational pluralism of the Dravidian parties, rather than their populism, which accounts for their positive impact on pluralist democracy.

[45] See Kohli (1990).

Populism, Economic Growth and Distribution

The darker side of Dravidian populism lay not only in the limits it placed on citizens' autonomy and the political agenda, but also in its impact on economic growth. The consequences of an expansion in entitlements for economic growth depend on the nature and manner of allocation of the entitlements. Subsidies for housing and education, and easy credit provision spurred economic growth in parts of Western Europe in the aftermath of World War II.[46] However, if subsidies for wage goods are not accompanied by fiscal measures to fund them over time, or preferential quotas are allocated with little regard to skill, economic growth is likely to decline. Major schemes adopted by the Dravidianists, such as a free lunch scheme which fed about a fifth of Tamil Nadu's population and the reservation of 69 per cent of government jobs for the intermediate and lower castes, were of the latter kind. Credit and housing schemes were implemented in ways that depleted the resources at the disposal of the agrarian cooperative credit system and restricted public housing provision to small pockets of the state. Such policies, and Tamil Nadu's fall from favour as a locus of major national government projects, resulted in a decline in industrial growth.

Even if populism curbs economic growth (which it does not always do), sustained political success can coexist with poor economic performance as populist clientelism enables rulers to purchase consent cheaply. Hence, populist regimes retained support, despite low economic growth, for long periods in Tamil Nadu and for shorter periods in the Indian Union.

Populist regimes may maintain support despite low economic growth if they distribute benefits more widely and effectively present this as part of the empowerment of plebeian groups. For instance, the ADMK regime's free lunch scheme gave poor children access to nutrition on a much wider scale than similar schemes of the earlier Congress government, although economic growth had been higher during Congress rule. Besides, support was generated for the scheme through sustained allusions to earlier promises in MGR's films to support the poor. As these films and mobilization with reference to them shaped the political sentiments of many citizens, the references to the films urged these voters to regard the

[46] See Esping-Andersen (1990).

lunch scheme and other welfare measures as evidence that their hopes for representation were finally being realized. So, many supporters tolerated shortcomings in policy outcomes and remained loyal to the ADMK. In the terrain of autonomous assocaitional activity which they helped shape, the populist clientelism of the Dravidian parties helped them retain power amidst low economic growth.

The Mixed Blessings of Bounded Internal Pluralism

The emergence of organizational pluralism crucially helped blunt the intolerant potential of early Dravidianism. It helped give Dravidianist ethnic appeals a more inclusive form, focused on revaluing plebeian culture rather than on policing ethnic boundaries. Moreover, the growth of internal pluralism means that there was more space for independent initiative while the Dravidian parties ruled. As a result, these parties were under pressure from those they had mobilized, as well as from others, to vindicate their populist promises by increasing entitlements for the intermediate and lower strata once they came to power. They increased such entitlements in many ways, and retained and augmented support only if they did so. Organizational pluralism had similar effects on reformist communist parties, urging them away from vanguardist strategies and making them responsive to some independently voiced demands. Thus, it redirected various potentially exclusionary political forces towards social pluralism.

However, the kind of internal pluralism which emerged within the Dravidian parties had its costs. While it reshaped notions of a popular/ethnic community so that they were more inclusive, it did so by making particular constructions of plebeian norms dominant in public culture. Anyone could adopt these norms, whatever their ancestry, but those who were uncomfortable with these norms and the vision of citizenship implicit in them were left with limited room for manoeuvre. They either swallowed their misgivings to retain a significant public voice, or were marginalized.

The Dravidin parties' populist clientelism reached benefits more directly to the intermediate and lower strata, but constricted the autonomy of its beneficiaries. As populism coexisted with internal pluralism in Tamil Nadu, citizens had greater autonomy than they had in regions dominated by populist organizations which lacked internal pluralism. But Dravidianist supporters had to avoid forms of mobilization inimical to the dominant agenda, which promoted social mobility without introducing major changes in property rights. Others were constrained in their efforts to promote alternative agendas by Dravidianist dominance. Not only did Dravidian populism restrict efforts to change property rights, it also limited economic growth. It compensated for restricting economic growth and the extent of redistribution only with piecemeal increases in entitlements. Although pluralistic populism increased political participation and enriched civic life, society was unable to reach many of the ends for which it got mobilized. The pluralist dream was realized, yet went sour in some respects.

Some of the bounds of internal pluralism were crucial to its blessings. They lent political organizations some coherence and helped maintain their integrity over fairly long periods. Besides, bounded internal pluralism reinforced pluralist democracy partly because it contained challenges to the interests of the dominant strata amidst considerable associational activity.

TYPES OF POPULIST MOBILIZATION

While populist forces have some common features, important differences have been noted in their support bases and appeals. Scholars have distinguished such forces from one another based on the social group from which they draw much of their support—urban labour, peasantry—or their position in the left-right spectrum—e.g., reactionary, progressive, socialist, fascist.[47] As the former approach implicitly assumes that populism occupies restricted social niches, it is irrelevant to understanding recent populist parties, which have drawn support from different strata in urban and rural areas. The latter approach, which understands populist forces in terms of other ideologies with which their appeals have an affinity, is misleading for two reasons. First, populist ideologies are invariably eclectic. Second, the sources from which populist appeals are drawn do not usually shape the sentiments of supporters directly, and are a poor guide to the policies populists advocate and implement. It is the way diverse ideological elements are rhetorically combined that influences populist supporters and determines populist policies. For instance, populism's egalitarian and collectivist features generally evoke

[47] See Allcock (1971), Coniff (1982).

images of a plebeian community, rather than motivating movements to undertake extensive property redistribution; while the definition of particular groups as ethnic outsiders may highlight populism's anti-élite thrust rather than lending it a fascist character.[48]

Contrary to existing approaches, I distinguish between two varieties of populism, *assertive populism* and *paternalist populism*, based on the social outlook and the patterns of action that appeals encourage in supporters. This typology describes systematic differences in types of appeal, organizational structures, social bases, supporters' attitudes, and policies promised and pursued.

Assertive Populism

Assertive populism urges excluded groups towards militant action to enter imperfectly inclusive public spheres. It creates entitlements to education, jobs, loans, subsidized producer goods, and sometimes small pieces of property. Due to the scarcity of such goods, they are usually rationed. As assertive populism often aims to reverse discrimination based on ascriptive criteria, such rationing tends to involve preferences based on ethnicity, status, territorial origin and evaluations of group deserts. Groups with some social capability, albeit modest, are best able to compete for these entitlements and are the key supporters. Assertive populist organizations have a strong social presence as they tap and extend social networks amongst such groups, in light of whose norms they seek to change standards of valuation.

Assertive populist regimes accommodate demands presented as those of a popular community more readily than those asserted on behalf of specific interest groups, giving such a form of patronage distribution its specifically populist character. Patronage is channelled through the networks within assertive populist subcultures, a prominent position within which gives one privileged access to patronage. The assertive populist outlook regards the activist's self-willed activity as the basis of the movement and the social changes

[48] Observers who understood the Dravidian parties in terms of their ideological sources claimed that they undertook neither significant property redistribution nor anti-Brahmin *pogroms* because they underwent substantial deradicalization, ignoring the fact that even early Dravidianists took neither step. See Spratt (1970), Barnett (1976).

it introduces. This is conducive to organizational pluralism and militates against patrimonialism. It serves to legitimize the distribution of patronage among activists, who are not required to defer to party bosses as they would to traditional patrons.

Paternalist Populism

Paternalist populism promises that a benevolent leader, party or state will enforce community norms. It takes these norms to require that the poor and powerless be provided subsidized wage goods and protection from repressive élites. This may be achieved through systematic subsidies or particular donations, repeated with some frequency. It gives the leader and party the initiative to both interpret the precise substance of these norms and to enforce them. So, its policies are less geared towards addressing immediate popular preferences than assertive populist policies are—for instance, food is typically distributed rather than liquor. In contrast with assertive populism, it encourages supporters to assume an attitude of reverence and gratitude towards the leader, party and state, depicted in the manner of a traditional patron writ large, rather than to engage in independent militant initiatives. So, it strikes less directly at the heart of social deference than assertive populism does, although it promotes a popular sense of entitlement to the goods distributed.

Paternalist populism appeals most to the lower strata and women, who are often unable to assert their demands independently, and to compete for the more substantial benefits assertive populism provides. Its welfare policies focus on addressing the basic needs of these groups. As the distribution of benefits is attributed to the leader's good will rather than the activities of the cadre, a person's entitlement to benefits does not tend to derive from his position in the movement subculture. Paternalist populist regimes disburse patronage to a larger number than assertive ones do, and entitlements to benefits are usually not defined by ascriptive standards. Nevertheless, the direction of patronage towards key support groups gives these welfare policies their clientelist character and the emphasis on the leader-as-donor in the accompanying rhetoric lends them a paternalist character.

Along with the relative passivity of paternalist populist supporters comes a weaker party organization having little ability to challenge the leader. The centrality of the leader rather than the activist in the paternalist vision and the relative weakness of the party organization makes the paternalist brand of populism more compatible with patrimonialism. As part of its intolerance of independent initiative, paternalist populism shows a greater inclination to control independent associations than assertive populism does. This inclination meets with varying degrees of success, depending on the strength of such associations.

Assertive Versus Paternalist Populism

Being ideal-types, the two strands of populism are often found interwoven with each other or with non-populist forms. While both types appeared in the course of the Dravidian movement, the distinction between them captures the contrasting features of the two major Dravidian parties—the DMK had an assertive core, while the ADMK was primarily paternalist.

While the DMK emphasized greater opportunities for middling groups, especially intermediate castes, the ADMK's appeals focused on protection for the powerless. The DMK was rooted primarily among intermediate castes of small property, while the ADMK gained greatest support from the SCs, those with little property, and women. The policy most closely associated with the DMK is the provision of quotas for intermediate castes in education and government jobs;[49] while the ADMK's most significant welfare scheme was the provision of free lunches for all public school children. The DMK built stronger party institutions, which were more autonomous of leaders, than the ADMK did. The efforts of the party leader to pass on the party leadership to a family member triggered three splits in the assertive Dravidianist organizations— once in the DK and twice in the DMK.[50] But, the original ADMK leader's charisma was readily transferred to his lover and no significant splits arose within this party. However, the two parties

[49] The DMK was the major electoral party which supported intermediate caste quotas most strongly, at least until 1989. Two parties formed since then, the PMK and the MDMK, which enjoy much less support, are also ardent supporters of such policies.

[50] While the DK leader's nomination of his wife as his successor led to the formation of the DMK in 1949, the efforts of the DMK leader to promote two of his sons to succeed him triggered two significant splits, one in 1972 and the other in 1994.

combined both the assertive and paternalist strands of populism when they were most successful—the DMK in the 1960s and the ADMK in the 1980s. It was the abandonment of paternalist promises on the part of the DMK in the 1970s which led to a split in the party, and enabled the ADMK to outflank it.

The assertive brand of populism is most likely to develop among the intermediate strata in semi-industrialized societies, an outcome earlier theories failed to explain. Many recent populist forces, like the Greek PASOK and the Peruvian APRA, exhibited primarily assertive features.[51] However, paternalist populisms is not episodic, a vestige of the past or rooted solely among atomized groups. Not only did the ADMK achieve sustained popularity in a relatively developed region of India, other populisms with pronounced paternalist features have arisen in even more industrialized areas— Brizola's political career in Brazil being the clearest instance. Besides, the lower strata attracted to paternalist populism often have strong social bonds—e.g. the ADMK's rural SC supporters and Andean Indian supporters of Peruvian President Fujimori.

As assertive populist organizations are more internally plural istic, they are more likely to coexist with social pluralism. Paternalist populist regimes such as the Brazilian *Estado Novo* contained social pluralism by repressing unions; while the first Peronist government, which had significant paternalist features, achieved the same effect by attracting most organized workers to state-affiliated unions. Assertive populist forces, both older ones like the APRA and more recent ones like the PASOK, have not had such an effect.

Recent populist forces with strong paternalist features, like the ADMK and the Fujimori regime in Peru, have not been able to exercise the extent of social control that earlier paternalist populist regimes could. The crucial difference is that the later paternalist populist forces have arisen in more pluralistic societies. Therefore, supporters have been able to appropriate even paternalist notions to further their autonomy, as in the earlier mentioned examples

---

[51] However, they had more paternalist characteristics than the DMK did. For instance, the founding leader dominated the PASOK (Papandreou) and the APRA (Haya). But, the initial leader's charisma was not transferred after his death to a relative in either case. Haya did not try to do so, and Papandreou failed in his efforts to hand over the torch to his second wife.

of artisanal fishermen and urban squatters rallying behind the ADMK flag. Thus, social pluralism has weathered the rise of paternalist populism. The prior tendency in Tamil Nadu towards the popular reappropriation of populist notions, set during the more assertive waves of Dravidianist mobilization, further aided autonomous responses to paternalist appeals.

Populism and Ethnic Militancy

Assertive populist forces show the greatest affinity with ethnic militancy as they tend to attract the petty intelligentsia, actual or aspiring white collar workers drawn from groups with a limited history of Western education. Not only is the petty intelligentsia attracted by assertive populist efforts to expand access to white collar employment, it is also drawn predominantly from the intermediate strata, whose outlook assertive populism more generally represents. This group has been at the forefront of language politics in colonial and post-colonial contexts, opposing the privileged language of the (former) colonizers and élite intellectuals more conversant with it. It has also spearheaded religious revivalism in such societies, by opposing secularization and religions of recent advent, or by upholding indigenized variants of religions introduced by colonizers.[52] From it have been drawn the ideologues of both assertive populism and ethno-nationalism, the militancy of whose cadences feed off each other readily as ethnic categories help in highlighting the distinctness of the élites populists aim to unseat. Assertive populism and ethnic militancy found their confluence in the DMK, as well as in Sinhala Buddhist revivalism, the Bulgarian Agrarian Union and the PASOK.

Some paternalist populist forces, like the ADMK and the Mexican PRI, promoted ethnic notions as part of official state ideology to augment the prestige of their patron-states, and others used them to highlight their affinity with the lower strata—such as Sanchez Cerro in Peru and Peron in Argentina. But, they resisted a militant appropriation of such notions, and other paternalist populists like Brizola in Brazil have hardly resorted to ethnic appeals.

[52] See Anderson (1983: 108–15), Marty & Appleby (1991), Jones (1989), Levine (1986) and Deats (1968).

Types of Populism and Pluralism

The two variants of populism have different implications for pluralism. Assertive populist organizations are more likely to be internally pluralistic, and to that extent are more likely to contribute to or coexist with social pluralism. However, the policies they advocate and implement typically pay less attention to the interests of the lower strata. As paternalist populism gives these interests greater centrality, it represents the lower strata more effectively. But, paternalist populism addresses the needs of its core supporters without giving them as much autonomy as assertive populism tends to. Even paternalist populist supporters may, however, enjoy some autonomy if social pluralism was strong before their party grew.

The greater affinity between the assertive version of populism and ethnic militancy has uncertain implications for social pluralism. If an assertive populist organization's ethnic militancy assumes exclusionary forms, it clearly impairs social pluralism. But, the internal pluralism which the assertive populist outlook promotes can blunt the intolerant potential of ethnic discourses.

ORGANIZATIONAL PLURALISM AND DEMOCRACY

The analysis presented in this book of the paths followed by the Dravidian parties in Tamil Nadu highlights certain features of intra-party relations and party-society transactions that orient ethnic and populist forces in ways conducive to pluralist democracy. It shows that the emergence of *organizational pluralism* aids the articulation of ethnic appeals in more inclusive ways, and helps contain the intolerant potential of various political forces. Specifically, internal pluralism makes parties and regimes more responsive to autonomous initiatives, and therefore increases accountability.

These arguments suggest that citizens who value pluralist democracy may intervene in potentially exclusionary movements to re-shape them. There are crucial moments when such political forces are more malleable, such as in the early stages of their growth, when new groups are being mobilized or when political opportunities change significantly. Dravidianism moved towards pluralistic populism at an early stage in its growth, and the DMK was formed soon after decolonization substantially changed the structure of political opportunities. The paternalist strand in Dravidian populism grew along with the mobilization of the lower strata and women, and the ADMK was formed when the DMK's abandonment of its paternalist promises made it easier for paternalist Dravidian populism to become an independent force. Such are the moments when citizens can most effectively redirect potentially exclusionary political forces towards the enhancement of social pluralism.

The craft of citizenship involves sensing such moments and responding to them effectively. If they are to gain greater autonomy, many citizens with limited social capabilities have to artfully engage and confront more powerful forces, whether they be states or strong movements and parties. In contrast with Marx's view of the situation of workers, such citizens have both worlds they could lose and worlds they might build. Since the potential losses as well as gains are high, they have compelling reasons to engage in citizencraft.

Opportunities have sometimes been missed when political forces which inflicted much violence could have been steered in more tolerant directions. Such moments arose in the history of Hindu revivalism, for instance. The introduction of universal suffrage after decolonization, and the disrepute which Hindu revivalist organizations suffered after one of their activists assassinated Gandhi in 1948, created such an opening. An opportunity was then missed to fashion more tolerant variants of Hindu revivalism, which could have attracted many voters. As with Gandhi's assassination, the demolition of the Babri Masjid by Hindu revivalists in 1992 and the riots that followed repelled many who had sympathies with some of the cultural dimensions of Hindu revivalism. However, intolerance of Muslims and others had become too central to the culture of movement organizations by then for it to be easy to alter this aspect of Hindu revivalism. Moreover, the absence of internal pluralism within the Hindu revivalist fold constricted the space for the pursuit of alternative strategies.

This study proceeds from an appreciation of many of the widely noted advantages of pluralist democracy. For instance, pluralist democracy facilitates the diffusion of conflict, and the maintenance of some degree of tolerance and accountability. It also creates the potential for improvements in social well-being, but does not ensure the realization of this end. This analysis also indicates the limitations of pluralist democracy. There must be scope for mobilization inspired by a wide range of visions to ensure that democratic institutions are sustained, and that these institutions fulfil their potential of providing citizens greater autonomy and enhancing their well-being. Organizational pluralism helps orient the initiatives of ethnic, populist and other potentially exclusionary forces so that pluralist democracy is maintained in the medium term. However, the bounded internal pluralism that emerged in some ethnic and reformist communist parties reinforced pluralist democracy partly because it restricted the autonomy of citizens and limited the policy agenda in ways conducive to gradual change amidst limited conflict. Such constraints on citizens' autonomy may weaken the participatory impulse, and thus endanger pluralist democracy in the long run. Besides, such limits on the policy agenda often prevent major improvements in social well-being. So, bounded internal pluralism is insufficient for the fuller realization of democracy's potential.

III

The Politics of Heresy: Non-Brahminism and Tamil Nationalism in the Late Colonial Period

> *Kadavul ozhiya vendum; madham ozhiya vendum;*
> *kaangirasu ozhiya vendum; gandhi ozhiya vendum;*
> *paarppaan ozhiya vendum.*
>
> (God should be destroyed; Religion should be destroyed:
> Congress should be destroyed; Gandhi should be destroyed;
> The Brahmin should be destroyed.)
>
> — E. V. Ramaswami Naicker,
> first mass leader of the Dravidian movement

Anti-Brahminism was the strongest aspect of mass Dravidianism in its formative phase, the late colonial period. While anti-Brahmin sentiments had existed for long in Tamil Nadu and elsewhere in India, it was some European missionaries who initially incorporated them into a systematic ideology in the nineteenth century. They argued that South Indian languages belong to a distinct Dravidian family; and, with less plausibility, that South Indians other than Brahmins constitute a distinct Dravidian race.[1] Early Dravidianist ideologues and organizations appropriated these notions from the turn of the century onwards. The South Indian Liberal Federation (also called the Justice Party), the Self Respect Association and the DK popularized visions of a 'Dravidian' or 'non-Brahmin' community they aimed to represent.

'Non-Brahminism', a term coined to signify the politicization of non-Brahmin identity, emerged only in Tamil Nadu and Maharashtra although movements with anti-Brahmin features arose elsewhere in India too.[2] Although Brahmins have enjoyed

[1] See Caldwell (1982), Nambi Arooran (1980), Irschick (1969).

[2] As non-Brahminism was popularized, the term non-Brahmin, initially coined in English, was translated into the inelegant Tamil term *paarppanarallaathaar*.

various privileges and been somewhat culturally distinctive throughout India, colonial society evidenced social strains conducive to the emergence of non-Brahminism only in these regions. These strains were reflected in the way Dravidian movement organizations emerged, and in the outlook of the movement's early mass leaders. Non-Brahminism endured in Tamil Nadu alone because it was linked to Tamil nationalism from the 1930s onwards in a populist discourse. A faction of the DK became associated with such a discourse in the last decade of colonial rule.

The politics of E. V. Ramaswami Naicker (*Periar*), the major Dravidianist leader of the colonial period, centred around ritual inversions of scriptural Hinduism, meant to shock society into insight about the links between religion and social dominance. I call this style of politics, in which Dravidianism was initially popularized, a 'politics of heresy'. As Periar placed himself at odds with demands for decolonization, the primary focus of late colonial politics, and his political style provided a poor basis for building broad coalitions, the organizations he led (the Self Respect Association and the DK) gained support only in small pockets. Partly because of their limited support, they attacked symbols of Brahmin and North Indian culture, rather than the property or persons of those they deemed outsiders. However, Periar's heretical style and emphasis on ethnic divisions might have provoked considerable conflict if Dravidianism had spread further based on his strategy. The DMK's rejection of the politics of heresy helped reconcile non-Brahminism with social pluralism.

THE SOCIO-HISTORICAL CONTEXT OF NON-BRAHMINISM

The grievances of the non-Brahminist movements of both Tamil Nadu and Maharashtra focused on the dominant position accorded Brahmins in Hindu scripture, Brahmin pre-eminence in ritual and the influential roles of Brahmins in the public spheres created during colonial rule. This urged scholars to identify non-Brahminism as a call for social equality arising in opposition to the barriers to social mobility resulting from 'traditional' Brahmin status dominance and 'modern' Brahmin professional dominance.[3] Such interpretations fail to explain why non-Brahminism did not emerge in

[3] See Rajagopal (1985: 2–3), Irschick (1969) and Hardgrave (1979). Barnett (1976) partly shares this view.

other parts of India where Brahmins enjoyed similar social eminence. Moreover, they are based on views of pre-colonial Indian society which have been seriously challenged lately.

Colonial knowledge, which understood Hindu tradition primarily in terms of the scriptures, interpreted caste in terms of varna categories. While scriptural prescriptions nowhere correspond exactly with practice, they do so less in regions like Tamil Nadu and Kerala, where intermediate castes had claimed no definite varna identities before colonial rule, and did so only in passing during last two centuries, mainly when prodded by persistent scholars and ethnic mobilizers. Yet, Indianist anthropologists have accorded varna a central role in their view of the caste system till recently. For instance, Dumont's classic accounts based on research done precisely in Tamil Nadu and Kerala characterize the Nairs of Kerala, many of whom were landholding chieftains who later entered the professions in large numbers, as well as the Piramalai Kallar of Tamil Nadu who suffered economic decline and official derision as a 'criminal tribe' in the nineteenth century, as Shudras who occupy occupying the fourth rung in the varna hierarchy. Besides, south India witnessed considerable social mobility at different points, contrary to Dumont's view that the caste system was static.[4]

Irschick's (1969) and Hardgrave's (1979) earlier accounts of the Dravidian movement derived their notions of 'traditional' Brahmin dominance from the Dumontian vision. Although Barnett's (1976) allusions to relative deprivation contained in germ a more tenable understanding, she largely accepted varna as the basis of stratification in Tamil society and viewed non-Brahminism as the self-assertion of groups accorded subordinate status until this century.[5] Barnett failed to see how the colonial project of preserving tradition reified status categories, how Congress's partial reliance on this ideology blurred the party's strategic vision, and how both these processes enabled the rise of Dravidianism. She took such megacaste categories as 'other backward caste' or

[4] Dumont (1970, 1971, 1983, 1986).

[5] Barnett (1976: 16) reproduced the vision of a varna-governed society, only with a difference: 'In south India, there are no Kshatriyas or Vaisyas, so all castes are either Brahmin, Suddhra, or Untouchable', not appreciating the fact that the shudra category accorded poorly with pre-colonial social relations in Tamil Nadu.

'backward caste' (henceforth OBC or BC)[6] and SC to be rooted in tradition, thus natural cleavages for mobilization. However, such cleavages became politically relevant due to processes to which the Dravidian movement was central. Therefore, they are outcomes to be explained, not premises on which an explanation can be built.

Recent work shows that while Brahmins enjoyed considerable social influence prior to the advent of colonialism, this influence was no greater in Tamil Nadu than in many other regions of India. Besides, other groups also shared such power with Brahmins in Tamil Nadu; and indeed enjoyed more power in certain respects in some Tamil speaking areas at points. Precisely because of these limits to pre-colonial Brahmin dominance, the gap was particularly large in Tamil Nadu between the pre-colonial patterns of status and power, on the one hand, and the scripturally prescribed caste structure underwritten by colonial legality, on the other. Brahmin dominance was also particularly strong in Tamil Nadu in institutions which emerged during the colonial period—Western educational institutions, the professions and Congress. These were the crucial sources of dissatisfaction on which non-Brahminism drew. Further, Tamil Brahmins have been culturally distinctive in a way that enabled them to be portrayed as alien to the Tamil community. Finally, some non-Brahmin castes enjoyed material and normative resources, which enabled them to cut on perceptions of Brahmins as unjustly privileged and alien.[7]

THE QUESTION OF BRAHMIN DOMINANCE: THE PRE-COLONIAL SITUATION[8]

Socio-Economic Power

Brahmins constituted about 3 per cent of the Tamil population, a good deal less than in much of northern India. Even in the Kaveri and Tamiraparani valleys, where they were more densely

[6] The intermediate castes are called 'other backward castes', i.e. backward castes other than the SCs in official accounts, and as backward castes (BCs) in popular discourse.

[7] Maharashtrian society also shared some of these features, but I consider this only in passing.

[8] This discussion draws from Weber's (1978) analysis of dominance, and the literature on the dominant caste fathered by Srinivas (1962).

concentrated, they accounted for no more than 6 per cent of the population. The tendency of Brahmins to settle in fertile areas, seen elsewhere in India too, indicates considerable social power.[9] The extent of Brahmin control over land was significantly less in Tamil Nadu than in regions like Kerala, Maharashtra, Uttar Pradesh and Bihar. Even in the valleys, where Brahmins owned more land, they shared land control with other castes. However, even in these valleys, Brahmins had a limited role in commerce, as was the case elsewhere in India. Both commerce and kingly power grew in influence in the late medieval period, enabling mercantile and warrior groups to acquire more land, the dominance that Brahmins and other landed castes had enjoyed over landed wealth until then declined.[10]

The Brahmins were thus only one of the many castes enjoying socio-economic power in pre-colonial Tamil Nadu. Such power was limited in the plains, where the majority of the Tamil population lived. While the most privileged Brahmins enjoyed considerable power, many other Brahmins, such as rural temple priests, lived in modest circumstances.[11]

Status

Status fluidity was greater in Tamil society than in non-peninsular India, partly due to the limited relevance of varna in status attribution. It increased with the growth in migration, the rise of new kingly powers and the opening of new routes to social mobility through the medieval period. The occupation associated with some jatis and the lifestyle associated with high status varied over space. For instance, the Mukkulathor were warrior-marauders who exercised dominance through their control over labour in parts of the southern plains, where they followed ritual practices typical of the middle and lower castes. Till recently, they performed animal sacrifices to semi-Hinduized folk deities and gave bride price rather than dowry. In the Kaveri valley, to which the

[9] Stein (1980).

[10] Brahmins shared dominance in land control with the Vellalas in early medieval times in the valleys. Immigrant castes from the Tamil plains and Telugu, Kannada and Maharashtrian areas dented the Brahmin–Vellala monopoly from the fourteenth to the eighteenth centuries in the Kaveri valley, but not in the Tamiraparani valley. See Baker (1984: 86–9), Ludden (1985).

[11] Appadurai (1983).

Mukkulathor migrated in large numbers during the medieval period, they became sedentary peasants and partially adopted upper caste habits. The sickle became for them primarily an agricultural implement rather than an instrument of theft, feud and warfare.[12]

The manner of allocation of rights to social precedence and property, the role of the temple in the definition of status and honour, and the influence of kings over property rights and the distribution of honour in temples contributed further to status fluidity in medieval Tamil Nadu. Rights to shares in property were assigned to families, kin, lineage, sect or other corporate groups based on generally accepted claims to prior settlement by their ancestors in an agrarian area, in a system called *kaniatchi*. Emergent élites attempted to validate such genealogical claims. Shares in the social product, increasingly transferable, passed to mercantile and warrior groups in late medieval times, and kings became more involved in building temples and supporting them through land grants. Contributions to temples brought honour, and this served as a means to redefine status. Kingly and economic power could be acquired by most castes and transmuted into higher status by concocting genealogies and gaining honour through donations to temples. Caste boundaries could be altered over time through such processes, as well as through the formation of sects associated with influential seers and the *bhakti* tradition of intense personal devotion to deities.

Many of these avenues to social mobility available in pre-colonial Tamil Nadu did not involve the adoption of the Sanskritic practices of locally dominant castes, a pattern that Srinivas initially discussed. Not only were the practices of many locally dominant non-Brahmin castes distinctly non-Sanskritic in the Tamil plains, efforts at upward mobility were not necessarily associated with claiming higher varna status.[13] The definition of status was a more

---

[12] Mukkulathor is a term of recent provenance meaning 'those of the three clans/castes'. It refers to three related caste-groups, the Kallar, Maravar and Ahamudaiyar, who typically adopt caste titles, such as Thevar, Pandian and Naattaar. See Dumont (1986).

[13] While Srinivas (1962) noted that claims to a Dravidian tradition in Tamil Nadu might follow a different logic, non-Sanskritic routes to social mobility were available in Tamil Nadu well before notions of a Dravidian tradition emerged.

open game in Tamil Nadu than in many other parts of India. Many non-Brahmin groups enjoyed high status and could press Brahmins into service as junior partners in their hegemonic ventures, especially in the plains.[14]

Political Power

Kingly power was accessible to most castes and medieval rulers had many means to legitimize their power. For instance, they tended to offer grants to temples and thereby present themselves as guarantors of the normative order. To the extent that Brahmins were crucial to temple worship, they were important to this process of legitimation. However, non-Brahmin priests officiated in many temples and temple priests of all castes often depended on temple benefactors.

While rulers were partly dependent on Brahmin priests for the legitimation of power, Brahmins in general did not play a major direct role in the upper reaches of the military or administration in pre-colonial Tamil kingdoms. This is in contrast to the more direct role played by Brahmin ministers in the Maratha and Mughal empires. Rulers of the sixteenth to eighteenth centuries forged alliances with a range of rural élites and absorbed some into the intermediate ranks of state personnel, but Brahmins were only one among the many castes which tasted political power through this process.[15]

BRAHMIN DOMINANCE IN COLONIAL SOCIETY

Socio-Economic Power

Although Brahmins did not monopolize the ownership of land, the most significant form of property in pre-colonial times, they virtually monopolized the scribal occupation. Other castes also played this role in much of northern and eastern India, but not in Maharashtra (where non-Brahminism also emerged). The scribal occupation was not a source of much power before British rule, but their monopoly over it helped Brahmins succeed in acquiring

---

[14] Stein (1975, 1978), Appadurai (1981, 1983), Appadurai & Breckenridge (1976), Champakalakshmi (1981), Silverberg (1968).
[15] See Appadurai (1981), Stein (1980), Ludden (1985).

Western education sooner than other castes did. The other major landed castes of the valleys, the Vellalas and some Telugu migrant castes, also adopted Western education and entered the professions to an equal extent at the same time. But, as their caste brethren elsewhere in the state lagged behind, a comparison of the educational attainments of megacastes showed Brahmins in the lead in the colonial period. Brahmin dominance in Western education ensured a similar early dominance in the professions in a context in which the white collar labour force was growing slowly.[16]

Brahmin dominance in education and the professions was greater in Tamil Nadu than in many parts of India where Brahmins enjoyed greater land control. In Kerala, Brahmins enjoyed greater land control, a more significant role in ritual legitimation, and a higher status in relation to other powerful groups than did their counterparts in Tamil Nadu. The extent of their dominance in pre-colonial society made them ill-disposed towards the changes wrought by colonial rule and the new avenues that these changes opened up. So, Nairs, rather than Brahmins, were the early leaders in education and the professions in Kerala.[17] This suggests that non-Brahminism, which emerged in Tamil Nadu and not in Kerala, arose primarily in response to the socio-economic power which Brahmins enjoyed in spheres associated with colonial rule, rather than to their situation before colonial rule.

While Brahmins gained an early lead in the professions, they did not gain such dominance in land ownership or commerce. Indeed, the extent of their control over land gradually diminished through this century even in the valleys. The ritual injunction against their direct participation in agriculture became more of an obstacle as share-cropping and tenancy declined and viable farming required closer supervision from the landowners, towards which other castes were more inclined. Further, Brahmins did not benefit significantly from the growth of commerce and money-lending, and were only one among the many castes that invested in

[16] See Suntharalingam (1974), Irschick (1969), Saraswathi (1974) and Ludden (1978a). While Brahmins entrenched in the bureaucracy did discriminate against members of other castes in recruitment into the bureaucracy in some cases, such discrimination was not systematic and was not the reason for Brahmin preponderance in the bureaucracy at this point. See Washbrook (1976: 38, 236–7, 274–5).

[17] Jeffrey (1976).

industry, once it began to develop in the early part of the century.[18]

The power of non-Brahmins in spheres other than the professions helped them act on their grievances. Many prominent merchants and landowners were patrons of the early non-Brahminist movement, particularly the élite Justice Party.[19] Others of more modest wealth aided the growth of mass non-Brahminism later.

Status

The fluidity of status which characterized pre-colonial Tamil society changed with the growth of the colonial state. As part of its proclaimed aim of protecting indigenous tradition, the colonial state gave legal validity to constructions of tradition based on scripture. The customary and religious laws which it adopted were influenced both by early orientalist anthropology and by the upper castes (in the Tamil case, mainly the Brahmins) which adopted Western education earliest and thus gained links with British officialdom soonest.[20]

The process of the legalization of tradition altered power, status and property throughout India, but especially so in Tamil Nadu where the logic of social action departed most from scriptural definitions. The legal interpretation of social cleavages in terms of varna placed all groups other than the Brahmins and the SCs at the fourth rung (Shudra) of the varna hierarchy. Groups that had enjoyed considerable access to property, kingly power and social esteem found to their dismay that they were placed three rungs below the Brahmins. Further, such groups found themselves on a par, in the eye of the law, with the peasant and artisanal groups, from which many of their social subordinates were drawn. The legalization of varna thus plebeianized previously privileged groups which could appeal to a 'non-Brahmin'/Shudra coalition, comprising about 67 per cent of the Tamil population.[21]

[18] Subrahmanian (1989), Baker (1984), Gough (1989), Mencher (1978).

[19] e.g. the Rajahs of Panagal and Bobbili, P. T. Rajan, W. P. A. Soundarapandia Nadar, Rajah Muthiah Chettiar, V. S. Thyagaraja Mudaliar, A. T. Panneerselvam.

[20] See Derrett (1968), Galanter (1989: Parts II & III).

[21] The share of the Tamil population accounted for by the 'minorities' (not clearly subsumed under the Shudra label) are as follows: SC and ST–

The colonial reification of caste categories abridged the scope for the revision of caste boundaries through such means as the formation of new sects. Even if such attempts to redefine status continued to gain some local acceptance, they could not get legal validation. The boundaries of the corporate-ethnic entities which owned shares in property became fixed.[22] Temples became subject to the control of the bureaucracy and elected local bodies, rendering it difficult to gain higher status by offering donations to temples.[23] Various non-Brahminical religious practices were branded heterodox—from the orgiastic worship of village deities to the *bhakti* tradition, from the conduct of prayers in Tamil to the long textually elaborated tradition of *saiva siddantham*, associated with the worship of Shiva. These traditions thus began to lose their influence over temples and other religious institutions. A range of legal disputes broke out through the nineteenth century over the control of property and social institutions such as temples. Although many non-Brahmin groups pressed their claims in terms previously regarded legitimate, they were usually rebuffed by the courts. These losses, often to other non-Brahmins, began to abridge their local influence too.

Brahmins gained pre-eminence for the first time due to the above processes associated with the construction of the colonial state. Although their cultural influence was not entirely new, it assumed many new and more exclusive dimensions. This was especially galling for groups that had enjoyed significant power. The outlook of such groups was only too familiar to Periar as he was the son of an affluent merchant from the Balija Naidu caste (an artisanal caste, many of whose members had turned to commerce), who was the patron of a temple in his home town of Erode. Periar's appeals reflected resentments evoked by the changes colonial rule introduced in status attribution. For instance, the Shudra category used by orthodox Brahmins and Anglo-Indian legality was central to his appeals. Periar frequently vented his indignation over the Shudra designation, but also located those deemed Shudras at the core of his conception of the 'Dravidian' community.[24]

---

19 per cent, Christian–6 per cent, Muslim–5 per cent, Brahmin–3 per cent. This leaves one with a 67 per cent Shudra-Hindu 'majority'.

[22] Washbrook (1981).

[23] See Presler (1987).

[24] See Ramaswami Naicker (1947); KA, 25 April 1926.

Some of the changes introduced by colonialism made it possible to focus the resentments of more modest groups too on the figure of the Brahmin. A wide range of groups experienced social decline during colonial rule. The autonomy and income of many artisanal groups declined with the onset of Company rule in the eighteenth century. Many peasant groups suffered due to the changes in the agrarian system resulting from the new legal foundations for landed property, and a shift to cash crops and export-oriented agriculture in many regions. These changes were associated with a move from tenancy and share-cropping to the greater use of daily wage labour in agriculture, a trend which sharply accelerated when the rice trade from the Tamil valleys to South-east Asia collapsed during the Great Depression.[25] The main alternative avenues available to distressed peasant and artisanal groups were the professions, in which they found little success initially. The problems of these groups, say indebtedness, frequently led them to the lawyer or the bureaucrat, who was often a Brahmin. This made it easy for such groups to associate their plight with the 'Brahminization' of the law and Brahmin dominance in the professions.

C. N. Annadurai, who was initially deemed Periar's heir and later founded the DMK, reflected the outlook of such distressed groups. He was one of the few from his weaver caste (the Senguntha Mudaliar) who had acquired a college education by the 1930s.[26] In his criticisms of Brahmin dominance, Annadurai not only focused on the changes introduced under British rule, but also explicitly recognized the role of British rule in these changes.[27]

Political Power

The changes associated with colonization enabled Brahmins to dominate some kinds of political activity in Tamil Nadu in the early twentieth century. The onset of British rule constricted the kingly path to political power. While some princelings continued

[25] See Baker (1984: 135–232, 421–533).

[26] The Sengunthar (also known as Kaikolar) are not among the so-called Sat-Shudra castes, traditionally of high status. They faced upper caste derision because of the modest nature of the weaving profession and because many girls of this caste were made *devadasis*, a form of temple servant/prostitute. See Mines (1984), Thurston (1975a, vol. III: 31–44).

[27] See Annadurai (1985a, 1985d, 1985e).

to enjoy limited political power under British paramountcy, few new lineages gained access to such power. However, some local notables of varying caste origins were regularly consulted by British administrators, and their influence increased in the first decades of limited self-government, from the 1880s to about World War I, when the electorate was defined by stringent property and educational qualifications.

The scope of associational activity and self-government increased in the early decades of the century. Brahmins set the tone of Madras city politics in the 1910s, of the Home Rule Leagues which sprouted during World War I and of nationalist mobilization, which grew rapidly after the war.[28] They controlled Congress's state-level leadership until World War II, although many from other castes joined the party and some of them became second-rung leaders in the 1920s and 1930s.

Non-Brahmins exercised autonomous political influence through the non-Brahminist parties and caste associations which arose through this period. As Congress did not participate in provincial governments until 1937, non-Brahminists enjoyed considerable access to the patronage which came with control over these governments in the 1920s and 1930s. But, the centre of political gravity shifted through this period from the institutions of self-government established by the colonial state to the differing forms of nationalist politics growing primarily outside them. The dominance of Congress in nationalist politics and the leading role of Brahmins in Congress ensured Brahmin political dominance until the 1940s.[29] This began to change in the last decade of colonial rule, when political participation increased rapidly, Congress led provincial governments at points (1937–9, 1946–7) and decolonization seemed increasingly imminent.

BRAHMIN CULTURAL DISTINCTIVENESS

While many castes have distinct dialects, the dialects of Brahmin sub-castes are largely invariant in vocabulary within Tamil Nadu, and are most distinct from other dialects, having a far greater Sanskritic content. The relative geographical uniformity of Brahmin dialects reflects the wider social networks to which Brahmins

[28] Suntharalingam (1974), Washbrook (1976), Saraswathi (1974).
[29] Baker (1976), Arnold (1977, 1988), Viswanathan (1983).

were linked, partly due to the strength of the religious institutions to which they owed allegiance. While religious institutions and military alliances also linked other castes to wider social networks, these networks tended to be less caste exclusionary, and so provided less of a basis for caste solidarity.

Brahmins had an important part in the introduction of Sanskritic elements into Tamil culture, as forest and mountain dwellers were incorporated into an emergent regional Hinduism and a growing agrarian culture through the later half of the first millennium.[30] The process of Sanskritization brought about some convergence in belief and ritual practice between Brahmins and many other castes, especially in the valleys where Brahmins exercised the greatest social influence. This partly attenuated Brahmin cultural distinctiveness.

Although Brahmins are culturally distinctive in most parts of India, this distinctiveness has specific dimensions in Tamil Nadu. Most relevant is the greater Sanskritic nature of the dialect, which was conducive to weaving together resentment of the Brahmin and fear of North Indian cultural hegemony in the course of the Dravidian movement. Many Tamil Brahmins were very conscious of the Sanskritic nature of their subculture and claimed with pride to be 'Aryans', suggesting a quasi-racial distinction from other Tamil castes. Along with popular conceptions of the historical role of Brahmins in the partial Sanskritization of Tamil culture, this provided fertile soil for the propagation of the non-Brahminist notions that Tamil Brahmins were alien Aryans who helped subjugate an ancient and autonomous Dravidian tradition. The superimposition of the varna framework only widened the perceived ritual distance between Brahmins and others.

A contrast between Tamil Nadu and Kerala highlights some factors which influenced perceptions of Brahmin cultural distinctiveness. While the ritual distance between Brahmins and other upper castes was greater in Kerala, the effect of this distance was reduced by the practice of hypergamy. Nairs and Thampirans, with whom Kerala's Namboodiri Brahmins have had a history of hypergamous relationships, considered themselves to have 'Namboodiri blood', though Namboodiris remained aloof and maintained a sense of their superiority. This made Nairs and

---

[30] See Stein (1980) and Champakalakshmi (1981) for differing accounts.

Thampirans more aware of their distinction from subordinate castes than from Brahmins and helped them shrug off attributions of Shudra status with some nonchalance. While hypergamy diminished Nairs' and Thampirans' perception of their cultural distance from Brahmins, it only strengthened Brahmin dominance. It not only gave Brahmins greater access to the proceeds of the landed wealth which Nairs and Thampirans enjoyed, but also restricted the autonomy and resistance of the latter castes which are immediately below the Brahmins in the social hierarchy.[31]

As caste (often sub-caste) endogamy is the rule in Tamil Nadu, there is a perception on all sides that castes are united by blood ties, thus that caste boundaries have an ethnic character. This also lent the Shudra epithet a sharper bite for the Tamil intermediate castes, which saw in it not only a demotion in status but also a challenge to the legitimacy of the endogamous non-Brahmin family. Powerful men from the upper castes had enjoyed sexual access to some women from the groups of lowest status now deemed Shudra. These practices did not enjoy in Tamil Nadu the social acceptance that Namboodiri–Nair conjugal links did in Kerala. The reduction of all non-Brahmins to Shudra status conjured up for some a male dystopia, in which the paternity of all non-Brahmin children would be open to question.

COLONIAL RULE AND THE EMERGENCE OF NON-BRAHMINISM

The preceding discussion of relations between Brahmins and others indicates factors crucial to the almost unique emergence of non-Brahminism in Tamil Nadu. The level of Brahmin dominance in pre-colonial Tamil society was not high in a comparative Indian perspective. Indeed, Brahmins were less dominant in many respects, and crucial institutions were more autonomous of Brahmin control in Tamil Nadu than elsewhere in India. But, upper non-Brahmin castes regarded Brahmin subculture as particularly distinct in Tamil Nadu, a distinctness marked by the extent of Sanskritic content.

The superimposition of the varna framework in the colonial interpretation of Indian society rendered the relative status of

---

[31] Dumont (1983: 104–44) notes the different attitudes of Namboodiris and Nairs regarding their relationship, though his account is excessively instrumental. Also see Thurston (1975a, vol. V: 152–241, 283–413).

Brahmins apparently greater in Tamil Nadu than elsewhere in India. This status gap was recognized by state institutions, though not always in society. The early lead gained by Brahmins in education, the professions and associational politics added to the picture of Brahmin dominance under colonialism. The gap between the profile of power and status in colonial society and in pre-colonial society was particularly large in Tamil Nadu. The contrast between the two pictures grated on many non-Brahmin groups, which tended to interpret many other social dislocations which occurred during colonial rule in terms of the 'Brahminization' of power.

The non-Brahminism which emerged in response to these circumstances viewed itself as battling a subjugation dating back centuries. The long history of Brahmin and Sanskritic influence and the conflation of various caste-related inequalities with Brahminism rendered this view plausible. Yet, the precipitants of non-Brahminism were not the inequalities between Brahmins and all other castes rooted in pre-colonial Tamil history. They were the specific changes introduced under colonial rule which were especially incongruous with the pre-existing character of power and status in Tamil Nadu. Further, the memory of greater autonomy in pre-colonial times and the residual autonomy that many non-Brahmin groups enjoyed even into the twentieth century aided the growth of non-Brahminism.

NON-BRAHMINISM AND THE ORIGINS OF THE DRAVIDIAN MOVEMENT

The precipitants of non-Brahminism shaped non-Brahminist ideology in its different versions and the trajectory of organizations that adopted this ideology. Non-Brahminism played a minor role within Congress prior to independence, but became more influential among Congress and communist factions thereafter.

Caste Associations

Colonial interpretations of Indian tradition influenced not only the state's efforts to preserve tradition, but also its modernizing efforts. Guided by its understanding of society's fundamental cleavages, the colonial state introduced preferences for the lower castes from the 1880s onwards in education, and later in government recruitment to promote the prospects of underprivileged groups.[32] The state's receptiveness to demands raised on behalf of castes motivated the formation of caste associations. Some of these associations claimed higher ritual status and more honourable appellations for the castes they represented to obtain for them both social prestige and access to public spheres which colonial knowledge deemed the preserve of castes enjoying a higher status (e.g. temples). Yet others (or the same ones in other contexts) claimed that their castes were socially underprivileged to benefit from caste preferences.[33] Many staked their claims in terms of varna, but some SCs tried to appropriate the term 'Dravidian', also a part of colonial knowledge.[34]

The demands of caste associations were closely linked to the precipitants of non-Brahminism. Claims to higher status were made in terms of recovering lost honour, even by associations of lower BCs, reflecting the sense of status dislocation. The primary material demands were for quotas in education and government recruitment, reflecting failure in new public arenas. Although many caste associations did not assume non-Brahminist stances, the late colonial context was conducive to the incorporation of their demands, with some modification, within a non-Brahminist framework.[35] Initially, most of these associations were supported by few other than the dependents of their leaders. But, their demands influenced public discourse and caste associations gained greater support over time.[36]

[32] See Radhakrishnan (1989).

[33] Baker & Washbrook (1975: 199–200 & passim), Rudolph & Rudolph (1967: 29–103).

[34] The periodical *Dravidan* was published from Kolar Gold Fields through the 1890s by some SC intellectuals led by Iyothi Dasan, who enjoyed some local support.

[35] There were tensions between non-Brahminist demands and policies of allocating quotas to categories like 'non-Brahmin' and 'OBC' and the concerns of caste associations to gain a greater share of resources for particular megacastes. While non-Brahminism exercised significant influence over various caste associations, the OBC quotas especially lost support over time from associations of the lower backward castes, which had benefited less from them. So, many caste associations have retained their vitality amidst Dravidianist dominance by demanding more tiered preferences.

[36] Some of the honourable caste names and titles claimed by caste associations have become a part of polite public discourse, reflecting changed

Emergence of the Self Respect Association

The first non-Brahminist organizations were the Dravidian Association (formed in 1912), the Justice Party (begun in 1916–17) and the Self Respect Association (formed in 1926). The first two were élite organizations of anglicized landlords and professionals who were important supporters of the colonial regime, and their demands and strategy were framed by colonial legality. They protested Brahmin dominance, demanded greater non-Brahmin shares in education and the professions, and referred at times to South Indian cultural specificity. But they were not deeply concerned with issues of status like the Shudra label and did not use a restorative idiom.

If some of the 'non-Brahmin grievances' identified earlier did not find a voice in the Justice Party, this showed the inability of the Justice Party to tap the roots of mass resentment effectively.[37] The Self Respect Association was the first non-Brahminist organization to fully articulate these grievances; thus also the first that gained some mass appeal. While it drew on colonial knowledge, its vision was not solely limited by the state's approach to social control. For instance, it paid little attention to electoral politics and reached significantly beyond the upper strata, constituting 3 per cent of the adult population, who could vote from 1919 to 1935.

The manner in which the Self Respect Association emerged reflects the dominant attitude towards non-Brahminism within the early Tamil Nadu Congress. After World War I, Gandhi assumed leadership over Congress, and C. Rajagopalachari (popularly called Rajaji), an orthodox Brahmin, became the leader of the Gandhian faction of the Tamil Nadu Congress.[38] Rajaji, on the lookout for lieutenants adept at mass mobilization, intrinsic to Gandhian

---

status attributions to some extent. However, claims to higher varna status, sometimes voiced by caste associations, have not appreciably influenced mass mentalities.

[37] The party did not have access to channels of mass communication and its non-Brahminism too obviously aimed at gaining its leaders and their cronies access to patronage. This was especially true of those like the Rajahs of Panagal and Bobbili who assumed leadership of the party and the provincial governments it formed, but not of some initial leaders like P. Theogaraya Chetty. Baker (1976).

[38] See Arnold (1977).

strategy, recruited Periar into Congress in 1919. Rajaji was influenced by Periar's roots among groups newly entering politics and his instinct for the popular phrase, which had already gained him prominence in the politics of Erode town.[39]

Periar became associated with a group of non-Brahmin Congress activists who hoped to address non-Brahminist concerns within a Gandhian framework. This group participated actively in major Gandhian campaigns between 1919 and 1923—the non-cooperation and Khilafat agitations, and campaigns to promote hand-spinning. However, many of them opted for an independent political route by the mid-1920s as their hopes to address non-Brahminist concerns were repeatedly belied by the postures that Gandhi and the state Congress leadership struck at different points.

Gandhi's compromise with the British and retreat from agitation in 1923 led his followers to concentrate on so-called 'constructive work', involving the improvement of rural social infrastructure, urging untouchables to adopt upper caste norms, and working towards the abolition of untouchability.[40] Gandhi conceived of constructive work as a step towards the realization of a reconstructed version of *varnashrama dharma*, the scripturally prescribed norms for interaction among the castes. Periar and his faction opposed the paternalistic aspects of Gandhi's social programme, which seemed conducive to demobilization and the legitimation of the status order introduced under colonial rule. Gandhi did clarify that he was proposing an idealized variant of varnashrama dharma, in which castes would be interdependent occupational groups, equal in social and ritual status.[41] Periar believed that, while Gandhi's version of varnashrama dharma was acceptable in the abstract, it was an idle construct because it did not correspond to the caste system as it has historically functioned; and misleading, as it distracted attention from addressing the injustice of the caste system. He argued that, as occupations were likely to remain unequally valued, caste-based occupational

---

[39] Viswanathan (1983: 21–4), Sithambaranar (1983: 70). Baker (1977) and Diehl (1978) discuss Periar's early career and his close and often ambidextrous relationship with Rajaji.

[40] Alternation between agitation and compromise was characteristic of Gandhian mobilization. See Low (1977) and Sarkar (1983).

[41] See Gandhi (1950, 1991: 56–65) and Ambedkar (1945: 286–8). For an account of changes in Gandhi's position, see Parekh (1989: 207–46).

interdependence would imply the perpetuation of existing patterns of dominance.[42]

Many actions of Congress leaders in this period seemed to accord well with Periar's interpretation. Despite the objections of Periar and others, Gandhi settled for less than full success during an agitation for the entry of the SCs into a temple at Vaikom in Kerala.[43] The Brahmin leaders of the Tamil Congress did not end the separate feeding of Brahmin and non-Brahmin children at a Congress sponsored nationalist school at Cheranmahadevi, run by a Brahmin leader.[44] Some of them opposed a move in 1926 to impose the control of the provincial government, then led by non-Congress politicians, over the administration of major temples and religious institutions, under considerable Brahmin influence at that point.[45] Further, Periar's efforts to get the Tamil Nadu Congress to adopt resolutions in favour of caste quotas in political representation were continually defeated between 1919 and 1925.[46]

The complaints which Periar frequently raised through the early and mid-1920s against these actions of Congress leaders reflected the range of characteristic non-Brahmin grievances of the late colonial period. His critique of the ritual status accorded non-Brahmins stemmed from the status incongruity caused by the imposition of varna categories on Tamil society. Unlike many other prominent non-Brahminists of the time, Periar also criticized untouchability as based on Brahminism. Periar's demands for greater political representation for non-Brahmins arose in response

[42] See Ramaswami Naicker (1975: 14–16).

[43] Gandhi settled for a compromise which allowed the SCs to enter the streets adjoining the temple, but not the temple itself. Periar insisted on full temple-entry rights. As a result, in Tamil Nadu, it was Periar who gained greatest credit for the agitation, gaining the title *Vaikkam Veerar* (hero of Vaikom), although the Brahmin Congressman Srinivasa Iyengar was the first Tamil politician to join the Vaikom agitation. See Viswanathan (1983: 42–6) and Irschick (1969: 336–9).

[44] Mangalamurugesan (n.d.: 38–43); Viswanathan (1983: 46–55); Ramaswami Naicker (1987c: 34); Ramanathan (1967: 65–6); KA, 30 April 1925, 12 July 1925; *Viduthalai*, 30 March 1950, 16 August 1950; Sudhanandha Bharathi (n.d.: 104–29, 190).

[45] See Mangalamurugesan (n.d.: 50–2), Sithambaranar (1983: 90–1), Presler (1987: 28–34) and Arnold (1977: 96–7).

[46] Sithambaranar (1983: 53, 92), Mangalamurugesan (n.d. 43–50), Viswanathan (1983: 55–62), KA, 24 November, 1, 8, 15 December 1925.

to Brahmin dominance in high politics. Periar's growing dissatisfaction with the Congress leadership, which he began to express from 1925 onwards in the journal *Kudi Arasu*, led him and his followers to leave Congress and found the Self Respect Association in 1926.[47]

NON-BRAHMINISM AND THE DISCOURSE OF MASS DRAVIDIANISM

'Hegemonic projects' present the particular interests of dominant groups as the general interest of a broader coalition. As populism presents itself as the opponent of dominant élites and ethnonationalism sometimes targets allegedly dominant ethnic groups as enemies, such ideologies have the capacity to inspire opposition to hegemonic projects by urging subordinate groups to challenge their subordination.[48] However, such movements might equally well be hegemonic in character—they might seek to replace old élites with emergent counter-élites, associated with somewhat different interests and outlooks, without the empowerment of subordinate groups.

The opposition of non-Brahminism to Brahmin dominance had the potential of serving as a banner for subordinate non-Brahmin groups. It was also susceptible to use by powerful non-Brahmin groups to buttress their dominance. The tussle between the

[47] Both Periar, the first President of the Self Respect Association, and S. Ramanathan, its first General Secretary, claim to have founded it. See Ramaswami Naicker (1975), *Kuttooci Guruswamy Ninaivu Malar* (1966: 39), Ramanathan (1967: 23), Mangalamurugesan (n.d.: 61–4). It is clear however that it was Periar's personality which shaped the Association. Anti-colonialism remained as important as non-Brahminism to S. Ramanathan, who returned to Congress in 1936 in disagreement with Periar's decision to support colonial rule.

There is some doubt about the year when the Self Respect Association was begun, but 1926 seems the best estimate. See Sithambaranar (1983: 77), Mangalamurugesan (n.d.: 64, 83).

[48] I do not presume that the concept of hegemony, drawn from Gramsci (1985, 1992), necessarily implies that subordinate groups accept the world view of dominant groups, only that they think and act in ways that reproduce existing patterns of dominance. This may happen even while the mentalities of subordinate groups are quite different from those of dominant groups. See Abercrombie, Hill & Turner (1980).

counter-hegemonic and counter-élite elements of Dravidianism was played out in the course of the movement's history in terms of tensions between the attempts of subordinate strata to assert their autonomy within the Dravidianist fold and the efforts of ascendant strata to maintain control over the Dravidianist agenda. Neither side ever won a complete victory, enabling the coexistence of a sense of mass political efficacy with limited changes in property rights. The simultaneous elaboration of homogeneous and layered social identities helped reconcile these two aspects of Dravidian populism. Periar posited a layered social identity and his ideology best revealed both the hegemonic and emancipatory aspects of Dravidianism. The tensions within this ideology prefigured some of the problems that later Dravidianists faced in cobbling diverse coalitions together.

Periar's Diverse Cadences

After leaving Congress, Periar interpreted Gandhian nationalism as a hegemonic project to maintain the dominance of Brahmins and 'Brahminism' in Indian society and the predominant influence of North Indians in national politics. He claimed that his brand of politics was oriented, on the contrary, towards the emancipation of subordinate groups in Tamil society, much as liberalism had opposed upper class and clerical dominance in the West.[49] Periar sought to associate himself with the enlightenment heritage by elaborating a materialist ontology and a genealogy of Brahminical morals as founded on a resentment of worldly non-Brahmin virtues. Further, he claimed Rousseau, Marx and Ingersoll as sources of inspiration and pointed to a future in which caste divisions and 'superstition' would yield place to pluralism, secularization and the acceptance of modern science and technology.[50] Such self-presentations prompted some scholars to view the

[49] Depending on context and audience, Dravidianists could present themselves as the Tamil variant of either the democratic revolution or the socialist revolution. Both interpretations were based on a vision of Dravidianism as anti-caste. The former interpretation equated caste with hierarchy and so regarded it as a barrier to social equality and contract, while the latter interpretation identified caste as the Indian incarnation of class.

[50] Ramaswami Naicker (1949, 1982b, 1983d, 1983e, 1984a, 1987g, 1987h); Personal Communication, Prof. Milton Singer.

Self Respect movement as consonant with 'British liberal assumptions'. If Dravidianists rose to political dominance later without seriously reducing social inequalities, these scholars took this to be a result of the movement's deradicalization over time.[51]

Important aspects of Periar's ideology and the manner in which it was deployed in mobilization were out of tune with liberalism. Far from relying on the concept of the abstract individual citizen central to British liberalism, Periar adopted ethnic categories drawn from colonial knowledge and sought to accord the Shudra primacy in the political community. Periar's vision of Shudra primacy provided the ideological basis on which later Dravidianists reinforced the dominance of non-Brahmin élites, both old and new, such as rich farmers, merchants and industrialists. While Periar's notions of social identity also had an emancipatory potential, this remained a subsidiary aspect of the Dravidianist project right through. An appreciation of the hegemonic aspects of Periar's politics makes resort to vaguely specified notions of deradicalization unnecessary to explain why the Dravidian parties stopped short of fundamentally changing the distribution of power in society.

The Definition of a Layered Social Identity

Periar conceived of the Dravidian community primarily in terms of a coalition of megacastes—the non-Brahmin Hindu castes of Tamil Nadu, i.e. Tamil speaking Hindus who were neither Brahmins nor SCs. The Dravidian was in other words the Tamil Hindu who was deemed a Shudra by Anglo-Indian legality and the varnashrama dharma that Periar wished to overthrow.[52] Indeed, Periar said that the DK, the successor of the Self Respect Association, might well be called the Shudra Kazhagam (Association of

[51] Barnett (1976: 51 & passim); Spratt (1970) and Pandian (1992) adopt a variant of this argument that sees in early Dravidianism an affinity with socialism.

[52] Periar's definition of Dravidian identity is especially clear in Ramaswami Naicker (1947): '*Dravidane, allathu Tamizhane, athaavathu paarppaanallaatha, Muslim allaatha, Kiristhuvan allaatha, adi-Dravidan (scheduled vaguppar) allaatha, Dravidane! "Soothirane"!*' (Dravidian, or Tamil, i.e. Dravidian who is neither Brahmin, Muslim, Christian, nor adi-Dravidan, i.e. SC)! 'Shudran'.) Also see Ramaswami Naicker (1937, 1987e); KA, 25 April 1926, 16 June 1929, 9 September 1930, 31 December 1939, 13 January 1945; *Viduthalai*, 6 March 1962.

the Shudras).[53] His indignation about varnashrama dharma was stronger as he claimed that it gave the rights of Brahmin men to cohabit with Shudra women priority over the claims of Shudra men to these women.[54] Such concern about the legitimacy of patriarchal authority within endogamous non-Brahmin families was at odds with, and tended to override, Periar's calls for women's rights.[55]

While Periar often demanded that a Shudra majority should enjoy political primacy, he also used more inclusive appeals at other times. For instance, he tended to use the term 'Tamil' in a more inclusive sense than the term 'Dravidian', to exclude only Brahmins and North Indians explicitly and the SCs implicitly (thus including members of minority religious groups).[56] He appealed to Muslims, Christians and SCs as allies in some contexts, arguing that only the DK and not the Brahmin dominated Congress, would give them an equal role in the political community.[57] But, he also treated these groups as obstacles to the interests of Shudras and the objectives of his movement at other times.[58] Periar used 'Dravidian' as a racial category too sometimes, to mean all South Indians who

[53] See Ramaswami Naicker (1987e: 5).

[54] This lent the insult of being called a Shudra its sharpest bite for many of Periar's followers. A constant motif of his speeches and writings, this was even the focus of Periar's last public speech, a week before his death (Ramaswami Naicker, 1987d).

[55] For instance, Periar defended women's conjugal rights in a debate with the prominent Tamil revivalist, V. Kalyanasundara Mudaliar, rejecting the notion of *karpu* (chastity) as the supreme feminine virtue, frequently asserted in Tamil literature. Also see Ramaswami Naicker (1987a, 1987g).

[56] KA, 31 December 1939: 'Non-Brahmin caste Hindus, Christians and Muslims are all Tamils as they originated here. That is not true of the Brahmins who are of Aryan descent. They came here only for survival.' The suggestion is that more honour and privilege are due to non-Brahmins as they are the original settlers of Tamil Nadu—shades of the mentality associated with *kaniatchi*. There is no mention of the SCs, who presumably are excluded. Periar did not employ these terms consistently, though, and sometimes equated 'Tamil' with 'Dravidan'.

[57] See KA, 9 January 1927; *Viduthalai*, 5 November 1948.

[58] The latter emphasis was evident in his appeal to the Dravidian-as-Shudra on the eve of Indian independence (Ramaswami Naicker, 1947). He urged the Shudra (also called Tamil or Dravidian) to treat Indian independence as a cause for mourning as it would bring the minority religious groups special privileges

were not Brahmins, based on Orientalist claims that these groups were descended from a distinct race.

A layered conception of 'Dravidian' identity underlies these apparently diverse conceptions of social identity. It contains at its centre the Tamil speaking Shudra of Tamil Nadu, and in successive concentric circles around this centre, South Indian Shudras who are non-Tamil speaking, Tamil Christians and Muslims, and Tamil speaking SCs. The groups clearly beyond the pale are Brahmins and 'North Indians', i.e. speakers of Indo-European languages derived partly from Sanskrit.[59] (As speaking a Sanskritic language was the crucial marker of a 'North Indian', North Indian Muslims could be allies).[60] The latter groups were deemed 'Aryans'. Periar called for the creation of a separate country in which the Dravidian-as-Shudra would enjoy primacy, and Christians, Muslims and SCs would also find a space.[61] This was at least the primary thrust of his statements, although he also referred to the future Dravida Nadu in more inclusionary terms. As for the 'Aryans', their ideological hold over the Dravidian was to be broken and, Periar said at times, those that resided in Tamil Nadu (or South India) were to be expelled.

The proportions of Tamil Nadu's population that occupy the different layers in the heretical conception of Dravidian identity cannot be precisely estimated as census categories are

---

and the SCs quotas at the national level, but no such entitlements for non-Brahmins. As Brahmins had their inherited privileges, Periar argued, only Dravidians (non-Brahmin caste Hindus) would be left high and dry. Also see *Viduthalai*, 6 March 1962.

[59] This is the loose sense in which the 'North Indian' figures in everyday speech among Tamils, and in Dravidianist demonology. This 'North Indian' is not a geographical category, as speakers of Sanskritic languages live in western and eastern India too. It is in this imprecise sense that references to the North Indian are to be understood in later discussions of Dravidianist ideology.

[60] Thus, Periar made common cause with the Muslim League at times, supporting its demand for Pakistan in return for the promise that the League would support the demand for a separate Dravida Nadu. Periar was also open to tactical alliances with the SCs and intermediate castes of Northern India at times, to the extent that he saw them as oppressed by the same varnashrama dharma that degraded Tamil Shudras.

[61] Anaimuthu (1974: 112); MM, 20 November 1939; KA, 17 December 1939.

not the same as those of Dravidianist ideology. Census figures
indicate that Brahmins and speakers of 'North Indian' languages
comprise about 6 per cent of Tamil Nadu's inhabitants, the SCs
and scheduled tribes (STs) 19.4 per cent, non-Hindus 11.2 per cent
and speakers of South Indian languages other than Tamil
12.7 per cent.[62] These figures overstate the number of current
inhabitants of Tamil Nadu outside the core of the early conception
of Dravidian identity for three reasons. First, some who report
languages other than Tamil as their native languages (especially
Telugu, Kannada and Marathi) are culturally indigenized and
generally regarded as 'Tamils'. Second, 'Brahmin' has not been a
category in post-colonial censuses, and the Brahmin share in the
population might have decreased slightly since decolonization
due to migration. Third, there is some overlap among the various
'out-groups' (some Christians are SCs, some Muslims are 'North
Indians', some non-Tamil speakers are Brahmins or SCs). Taking
these caveats into account, Periar's 'Aryans' probably constitute
no more than 4 per cent and others beyond the core conception
of Dravidian identity a little over 30 per cent of the state's
inhabitants.[63]

If heretical Dravidianism had acquired the power to unleash
massive violence against 'Aryans', their relatively small numbers
would have rendered them vulnerable. If it had turned against other
groups not part of the core conception of Dravidian identity, larger
numbers would have been affected, and the higher numerical
strength of those attacked might have helped them respond more
effectively, perhaps leading to prolonged ethnic violence. So, the

[62] Department of Statistics (1994: 62–4, 73).

[63] I guesstimate 'Aryans' at 4 per cent because Periar did not include Urdu-
speaking Muslims (about 1.8 per cent) under this rubric. The second figure is
based on the following assumptions: the majority of those the censuses report
as Telugu speakers (8.7 per cent) and some 'Kannada speakers' (2.6 per cent)
are generally regarded as Tamils as they are literate only in Tamil and/or
English, speak a Tamilized variant of the languages of their ancestors (who
migrated to the Tamil majority areas centuries back) and do not closely
identify themselves with the latter languages; a significant minority of the
Telugu and Kannada speakers who are not considered Tamils are Brahmins
or SCs; and there is at least as high a proportion of SCs among Christians
(5.8 per cent) as in the general population. These assumptions should seem
reasonable to those familiar with Tamil society.

limited extent of the violence Dravidianists visited upon their 'others' should not lead one to underestimate the potential that early Dravidianist discourse had for provoking ethnic violence. The way in which Dravidianism turned towards populism was crucial in containing this potential.

Hinduism and Early Dravidianism: An Ambivalent Relationship

'Hinduism' plays a role in the construction of social identity detailed above for the layers of which this identity is composed are defined by the Orientalist vision of a Hindu community, and the Shudra is accorded priority in relation to the Brahmins, the SCs and non-Hindus. This may seem perplexing as Periar rejected religion as the root of caste distinctions and injustice in Tamil society around the time he left Congress and asserted his atheism with acerbic frequency for decades thereafter.[64]

A key to this puzzle is to be found in the motivations underlying Periar's atheism. Periar rejected religion primarily because he wished to oppose the caste system and the 'Brahmin dominance' brought by colonization. So, the religion which he opposed most vociferously was Hinduism, especially the 'Brahminical Hinduism' associated with varnashrama dharma. While a significant chunk of his speeches and writings were devoted to criticizing various aspects of Brahminical Hinduism, and DK meetings and conferences reviled Hindu gods, epics and scriptures,[65] Periar devoted little attention to the criticism of other religions.[66] Indeed, he found aspects of Islam and Christianity more acceptable than

---

[64] KA, 15 August 1926, 9 January 1927, 9 September 1930; and Ramaswami Naicker (1987h) are among Periar's early atheistic pronouncements. Also see Ramaswami Naicker (1982a, 1983b, 1984a, 1985a, 1985c, 1987a, 1987h, 1987i).

[65] See Ramaswami Naicker (1947, 1975, 1982b, 1983a, 1983c, 1985a, 1985b, 1985c, 1987b, 1987c, 1987h, 1987i, 1987j). Even Periar's exposition of a materialist ontology (Ramaswami Naicker (1984a, 1985a)), which rejected religion *tout court*, was elaborated through arguments against elements of Hindu philosophy.

[66] For instance, Periar frequently criticized the unequal status accorded women in Hindu society and scripture (Ramaswami Naicker (1978, 1983c, 1987c)), but rarely criticized female seclusion and marginalization among Muslims.

Hindu beliefs and practices—the applicability of a uniform moral code to all of the religion's adherents, non-personified notions of the deity, and the lack of animistic beliefs and idol worship. This led Periar to urge Hindus to convert to some other religion if they could not do without the consolations of faith.[67] Periar's denunciation of Hinduism echoed some of the tones of Christian missionaries and Hindu revivalists who wished to reconstruct Hinduism on a Semitic model. His critique of Tamil society was influenced more by colonial paternalism and the Semitic interpretation of Hinduism than by liberalism.[68]

If the reform of varnashrama dharma was Periar's primary focus, the Hindus whose actions these norms are supposed to govern were his main target audience. A vision of the movement as focused on reforming Hindu practices shaped many of Periar's positions. For instance, Periar regarded the so-called 'self respect marriages', wedding ceremonies conducted in Dravidianist families ritually validated by the speeches of political leaders rather than religious rituals performed by priests, as a reform of Hindu practices.[69] Although these ceremonies were sometimes presented as a move towards secularization, they were rarely conceived as alternatives to orthodox Christian or Muslim weddings. When the DMK came to power and gave legal recognition to Self Respect weddings, this took the form of an amendment to the Hindu Marriages Act, rather than being recognized as a form of civil marriage—a move congruous with the initial vision of such ceremonies.

Periar vehemently opposed Hindu revivalists for their acclamation of scriptural Hinduism and the patterns of belief common among the 'North Indian' upper castes, their upper caste leadership, commitment to Indian unity and disregard of South Indian cultural specificity.[70] However, he assumed some postures similar to those of the Hindu revivalists because of the indirect role that a notion of a Hindu community played in his discourse. For instance, Periar bemoaned the barriers that caste differences placed to the emergence of an integral Hindu community, comparable to the community of the faithful said to be associated with the Semitic

---

[67] See, for instance, Ramaswami Naicker (1947).
[68] One might say he espoused a Semitic atheism.
[69] Ramaswami Naicker (1983e).
[70] See Ramaswami Naicker (1937, 1983b, 1985b).

religions. Further, he opposed the extension of special rights to religious minorities and preferential quotas to the SCs in the Indian constitution, which mandated no such preferences for the BCs.[71] When both Hindu and Muslim religious leaders denounced a DK campaign to break idols of the Hindu Pillayar deity, Periar warned Muslims not to impede a movement that had arisen from within the Hindu community. Following this definition of his movement, he instructed Mulim party members to keep away from the agitation. Further, he threatened that DK activists would play music in front of mosques if Muslim religious leaders did not withdraw their objections to the agitation, reaching down into the bag of tricks Hindu chauvinists had assembled well before.[72]

The subtle similarities between early Dravidianism and Hindu revivalism, little remarked upon because of the more obvious differences, help one understand the weakness of Hindu revivalism in Tamil Nadu. Assertive Dravidianism inhibited the growth of Hindu revivalism in Tamil Nadu not only (as is often popularly asserted) due to its opposition to Brahminism and Hindu chauvinism, but also because it deployed notions of community resembling in some respects those of the Hindu revivalists. It thereby gained the durable support of some groups which support Hindu revivalism elsewhere in India (e.g. urban shopkeepers).[73]

Periar's appeals neither presumed nor necessarily promoted the recession of faith into the private sphere, the reduction of religious motifs in political mobilization or the exclusion of religious institutions from political contention. Like other heresies, Periar's were contingent on faith, at least the faith of others. Periar made tactical alliances with non-Brahmin Hindu sects and institutions and recognized boundaries distinguishing 'Hindus' from 'non-Hindus'. He recognized as legitimate and himself made claims on behalf of caste groups which, by his own argument, owe their definition ultimately to Hindu religious beliefs. After decolonization, he proceeded to demand that freedom of religion be constrained

[71] See Ramaswami Naicker (1947, 1982b: 22–4), *Viduthalai*, 6 March 1962.

[72] See *Viduthalai*, issues of March and May 1953; interviews: K. Veeramani, 'Tiruvarur' Thangarasu (Madras); A. M. Muthusami (Tiruvannamalai).

[73] However, shopkeeper supporters of the Hindu revivalists tend to be from the upper and upper-middle castes, while those of the DK and the DMK are predominantly from the intermediate castes. Chapter VI elaborates on how assertive Dravidianism 'inoculated' Tamil society against Hindu revivalism.

according to the specific content of religions. He argued that freedom of religious belief and practice was incompatible with equality of opportunity as caste-based dominance has been intrinsic to Hindu practice. Despite his atheism, Periar was no secularist. If his followers failed to effect secularization when they came to dominate Tamil politics, this was prefigured by Periar's own politics.[74]

The SCs and the 'Shudra Kazhagam'

Periar considered Shudras the natural vanguard of a movement arisen to overturn the world of varnashrama dharma. The relegation of non-Hindus to the margins of such a movement is readily understandable, but not that of the SCs who presumably share an interest in opposing upper caste hegemony. A consideration of this puzzle leads us back to the historical pre-conditions of non-Brahminism. It was the Shudras, many of whom enjoyed considerable power, who were most affected by the inscription of aspects of varnashrama dharma into Anglo-Indian legality and the dominance of Brahmins in new public spheres. While the SCs occupied a liminal position within the varna framework, they had little power even before the onset of British rule, and so suffered no comparable loss in status due to the changes wrought by colonization.

Periar's discussion of the situation of the SCs clarifies why he accorded them a marginal role in his transformative project. His references to the SCs were ambidextrous, much like those to Muslims and Christians.[75] He urged the SCs to distrust paternalistic efforts, of the sort undertaken by the Gandhians, to improve their lot by adopting upper caste practices. He argued that their problems arose not from unenlightened practices, but from the segregation and poverty to which caste discrimination condemned them. To the extent that he, as a Shudra, was oppressed by the same Brahminism which condemned the SC to the status of a *parayan* (pariah), he urged the SCs to treat him as a tactical ally

[74] For discussions of secularization, see Martin (1979) and Berger (1987).

[75] For Periar's statements regarding untouchability and the SCs' situation, see Anaimuthu (1974); Aadalarasan (1986); Ramaswami Naicker (1947); KA, 18 October, 6 December 1925; 25 April 1926; 16 June 1929; 12 April, 24 May 1931; 8 May 1932; 28 July 1935.

in the struggle against varnashrama dharma, and no more.[76] Periar criticized the discriminatory treatment meted out to the SCs by non-Brahmin caste Hindus, not just by Brahmins. He claimed that the Shudra had been beguiled by the Brahmin into a sense of higher status as a means to ensure his acceptance of the caste system. Urging the Shudra to shed the veil of Aryan illusion, he demanded that the Shudra extend whatever rights he gained to the SCs too.[77]

The above features of Periar's discussion of the situation of the SCs could be read as a call for the independent mobilization and self-assertion of the SCs through a rejection of Hinduism. Indeed, he suggested at times that the SC would enjoy parity with the non-Brahmin in the future Dravida Nadu.[78] This was the vision which inspired the considerable entry of SC bonded agricultural workers from the Kaveri valley into the DK through the 1940s and 1950s. This occurred especially in parts of the Kaveri valley with a limited communist presence—in scattered pockets in Tiruvarur, Nagaipattinam, Nannilam, Kodavasal, Kumbakonam and Mayuram taluks.[79]

However, Periar could also be read as relegating SC concerns to a secondary status. We saw that he rarely included the SCs within the core of his layered conception of Dravidian or Tamil identity. His discussions of the situation of the SCs were invariably couched in terms of 'us' and 'them' while speaking to a primarily caste Hindu audience; in terms of 'you' and 'us' while addressing a primarily SC audience, even while he urged the SCs to be

[76] KA, 25 April 1926; 16 June 1929; 25 May 1931; 8 May 1932.

[77] KA, 9 December 1928.

[78] Periar was in the habit of answering questions sent to him on slips of paper by individuals in the audience after his speeches. One of the questions he was posed after a speech in Madras was: 'Will the *adi-Dravidas* gain or lose from the creation of Dravida Nadu?' Periar responded, 'They will only lose,' and, after a dramatic pause, added, 'They will lose the prefix *adi* and gain their rightful place as equal members of the Dravidian community.' Interviews: 'Kavignar' Kudi Arasu (Madras), A. M. Muthuswami (Tiruvannamalai).

[79] Interviews: 'Nagai' Kaliappan (Madukkur), 'Tirumangalakkudi' Ku. Govindarajan (Tirumangalakkudi, Kumbakonam), Thangarasu (Rajagiri), S. S. Batcha (Nagaipattinam), Ka. Ma. Kuppusamy (Vallam), 'Tiruvarur' Thangarasu (Madras), G. N. Sami (Darasuram), P. Sivasankaran, 'Kavalakkudi' Marimuthu, V. Subramaniam, S. S. Maniam, Kamaraj, 'Malliam' Kannayyan, 'Neikuppai' Ganesan (Tiruvarur).

self-assertive.[80] He initially argued for extending preferential quotas to the SCs; but was critical when the SCs gained quotas in national government employment and the BCs did not.[81] To justify according centrality to the BCs in his struggle against Brahminism, he argued speciously that the status of a Shudra was more demeaning than that of an untouchable. As earlier stated, non-Brahminist indignation at the Shudra label included the concern that it implied the denial of the legitimacy of the endogamous non-Brahmin family. Alluding to such male non-Brahmin anxieties regarding subtle challenges to their control over their women, Periar claimed that, in the Brahminical lexicon, the term 'Shudra' implies that one was born out of wedlock, but that the term *parayan* carries no such connotation. Periar argued on this basis that the Shudra was dishonoured more by Brahminism than the *parayan* was.[82]

To the extent that Periar gave the BC primacy over the SC, his discourse was amenable to appropriation for the hegemonic projects of the ascendant BCs. He could be interpreted in tune with the BCs' jealousy of their privileges and envy of the quotas SCs gained. Such an interpretation was common among the predominantly BC base that the DK built in commercial towns all around the state, and in some villages of the northern plains and the new delta of the Kaveri valley (whose social structure resembled that of the plains). Among my case areas, the DK had such a base in some of the small towns and larger villages of northern and western Mannargudi and Chengam taluks (near Tiruvannamalai).[83] The

[80] Diehl's (1978) remarks upon such usage, evident in KA, 25 April 1926, 9 December 1928, 8 May 1932; and Periar's addresses to Adi-Dravida conferences on 16 June 1929 and 29 September 1935.

[81] KA, 9 December 1928; Ramaswami Naicker (1947).

[82] KA, 25 April 1926; 16 June 1929.

[83] Among these predominantly BC bases of the DK were the villages of Nidamangalam, Idamelayur, Idakeelayur, Idaannavaasal, Ullikottai, Koilvenni and Paravakottai in the new Kaveri delta portions of Mannargudi constituency; and Tirupathur, Tandrambattu, and Narayanakuppam in the northern plains. Interviews, 'Nagai' Kaliappan, Balasubramaniam (Madukkur), Ka. Ma. Kuppuswami (Vallam), R. P. Sarangan, K. Nallathambi, 'Mannai' Narayanaswami (Mannargudi), Aa. Subramaniam, Venkatesan (Nidamangalam), Sivanandan Saluvar, Azhagu Tirunavukkarasu (Idamelayur), B. Neelakantan, B. Vaiyapuri, Uthirandam Arunachalam (Tiruvannamalai), Ganapathi,

interpretation of Dravidianism as a vehicle for BC preeminence was even stronger among those who later embraced the DMK.

Heresy as Politics

The inversion, sometimes ritualistic, of dominant ideologies and their symbols was crucial to the articulation of Periar's cultural politics. These gestures were intended to shock society into insight regarding the deeper roots of caste-based domination, much as Bertolt Brecht attempted to confront European audiences with stark images of the social roles of class, power and gender around the same time through the dramaturgical device of the 'alienation effect'.[84] They did not necessarily subvert existing structures of dominance, as is often the case with inversion rituals.[85] Rather, they evoked far more antagonism than support and often placed the DK at odds with attempts to build a tolerant society.

Periar and his followers inverted religious orthodoxy through the denigration of Brahminical norms, the abuse of Hindu deities, epics and scriptures, and the derision of the acts of godmen who claimed divine inspiration (for instance, by replicating their acts to show that they were merely the result of physical prowess or sleight of hand). The Ramayana was reinterpreted in a way that transposed the characters of Rama and Ravana as hero and villain;[86] and Periar's followers gave their children names deemed inauspicious by the orthodox.[87] Early Dravidianist inversion rituals included beginning ceremonies at inauspicious hours, garlanding idols with slippers rather than flowers, parading idols around town while beating them with slippers, breaking idols, ceremonially cutting (rather than putting on) the sacred thread worn by Brahmins, displaying placards depicting deities engaged in sexual orgies and, where the DK was strong enough to permit it, beating

---

Ramachandran (Tandrambattu), Dhanakoti Gounder (Tanipadi), Balakrishnan (Narayanakuppam), Venkatrama Naidu (Bondai), G. Sami Naidu (Tirupathur).

[84] See Brecht (1964).

[85] Turner (1969) argues that inversion rituals serve to bind community rather than challenge patterns of dominance.

[86] Ramaswami Naicker (1987b, 1987j), Richman (1991: 175–201).

[87] e.g. Moodevi (the name of a goddess of the inauspicious, usually used as a term of abuse) and Ravana Das (a name which initially aroused my curiosity about Dravidianist ideology at the age of six—see the Preface).

up rather than honouring visiting religious mendicants.[88] The peasants of medieval Europe could not have done better at turning the world upside down. Indeed, Periar's determination to embarrass and outrage the orthodox did not end with his death. To fulfil his wish, the following statement of his was inscribed under the many statues erected throughout Tamil Nadu by of his later Dravidianist regimes: 'He who created god was a fool; he who propagates god is a scoundrel; he who worships god is a barbarian.'

Periar's iconoclasm extended to attacks on the emerging political orthodoxy of pan-Indian nationalism and its most popular exponent, Gandhi. From ardent support of Gandhi, Periar moved to a view of him as a symbol of Brahminism and North Indian domination, which he claimed Congress rule would bring.[89] While Gandhi aimed to build a pan-Indian national community which would shake off the British yoke, Periar asserted a distinct Dravidian identity and embraced colonial rule as a necessary buffer against Brahmin and North Indian domination. When independence came, Periar directed his followers to mourn the departure of the British, in contrast with the popular celebrations sponsored by the newborn post-colonial government.[90] Gandhi aimed to inspire a cosmopolitan order through the neo-Hindu myth of *Ram Rajya* (the rule of Rama). Periar attacked Hindu epics and festivals, focusing his ire on the Ramayana, and insisted that the retention of Hinduism, even in private belief, would be necessarily divisive along religious and caste lines.[91] While Gandhi urged the SCs to use the Brahminical channels to caste mobility without changing their logic, Periar warned them against such paternalistic strategies

[88] V. S. Anandan, who later joined the DMK, gave idol-breaking an innovative twist. He stole into a Pillayar temple in Washermanpet (north Madras) at night and strung up the idol on a nearby tree with a supposed suicide note from Pillayar saying that he was giving up the struggle as the rising prices of rice and sugar invariably left him short of the sweetmeats which are considered this god's favourite food item.

[89] That Gandhi was neither a Brahmin nor a North Indian did not deter Periar as he found Brahminical and North Indian biases in Gandhi's cultural politics. While he was from a mercantile caste, Gandhi did fit the Dravidianist vision of the North Indian as Gujarati, his native language, is considered Indo-European.

[90] Ramaswami Naicker (1937), *Viduthalai*, 5 August 1947.

[91] Ramaswami Naicker (1937, 1985c, 1987a, 1987j).

and exhorted them towards self-assertion. While Gandhi urged the adoption of upper caste habits, Periar organized beef-eating sessions. While Gandhi wore white, Periar and his followers wore black. Periar summarized the five cardinal principles of his movement as: 'Destroy god; Destroy religion; Destroy Congress; Destroy Gandhi; Destroy the Brahmin.'[92]

As they attacked the prevailing social and political orthodoxies, Periar's gestures of inversion were heretical. It was Periar's gestures of heresy rather than his ventures into social critique that left a lasting mark on the popular imagination. So, to characterize Periar, I borrow from Borges the term 'heresiarch,'[93] presumably coined by conjoining the words heresy and patriarch. A heresiarch could only be an inspired virtuoso, whose harsh cadences haunted the nightmares of the pious, the proper and (sometimes) the powerful. Periar's allusions to a popular Dravidian community, represented in the title of the first journal he edited, *Kudi Arasu* (which may be translated as 'The Republic of the Popular Community'), anticipated the later populist articulation of Dravidianism. However, unlike his populist successors, Periar did not mobilize large numbers or build a well organized party.

Periar's support of colonial rule from 1934 onwards prevented the DK from challenging the dominance of pan-Indian nationalism in the late colonial period when expelling the colonizer had become the focus of mass politics.[94] Besides, the politics of heresy was unfavourable to coalition building. While populist appeals may be flexibly deployed to address the specific concerns of many groups, the politics of heresy is likely to alienate potential supporters by attacking symbols that much of society holds sacred. Where each new way of articulating populist appeal may help attract further supporters, every heretical gesture is likely to alienate more groups which share some of the movement's aims. These features of the politics of heresy restricted the membership and base of the

---

[92] See Ramaswami Naicker (1975: 16). I am indebted to David Washbrook for the suggestion that Periar constructed an image of himself as an 'anti-Gandhi', an expression I use as a takeoff on 'anti-Christ'. Periar envisioned himself as a Nietzschean figure showing his social world of Shudra Tamils the hollowness of the morals they had accepted out of weakness.

[93] Borges (1981).

[94] Mangalamurugesan (n.d.: 122–30), Ramamurthi (1983: 152–3), Irschick (1986: 102–3).

organizations Periar led, despite the wide popularity that features of his militant non-Brahminism acquired. So, his politics of heresy remained a vehicle of protest rather than of social change.

The Self Respect Association and the DK relied on the patronage of notables in ways incompatible with their plebeian rhetoric, partly to compensate for their organizational weakness and limited support. The social influence and mercantile links of his family helped Periar launch his early political career.[95] Big landlords like Samiappa Mudaliar of Nedumbalam and Kayaroganan Pillai of Tiruvarur provided material support and social protection for DK mobilization in the early strongholds in the Kaveri valley. The wavering support of other such landlords like P. T. Rajan of Madurai and W. P. A. Soundarapandia Nadar of Pattiveerampatti enabled some level of party activity even in the inhospitable Madurai district.[96] The resistance of the locally dominant Kongu Vellala Gounders to the DK in parts of Coimbatore and Madurai districts was diminished by the support of N. Arjunan, the princeling of Pazhayakottai.[97] Less wealthy notables also helped build the DK in its pockets of strength—the landlord/merchant A. Arumuga Chettiar in Nidamangalam, the cigar factory owner K. K. Neelamegam in Kumbakonam (in Thanjavur district), the soda company owners R. D. Gopal and R. D. Umapathi Naicker, the landlord and lawyer G. Sami Naidu and the liquor store contractor C. M. Subramania Naidu in Tirupattur, and the minor landlords M. D. Rangaswami Reddiar and Pa. Seethapathi Reddiar of Tandrambattu and Balakrishna Naidu of Narayanakuppam (in North Arcot district).[98]

[95] Baker (1977) shows this, but neglects the significance of Periar's ideology.

[96] See *Mannai Narayanaswamy Pon Vizha Malar* (n.d.); Iraiyan (1981: 56–8); Interviews: P. T. R. Palanivel Rajan, S. Kaverimaniam (Madurai); P. Sivasankaran (Tiruvarur); 'Mannai' Narayanaswamy, P. Venkatesa Solagar (Mannargudi); Thangarasu (Rajagiri); Nagai Kaliappan (Madras, Madukkur); T. Govindarajan (Tirumangalakkudi, Kumbakonam).

[97] Iraiyan (1981: 179–80); Interviews: Kovai Sezhiyan (Madras), Angusami, G. Lakshmanan, Govindammal (Dindigul).

[98] Iraiyan (1981: 214–19, 249–50, 286–7); Interviews: G. Sami Naidu, T. S. Kittayyar, K. Annamalai Gounder, Marappan, Shankar, Dr. M. Krishnan, Radhakrishnan, Muni Chetty (Tirupattur); A. M. Muthuswami, Uthirandam Arunachalam, Narayanaswami Reddiar (Tiruvannamalai); N. C. Ramaswami Gounder, Ramachandran, Ganapathi (Tandrambattu); Dhanakoti Gounder

Periar regarded the organizations he led as his patrimony, not distinguishing his personal wealth from party funds. He likened his bond with his followers to a master-servant relationship (and treated many of them little better than domestic servants typically were), even while expecting them to fend for themselves financially.[99] His organizations were held together by his followers' reverence for him, their respect for his ideals and the statements that appeared in the party organ. He resisted the efforts of the likes of Annadurai to routinize party organization as it could have diluted his personal authority. If some organizational pluralism developed nevertheless, it was due to the efforts and popularity of his populist successors, whose outlook differed from his because they matured while decolonization was impending.

If Periar's heretical gestures shocked many and hindered the DK's growth, why did he, and not others who expressed non-Brahmin grievances in a more prosaic and socially acceptable idiom, become the most popular non-Brahminist leader of the late colonial period? Periar could acquire mass support despite his heretical gestures because the DK's demonstrations of unbelief did not constitute as much of a departure from past experience as they appeared at the first sight. Tales of inversion rituals involving the

---

(Tanipadi); Venkatrama Naidu (Bondhai); Ko. Si. Mani, Stalin, 'Mundasu' Natarajan (Kumbakonam); R. P. Sarangan, 'Mannai' Narayanaswamy, K. Nallathambi (Mannargudi); Aa. Subramaniam, Venkatesan (Nidamangalam); P. Sivasankaran, 'Malliam' Kannayyan, Thangaraj (Tiruvarur); Tiruvarur Thangarasu (Madras).

[99] '*Yennaip pinpattrukiravarkal thangal sontha pakuththarivaikkooda koncham thyagam seyya vendum. Yaaraavathu oruvanthaan nadaththakkoodiyavanaaka irukka mudiyume thavira, yellorume thalaivarkalaaka irukka mudiyathu*' (Those who follow me have to sacrifice their independent judgement to some extent. Only one person can lead, not everyone). KA, 29 May 1948.

However, Periar frequently told his supporters: '*Un veettil saappittuvittu yen veettukku vanthu velai sey*' (Eat at your house, and then come to mine to work). Those without independent means who worked on the party newspaper were fed at Periar's home, but had to sleep on sacks containing agricultural produce in the godown adjoining the house. See Karunanidhi (1986); Interviews: K. Veeramani, Tiruvarur Thangarasu (Madras); A. M. Muthuswami (Tiruvannamalai), K. Nallathambi (Mannargudi), R. Rathnagiri (Thanjavur).

reversal of textually approved forms of worship occupy an important place in the genealogies of emergent groups in Tamil Nadu. Stories of such practices, which would be regarded as tantamount to the abuse of deities from the orthodox Brahminical standpoint, served to exalt saintly devotion and accommodate departures from approved forms of ritual in the *bhakti* tradition of the early second millennium and marked the incorporation of 'non-Brahmin' lineages into high Hindu culture.[100] Specifically, alternative versions of the Ramayana which praised Ravana's heroic qualities, portrayed Rama as an uncouth invader, and did not validate varnashrama dharma and Brahmin supremacy were written by Jain poets and similar tales were transmitted through the oral traditions of the lower and intermediate castes in some regions.[101] Periar's inversions differed from the earlier instances as they were not founded on the acceptance of religious belief. Yet, many regarded the DK's heresies sympathetically as a continuation of an earlier tradition without joining the party or rejecting their religious faith.

After the majority of Periar's followers split from him in 1949 to form the DMK, they drew selectively from his stream of heresies to forge an alternative orthodoxy, of which they enshrined Periar the grey bearded patriarch.[102] In the process, they augmented the

[100] Dirks (1987: 75–96 and passim) offers a careful analysis of such genealogies. Also see Blackburn and Ramanujan (1986) and Zvelebil (1973).

[101] Thapar (1987: 14–15) and Ramanujan (1991: 22–49) discuss the Jain Ramayana, while O'Hanlon (1985: 169–74 and passim) indicates the presence of such alternative interpretations of characters appearing in the Ramayana in Marathi ballads. Tamil poems of Jain and Buddhist inspiration are part of the literary heritage acclaimed by some Dravidianist ideologues.

[102] The ideology and career of Victor Raul Haya de la Torre, the founding leader of the Peruvian APRA, parallels that of Periar's to some extent. Both combined materialist and indigenist notions, deployed discourses about marginal groups to mobilize mainly groups of intermediate status, and were supreme charismatic leaders of their loosely structured organizations. The careers of both spanned the long period extending from the interwar period to the 1970s, when their respective societies went through many phases of mass mobilization, over which they exercised considerable influence without gaining direct access to state power. They remained somewhat naive about the nature of state power, leading them to support rulers they once abhorred (in Periar's case, the British and then Congress; in Haya's case, Odria, a Peruvian dictator). See Pike (1986) and Stein (1980).

hegemonic features of early Dravidianism and attenuated its emancipatory elements. Such aspects of Periar's programme as the transformation of BC–SC relations and the liberation of women, never the foci of even DK mobilization, were largely cast by the wayside. However, the reorientation of Dravidianism from heresy to populism helped curtail threats to tolerance and enabled effective coalition building.

The Tamil Variant of Fascism?

Some features of non-Brahminism, particularly its heretical variant, have invited comparisons with European fascism.[103] The main such feature was the definition as an outsider of an ethnic group (the Brahmins in the one case and the Jews in the other) whose members had inhabited the region for centuries, contributed significantly to its high culture, and considered themselves and were partly accepted as belonging to the region prior to the emergence of these movements. Opposition to the out-group was associated in both cases with a rhetorical rejection of an emergent bourgeois cosmopolitanism, perceived colonial Brahminization in Tamil Nadu and the feared eclipse of German culture by West European civilization in Germany. The DK's calls, albeit infrequent, for the expulsion of Brahmins, and Periar's professed admiration for Mussolini and Hitler made the parallel seem even closer.

Despite these ideological similarities, the respective movements' approaches to mobilization were significantly different.[104] Even while denouncing Brahmin perfidy from platforms, Periar and some of his followers maintained social relations with Brahmins that were cordial, and in some cases close. Not only did Periar rent out many of the houses he owned to Brahmins,[105] but he also had a long and close personal association with the leading Tamil Brahmin politician of his time, Rajaji, who he opposed politically

---

[103] However, no scholar familiar with South India considers the affinities close.

[104] Besides, the social situation of Tamil Brahmins, who enjoyed considerable power especially during colonial rule, was quite different from that of the European Jewry, which suffered different forms of discrimination.

[105] He defended this practice by saying that Brahmins are known to be the most reliable tenants.

through much of his career.[106] He remained open to political cooperation with individual Brahmins, campaigning for some in different elections.

The DK's heretical gestures hurt the sensibilities of many, including Brahmins, but rarely involved violence against property or person. Incidents of DK violence against Brahmins were few and far between, involving the destruction of a few houses or attacks on a few individuals, mostly during two phases after the DK had lost much of its strength—during a wave of agitations in 1957–8 and again in 1971. The limited nature of the DK's actions against Brahmins was not due to the party's lack of strength, for the DK was able to overcome considerable social opposition in its areas of strength from the 1930s to the 1950s, or due to the fear of state repression, which the DK had faced to a significant extent at times.

The DK's anti-Brahmin propaganda was evidently meant to protest 'Brahmin dominance' rather than to evoke massive attacks against Brahmins. The definition of the Brahmin as an outsider was meant to highlight this protest, rather than to expel Brahmins or seriously abridge their civil rights. This obviously differs deeply from the record of European fascism. Further, Periar lacked a clear conception of state power and a strategy to acquire and exercise it, the demand for Dravida Nadu notwithstanding. He saw the state primarily as a source of patronage to be tapped, leading him into compromising alliances with various rulers he once opposed—first the British, then the Congress regime, and finally the DMK regime. The Nazis, on the contrary, had the definite ambition of capturing state power, used electoral fora effectively to this end and, once ensconced in power, systematically heightened attacks against ethnic out-groups, leading to the holocaust.

If Periar's politics was so different from that of European fascism, why did he claim an affinity with it? Not only did these claims draw further attention to anti-Brahminism, they helped Periar distinguish himself from British liberalism even while he tactically supported the colonial state. While his allusions to the enlightenment served to reassure the colonial state and some Tamil

[106] Among the notable points in Periar's long friendship with Rajaji were: Rajaji recruiting Periar into Congress in 1916; Periar seeking advice solely from Rajaji in deciding on his controversial second marriage in 1949 (two decades after he had left Congress), and Periar staying with Rajaji's body throughout the latter's funeral ceremonies in 1972.

intellectuals, positive references to fascists and communists signalled to potential supporters that he was motivated more by the concerns of plebeian groups than by the rewards offered by the colonial state. Despite certain ideological similarities with fascism, ethnic antagonism was not central to early Dravidianism. It could have become so later, but did not due to the populist turn the DMK initiated. Unlike in the Nazi case, the growth of Dravidianist support was attended by a growing acceptance of tolerance.

THE POPULIST TURN PREFIGURED: THE EARLY OUTLOOK OF C. N. ANNADURAI

While heretical non-Brahminism reflected tensions arising from the peculiar nature of colonial state-society relations, Periar relied too heavily on colonial paternalism to be able to recognize the colonial origins of many of the problems he addressed. However, non-Brahminism also attracted a younger generation which matured politically through the 1930s and 1940s, when opposition to colonialism had become the focal point of mass politics. While accepting Periar's leadership, this group developed an autonomous perspective which paid greater attention to language, territory and the state. Annadurai, who assumed leadership over this group, was introduced to Dravidianism by Justice Party notables like the trade unionist C. Basudev and the mercantile/industrial tycoon, Raja Muthiah Chettiar.[107] His relationship with Periar, which began a few years later, was crucial but often fraught with tension due to their many strategic and ideological differences.

Annadurai addressed the range of non-Brahminist grievances typical of the period. He not only criticized the attribution of low status to non-Brahmins, Periar's focus, but also the destruction of the crafts and growing land concentration (a difference in emphasis related to Periar's origins in a wealthy mercantile caste and Annadurai's in a modest weaver/peasant caste). Further, Annadurai traced these problems not just to the dominance of North Indians and Brahmins but also to the impact of British colonization,[108] and recognized the role of British rule in enabling the dominance of some North Indian castes in trade, the rise of Brahmins in the

[107] Maraimalaiyan (1967: 63, 96), Chinnasami (1983: 15–21), *Manram*, 9 November 1969.
[108] See Annadurai (1985d, 1985e, 1986c).

professions, and the influence of Brahminical norms on the law. He wrote in a pamphlet entitled *Aariya Maayai* (Aryan Mystification): 'It is only after British rule began to take root in this country that the speakers of Sanskritic languages (Aryans) were able to become government officials, lawyers and judges; and introduce their scriptures. It is only after this that the contents of scripture themselves became law.'[109]

Based on these arguments, Annadurai pushed Dravidianists to distance themselves from the colonial state and from notables closely associated with this state, the likes of whom had dominated the Justice Party until Periar took over the leadership of the party in 1938 and filled its ranks with his own followers from the Self Respect Association. To achieve this end, Annadurai successfully moved a resolution at a Justice Party conference in 1944 that (besides changing the party's name to the DK) required party members to forsake honorific titles bestowed by the British Raj.[110] At the same conference, Annadurai successfully pleaded for the formalization of party institutions and the strengthening of its youth wing (formed in 1942), enabling the recruitment of more youth sympathetic to his vision and gaining his faction greater autonomy from Periar. Periar grudgingly accommodated Annadurai as the latter enjoyed considerable influence among the cadre.

Annadurai's understanding of colonial rule led him to oppose Periar's directive to his followers in 1947 to mourn decolonization. He argued that the Dravidians were oppressed by the Brahmin, the Bania (a North Indian merchant caste) and the British, and that the departure of one of the oppressors could only be an occasion to rejoice. He wished to continue the struggle for secession, to free Dravida Nadu of the other two oppressors, and expected that an independent, democratic and federal India would offer a more favourable terrain for this struggle. Some DK members followed his call to celebrate Indian independence.[111]

[109] While Annadurai (1985a: 51) argues for the colonial origins of the dominance of Sanskritic norms, Annadurai (1985d) discusses the rise of Brahmins in the professions and North Indians in trade during British rule.

[110] This led many pro-colonial notables to leave the DK and deny it their patronage. See KA, 2 September 1944, Maraimalaiyan (1967: 139–40), Visswanathan (1983: 294–7) and Barnett (1976: 65–7).

[111] DN, 10 August 1947; 'Mannai' Narayanaswami read this article of Annadurai's as he chaired a DK meeting mourning decolonization in

Tensions arose periodically within the DK through the 1940s due to differences between Periar and Annadurai, which extended beyond their assessments of colonial rule.[112] Annadurai did not associate the Dravidian community primarily with the Shudra category, but with a distinctive non-Sanskritic language and cultural tradition, held in low esteem in the colonial order and little recognized in pan-Indian nationalist discourse. While Annadurai's early vision drew upon colonial ethnic categories, much as Periar's did, he and his followers recast these categories in a way that focused not so much on putative blood ties but on a cultural logic marginalized by colonial Sanskritization. They focused not so much on 'being Dravidian/Tamil' (in terms of descent) as on 'doing Dravidian/Tamil' (to paraphrase Barth), i.e. on the mores of intermediate status groups which they deemed authentically indigenous.[113]

Unlike the strict notions of custom which tend to bind small culturally homogeneous groups with limited contact with outsiders, the norms which Annadurai appealed to were loose, and so more appropriate to mobilize a large group of people embedded in widespread social networks whose practices varied considerably such as Tamils have been in the twentieth century.[114] This rendered Annadurai's discourse 'open', giving supporters considerable scope to appropriate it in ways attuned to their concerns.

Mannargudi and, convinced by the argument, left the platform announcing his change of heart and proceeded to organize celebration rallies. He had earlier defied Periar's dictates and participated in the anti-colonial Quit India agitation. Interviews: 'Mannai' P. Narayanaswami, P. Venkatesa Solagar, Amirthalingam Pillai, Kakkaji. (Mannargudi)

[112] See Visswanathan (1983: 328–36).

[113] See Barth (1969: 119): '(A) Pathan is a man who lives by a body of customs which is thought of as common and distinctive to all Pathans. The Pashto language may be included under this heading—it is a necessary and diacritical feature, but in itself not sufficient: we are not dealing simply with a linguistic group. Pathans have an explicit saying: "He is a Pathan who *does* Pashto, not (merely) who *speaks* Pashto", and 'doing' Pashto in this sense means living by a rather exacting code, in terms of which some Pashto speakers consistently fall short.'

[114] In this regard, the 'doing Tamil' which Annadurai appealed to was different from the 'doing Pashto' of Barth's mountain Pashthoons, who had limited contacts both with economic élites from elsewhere and with political mobilizers such as the Pashthoon nationalists.

The shift in emphasis from putative blood ties to the norms of intermediate status groups paved the way for the DMK's later populist articulation of ethnicity. By associating the notion of a non-Sanskritic cultural model with plebeian groups marginal to state-society networks, this shift inaugurated a full-blown populist discourse which could appeal to the numerous groups at the margins or beyond the pale of pan-Indianist subcultures around the time of decolonization. Along with the reassessment of colonialism, electoral politics and mass culture, it enabled the DMK to adopt flexible strategies which were sensitive to prior patterns of local contention and issues relevant to emergent strata in the post-colonial age. Such strategies helped the DMK recruit new groups without a heavy reliance on non-Brahmin notables, a further break from the DK's approach. These ideological and strategic shifts, brewing through the 1940s, were completed only with the formation of the DMK in 1949.

THE DURABILITY OF NON-BRAHMINISM

While the ideological reorientations initiated by the early DMK leaders shifted the movement's focus away from militant opposition to Brahmins, the cultural model these leaders and their successors exalted retained a non-Brahminical and non-Sanskritic character. So, non-Brahminism remained closely associated with assertive Dravidianism, even if it ceased to be its primary banner. The sustained salience of non-Brahminism in Tamil Nadu stands in contrast with the experience of Maharashtra, non-Brahminism's initial cradle, where the Satya Shodhak Samaj withered away in the 1930s in the face of growing Indian nationalist mass mobilization. Individuals from the Samaj largely joined the growing pan-Indianist parties—Congress and the CPI.

Non-Brahminism appeared headed for oblivion in Tamil Nadu too by the mid-1930s as the Justice Party and the Self Respect Association supported a colonial state whose demise appeared imminent; the demand for caste quotas was partially implemented in the 1920s, potentially diminishing the force behind some non-Brahminist grievances; and non-Brahmins rose to district-level leadership (and, by the 1940s, to state-level leadership) within Congress, which had gained the support of most politicized non-Brahmin Tamils by then. The Justice Party had performed well in elections to the provincial government in the 1920s, leading many of the governments of the decade, only because property and educational criteria restricted the electorate to just 3 per cent of the adult population, excluding much of the intermediate strata which were drawn largely to pan-Indian nationalism. Further, Congress did not contest these elections under its own banner.[115] Nationalist mobilization grew through the 1920s, largely outside the framework of electoral politics, among the upper and intermediate strata, especially in the valleys and the western plains.[116] Congress was so popular that by 1927 the Justic Party was forced for reasons of survival to allow its members to have parallel membership in Congress.[117] When the electorate was broadened to about 15 per cent of the adult population and the powers of the provincial governments expanded, Congress chose to contest the polls and convincingly defeated the Justice Party, by then allied with the Self Respect Association, in 1936.[118]

These developments could have led to the successful incorporation of non-Brahminism within the Congress fold. While Congress was successfully wooing Maharashtra's non-Brahminists, Rajaji made similar overtures towards Periar in 1934. His effort failed as Periar insisted that the Tamil Congress commit itself to the introduction of caste quotas in the bureaucracy and the professions; and the state Congress leadership remained intransigent

---

[115] While Congress did not contest these elections, individual party members and a faction called the Swarajya party did contest some of them.

[116] Arnold (1977), Baker (1976), Sivagnanam (1982), Somayajulu (1982); Interviews; C. Subramaniam, Ma. Po. Sivagnanam, A. Chengalvorayan, S. C. C. Anthony Pillai, Dr. T. Kannan, C. Harihara Subramania Iyer (Madras); Sivarama Reddiar, Tirunavukkarasu (Tiruvannamalai); Kakkaji, P. Venkatesa Solagar (Mannargudi); Swaminatha Udayar (Thanjavur); S. Chellapandian, N. Somayajulu (Tirunelveli); K. A. Vasimalai, P.V. Das, A. Chinnasami (Dindigul).

[117] Irschick (1969: 316–17).

[118] The popularity Congress acquired, although it initially opposed non-Brahminism and later included non-Brahminist demands as merely subsidiary features of its programme, renders untenable accounts of late colonial politics as dominated by the 'non-Brahmin community' and the Brahmin/non-Brahmin conflict. See Barnett (1976: 15), Irschick (1969) and Baker (1976). Congress achieved such popularity although its strategy was not set by the rewards offered by the colonial state, contrary to Baker's (1976: 245–316 & passim) argument that institutions created by the colonial state shaped the focus of mobilization.

on this issue.[119] Periar exercised tight control over the Self Respect Association at this point—for instance, only a few opposed his momentous decision during the same year to support the colonial government.[120] If he had shifted to Congress, most of his organization was likely to have done so. As the Justice Party was in decline, an independent constellation of non-Brahminist parties might not have emerged after independence.

Three factors prevented the absorption of non-Brahminism within the Tamil Nadu Congress at this stage. First, the resistance to non-Brahminist demands was greater within Congress in Tamil Nadu than in Maharashtra in the 1930s, inhibiting accommodation. Second, the heretical articulation of mass non-Brahminism was especially difficult to accommodate. Third, an incipient populist ethno-nationalism had emerged, which associated non-Brahminism with appeals to the Tamil language and a non-Sanskritic cultural model, and with opposition to variously defined élites. The last factor was crucial to the Dravidianists maintaining an ideological profile distinct from pan-Indian nationalism and Congress, which did not identify itself primarily with linguistic or anti-élite appeals. Maharashtrian non-Brahminism, by contrast, did not associate itself as closely (and exclusively) with a discourse of language, territory and the 'people', and so failed to present a distinct ideological alternative to Congress.[121]

Language Politics and the Persistence of Non-Brahminism

Populist ethno-nationalism gained momentum in Tamil Nadu after 1937, when the Congress-led provincial government mandated Hindi instruction in primary schools. This decision triggered an agitation in which diverse Tamil nationalists united under Dravidianist leadership to oppose 'Hindi imposition', in a pattern which was to repeat itself many times until the late 1960s. The Dravidianists challenged Congress's monopoly of the streets for

[119] See Visswanathan (1983: 156–7). The Tamil Congress changed its attitude towards caste quotas later, but by then Dravidianism was too strong to be readily assimilated.

[120] Mangalamurugesan (n.d.: 130), Arnold (1977: 159), Irschick (1986: 103).

[121] Arnold (1988: 219–20) emphasizes only the problems that Periar's 'maverick individualism' posed to the Tamil Congress in accommodating non-Brahminism.

the first time in this agitation, which gave the incipient Dravidian populists their first taste of 'battle' and shaped the alternative Dravidianist vision they adopted, in which language demands were far more central.[122] Although Periar led this agitation, the use of the Tamil language played a more limited role in his appeals, partly because his family spoke Kannada at home.

The change in language policy gave the Dravidianists a chance to recover from their disarray following their resounding defeat in the 1936 elections. Far from being an isolated instance of poor political judgement, this move was an intrinsic part of the policies the national leadership of Congress had for long envisioned to effect cultural decolonization and pan-Indian integration. The debates which raged within the all-India Congress regarding the comparative virtues of a Sanskritic Hindi and a Hindustani more influenced by Persian and Urdu as national languages seemed largely irrelevant to most Tamils, to whom the two languages were equally incomprehensible. Gandhi was the major proponent of the adoption of Hindustani as the national language, and urged Tamils to study the language during every visit of his to Tamil Nadu.[123] Under his inspiration, the Dakshin Bharat Hindi Prachar Sabha was established in 1918 to promote Hindi learning outside the schooling system in non-Hindi speaking areas.[124] Those Tamil Congress members inclined towards assimilation within a pan-Indian culture considered learning Hindi central to the 'Congress culture', much as wearing handspun cloth was. Even those like Rajaji more attuned to Tamil cultural pride urged Tamils to learn Hindi, feeling that Hindi would inevitably be the official language of the post-colonial future.[125] These remained the dominant positions on language policy within the Tamil Congress into the 1960s, although Rajaji himself left Congress and defected to the Tamil nationalist camp in the late 1950s.

As Tamil is the major Indian language which is linguistically most different from Hindi, the compulsory introduction of Hindi

---

[122] Visswanathan (1983: 187–265), Azhagarasan (1985), Ilanchezhian (1986).

[123] While Gandhi learnt eight Indian languages to help him understand and communicate with people, neither Tamil nor any other South Indian language were among them. See Visswanathan (1983: 188–94).

[124] See Mohan Ram (1968).

[125] Rajaji made this argument in his introduction to a Hindi primer for Tamil children. See Visswanathan (1983: 192–3), Azhagarasan (1985).

instruction as a means of cultural assimilation became in Tamil Nadu a powerful symbol of the devaluation of local culture and the attenuation of Tamil autonomy. Many Tamils who took pride in their language and culture, while also having pan-Indian sympathies, desired the indefinite retention of English as an official language and the simultaneous use of many Indian languages. But this option was ruled out by most pan-Indianist political forces at the national level. As the pan-Indianists seemed unprepared for an accommodation, a demand emerged for the secession of Dravida Nadu in the course of the first anti-Hindi agitation of 1937–8. While it was never Dravidianism's most important source of appeal, it remained an important rallying cry of the Dravidianists until the 1960s, and was used to argue that the question of a 'national' Indian language was irrelevant to Tamils.[126] The Dravidianists were able to link non-Brahminism and anti-Hindi as Brahmins took to Hindi quicker than other Tamils did (much as happened earlier in the case of English), partly because Brahmin dialects share more of Hindi's Sanskrit roots. They were thus able to present non-Brahminism as part of the authentic politics of the Tamil nation.

The first anti-Hindi agitation, which led the provincial government to temporarily abandon its plan for compulsory Hindi instruction, had a lasting impact on the lines of political contention and the Dravidianist agenda. The persistent efforts of Congress-led state governments to introduce Hindi instruction through the first two post-colonial decades, occasioned by the mandate of the post-colonial constitution to switch by 1965 to Hindi as the national government's sole official language, provoked periodic anti-Hindi agitations over which the Dravidianists exercised leadership. The language agitations, and the secession demand which arose in connection with them, highlighted the DMK's growing political influence and lent greater emphasis to images of territory and nationhood in Dravidianist discourse. They helped focus Dravidianist mobilization against the state and central governments rather than against groups deemed ethnic outsiders, especially as the non-Tamil speaking groups which might have opposed

---

[126] Nambi Arooran (1980: 233–51), Visswanathan (1983: 235), Barnett (1976: 51–3).

these agitations accounted for less than 10 per cent of the state's population.

Although the main demand of the agitators was the retention of English as an official language, the agitators were drawn primarily from the vernacular intelligentsia, whose outlook shaped the slogans and idioms of struggle.[127] As the agitators gained increasing support, the repression they had encountered generated sympathy and the language of the agitators acquired the power to shape the popular imagination. In the drama of battle, as Tamil society was invited to imagine these political struggles, the Dravidianists were assigned the role of the champions of the plebeian community, and the state and central governments and Congress, which led them, were cast as alien forces insensitive to the concerns of this community. This completed the populist image of the world—the righteous representatives of the 'people', rooted in local culture, challenging an effete and deracinated élite.

The language agitations thus played an important role in Dravidianism's turn towards a full-blown populist project, within which were subsumed both non-Brahminism and Tamil nationalism. This turn was completed with the formation in 1949 of the DMK, which adopted a flexible strategy attuned to a rapidly mobilizing society and the post-colonial political order. Such a strategy enabled the DMK's rapid growth through the 1950s and 1960s, and ensured that non-Brahminism would remain an important part of Tamil political culture through the rest of the century.

[127] See Ramaswamy (1993).

IV

The Ascent of Assertive Populism: The DMK in the Nehruvian Period

Naan yezhaiyin punnagaiyil iraivanaik kaankireen.
(I see god in the smile of the poor.)

Yellorum innaattu mannar.
(All are kings in this land.)

— C. N. Annadurai, founding leader of the DMK

When India became independent, the Dravidianists had but a limited foothold in Tamil Nadu as the DK placed itself at odds with the dominant thrust of Indian politics—towards decolonization and post-colonial nation-building. Pan-Indian parties—Congress and its centrist offshoots, the CPI and the Socialist Party—dominated the first elections based on universal suffrage in 1952.[1] While the DK was disinclined towards electoral politics, the DMK lacked the organizational capacity and support to compete in these elections. Yet, within a decade, a Dravidian party became Congress's major electoral challenger, polling 27.1 per cent of the popular vote and capturing 50 of the 206 seats in the state assembly.[2]

Dravidianist growth was rapid after decolonization because the DMK, formed in 1949, adopted a strategy appropriate to the post-colonial political order. The DMK's incorporation of non-Brahminism and Tamil nationalism within a populist discourse

---

[1] Pan-Indian parties with support beyond Tamil Nadu gained 69.2 per cent of the popular vote in 1952 (Congress polled 34.6 per cent, CPI 13 per cent, the socialists 6.4 per cent and two Congress offshoots 9 per cent and 3 per cent respectively). The sole autonomist party contesting the elections (the Justice Party's élite remnant) polled a mere 0.4 per cent of the vote, caste parties with support in pockets of Tamil Nadu gained 6 per cent and independents 24.3 per cent. See Table II, Singh & Bose (1988: 42, 45) and Government of Tamil Nadu Public (Elections) Department (1989).

[2] Singh & Bose (1988: 41, 45)

shifted the focus of the Dravidianist critique from Brahmin dominance to bureaucratic clientelism. Due to these strategic shifts, groups hardly mobilized by political parties until independence began to flock predominantly towards the DMK, particularly in the northern plains where pan-Indianist subcultures were the shallowest.

Growth in political participation of different kinds (voting, associational activity and street protest) accompanied early DMK growth. While considerable conflict erupted between the Dravidianists and the state and national governments through this period, conflict among the state's major social groups remained limited. The state government's introduction of preferential quotas for the BCs in this period, a move urged by Dravidianist pressure, did not lead to heightened caste conflict; and class conflict declined along with communist militancy by the mid-1950s.

Tamil Nadu was the first Indian state in which secessionist/ autonomist impulses developed despite initial enthusiasm about the creation of the Indian union.[3] However, the DMK's secessionist demand was never resolute, with party leaders seemingly willing to settle for considerable state autonomy. While some activists desired secession fervently, the party's primary appeal never lay in its secession demand.[4]

The emergence of strong and early autonomist sentiment in Tamil Nadu appeared surprising in light of early pan-Indianist electoral dominance and relatively high economic growth during the two decades of Congress rule in Tamil Nadu (1946–67). Congress gained its most spectacular victory in the 1937 elections in the former Madras Presidency, which included most of today's Tamil Nadu. Tamil Nadu was the second or third most industrialized Indian state, the second most urbanized state, and experienced relatively high agricultural growth during Congress rule.

---

[3] While secessionist demands were also raised from the 1940s onwards in Jammu & Kashmir and Nagaland, even the initial attitude towards nation-formation was ambiguous in these border states. The National Conference, the dominant party in Kashmir in the 1940s, accepted accession to the Indian union as preferable to integration in Pakistan. A separate Kashmir seemed the preferred option of party leaders, but they lacked the military capability and international support to achieve this end. A separatist movement began in 1946 in Nagaland. See Ganguly (1997), Buchheit (1978).

[4] Barnett (1976: 214).

However, both pan-Indianist dominance and socio-economic growth rested on thin foundations. Political participation was low during pan-Indianist dominance (which declined as political participation increased); and the high rates of industrialization and urbanization coexisted with relatively high levels of poverty and inequality. The slack this indicates in the political system enabled early DMK growth.

Parties that did not focus on regionally rooted identities capitalized on a similar slack in the political system in some other Indian states through the 1950s and 1960s—the communists in West Bengal and Kerala; Hindu revivalists in the Hindi belt, Maharashtra and Gujarat; farmerist parties and socialists in the Hindi belt, and centrist Congress offshoots in Orissa, Bengal and Kerala. The communists were Congress's strongest opponents in Tamil Nadu in the late 1940s and early 1950s. The DMK outdid them as its ethnic and populist appeals attracted the intermediate strata more effectively, unlike in West Bengal and Kerala where it was the communists who gained considerable support from such groups.[5]

THE FRAGILITY OF CONGRESS DOMINANCE

Tamil Nadu witnessed relatively limited nationalist agitations during the colonial period, and the Tamil Congress did not produce charismatic leaders remotely comparable to Gandhi and Nehru, both from regions (Gujarat and Uttar Pradesh) where such agitations were more extensive.[6] The faction of the Tamil Congress primarily involved in Gandhian agitations was weaker than that which participated in colonial institutions of self-government.[7] If Congress nevertheless dominated the last two elections of the colonial era in the Tamil areas, this was partly because levels of mobilization were low and the electorate was restricted to about 15 per cent of the adult population based on property and literacy criteria.[8] Congress's margin of victory diminished with the advent of universal suffrage.

[5] Regarding communism in Kerala, see Nossiter (1982); in Bengal, see Franda (1971) and Sengupta (1980); and in Tamil Nadu, see Bouton (1985).

[6] See Pandey (1978) and Low (1977). The considerable respect accorded Rajaji and Kamaraj did not bring Congress the support of many outside the Congress subculture, unlike the case with more popular Congress leaders.

[7] Arnold (1977).

[8] Walch (1976: 157), Barnett (1976: 77).

Due to these features of late colonial politics, Congress's subculture was relatively shallow and its party organization less cohesive in Tamil Nadu in the early post-colonial period. The glory of having led the nationalist movement faded sooner here as nationalist activity had been more limited and anti-colonial agitators played less decisive roles in the party after independence, being subordinated to party bosses and local notables, many of whom played nominal roles, if any, in the agitations.[9] This was symbolized by the emergence of K. Kamaraj, the machine politician, rather than Rajaji, the leader of the Gandhian agitations of the 1920s and 1930s, as the leader of the post-colonial Tamil Congress.[10]

Considerable patronage was disbursed through party channels after decolonization, but propaganda did not clearly identify the patronage with the party. This bolstered the power of party bosses without ensuring their loyalty or that of activists to the party.[11] So, Congress dominance was more fragile in Tamil Nadu than in many other states. Further, in Tamil Nadu, unlike in most other states, Congress faced the opposition of an ethnic party which developed deep roots in society. The DMK's populist challenge ensured that Congress did not live down its élite paternalist past in Tamil Nadu, although it recruited BCs in large numbers from the 1930s onwards.

Nehruvian Nation-Building and Its Limits

The development strategy of the Nehruvian period focused on large public sector projects, whose gestation periods were long and the percolation of whose benefits to the intermediate and lower strata

[9] Many Tamil politicians lament the political decline of anti-colonial agitators, who continue to be regarded with much respect—some Congressmen to indicate their party's moral decline, and others to divest the post-independence Congress of the residual sheen of its anti-colonial past. See, for instance, Karunanidhi (1986: 61).

[10] While Kamaraj participated in nationalist agitations of the 1930s and 1940s, his strategic focus (as that of his mentor, S. Sathyamurthi) was on party-building, through forging links with the propertied, and participating in elections and governments.

[11] Weiner (1967: 422–51) remarks on the inability of patronage to cement Congress in Madurai, unlike in Calcutta.

often lay in the uncertain future.[12] Tamil Nadu's experience typified the tensions in this strategy, as economic growth benefited only small sections of the intermediate and lower strata through the early post-colonial decades.[13] Nehru aimed to cement the Indian nation primarily through cooperation in this economic strategy, and only secondarily by propagating myths of nationhood. Not only was Nehruvian nationalist mythology sparse in its reference to specific cultural symbols, but it was also drawn largely from the syncretic *Mughlai* culture of the North Indian élite, with which few Tamils felt an affinity.[14] Nehru could only respond with perplexity and anger to Dravidianist mytho-history, which he decried as 'nonsense', provoking one of the DMK's major early agitations.[15]

Both the gains of the development strategy and the vision of the Indian nation associated with Nehru appeared distant to many of the Tamil middling and lower strata. The DMK's critique of an aloof state, operating from Delhi and in contact only with Congress oriented Tamil élites, and its reference to more proximate cultural symbols made it more appealing to a wide range of groups in Tamil society.[16]

Seminal analyses have attributed the growth of populist and ethnic forces in India mainly to changes that took place during and after Indira Gandhi's rule—the dismantling of party institutions,

[12] Frankel (1978), Singh (1974), Gopal (1984: 106–26; 1980: 291–319). The plan to alleviate poverty and generate employment by assigning wage goods production to labour intensive small-scale industries and forming agricultural cooperatives was barely implemented and failed.

[13] See MIDS (1988), Department of Statistics (1994), Kurien (1981), Vaidyanathan (1986) and Guhan (1981, 1983).

[14] See Nehru (1989a), Gopal (1980: 320–37, 467–504, 526–39) and Chatterjee (1986: 131–63). Nehru's (1989b) ventures into mytho-history celebrate equally the enduring spirit of various colonized Asian nations. The education policies adopted under his rule to form the Indian citizen focused on the cultivation of a secular 'scientific temper', not on fostering attachment to culturally specific visions of nationhood.

[15] The deep differences between Nehruvian and Dravidianist mytho-history are illustrated by their different interpretations of the Indus valley civilization. Contrast Nehru (1989a) with Sesha Iyengar (1925) and Annadurai (1985a).

[16] This critique of Nehruvian bureaucratic clientelism, represented in Annadurai (1985e, 1986b), to some extent resembles those of Gandhian socialists and farmerists, though the latter groups did not focus on regional biases.

the centralization of power in the political system, the state's partial retreat from multicultural policies and its increasing resort to repression rather than accommodation.[17] The timing of DMK growth, which was most rapid prior to these developments, accords poorly with this interpretation. Although many policies were more cosmopolitan in inspiration during the Nehruvian period, the DMK grew in response to the limits of Nehru's nation-building project. This suggests that other populist and ethnic forces have grown more recently in other parts of India in response to these limits, not merely as a result of institutional and policy changes since the late 1960s. As the Nehruvian strategy of incorporation reached its limits in the middle to late 1960s, the populism of Indira and Rajiv Gandhi, the backward casteism of parts of the Janata and the Janata Dal, and the farmerism of Charan Singh arose as different alternatives, as did a variety of ethnic forces propagating identification with language and religion.

FROM THE POLITICS OF HERESY TO THE POLITICS OF COMMUNITY

Differences regarding ideology, strategy and political style led to the DK split of 1949. The immediate precipitant of the split was Periar's marriage to his personal secretary, Maniammai, a woman over forty years younger than he, a move many Dravidianists considered contrary to the ideals Periar himself propagated. What perhaps offended Periar's critics even more was his peremptory replacement of Annadurai with Maniammai as his nominated successor as party leader and treasurer.[18] The DMK, formed in response under Annadurai's leadership, took with it over three fourths of the DK's membership and an even greater proportion of its support right at the outset.[19] While the DK stagnated thereafter and later declined, the DMK grew.

---

[17] Weiner (1989) and Kohli (1990, 1997) are among the best examples.

[18] See *Viduthalai*, 19, 28 June 1949 (Periar's announcements); DN, July–September 1949 (in which Periar's prominent critics listed their names as *kanneer thulighal* (tear drops)); *Kilarchchi*, 15 July 1949; Chittibabu (1975: 38–44).

[19] Chittibabu (1975: 45–57), Karunanidhi (1986: 121–6); Interviews: V. R. Nedunchezhian, Sathyavani Muthu, P. A. K. Palanisami, Nagai Kaliappan (Madras).

DMK leaders claimed that they were committed to the DK's ideals, but were rejecting Periar's autocratic style. Indeed, Annadurai claimed that he would welcome reunification with the DK if Periar gave up his authoritarian style and left the post of party president open through his lifetime for Periar to assume, were he to so choose.[20] These rhetorical gestures helped portray the split as motivated by adherence to movement principles. But, strategic differences were evident even then and became more pronounced after the split.

Identity Reconfigured

The DMK differed from the DK in its understanding of Dravidian identity, Tamil cultural history and religion's social role, as well as of the colonial impact and the significance of Indian independence. The DMK's ideological shifts changed the focus of opposition from Tamil Brahmins (and other local inhabitants) to the state and central governments, containing Dravidianism's potential to provoke conflict within Tamil society. While Periar's heresies relied on systematic inversion, the DMK's discourse of community was eclectic, linking diverse ideological propositions through recourse to allusion and alliteration.

The DMK's vision of the Dravidian community was overtly homogeneous, including all Tamils/South Indians, as expressed in a slogan Annadurai adopted from a seventh century Tamil mystic— '*Onre kulam, oruvane dhevan*' (There is but one community/caste and one god). However, the identity to which party propaganda alluded also had a layered character, which was less explicit than in the DK's appeals. The BCs lay at the core of the Dravidian community for the DMK, as for the DK. But, DMK propagandists elaborated their conception of the Dravidian community through references to categories of status ('plebeian'), class (e.g. small property owners) and social marginality, in addition to ethnic categories.

If the layers of Dravidian identity resembled concentric circles around the core composed of the BC megacastes in Periar's vision,

[20] The DMK's formation was even announced on Periar's birthday, 17 September 1949. DMK leaders admit now that ideological and strategic differences motivated the split. See DN, October 1949; Parthasarathi (1961) and Chittibabu (1975).

they overlapped partially in the picture portrayed by DMK ideologues. The latter form of layering made ethnic conceptions especially conducive to populist articulation. The symbol of Tamil language use could for instance serve to exclude from the core of the community landed groups which spoke Telugu at home or the professional élite that used English rather than Tamil for formal purposes, without precluding their reincorporation in a different context or at a later date. The groups included within the popular coalition and those deemed the unfairly privileged élite varied across region, depending on pre-existing lines of solidarity and contention. In the Kaveri valley, the simple Dravidians were those who did not enjoy eminence in the interlocking structures of temple Brahminism and landlordism. This placed big non-Brahmin landlords beyond the pale, or at least not clearly within it, in contrast with Periar's reliance on the patronage of such landlords.[21] In parts of the southern plains, the Dravidian image became identified by the late 1960s with the Mukkulathor, while largely excluding the Nadars, who were traditionally of lower status than the Mukkulathor but had aligned themselves with Congress.[22] The DMK's discourse acquired its mobilizing power primarily from its layered character and its populist articulation.

Homogeneous ethnic notions focused on the Tamil language did, however, provide the DMK's coalition some coherence and aided a partial reconciliation with Tamil Brahmins. Annadurai avoided derogatory references in public to Brahmins (as *paarppanar*) from the late 1950s, calling them *mettukkudi makkal* (esteemed

[21] Thus, the SC district-level leader of the DMK from Mannargudi taluk, N. 'Sithamalli' Somasundaram, could claim that the DMK's growth had helped end the repressive dominance of local landlord families, both Brahmin (Kunniyur Sambasiva Iyer) and BC (Krishnaswamy Vandayar, to whose family his was once bonded in slavery); and DMK activists in the Tiruvannamalai region saw the party benefit from the social decline of local Reddiar landlords. *Mannai Narayanaswami Ponvizha Malar* (n.d.). Interviews: Sithamalli Somasundaram (Nidamangalam); Mannai Narayanaswamy (Mannargudi); K. P. Kannan (Kilpennathur); V. Kumaraswamy (Tiruvannamalai).

[22] Many among the less prosperous 'southern Nadars' of southern Tirunelveli district became sympathetic to Congress as early as the 1930s. The 'northern Nadars' of northern Tirunelveli, Ramnad and Madurai districts, who initially favoured the Justice Party, flocked to Congress in the 1950s after one of them, Kamaraj, became the Chief Minister. See Hardgrave (1969).

upper caste people) instead, and exhorted party activists to adopt such usage. He stressed that he opposed Brahminism, not Brahmins, appealed to Brahmin youth (although he achieved significant success in this regard only in the 1960s) and pointed towards a non-hierarchical popular religion through his usual retort to questions about his religious convictions: *'Naan yezhaiyin punnagaiyil iraivanaik kaankireen'* (I see god in the smile of the poor).[23] While the DK broke Pillayar idols, DMK leaders periodically upheld Pillayar and Murugan (deities incorporated into the Hindu pantheon relatively late) as indigenous deities, contrasting them with deities worshipped more often in northern India.[24] They also made overtures to the heads of religious institutions by the 1960s and 1970s.[25] The DMK thus extended an arm towards the upper castes and the religious, and avoided associating itself exclusively with the intermediate strata.

As the DK's atheist and anti-caste rhetoric had gained popularity mainly because it highlighted Dravidianism's plebeian and assertive thrust, the DMK could abandon some of this rhetoric, yet attract many old DK supporters, so long as the vision remained of a plebeian and indigenous community. The retention (after some debate) of the 'Dravidian' rather than the 'Tamil' label in the party name helped in this regard, indicating claims to a distinct 'great tradition' and to the fact that plebeian norms defined the cultural core of the community.[26] Such a discourse helped the DMK better mask the thrust of its hegemonic project, which became more viable as a result.

Assertive Populism and the Backward Castes

The DMK drew its early support mainly from intermediate castes of small property, especially in the northern plains. As the BCs

[23] See for instance NN, 13 April 1957. Karunanidhi (1988); Interview: T. S. Kittayyar (Tirupattur).

[24] For instance, Karunanidhi claimed that the Brahmin Rajaji was more attached to the Aryan god Rama than to Pillayar, the common man's deity (*Murasoli*, 25 February 1971; *Kumudham*, 3 June 1974). Basham (1959: 330–1) and Ryerson (1988: 33–4, 37, 46–50) discuss the historical basis for interpreting Murugan as a Tamil god.

[25] These religious leaders were usually non-Brahmins, but sometimes Brahmins too. See Ryerson (1988).

[26] Interview: K. Appadurai (Madras); Parthasarathi (1961).

account for 51 per cent to 67 per cent of the state's population, and groups of small property and white collar workers constitute 50 per cent to 60 per cent of the population, the DMK's assertive populism gave it an affinity with a large chunk of the electorate.[27]

Barnett claimed that envy of Brahmin ritual privilege and indignation about the Shudra label were mainly found among otherwise powerful 'upper non-Brahmins', whom the Dravidianists primarily mobilized using caste-based appeals in the 1930s and 1940s. As such appeals were likely to alienate the BCs from the upper non-Brahmin castes leading the Dravidianist project, she argued that the DMK abandoned radical non-Brahminism for an ethnic discourse with a conveniently vague caste content. Barnett contended that the DMK gained considerable BC support from the 1950s onwards because of adopting such a definition of Dravidian identity, rather than due to its identification with the lower and intermediate strata.[28]

Contrary to Barnett's claims, the focus of DMK propaganda of the 1950s on Dravidian identity did not mask conflicts between the BCs and upper non-Brahmins. Despite emphasizing criticisms of varnashrama dharma less than Periar did, the DMK did voice the BCs' specific status aspirations, which sometimes conflicted with those of more powerful non-Brahmin groups. In its early bases, the DMK was recognized as a plebeian party, which contested traditional and bureaucratic clientelism, and thus the dominance of

---

[27] Estimates of the BCs' share in the state's population vary as different criteria are used, in varying ways, to assess the position of castes. The first State Backward Classes Commission offered the smaller figure (51 per cent), which comes closer to the share of groups that are indeed socially and educationally backward. The second Commission's larger estimate (67 per cent) better captures the range of castes whose position gave them an affinity with Dravidianist ideology. Backward Classes Commission Report (1975–5; 1985a: 3, 5–6, 8–15; 1985b: 23–8, 87–90); G.O.Ms. No. 73, Social Welfare (1 February 1980).

[28] '(The) status [of BCs] was not threatened by the wealthy landlord or the proud and orthodox Brahmin, but by the previously subservient Untouchable. The social base of the radical Dravidian ideology during its period of origin in the early twentieth century was the élite non-Brahmin groups who felt a sense of relative loss... The symbols of oppression (particularly the symbol, 'Suddhra'), so important in shaping a radical support structure for the Dravidian movement, were irrelevant for the backward castes'. Barnett (1976: 83–4, 115 & passim).

some non-Brahmin landowning and mercantile groups. This was crucial to the DMK's growing support. While the DMK opposed the hold of local notables (Brahmin and non-Brahmin) at crucial points in Mannargudi (Kaveri valley) and Tiruvannamalai (northern plains), it was closely associated with a fishermen's caste association in Royapuram. Thus, the DMK's strategic and discursive shifts were not aimed at diffusing contradictions within the non-Brahmin coalition, for which Periar's discourse had anyway left sufficient scope.

DMK leaders and many BCs of lower status took offense at aspects of Brahmin privilege and varnashrama dharma. These concerns were important both to Annadurai and his successor, M. Karunanidhi, and influenced the ideological formation of the early DMK cadre, many of them of BC origin.[29] Karunanidhi, from the lowly Isai Vellalar caste, many members of which used to be temple servants, most forcefully expressed the DMK's plebeian character, of which he took the coarser aspects of the party's culture to be a natural reflection. Thus, when a Congress minister derided the DMK as a 'naankaam thara' (fourth rate) party, Karunanidhi retorted with belligerent pride that this was indeed so, as it was a party of 'naankaam thara makkal' (people of the forth rank), i.e. Shudras, who occupy the fourth rung in the varna hierarchy.[30]

Clearly, Periar's vision of a Shudra party lurked just below the surface in the DMK and was asserted by a 'backward non-Brahmin'. While this does not concur well with Barnett's explanation of grievance based on relative deprivation, it is quite understandable because BCs of lower status, not 'upper non-Brahmins', have faced the worst caste-based indignities. For instance, many Isai Vellalar women were sexually exploited by temple priests, making Karunanidhi's opposition to the Shudra label and its insidious implications hardly surprising.[31] The mobilization of the lower and intermediate strata by the DMK and other forces popularized non-Brahminist interpretations of the Shudra

[29] See Annadurai (1985a: 54 and passim, 1986a).

[30] See Karunanidhi (1988). Thurston (1975a, vol. v: 59–60) discusses the practices of the Isai Vellalar, also called Melakkarar.

[31] It is revealing that the term *thevar adiyaal* (servant of the gods), used to refer to women dedicated to temple service, is also the contemporary Tamil word for a prostitute.

epithet and brought the more egregious instances of caste-based exploitation into disrepute.[32] The depiction of a temple priest's attempt to rape a poor widow in *Paraasakthi*, a film Karunanidhi scripted, and similar scenes critical of exploitative upper caste élites brought Dravidianist films great popularity. Such films and their message contributed to the DMK's growth and the outlook of its early supporters.

Barnett misunderstood the DMK's appeal, taking the BCs to be aiming mainly for a defence of their status in the varna hierarchy and society.[33] Many BCs have risen to the ranks of the rich peasantry/tenantry, and white collar and organized industrial labour through the century. Others among them have experienced social decline as the erosion of the customary bases of land tenure and agrarian labour recruitment have increasingly placed the poorer BCs economically on par with the SCs.[34] These changes certainly made many BCs wary of their relative position vis-à-vis the SCs. But, the DMK provided the BCs an assertive rather than a defensive response to their predicament. It promised the intermediate strata, as its electoral symbol (the rising sun) suggested, that their sun would rise on the morrow, rather than the preservation of an inexorably changing old society and its attendant anxieties. Therein lay the assertiveness of the DMK's populism and the key to its success.

Although the BCs were important in the DMK's discourse and support base, the party differed significantly from 'backward casteist' organizations aiming to promote the interests of particular castes or caste coalitions, such as caste associations and parties like the Socialist Party in Bihar and Uttar Pradesh until the 1970s, and

[32] Karunanidhi's criticisms were echoed by Ramamirthammal, a prominent early Dravidianist woman activist who had been a temple servant. See Iraiyan (1981: 59–60). Non-Brahminist opposition to the Shudra epithet is shared by many BCs outside Dravidianist subcultures. For instance, a 'lower BC' (Christian Nadar) school teacher of mine erupted in anger and beat a Brahmin student for using the word 'soothirhan' in his examination answer, giving me my first exposure to the non-Brahminist reading of the 'Shudra' category.

[33] Barnett (1976: 83): 'The orientation of backward castes was toward maintaining their position in the face of competition from Untouchables and other backward groups'.

[34] These trends are documented in such village studies as Beteille (1965), Harriss (1982) and Venkatesh Athreya et al. (1990).

the Janata party, Janata Dal, Samajvadi Janata Party and Rashtriya Janata Dal in these states later. The DMK differed from such organizations as it incorporated caste and other categories within a vision of a popular community, which gave it a broader potential base and more strategic flexibility, and therefore greater and more durable success. It had an ambivalent relationship with Tamil Nadu's backward casteist organizations and enjoyed limited early success in regions where it emphasized appeals to particular backward castes. The leaders of the DMK and caste associations jealously guarded their autonomy in their dealings with one another, due to the tension between Dravidianism and the interests of particular castes.

Ethno-Nationalism and Assertive Populism

Annadurai and his followers were the first to give Dravidianism a full-blown nationalist articulation. While the DK appealed to an aggregate of megacastes, the DMK envisioned a territorially rooted nation. This distinction is highlighted by the respective party names, *Dravidar* Kazhagam referring to a group of people (the Dravidians), while *Dravida* Munnetra Kazhagam refers to a country (Dravidam). Periar envisioned Dravida Nadu as a place where his ideals would be realized, without clearly and consistently specifying its boundaries.[35] It was the DMK's leaders who first specified Dravida Nadu's territorial compass (until they abandoned secessionism in 1963), though it too shrank from comprising all of south India to just Tamil Nadu due to lack of support in the other southern states.[36] Symbols of the soil and a motherland demarcated by ancient hero-stones figured prominently in the DMK's discourse, unlike in the DK's.[37]

Periar considered myths of past glory dangerous opiates likely to entwine Dravidians further in the web of Aryan illusion. He often argued that the practices of Tamil kings, southern Saivite

[35] He insisted that Tamil Nadu and Dravida Nadu were the same as all Dravidians (South Indians) initially spoke Tamil, and defended the Dravida Nadu demand as resting on the same principle as an individual's proprietary rights in land. See Anaimuthu (1974: 112); KA, 17 December 1939.

[36] See Annadurai (1985a), Maran (1962).

[37] This is evident in Annadurai (1986d, 1986e, 1986f, 1986g), novels on the basis of which films were produced, Karunanidhi (1985) and two films that Karunanidhi scripted, *Paraasakthi* and *Manohara*.

religious beliefs and much of Tamil literature were parasitic on Brahminical norms, though he also alluded less frequently to autonomous elements in non-Brahmin kingly and religious traditions.[38] DMK leaders were more open to the selective appropriation of Tamil cultural history. Even while endorsing Periar's call to burn two major 'Brahminical' Tamil epics while he was in the DK, Annadurai distinguished these from earlier Tamil literature which bore less of a Sanskritic/Brahminical imprint.[39] Karunanidhi interpreted one of these earlier works, the *Silappathikaaram*, as an expression of uniquely Dravidian virtues.[40] An assertion of past Tamil glory and wealth was central to the DMK's justification of its demand for secession.[41]

To Periar's critique of the cultural chauvinism inherent in Indian nationalism, the DMK added one of the alleged economic neglect of South India, highlighted by the slogan '*Vadakku vaazhkirathu; Therkku theykirathu*' (The north prospers, while the south decays). By contrasting Tamil Nadu with the two Indian regions which were more industrialized until the mid-1960s (the industrial belts around Bombay and Ahmedabad), the DMK glossed over the relatively high levels of industrialization in Tamil Nadu at the time. The contrast between the textile mills of Bombay and Ahmedabad and Tamil Nadu's handlooms suggestively linked a critique of uneven development to an opposition to large-scale industry, and associated an appeal to small property with the demand for secession. DMK ideologues argued that Nehruvian economic policy, focused on large-scale enterprises, was irrelevant to the needs of the emergent strata, and contrary to the property regime rooted in Tamil tradition.[42] Party activists wore handloom cloth (and organized campaigns to sell it) from the mid-1950s to show their solidarity with distressed weavers, thereby offering a symbolic alternative to the Congress tradition of wearing handspun cloth.

[38] See Ramaswami Naicker (1987i: 14–16); Anaimuthu (1974).

[39] See Annadurai (1986a: 9–14 & passim).

[40] He says that he was motivated to write this film script (which later became a play) to rebut a more Brahminical reading of the *Silappathikaaram* in an earlier film. See Karunanidhi (1986: 140–2).

[41] For example Annadurai (1985a) and the 'Dravida Nadu' song in the film *Paraasakthi*.

[42] See Annadurai (1985d, 1985e). Washbrook (1989) points to links between the DMK's economic ideology and property rights in pre-colonial Tamil Nadu.

Tamil linguistic nationalism influenced the petty intelligentsia, from which most DMK leaders and ideologues were drawn, as were many activists in the language agitations which dramatized the party's social presence. However, the DMK's opposition to North Indian culture and rule from Delhi appealed to many core supporters (especially those of small property) not primarily due to the defence of language rights or the demand for greater state autonomy, but because it connoted the revaluation of local mores and dissatisfaction with an aloof post-colonial state. It was because ethno-national demands did not crucially motivate many core supporters that the DMK was able to make major compromises regarding them without losing much support. Not only did the DMK abandon secessionism in 1963, it also settled for a stalemate rather than decisive victory on language policy upon assuming power in the state.

From Plebeian Rhetoric to Plebeian Party

The changes that accompanied decolonization rendered Periar's politics of heresy even more incompatible with viable party building. Periar gave priority to his goals of social reform over popular opinion, which he always considered suspect, partly because it never favoured him. It was on such a vanguardist basis that he rejected universal suffrage and Indian independence, although they enjoyed overwhelming support in Tamil Nadu. So, the DK never contested elections (though it campaigned for other parties), which Periar felt would necessitate catering to popular prejudice.[43]

Unlike Periar, DMK leaders embraced electoral politics, which was regarded as the primary legitimate arena for political competition. They regarded election campaigns as opportune moments to gain the ear of the less politicized and gain support for the party's goals, including secession.[44] If they chose to contest elections to the state assembly and parliament only in 1957, and to local bodies in

[43] Although Periar was the Justice Party's most important campaigner in the 1936 elections, he was not a member of the party then.

[44] Annadurai used these arguments to urge the party to contest the 1957 state assembly elections. See NN, 18 June 1956; Karunanidhi (1986: 275–6) and Parthasarathi (1961). Karunanidhi (1986: 287) thinks subsequent events have validated these arguments.

1959, this was only because they felt they had limited resources and support earlier.[45]

Learning from the DK's limited growth, the DMK leaders organized the party according to clearly specified democratic norms. All party posts from the party branch upwards were filled through open elections. While Annadurai's leadership was unquestioned, activists not of his choice could assume positions of influence. In its early bases, the DMK had a stronger party organization than Congress by the late 1950s, maintaining mass contact and running election campaigns more effectively.

Periar was averse to the use of artistic fora for propaganda as he considered fiction the currency of the Aryan illusionists, to which the stark prose of heresy was the only appropriate Dravidian response. The DMK set out to conquer the realm of the mythic from the priest and the genealogist. Every state-level leader edited a journal;[46] and many (notably Annadurai and Karunanidhi) were script writers for plays and films. Many popular litterateurs, singers and theatre and movie actors were DMK people by the late 1950s.[47] While journals, short stories and novels reached the literate, the party reached the illiterate and semi-literate majority through theatre and films. Especially in the early years, party meetings in street corners were accompanied by songs and plays, with even major leaders wearing the players' make-up. The DMK elevated oratory and debate (*pattimanram*) to alliterative fine arts, providing many members systematic training.[48] Many of these popular

[45] NN. 4 July 1955; TH, 17 April 1957; Karunanidhi (1986).

[46] Annadurai edited *Dravida Nadu, Maalai Mani, Nam Nadu, Kaanchi* and *Homeland*; V. R. Nedunchezhian and Era. Sezhiyan edited *Manram*; M. Karunanidhi edited *Murasoli*; K. A. Mathiazhagan and K. A. Krishnaswamy edited *Thennagam* and N. V. Natarajan edited *Dravidan*. The networks for circulating these journals often became bases for party factions. Many intellectually inclined DMK activists also edited journals, some of them short-lived. See Chittibabu (1975: 93–4); Interviews: V. R. Nedunchezhian, Era. Sezhiyan, K. A. Krishnaswamy, C. V. M. Annamalai, 'Murasoli' Maran, N. V. N. Somu, 'Naathikam' Ramaswami, Rama. Arangannal.

[47] For example M. G. Ramachandran, K. R. Ramaswamy, S. S. Rajendran (film actors); Kannadasan, T. K. Srinivasan, Annadurai, Karunanidhi (litterateurs and film script and song writers); 'Nagore' Hanifa and Sellamuthu (singers).

[48] The *pattimanram*, a form of debate which became ubiquitous with the growth of Tamil revivalism, typically concerns literary themes such as the

artistic productions involved the reinterpretation of Tamil cultural history. The DMK's prominence in the arts led opponents to deride the party as a *koothaadi katchi* (party of players/clowns). The DMK leaders gladly pocketed the insult and raked in the vote.

Unlike the DK, the DMK did not enjoy significant support from the affluent in its formative phase. Rather, such groups largely rallied behind Congress—the Brahmin and Vellala landlords of the Tamiraparani valley (many of whom became prominent industrialists through the century) from the 1920s,[49] the major industrialists and prosperous farmers of the western plains (largely Kongu Vellala Gounder and Naidu) from the 1930s,[50] and most major landlords of the Kaveri valley (of all castes) at least since independence.[51] Even in the poorer northern plains, the smaller landlords of the Tiruvannamalai area (the *zamindar* of Vettavalam and the Reddiars of the Kilpennathur region) supported Congress through the 1950s;[52] while the more influential notables from the numerous Vanniar caste, who initially gathered under the caste umbrella of

---

relative virtues of characters in epics. While exhibiting their command over literary and cultural history, participants often situate those themes in a current social context.

[49] Somayajulu (1982); *A. P. C. Veerababu Ninaivu Malar* (n.d.); Interviews: A. N. Sivaraman, C. Hariharasubramania Iyer, A. Nallasivan (Madras); M. S. Selvaraj (Arumuganeri); Shanmugam Pillai, V. P. Nayakam (Ambasamudram); S. Thangam Pillai, Ananthanarayanan, K. S. Subramaniam (Kallidaikurichi); S. Swaminathan (Palayamcottai); N. Somayajulu, A. Chellapandian (Tirunelveli); A. P. C. V. Chockalingam, M. S. Sivaswami (Tuticorin).

[50] Interviews: C. Subramaniam, K. A. Krishnaswamy, Kovai Sezhiyan (Madras), K. Ramani (Coimbatore).

[51] While some supported Congress from the 1930s or earlier (e.g. families of Sambasiva Iyer of Kunniyur, Nadimuthu Pillai of Pattukottai, the Moopanars of Kapisthalam and Papanasam, and Swaminatha Udayar of Mannargudi), others did so once decolonization seemed imminent in the 1940s (e.g. families of Krishnaswamy Vandayar of Poondi and V. S. Thyagaraja Mudaliar), following the lead of P. Subbaroyan (zamindar of Kumaramangalam). *Thanjavur Maavatta Thyagigal Malar* (n.d.); Interviews, G. K. Moopanar (Madras); Thulasi Ayya Vandayar (Poondi); K. S. Ramaswamy, K. S. Rajagopala Mudaliar, P. Venkatesa Solagar (Mannargudi); T. Govindarajan (Tirumangalakkudi), 'Kombur' Venkatesan (Kombur).

[52] Interviews: Sivarama Reddiar, Narayanaswami Reddiar, Rangaswami Reddiar, K. V. Ghaffar, T. S. Tirunavukkarasu, Veeraraghavan, V. Kumarasamy

the Commonweal and Tamilnad Toilers' Parties, shifted to Congress in the mid-1950s.[53]

The DMK successfully overcame the influence of such notables in the 1950s in areas where it built networks among those of less wealth and status. Some individuals of moderate wealth aided the party then. But, the DMK drew its primary support from small shopkeepers in Tiruvannamalai town and small peasants in the vicinity;[54] small shopkeepers and urban casual labour in Royapuram, and Mannargudi and Dindigul towns;[55] and small and medium peasants and tenants in the new delta villages around Mannargudi, mostly from the BCs.[56] Early DMK activists in Tiruvannamalai proudly emphasized their modest origins by rattling off a list of their names and occupations (in all but two cases, owners of very small shops): *'Javuli kadai* Venkatachalam, *podi kadai* Annamalai, *rotti kadai* Radha, *pena kadai* Qutubuddin, *cycle kadai* Azizullah, *arisi kadai* Govunandam, *javuli kadai* Thyagarajan, *cycle kadai*

(Tiruvannamalai); Dhanakoti Chettiar, V. A. Krishnan (Vettavalam); C. Kannan (Kilpennathur).

[53] For example, Manickavel Naicker, S. S. Ramaswami Padayachi (ministers in state cabinets of the 1950s). Interviews: N. M. Mani Varma, Vazhappadi K. Ramamurthi, 'Pulavar' Govindan (Madras); T. S. Tirunavukkarasu, Sivarama Reddiar, S. Murugayyan, S. Tiruvengadam (Tiruvannamalai); N. C. Ramaswami Gounder (Tandrambattu); Sahadeva Gounder (Edathanoor); Dhanakoti Gounder (Tanipadi).

[54] Interviews: S. Murugayyan, Santhanam, N. Venkatachalam, Qutubuddin, Azizullah, Sattar, V. Kumaraswami, S. Tiruvengadam, B. Vaiyapuri, B. Neelakantan, 'Avur' Ramalingam, Murugan, D. Venugopal Gounder (Tiruvannamalai); P. U. Shanmugam (Madras); K. Manickam (Konalur); V. A. Krishnan (Vettavalam); C. Kannan (Kilpennathur); C. Jayaraman, Ramadas (Tandrambattu); Dhanakoti Gounder (Tanipadi); Rajamani (Endhal); Nainar (Somasipadi).

[55] Interviews: S. D. Somasundaram, Sathyavani Muthu, P. A. K. Palaniswami, V. S. Anadan, N. Vedachalam, Era. Manoharan, Kapada Raje, P. Ponnurangam, M. Pavadaiswami (Madras); Mannai Narayanaswami, Ku. Balakrishnan, Pazha. Balasubramaniam, N. Govindarajan (Mannargudi); Samadharmam, Anguswami, Abdul Samad, Muthuswami, Manimaran, O. N. Sivagnanam, G. Lakshmanan, Oomer Shah, V. S. Lakshmanan, N. N. Alagar (Dindigul).

[56] Interviews: L. Ganesan (Madras); Ullikottai Arunachalam, P. Venkatesa Solagar (Mannargudi); Sithamalli Somasundaram, S. S. Nathan, Krishnan (Nidamangalam); A. K. Subbiah (Perugavazhndan-Sithamalli); Sivanandan Saluvar (Idamelayur); 'Mundasu' Natarajan (Kumbakonam).

Kumaraswami, *thavuttu kadai* Natarajan, *javuli kadai* Dharmalingam, *kaay kadai* Annamalai, *arisi kadai* Murugaiyan, *tea kadai* Sattar' (Textile shop Venkatachalam, snuff shop Annamalai, bread shop Radha, pen shop Qutubuddin, cycle shop Azizullah, rice shop Govunandam, textile shop Thyagarajan, cycle shop Kumaraswami, grain shop Natarajan, textile shop Dharmalingam, vegetable shop Annamalai, rice shop Murugaiyan, tea stall Sattar). The easy move back and forth from 'Hindu' to 'Muslim' names is notable and indicates that the DMK built strong social networks extending across religious boundaries. We will see later that this helped inhibit Hindu revivalist mobilization, which relied significantly on the cultivation of animosities between Hindus and Muslims. The DMK built a plebeian base to match its plebeian rhetoric, something the DK approximated only in small pockets.

Periar's vanguardism, disdain for maximizing mass support, opposition to universal suffrage and to using many channels of mass communication, and his frequent resort to notable support made him in many respects a creature of the colonial period (although he outlived it by twenty-six years). His reflexes formed in a period of limited political participation and sixty-nine years old when India achieved independence, he failed to alter his strategy in light of post-colonial realities. The DMK's growing success and his own evident failures led Periar to abandon hope of acquiring sufficient support to effect many of the changes he desired in his lifetime. So, he became even less concerned with broadening support, and gestures of heresy and protest dominated his political style more.

The DMK's leaders entered politics just prior to decolonization and adapted effectively to the post-colonial era. Annadurai was only thirty-seven when India attained independence and forty when the DMK was formed, and almost all who joined the DMK upon its formation were younger than Annadurai.[57] So, the diminutive form of his name, Anna (which also means elder brother), could suggest a proximate, albeit hierarchical, relation to

[57] Many older DK members who agreed with some of Annadurai's criticisms of Periar stayed with the DK out of a sense of personal loyalty to Periar or ideological affinity with him—e.g. S. 'Kuttooci' Guruswami, the editor of the DK organ *Viduthalai,* and the renowned poet Bharathi Dasan (alias Kanaka. Subburathinam). See Iraiyan (1981: 46–51, 82–7); Karunanidhi (1986: 121–4), Selvaraji (1986).

his cadre.[58] The DMK's strategic shifts, involving electoral participation and building networks largely independent of notable
influence, helped the party mobilize groups outside pan-Indianist
subcultures and challenge Congress dominance.

PARTIES AND THEIR STRATEGIES

Socialism, Backward Casteism and Congress

Congress attempted to use its hold over state power to consolidate
its dominance over Tamil politics during the initial phase of DMK
growth. The Indian government initiated a drive to develop
industry and infrastructure from the Second Five Year Plan (1956–
60) onwards as part of its efforts to build a 'socialistic pattern of
society'. The patronage associated with these development schemes
helped Congress consolidate support throughout India. Tamil
Nadu got a significant share of the government's industrial and
dam-building projects during the second plan, becoming the second
most industrialized state by the late 1950s.[59]

Rajaji led the libertarian opposition to Congress's socialist turn
in intra-party debates of the late 1950s, which he lost. As he had
also lost factional battles within the Tamil Nadu Congress just
before this, he left Congress in 1956 and founded the Swatantra
party (henceforth Swatantra) in 1959, taking with him many of the
libertarians in the Tamil Nadu Congress.[60]

Rajaji's departure from Congress was linked to the increasing
recruitment of BCs into the Tamil Congress leadership from the
1930s, a trend symbolized by the emergence of Kamaraj, a Nadar,
as the state Congress President in 1939. A rivalry developed
between Kamaraj and Rajaji, primarily based on differences in
political style, but assumed caste overtones though the two leaders
did not clearly disagree in their vision of caste relations.[61] Kamaraj

---

[58] Annadurai's editorials letters in *Dravida Nadu*, composed as letters to
activists, were addressed '*Thambikku*' (To my younger brother), and signed
'Anna'. In a variation on this theme, his succcessor, Karunanidhi, addressed
his editorial letters in *Murasoli* '*Udanpirappe*' (sibling).

[59] MIDS (1988: 190–234).

[60] TH, 21, 22 January, 22 April, 13 October 1957; 1, 5, 6 June 1959; Gandhi
(1978: 250–3, 280–5); Frankel (1978: 122–55, 163–79).

[61] Rajaji opposed the endorsement of caste barriers by many Tamil
Brahmin Congress leaders in the 1920s. Kamaraj was initially the protege of

gained increasing control of the party through the 1940s and 1950s, while Rajaji became marginalized by his lack of talent for machine politics, his statesmanlike postures and periods he spent outside Congress and Tamil Nadu.[62] Nevertheless, Rajaji became the Chief Minister after the 1952 elections as Congress failed to win an absolute majority in Madras Presidency, and his influence was needed to lure some small parties into a coalition government.

While he was the Chief Minister, Rajaji introduced a scheme for part-time craft education during school hours to train students for non-white collar careers. The Dravidianists portrayed the scheme as intended to perpetuate caste barriers to occupational mobility as lower caste children were likely to learn their fathers' crafts. Although Rajaji opposed caste discrimination and participated in Gandhian social work among SCs before decolonization, his Brahmin origins and Sanskritic idiom lent this criticism credence. The DK and the DMK spearheaded a major agitation against the craft-education scheme, which Kamaraj used to replace Rajaji as the Chief Minister in 1954.[63] This change in leadership enabled the Tamil Congress to ally itself with non-Brahminism.

The Tamil Congress fit the bureaucratic clientelist mould under Kamaraj's leadership. Contracts and industrial licenses associated with Second Plan projects were distributed to habitual supporters and to win over other industrialists. These industrialists sent some workers from their factories to help in Congress election campaigns, and are rumoured to have made handsome contributions to party coffers.

The Congress government introduced a 25 per cent quota for BCs in educational institutions and state government jobs in 1951 owing to the influence of Kamaraj and other BC legislators, whose ranks were growing, as was Dravidianist pressure. This made the

---

a Brahmin politician, S. Satyamurthi, and was not committed to non-Brahminism, but played the non-Brahmin card when it suited him. See Gandhi (1978) and Parthasarathi (1982).

[62] Rajaji was not in Congress between 1942 and 1946 as he disagreed with the party's Quit India agitation and its initial opposition to the demand for Pakistan. Being India's Governor General from 1947 to 1952 also distanced him from state politics. Gandhi (1978: 75–90).

[63] Gandhi (1978: 224–55), Barnett (1976: 77–80); Interviews: C. Subramaniam, A. N. Sivaraman.

growth of white collar government employment attendant on state-building more attractive to the BCs. Quotas had already been introduced for all non-Brahmins in the 1920s in Madras Presidency and other parts of the south Indian peninsula.[64] Along with mandating quotas for the SCs, the post-colonial constitution enabled state governments to introduce quotas for other groups deemed backward. BC quotas were introduced in the peninsular states and in Jammu and Kashmir in the early 1950s, decades earlier than in much of North India. Only in Madras and Maharashtra were the quotas based exclusively on caste criteria; and a much higher proportion of the population was included in the BC list in Madras (51 per cent) than in Maharashtra (14 per cent).[65]

Congress's socialist turn urged most members of Tamil Nadu's Socialist Party (which got 6.4 per cent of the vote in the state in 1952) to join Congress by 1956.[66] Backward casteism and patronage urged some caste parties and independent candidates to join Congress, and their vote share declined from 32 per cent in 1952 to 6.7 per cent in 1962. Congress thus consolidated its support through the 1950s, and, unlike in 1952, won comfortably in the 1957 and the 1962 elections, despite the DMK's growth through this decade. Congress's share of the vote increased from 34.6 per cent in 1952 to 45.3 per cent in 1957 and 46.1 per cent in 1962.[67]

Kamaraj's ascent and the introduction of the BC quotas were given a Dravidianist slant when Periar decided to back Kamaraj, calling him a '*pachchai Tamizhan*' (pure Tamil), when he became the Chief Minister. Periar justified this move much as he had justified his earlier support for the colonial state, claiming that a government inclined towards preferential policies could act as a counterweight to Brahmin social power, and he had sufficient control over DK activists by then to ensure their acceptance of the

---

[64] i.e. Bombay Presidency and the princely states of Mysore, Travancore and Cochin. See Galanter (1984: 27); Irschick (1969: 218–44) and Baker (1976: 50–4).

[65] Kerala employed an income ceiling, Jammu & Kashmir used religion and geographical origin as additional criteria, and Andhra reverted in the 1960s to income tests, rather than criteria of 'traditional' social backwardness and educational attainment, to determine the backwardness of castes. See Galanter (1984: 158–87).

[66] Fickett (1976).

[67] Singh and Bose (1988: 42, 45).

move. He claimed to support Kamaraj and not Congress, but campaigned in favour of all Congress candidates, including Brahmins.[68] His motives were many—Kamaraj was the first non-upper caste Tamil to head the government of Tamil Nadu/Madras Presidency;[69] Periar hoped to enhance Kamaraj's weak non-Brahminist inclinations; and wished to contain the DMK's growth, which embittered him. Further, the DK thereby gained limited influence over bureaucratic appointments, and might have helped urge the government in 1957 to declare concessions in college fees for some castes deemed 'most backward'.[70]

The DK's support for the state government while demanding secession inevitably led to awkward postures. Besides, the party lost the appeal it had by virtue of its militant opposition to Congress. This, along with the desire to enjoy political office, led some DK activists to join the DMK, to counter which trend Periar urged his supporters to join Congress instead. This only denuded the DK further.[71]

Kamaraj neither publicly sought nor acknowledged the DK's support, though it benefited him. This helped him dissociate himself from the DK's more unpopular acts and avoid the wrath of the Congressmen more implacably opposed to the DK.[72]

[68] The DMK criticized Periar's inconsistency in supporting Brahmin candidates. See TH, 24 December 1957.

[69] All Premiers/Chief Ministers of Madras Presidency had until then either been Telugu speakers (the Rajahs of Panagal and Bobbili, B. Munuswamy Naidu, T. Prakasam, O. Ramaswami Reddiar, P. S. Kumaraswami Raja) or from the upper castes (Rajaji, T. Prakasam, P. Subbaroyan).

[70] See TH, 13 July 1957; Interview: N. D. Sundaravadivelu (Madras), former Director of Collegiate Education (a Dravidianist bureaucrat reputedly appointed on Periar's recommendation).

[71] DK members joined the DMK through the 1950s also because it was clearly the more influential Dravidianist party. Periar ritualized the shift of some DK activists to Congress by helping them out of their black DK shirts and into the *khadi* shirts associated with Congress in public meetings. Interviews: K. Rajaram, 'Naathikam' Ramaswami (Madras); K. Nallathambi (Mannargudi); Aa. Subramaniam (Nidamangalam).

[72] Distancing himself from Periar helped Kamaraj, for instance when Periar threatened Brahmins not to vote in the 1962 elections. Periar however claimed that Kamaraj sought his support, promising to help realize the DK's goals. TH, 10 March 1957; 19 February 1962; *Viduthalai*, 1 January 1962.

The Last Gasp of Dravidian Heresy

The DK conducted idol-breaking processions in many towns in 1953, just before it linked itself to Congress.[73] Periar felt freer to play out his heretical fancies due to his tacit alliance with Congress, leading to a series of DK agitations which proved to be the party's undoing. In 1957, the DK agitated to remove the 'Brahmin' designation from signs on restaurants run by Brahmins and specializing in Brahmin cuisine.[74] Later that year, it burnt copies of the Indian constitution in public, claiming that the provision for freedom of religion tacitly permits the caste discrimination intrinsic to Hinduism.[75] By early 1958, DK activists burnt maps of India without Tamil Nadu to press the demand for secession.[76] In the midst of these frenzied agitations, Periar was reported to demand that ten to twenty *agraharams* (Brahmin residential areas) be set afire and at least a thousand Brahmins killed.[77] While this report was not reliably verified, some DK zealots cut off the tufts (*kudumi*) and sacred threads (*poonool*) of some Brahmins and launched minor attacks on Brahmin households soon after-wards.[78]

The DK put its meagre resources fully into these agitations. The state government arrested large numbers of the agitators, mandating the longest prison terms in Thanjavur district, the sole

[73] See Sithambaranar (1983: 330); Interviews: K. Veeramani, Nagai Kaliappan, Tiruvarur Thangarasu, V. S. Anandan (Madras); Ka. Ma. Kuppuswami (Vallam); A. M. Muthuswami, B. Vaiyapuri (Tiruvannamalai); R. P. Sarangan (Mannargudi); Thangaraj (Rajagiri); G.N. Sami (Darasuram); Venkatesan (Nidamangalam).

[74] TH, 3, 6, 8, 9, 10, 12 May; 2, 3 August 1957; 1 January 1958.

[75] TH, 5, 7, 12, 27, 28, 29 November; 5, 9, 10, 11, 12, 14, 15 December 1957.

[76] TH, 12 December 1957; 24 January 1958.

[77] This claim, contained in a police report, was denied by Periar in court. See TH, 29, 30 October; 8, 16, 21 November; 15, 22 December 1957.

[78] TH, 30 November; 1, 5, 9, 12, 24, 25 December 1957; Periar said these attacks were legitimate in principle, but condemned them as they were launched before he called for them (TH, 30 November 1957). He altered his position later, saying that the social boycott of Brahmins was sufficient, as killing a few of them or burning their houses would not remove caste dominance, and would only be used by the DK's enemies (TH, 12 December 1957).

remaining pocket of DK strength.[79] Not structured to face such repression effectively, the DK never recovered from it and ceased thereafter to be an effective political force.[80] Periar's continued support for Kamaraj (until 1967) despite the repression only undermined his prestige further.

The Communists: A Parliamentary Path to Oblivion

As the CPI launched armed peasant revolts in parts of Andhra and Bengal from 1946 to 1953, it was banned and made the main target of police repression throughout India. Rajaji declared that 'communists are my enemy number one' while he was the Tamil Nadu Chief Minister.[81] The repression had an ambiguous impact on the communists. While impeding communist mobilization among their primary supporters, peasants and industrial labour, it led many whom communists had not directly mobilized to view them with sympathy as Congress's most resolute opponents. The DK and the DMK publicized the plight of the communists and provided communist fugitives refuge through this period. Further the DK campaigned for CPI candidates in some constituencies during the 1952 elections. These factors gained the CPI significant support during these elections, which most communist candidates contested from prison, especially in the Kaveri valley where both the communists and Dravidianists enjoyed greatest early support.[82]

[79] The Union Home Minister reported that 2,884 had been arrested in connection with the Brahmin hotel agitation until 26 November 1957, i.e. before the constitution burning agitation began (TH, 8, 9, 10, 12, 14, 16, 23 May; 1, 12 June; 2, 3, 23 August; 5 December 1957). DK leaders estimate that 5,000 to 10,000 activists were arrested in connection with the three agitations of 1957–8. Interviews: K. Veeramani, Nagai Kaliappan, Tiruvarur Thangarasu (Madras); K. Nallathambi (Mannargudi).

[80] C. Subramaniam, then a state cabinet minister, said with some prescience that Periar was 'performing the last rites of his party'. See TH, 29 November 1957.

[81] Mohan Ram (1969: 22–32), Bouton (1985).

[82] Voters were especially moved as the wives of communist candidates went from door to door, requesting voters to help save their husbands (as legislators could not be imprisoned). Eight of the fourteen seats communists won in Tamil areas were in the Kaveri valley. Ironically, the DMK might have gained more long-term support from helping cultivate an aura of communist martyrdom than the communists themselves did. See Ponneelan (1974),

After the peasant revolts were quelled, the CPI opted for peaceful electoral participation in 1953, helping it consolidate support among industrial and agricultural workers and the intermediate strata in Kerala and West Bengal. But, in Tamil Nadu, the party faced increasing competition in trade unions, and the electoral support of many outside the communist subculture shifted over the next decade to the DMK.

Some of the DMK's criticisms of Congress were applicable to the communists too. The communists, like Nehru, focused on economic issues to the detriment of cultural ones, and considered the Indian nation the only natural and appropriate focus of identification. The DMK criticized these features of communist ideology, as well as its internationalism. The Dravidianists portrayed the communists as blind to caste (rather than class) divisions, which they considered Indian society's primary fault lines; and claimed on this basis that their caste appeals made them Tamil Nadu's authentic communists. The communists were unable to outdo this combination of indigenist and subaltern rhetoric, which they did not confront in states like West Bengal and Kerala, where they prospered more.[83]

Caste-based mobilization was weak and communists became linked to regional identity in West Bengal, the latter factor especially attracting middle class support.[84] While mobilization along caste lines was even stronger in Kerala than in Tamil Nadu, communists participated more actively in caste associations and tapped the emerging solidarity of a wider range of castes in Kerala, doing so only among the Kaveri valley SCs in Tamil Nadu. Further, communists became more influential in cultural fora in Kerala, Bengal and Andhra than in Tamil Nadu, and the absence

---

Ramamurthi (1983), Veeramani (1985); Interviews: Nagai Murugesan (Madras); Venkatesa Solagar, N. Govindarajan (Mannargudi); Charles (Dindigul); V. P. Nayakam (Ambasamudram).

[83] Communists invariably lost battles of mutual caricature and calumny with the Dravidianists. For instance, the DMK leader V. R. Nedunchezhian and the communist leader (and former Dravidianist) P. Jeevanandam debated each other, in *pattimanram* style (though in print, in issues of *Manram* and *Janasakthi*), on what is most indispensable to man, food (the supposed communist view) or *maanam* (dignity—the putative Dravidianist view). The terms of the debate clearly gave the DMK the moral high ground.

[84] See Sengupta (1972: 136–71, 203–64; 1980).

of a strong regionalist challenger in the former states gave them greater space to express the specificities of regional culture while remaining committed to Indian nationalism.[85] In contrast, competition with the DMK drove Tamil Nadu's communists to oppose secession with a shrillness that appeared insensitive to regional sentiment. After the DMK overtook the CPI in the 1957 elections, the CPI propagated commitment to Indian unity more systematically than even Congress did, countering DMK's 'Dravida Nadu weeks' and conferences with 'anti-Dravida Nadu' conferences.[86]

The All India Trade Union Congress (AITUC), which dominated the support of unionized industrial workers, came under communist control in the 1940s. Although the AITUC conducted organizing drives in new factories after independence, communist strength declined in industrial unions due to the emergence of rival unions. The main competitor was the Indian National Trade Union Congress (INTUC), affiliated with Congress, which both employers and the government often supported to curtail communist influence. While most workers in communist-affiliated unions supported the CPI in the early 1950s, the party affiliations of many diverged from their union affiliations through the next decade. Although the communists continued to be a major force in industrial unions in the early 1960s, many of their union members voted for other parties, especially the DMK, despite the limited involvement of the DMK in trade unions.[87]

Differences regarding the strategy to be pursued in India and the Sino-Soviet rift deepened within the CPI by the late 1950s, affecting routine party activities, particularly outside the communist bastions.

[85] Communist support had declined much before the regionalist Telugu Desam emerged in Andhra in the 1980s. Fic (1970: 8–30) attributes the indigenous image of Kerala's communists also to their early indifference to Comintern dictates.

[86] During the CPI's many 'anti-Dravida Nadu' conferences, conducted from 1957 to 1963, processions wound their way through many Tamil towns chanting 'Ketkaathe! Ketkaathe! Dravida Nadu ketkaathe!' (Don't demand Dravida Nadu). *Janasakthi*, 12 April 1958, 15 August 1961; TH, 8 March, 11 April 1962; NN, 5 August 1961, 8, 10 March, 13 April 1962; interviews: C. S. Subrahmanyam (Madras); P. Venkatesa Solagar, Duraiarasan (Mannargudi); V. Madanagopal (Dindigul).

[87] Annadurai frequently gloated over this trend: '*Sandhaa avanukku; vaakku yenakku*' (The union subscription goes to him; the vote comes to me).

In Tamil Nadu, they were given a Dravidianist twist by some leaders of the 'right-wing' pro-Soviet faction, which stayed with the CPI after 1964.[88] Such problems hastened the CPI's decline in Tamil Nadu though its first 'parliamentarist' decade, which brought the party much success elsewhere.

The DMK and Agitational Politics

The agitational activities of the pan-Indian parties declined as Congress became the ruling party, the socialists were tamed by their return to Congress, and the first wave of communist peasant agitations ended. While communist agitations continued, they attracted diminishing attention as the party declined. The DMK began to dominate the politics of the streets from the mid-1950s. It launched a series of state-wide agitations through this period which highlighted its positions and growing importance. Its first major agitation in 1953–4 encompassed the major themes of Dravidianism. Called the *mummunai poraattam* (three-cornered agitation), it had three distinct targets. First, it demanded that the original name of a train station be restored. The station had been named Dalmiapuram, after the nearby cement factory owned by a major North Indian industrial house. In demanding the restitution of the original name of the village (Kallakudi), the DMK highlighted its opposition to the North Indian economic and cultural presence.[89]

Second, the *mummunai poraattam* protested Nehru's alleged denigration of Tamil and South Indian culture in calling Dravidianist demands for giving Tamil cultural history greater importance in school curricula 'nonsense'.[90] Third, it opposed the craft education scheme introduced by the state government, deemed it a '*kula kalvi*

---

[88] M. Kalyanasundaram pointed derisively to the non-Tamil and Brahmin origins of many leaders of the 'left' faction, which later became the CPI-M.

[89] It also suggested the affinity of the DMK with the BCs as the name of the village, Kallakudi, alludes to the Kallar caste (one of the constituents of the Mukkulathor caste cluster). See Karunanidhi (1986: 180–255); Subbiah (1985: 69–76); NN and *Murasoli*, 14 June to 18 July 1953.

[90] The DMK protested against Nehru's visit to Madras in 1953 to inaugurate a science exhibition, demanding that an exhibition also be conducted on Tamil cultural history, and criticizing the neglect of South Indian history in textbooks. The postures of the parties to this confrontation—Nehru inaugurating a science exhibition, and the DMK demanding attention to

thittam' (a caste-based education scheme), and linked it to the Brahminical social outlook of the Chief Minister Rajaji.[91] By linking these three agitations, the DMK suggested that the alleged upper caste and North Indian biases of Congress were of a piece. The first two prongs of the agitation involved only the DMK, evoked limited response, and did not achieve their stated aims.[92] But, the third brought together a coalition of non-Brahminists including the DK, and led to Rajaji's ouster as the Chief Minister, the first major change in which the DMK played a part.[93]

The DMK periodically agitated—in 1950, 1952, 1959, 1960 and 1963—against the commitment of the Indian constitution to change the official language of India from English to Hindi in 1965; and opposed the Official Languages Commission for limiting its purview to the timing of the change to Hindi, rather than permitting those deposing before it to dispute the wisdom of such a switch.[94]

State boundaries were redrawn to conform to linguistic ones between 1953 and 1956. The state of Tamil Nadu was formed through the excision of predominantly Telugu, Malayalam and Kannada speaking areas from Madras Presidency, and the inclusion of some predominantly Tamil speaking areas from the former

---

Dravidianist cultural history—reflect their contrasting approaches to the formation of the citizen. To Nehru, who placed the spirit of science and rationality at the core of nation-building, the DMK's demands could only appear nonsensical. NN, 5, 8, 12 August 1953; Chittibabu (1975).

[91] Rajaji's scheme was intended to impart artisanal skills and prevent the decline of the crafts. C. Subramaniam, who became the Education Minister as the scheme was being implemented, insists to this day that caste was not relevant to this scheme. But non-Brahminists argued that most students would learn their parents' crafts, perpetuating a caste-based occupational structure. The DMK's interpretation of the scheme so successfully influenced Tamil political memory that even many non-Dravidianists refer to the scheme today as the '*kula kalvi thittam*'. NN, 13–20 July 1953; TH, 15, 16, 17 July 1953; Interview: C. Subramaniam (Madras).

[92] The train station was renamed only in 1970, after the DMK assumed power.

[93] See Chittibabu (1975: 98–114, 125–6), Karunanidhi (1986: 180–225), Barnett (1976: 79–81).

[94] TH, 13 August 1957; NN, 12 August 1955; 18, 31 July 1959; 1, 3, 14 August 1960; Chittibabu (1975: 62–3, 88–90, 214, 231–7, 299–309); Interviews: L. Ganesan, K. Kalimuthu, A. N. Sivaraman (Madras).

princely state of Travancore. The DMK, along with other Tamil nationalist forces, demanded the inclusion of more areas in Tamil Nadu in a series of agitations between 1953 and 1958. Unlike some of its allies, the DMK demanded only the inclusion of areas with substantial Tamil-speaking populations and not those that were of religious importance like Tirupathi.[95] These agitations strengthened the political salience of linguistic bonds and solidified linguistic identities along Tamil Nadu's borders.

While the DMK's agitations focused on cultural issues in the Nehruvian period, some of them addressed economic problems too. The party was serendipitously associated with a peasant agitation (in Nangavaram, Tiruchi district), and supported distressed handloom weavers and striking *beedi* and transport workers.[96] A state-wide agitation launched in 1962 against inflationary trends drew significant support.

But, the DMK did not mobilize specific occupational groups around their economic demands through this period, forming no party-affiliated unions among industrial, agricultural or white collar workers. Some party activists organized small industrial unions and cultural associations on their own initiative in a few factories, especially in Coimbatore, Madras, Tuticorin and Ponmalai. But, the party did not provide systematic material or legal support to these early unionists, and party leaders rejected their proposals to form a party-affiliated umbrella organization for these unions. Annadurai preferred easier routes to recruiting workers, wishing to avoid repression and entanglement in court cases. It was only after the DMK assumed power, and Karunanidhi assumed the leadership of the party and the state government, that a party-affiliated umbrella organization was formed, whose main purpose was not mobilization but social control.[97]

[95] See Sharma (1969), Sivagnanam (1986), Chittibabu (1975: 94, 130–6), TH, 11 January, 2, 4, 5 May, 15, 29 June, 21, 28 August, 1, 13, 29 September, 1 October, 18 November 1957.

[96] Support for handloom weavers was in tune with the DMK's criticism of large industry and Annadurai's origins in a weaver caste. Karunanidhi (1986: 171, 287–8); Chittibabu (1975: 92, 145, 179, 195–7, 212, 215); TH, 5 May, 5 September 1957; Interview, Devasagayam (Lalgudi).

[97] TH, 2 May, 11 October 1957; NN, 2, 3 May 1958; Interviews: K. Raghavanandam, Kovai Sezhiyan, T. K. Ponnuvelu, Kuppuswami (Madras); M. S. Sivaswami (Tuticorin).

The DMK's early agitations brought the party to popular attention and shaped the self-conceptions of activists. But these involved only party activists (except the agitation against the craft-education scheme), drawing few into politics or the DMK.[98] They introduced no new forms of protest, though they were often publicized in a novel idiom. These agitations aided party growth more once the anti-Hindi battles grew fierce in the mid-1960s, thereby spinning out of the control of party leaders.

State Responses to the DMK and the Limits of DMK Militancy

Although the DMK claimed until 1963 that secession was its ultimate goal, the party neither conducted agitations to press this demand nor ever considered resorting to armed rebellion. Such agitations would have inevitably invited concerted state repression, and the DMK (unlike the CPI) was not structured with a view to illegal functioning. Conscious of the limits of the repression they could endure, party leaders avoided activities which might provoke repression in excess of these limits. So, they restricted themselves to voicing secessionist demands from conference and electoral platforms, even while calling their agitations just wars (arappor), much as they avoided militant trade unionism even while eloquently depicting the plight of workers.

The state reciprocated by limiting its repression of the DMK, imprisoning agitators for brief periods but not seeking to crush the party.[99] During the 1962 elections, Kamaraj channelled Congress's resources to constituencies where the DMK was strong, and Congress won in all the fifteen constituencies where the DMK had won in 1957. But, the government did not hamper DMK propaganda even if it was conducted by government employees, who were forbidden from participating in partisan politics. Many white collar workers joined the DMK during this period, and school and

[98] The location of DMK agitations in this period—all around the state—does not correspond to the foci of party growth, which accords with the insignificant direct role of agitations in gaining support.

[99] This was its response to the DK too, except during the agitations of 1957–8.

college teachers were crucial in urging the youth towards the DMK.[100]

In contrast with its treatment of the DMK, the state government harassed communists even after they abandoned armed warfare, frequently punishing communist government employees for instance. It treated the CPI and the DMK differently as many Congress leaders viewed the CPI as a greater threat even though the DMK was outdoing the CPI electorally by the late 1950s. These leaders considered the communists more formidable opponents as the communists' methods and goals were greater threats to the interests dominating Congress's coalition, the CPI was a competitor at the national as well as state levels, and its activists had withstood more repression. They tended to discount the DMK's prospects as parties issuing appeals through films and pulp literature had not yet gained prominence in India. The differing state responses to the two parties further helped the DMK outdo the CPI.

The DMK's emergence as a serious threat to Congress in the 1962 elections (in which the DMK polled 27.1 per cent of the vote and won 50 of the 206 seats in the state assembly) shocked the national government into amending the constitution to prohibit secessionists from holding public office. As the DMK had conducted no secessionist agitations, this move was meant to curb the electoral growth of the DMK and other potential secessionist parties, rather than to confront an immediate threat of secession. DMK leaders had decided in private to drop the secession demand in 1961, but had not announced the decision for fear of adverse response from activists. The constitutional amendment banning secessionism only pushed these leaders to announce their decision sooner (in 1963), arguing that the party would be destroyed were it to defy the government.[101]

[100] Some Tamil teachers (most of them government employees) wrote Dravidianist poems in the red and black colours of the DMK flag on school blackboards. The Congress regime paid dearly for overlooking such practices. N. Karuppannan kindly let me consult letters Tamil teachers addressed to the DMK regimes of the 1960s and 1970s, which highlight their contribution to DMK growth. Interviews: Rama. Subramaniam (Thanjavur); Vriddhachalam (Karanthattankudi).

[101] Annadurai (1963); TH 19 November, 31 December 1962; 2, 22, 26 January, 3 May, 8 August, 24, 26, 28 October; 4 November 1963; Kannadasan (1972); Barnett (1976: 109–10, 126–9).

The Talk Shop

DMK leaders realized by the early 1960s that the party had grown less through militant agitation and separatism than through election campaigns, street corner meetings and conversations in shops run by party adherents.[102] The shops of some early activists served as the party's primary recruiting grounds, where Dravidianist journals were available, people congregated to gossip and discuss social issues, and the latest statements and directives of party leaders were made known. These included tea stalls, barber shops and cycle repair/rental shops (where people tend to linger) and wholesale and retail shops dealing in grains, spices and produce (*mandis*).[103] Some of these shopkeepers ran their shops in ways that maximized political support rather than profits.[104]

Like Weber's German lawyer, the shopkeeper was the natural politician of the plebeian Tamil society to which the DMK appealed. The shops gave their owners some economic independence and social contact, and they could deal with political activities while attending to business. While deriving his local influence mainly from his role in the party, the shopkeeper-activist also had independent professional and kin links, which he could use not only to gain the party more support, but also to maintain

---

[102] They emphasized this to activists. DN, 5 November 1961; Karunanidhi (1986: 170; 1988: 21–3).

[103] For example, the shops of some of my interviewees—the tailors Paramasivam in Pathamadai and Arumugam in Royapuram, the cycle repair/rental shop owners Azizullah and V. Kumaraswami in Tiruvannamalai, the barbers Karuppiah and Abdul Razack in Dindigul, the tea stall owners Dass in Mukkoodal and Sattar in Tiruvannamalai, the restaurant owner Krishnan in Nidamangalam, the textile shop owners P. A. K. Palaniswami in Royapuram and P. U. Shanmugam in Tiruvannamalai, the optical goods merchant Qutubuddin and the grain merchants Ti. Ma. Natarajan and J. Malik in Tiruvannamalai, the rice mill owners Dhanakoti Gounder in Tanipadi and Ramalingam in Avur, the soda shop owners Manickam in Konalur and Nainar in Somasipadi, the iron merchant Velayudhan, the small tobacco company owner Qadir Shah and the utensil shop owner Ma. Velayudhan in Dindigul.

[104] For instance, a cycle repair shop owner recalled at a public meeting at Choolai (north Madras) that he used to repair cycles slowly whenever a new customer came by, in the hope that the waiting customer would pick up some of the party literature lying around and ask a question, which would give him an opening to subject the hapless victim to his political pitch.

his autonomy of party leaders. He was anything but the atomized individual whom Kornhauser (1959) considered populism's typical supporter.

Reading rooms and party offices also served as talk shops. Through informal gatherings in the talk shops, the DMK subculture was formed and prior social networks incorporated within the subculture and party. Some recruits were trained in oratory and party ideology in *manrams* (associations) and schools formally or informally affiliated with the party. Once such activities had attracted at least twenty-five activists in an area, a party branch was established there and meetings held in which the party flag was ·hoisted in a street corner, signalling the party's presence in the area. The nature of the networks incorporated into the party shaped the social composition of its local membership and base, and the direction of local party activities. The discourse of party leaders passed through the sieve of local interpretation as it entered conversations in the talk shops. So, the motivations of those recruited through talk shops were particularly shaped by local realities. Even those inspired directly by leaders' speeches and writings often found in them what was relevant to their situation.

Sensing the party's growth, DMK members decided in 1956 to participate in elections.[105] As DMK members got elected to local government institutions from the late 1950s, Annadurai urged activists to meet people in every street in their area periodically, to represent local demands.[106] The party's local government representatives mediated effectively with government officials, to benefit those in the DMK subculture and through them others from the intermediate and lower strata.[107] This strengthened the party's social roots, which began in towns and larger villages in the northern plains and Kaveri valley in the mid-1950s and spread to smaller villages in these regions by the early 1960s.

[105] The decision was left to party members, 56,942 of whom voted for participation and 4,203 against. See NN, 19 November 1955; 19, 20 May 1956; Chittibabu (1975: 128, 143–4, 150–1, 216); Karunanidhi (1986: 276).

[106] Annadurai (1986b, vol. 11: 109–10); Chittibabu (1975: 217–25).

[107] Interviews: Manikkavasagam (Thanjavur); Balasubramaniam, V. S. Anandan, Radhakrishnan (Madras); S. Murugayyan, Avur Ramalingam, Azizullah, V. Kumaraswamy (Tiruvannamalai); K. Balakrishnan (Mannargudi), N. Sundaram (Tirupattur).

The DMK: Cultural Politics and Language

Dravidianists played an increasing role in expressive arenas. Films that DMK leaders scripted were among the major commercial successes of the 1950s. These leaders courted the support of actors and others associated with the cinema, and helped make them popular. The most significant example was that of Karunanidhi attracting to the party in 1953 M. G. Ramachandran (MGR), the most popular film star and public figure of modern Tamil Nadu. By giving MGR the title '*puratchi nadikar*' (revolutionary actor) in 1954, Karunanidhi associated him with Dravidianist militancy, an association reinforced by allusions in MGR's films. By the late 1950s, MGR fan clubs had begun to form spontaneously around the state, and were brought under the rubric of a unified organization in 1961. Many supporters and activists were attracted to the party through MGR's films, and the fan clubs provided considerable manpower for election campaigns. By the early 1960s, MGR had become a magnet drawing crowds to party meetings and voters, especially women, to the polling booths.[108]

MGR and cinema were only the most obvious indications of the DMK's growing influence in cultural fora. Party members were active in other mass cultural fora such as street theatre, hack journalism and cultural debate (*pattimanram*). Many from newly educated groups were politicized through exposure to these fora, which were dominated by Dravidianist ideas and the alliterative, non-Sanskritic Tamil associated with the DMK.

While Congress had also politicized people through the use of cultural media during the nationalist movement,[109] its strength in cultural fora declined after it assumed power and focused less on mobilization. Partly due to changes in the party leadership, Congress leaders maintained close contacts with fewer journalists, litterateurs and actors. While their contact with the film world declined with the death of S. Sathyamurthi in 1943, the primary architect of the late colonial Tamil Congress, Rajaji's departure in

[108] For instance, MGR's last minute campaigning is said to have been crucial to the DMK winning the by-election in Tiruvannamalai in 1963, after which many party leaders began to consider state power within their reach. NN, 1 July 1963; Karunanidhi (1986: 438–40); Interviews: R. M. Veerappan, P. U. Shanmugam (Madras); S. Murugaiyan (Tiruvannamalai), V. K. Krishnan (Vettavalam).

[109] See Bhaskaran (1984).

1956 weakened the party's links with journalists.[110] Kamaraj preferred to gather support by maintaining activist loyalty and transacting with influential groups. While a major film star, 'Sivaji' Ganesan, was a Congress member from the mid-1950s and his fans participated in election campaigns, he was not accorded the significance given to MGR in DMK propaganda.[111] Many theatre and music groups inclined towards Congress became moribund, and others focused less on politicization.

Some of Congress's positions on language policy and state boundaries alienated the party from growing Tamil nationalist sentiment. While a range of opinions existed among Tamil Congressmen on these issues, the Tamil Congress was constrained by the basic positions of the national party and government. When the Tamil Arasu Kazhagam faction disregarded these constraints and agitated for redrawing state boundaries, it was expelled from the party.[112] Although a Congressman, Sankaralinga Nadar, fasted to death to press the demand that the state be renamed Tamil Nadu, his death was seen as a result of Congress's obduracy on the issue and produced antipathy towards the party. The DMK adopted Sankaralinga Nadar as a hero and conducted functions to mark his death anniversary.[113]

The Congress regime did take many steps to shift from English to Tamil as the official language of the state. Textbooks were published in Tamil especially in the scientific and technical subjects, enabling the Tamil language to be made the medium of instruction in most schools and colleges. The Tamil typewriter was introduced and Tamil made the language of administration in many

[110] Some like N. S. Krishnan and T. R. Madhuram, major Indian nationalist theatre and film actors of the 1930s and 1940s, became altogether alienated from Congress and campaigned for the DMK in the 1957 elections. Aranthai Narayanan (1981), Karunanidhi (1986: 289), Gandhi (1978); Interview: A. N. Sivaraman.

[111] Aranthai Narayanan (1981); Interview: 'Sivaji' Ganesan.

[112] The expulsion of the Tamil Arasu Kazhagam faction was significant, despite the factions's limited support, as it widened the gap between Congress and Tamil nationalism in public perception. Mainstream Congress politicians regarded this faction as quixotic and did not regret its expulsion. Sivagnanam (1986: 382–6, 447–64); Interviews: Ma. Po. Sivagnanam, C. Subramaniam, A. Chengalvorayan.

[113] TH, 28 July 1956; NN, 29 July, 23 August 1956; Chittibabu (1975: 162), Karunanidhi (1986: 282–3).

government departments.[114] The steps taken in these directions during Congress rule were in fact more significant than those adopted by the DMK after it assumed power. The Congress government paid little attention, however, to Tamil nationalist mytho-history in education and propaganda. Part of the DMK's success lay in the fact that most Tamils paid greater attention to mytho-history than to administrative and educational policies in judging a party's Tamil nationalist credentials, and by those standards the DMK was not to be outdone.

The state government and many Tamil Congress leaders protested the plans of the national government to follow the constitutional commitment to shift from English to Hindi as the official language for national administration in 1965. Due to their arguments and those of Congressmen from other southern states, Nehru agreed in 1958 that such a shift would not occur until the people of the southern states were ready for it. Besides, he informally assured southern Congress leaders that people from their regions would be allowed to judge whether they were ready for such a shift.[115] However, the Tamil Nadu Congress only argued that the shift to Hindi be postponed indefinitely, rather than abandoned. To enable such an eventual shift, the state government included a third language, expected to be Hindi, in the education scheme it announced in 1958.[116] The parliament passed a bill in 1963 which enabled the use of both English and Hindi as official languages. But it did not mandate the continued use of English, or give English the status of an associate language as some demanded, or postpone the introduction of Hindi. Thus, it fell well short of Nehru's earlier assurance, and did not meet the demand of the DMK and other Tamil nationalists for a constitutional amendment embodying this assurance.[117]

---

[114] Rajaji even wrote a science textbook in the Tamil language. TH, 16 January, 4 May, 29 June, 21, 22 August 1957; 21 March 1962; interviews: C. Subramaniam, K. S. Ramanujam.

[115] TH, 12, 24 October, 9 November, 31 December 1957; 2, 3, 4, 7, 17, 18, 19 January, 1, 8 February 1958; 5 September 1959; 12 September 1962; NN, 11, 31 December 1957; Subramaniam (1978); Interview: C. Subramaniam.

[116] TH, 4 January 1958.

[117] Clause 3 of the bill said: 'Notwithstanding the expiry of the fifteen years from the commencement of the constitution, English *may*, from the day notified, continue to be used in addition to Hindi' (emphasis mine). The use

In its deliberations on language policy, the Official Languages Commission only considered those objections to the introduction of Hindi which were based on the extent of growth in competence in Hindi in the non-Hindi-speaking states, rejecting autonomist arguments that the popular preference in some non-Hindi states for the indefinite continuation of English as the sole official language should influence policy. So, no accommodation was offered to autonomist sentiment, and the concerns that non-Hindi speakers would be at a disadvantage in competition for the professions if Hindi were to become the sole official language were not addressed.

The Tamil nationalists felt threatened as the majority of Congress members throughout India seemed to favour a quick transition to Hindi, perhaps even by 1965. Their disquiet increased as the influence of Nehru, who was willing to introduce Hindi gradually in non-Hindi-speaking states, declined after India's defeat in the war with China, and his health deteriorated. They found the efforts and commitment of the Tamil Congress to forestall the introduction of Hindi inadequate. By now, their growing ranks included even Rajaji, whose introduction of Hindi into the school curriculum in 1937 had provoked the first anti-Hindi agitation.[118] Most of them found the DMK's unconditional opposition to the introduction of Hindi, which outlived its secession demand, more attractive than the Tamil Congress's ambivalent posture.

However, language demands were not the primary reasons for DMK growth and partisanship was not closely linked to the economic relevance of these demands until the early 1960s, unlike in the more linguistically heterogeneous Assam, where the majority of the Assamiya middle class supported the Asom Gana Parishad since its emergence and most non-Assamiyas opposed it.[119] The DMK could not claim a monopoly on the demand to

---

of 'may' rather than 'shall' disturbed Tamil nationalists. Nehru claimed in an explanatory note to parliamentarians that 'may' and 'shall' are interchangeable! TH, 12 September 1962, 15 February 1963.

[118] Rajaji changed his position on the wisdom of introducing Hindi as the national language in 1956, just after he left Congress. See TH, 12, 24 October 1957; NN, 1, 12 October 1957; Gandhi (1978: 263–5).

[119] See Baruah (1986, 1994).

increase the official use of Tamil in the state as the state government actively promoted it. The economic appeal of the demand to restrain the introduction of Hindi at the national level was greatest for Tamils fluent in English who entered the professions, particularly the national bureaucracy. Yet, professionals were predominantly aligned with Congress rather than with the DMK until the early 1960s. Indeed, the first activist with a college degree did not join DMK until 1962 in the early party bases of Tiruvannamalai and Royapuram. The geographical concentration of DMK support in the Nehruvian period also bears no relation to the relevance of the party's language demands, which was the same throughout the state. Further, the social profiles of DMK and Congress support were not closely related to language use. Native speakers of Tamil, who account for 84.5 per cent of the state's residents, dominated the social bases of both partie. although the majority of non-Tamil speakers continued to favour Congress (as was the case until the early 1960s with most other groups marginal to the early Dravidianist vision—Brahmins, SCs and Christians, though Muslims had begun to move in larger numbers towards the DMK in its regions of strength).

The DMK's Tamil revivalism was nevertheless relevant to the party's early supporters, especially the petty intelligentsia, because it aimed to give the Tamil language preeminence in the public sphere, signified the party's association with plebeian groups not well versed in English, and highlighted its opposition to the national government.

Just before Nehru's death, the DMK announced its plans for an agitation to oppose the switch to Hindi in 1965.[120] The national government's minor concessions regarding language demands and the growing prospect of capturing the state government failed to deter the DMK from embarking on its most dramatic and violent confrontation with the state in the language agitations of the mid-1960s. Far from losing the party support, these agitations, along with other features of the conjuncture of the mid-1960s, saw the DMK extend its reach beyond its early bastions and assume power in the state.

[120] TH, 21 October, 17 November, 1 December 1963; 9 May, 3 August 1964; Chittibabu (1975: 299–313).

CHANGING PARTISANSHIP DURING
THE DMK'S ASCENT

The Political Map at Independence

We saw that Congress's dominance at the point of decolonization rested on shallow and somewhat uncertain foundations. Congress had deeper subcultures in areas of flourishing agriculture, the valleys and western plains. While the dominant strata were at the forefront in local party organizations, middling strata also played a significant role and support extended across the social spectrum. Congress enjoyed the greatest support around the state among the landed upper castes and the SCs, largely passive in the case of the latter. The majority of those not part of any party's subculture also favoured Congress because it led the nationalist movement and had gained the support of the dominant strata when it controlled the provincial government in the last decade of colonial rule. Such passive support for Congress was greatest in the western and southern plains.[121]

The CPI and the DK had developed nuclei of support from which they could expand into uncharted territory. The communists had a strong presence among agricultural workers and peasants (especially the SCs) in the Kaveri valley and more restricted support among these groups in the Tamiraparani valley and among industrial and other ranks of urban labour in the major industrial centres.[122] The DK had greatest support among BCs and SCs in rural pockets in the Kavery valley, and more limited support among the BCs in commercial towns, especially in the Kavery valley and northern plains.

---

[121] Interviews: C. Subramaniam, N. Somayajulu, G. K. Moopanar, A. R. Marimuthu, A. Chengalvorayan, M. P. Subramaniam (Madras).

[122] Support for the CPI was greatest in the industrial centres of Coimbatore/ Singanallur, Madurai, north Madras and Vikramasingapuram; and more limited in Salem, Dindigul, Valparai, Tuticorin, Ponmalai, Nagaipattinam, Gudiyatham, Ranipet, Vellore and Nellikuppam. Ramamurthi (1983), Ramaswamy (1988); Interviews: A. Nallasivan, A. Srinivasan, C. S. Subrahmanyam (Madras); K. Ramani (Coimbatore); R. V. Ananthakrishnan (Vikramasingapuram); V. P. Nayakam (Ambasamudram); S. K. Palaniswami (Veeravanallur); V. Madanagopal, Charles, K. Ramaswami, A. Narayanan (Dindigul).

While the lower classes and castes were least extensively mobilized by parties, this was less true in the more politicized regions (the valleys and western plains), where stronger party loyalties had developed.[123] The majority of the intermediate strata favoured Congress and some supported the DK in a few pockets. Political organization and solidarity were strongest among the two most numerous backward caste clusters, the Mukkulathor and the Vanniar. So, parties based primarily among these castes (the Forward Bloc among the Mukkulathor, and the Commonweal Party and the Tamil Nadu Toilers' Party among the Vanniar) were strong just after independence in areas where these castes are concentrated.

The DMK got the lion's share of the DK's cadre and support in much of the state, where the DK had grown on a thin base of notable support and some BC solidarity. The only exception was the Kaveri valley, where heretical Dravidianism had developed deepest social roots. Dravidianism's opposition to ritualistic upper caste Hinduism and its image as a proponent of the ritually lower castes were most appreciated in this region, where Brahminical ritual practices had greatest influence and social polarization was most pronounced.[124] As these features of Dravidianism continued to be closely associated with Periar, Dravidianism's first heretical call continued to echo loudly through the 1950s in the Kaveri valley, where the DK provided the DMK some of its bitterest initial resistance.[125]

Growth in Political Participation

New groups, mostly from the intermediate strata, were mobilized through the Nehruvian period, often attracted by the new forms

[123] The least mobilized groups were, in terms of caste, the SCs and many of the lower BCs; and in terms of class, the landless and the land-poor in poorer rural areas and urban casual labour.

[124] For instance, many pro-DK families did not celebrate Hindu festivals like Deepavali in parts of northern Mannargudi taluk (e.g. Nidamangalam) through the 1950s, and the DK had sufficient strength in some villages there (e.g. Idamelayur) for its activists to habitually expel religious mendicants. Interviews: Aa. Subramaniam, Venkatesan, S. S. Nathan (Nidamangalam); R. P. Sarangan, K. Nallathambi (Mannargudi); 'Mundasu' Natarajan (Kumbakonam).

[125] Karunanidhi (1986: 177); Interviews: 'Mannai' Narayanaswamy (Mannargudi); L. Ganesan (Madras).

of appeal characteristic of the DMK. The majority among them supported the DMK, but some preferred other parties, some of whose leaders and ideologues adopted the DMK's mobilizing methods. Aware of the growth in the party's support, DMK leaders initiated a massive voter registration drive concentrated in poorer residential areas on the eve of the 1962 elections. Activists showed many new voters how to stamp ballots, assured them that the ballot was secret and promised to ensure that Congress activists and social élites would not invalidate their ballots.[126]

The voter registration drive led to the largest increase in voter participation in the state's electoral history, which extended across the gender and rural/urban gaps. Turnout rates surged from 49.3 per cent in 1957 to 70.7 per cent in 1962, never to return to the sluggish levels of the 1950s. The gender gap in voter participation was narrowed, from about 10 percentage points through the 1950s to around 5 percentage points in 1967 and most later elections. However, the habitual gap in participation rates between the general constituencies and those reserved for SC/ST candidates did not decline until later.[127]

[126] DN, 5 November 1961; Annadurai (1986b, vol. 11: 137–9; vol 12: 149); interviews: Rama. Subbiah, Balasubramaniam (Madras); Manikkavasagam (Thanjavur); Ullikott i Arunachalam (Mannargudi); S. Murugayyan, N. Venkatachalam (Tiruvannamalai); C. Jayaraman (Tandrambattu); V. A. Krishnan (Vettavalam).

[127] Turnout rates in constituencies reserved for SC/ST candidates are an uncertain index of electoral participation levels among the SCs and STs themselves as the electorate is not restricted in these constituencies. They serve as a rough index, nevertheless (see Weiner and Field: 1975, vol. IV: 78–164) as the reserved constituencies have a greater concentration of SC/STs than the general population (while these groups account for 18 per cent of Tamil Nadu's population, they constitute about 25 per cent to 35 per cent of the population in SC constituencies and a higher proportion in the ST constituencies). However, other factors might contribute to lower turnouts in reserved constituencies—e.g. lower participation among non-SC/STs due to the absence of non-SC/ST candidates, parties spending less on campaigning in these less prestigious constituencies. Interviews in my case constituencies (of which two were reserved for the SCs at times) and polling booth-wise voting data in ten constituencies for the 1984, 1989 and 1991 assembly elections suggested that turnout rates continued to be lower among the SCs. The gap in turnout rates between general and reserved constituencies was always lowest in the Kaveri valley, where the SCs have been most politicized.

The increase in voter participation in this period was far greater in Tamil Nadu than in India as a whole and participation rates continue to be significantly higher in Tamil Nadu (see Table 1.5). Its coincidence with the emergence of the DMK as a major electoral contender, the voter registration drive the DMK conducted prior to it, and the high levels of correlation between increases in turnout and the number of times a DMK candidate contested from a constituency show the intimate link between this trend and the DMK's growth.[128]

DMK mobilization through the 1950s and early 1960s and the party's voter registration drive of 1962 not only increased electoral participation, but also helped reduce the influence of traditional clientelist bonds, already weakened by the ongoing commercialization of class relations, on voting. Congress and notables who were independent candidates had relied heavily on such ties in the 1950s, particularly in rural areas. The decline in the independent candidates' share of the popular vote, from 24.3 per cent in 1952 to 5.3 per cent in 1962, reflects the sharp reduction in the influence of traditional clientelism on voting.[129] Such influence remained strong by the early 1960s only in the poorest regions, where party allegiances solidified latest.[130] These changes contributed to the DMK's growth and Congress's decline.

More individuals from the intermediate and lower strata became local party leaders, mainly in the DMK and the CPI. This trend was strongest in the Kaveri valley, where these groups entered politics earliest. It created a stark contrast between the social composition of the local leadership of Congress and other parties, particularly in the valleys where Congress bore the stamp of landlord dominance. In Mannargudi, N. Somasundaram, from an SC bonded agrarian tenant family, became an important figure in the local DMK; and the lower BC tenant farmer P. Venkatesa Solagar, the SC small peasant A. K. Subbiah and the former SC

---

[128] See Barnett (1975: 93–5).

[129] Singh & Bose (1988: 42).

[130] For instance, local *beedi* magnates exercised decisive influence as late as 1962 in Kadayam, a poorly developed constituency in the southern plains. The support of Chockalinga Nadar, who owned the area's largest *beedi* company, ensured resounding victories for his relative D. S. Adimoolam in 1957 and 1962, though Adimoolam opposed Congress as an independent in 1957 and was the Congress candidate in 1962. Singh & Bose (1988: 498).

bonded worker K. Murugaiyan in the CPI.[131] In contrast, Congress continued to be dominated by landlords and professionals from landed families in Mannargudi and Sermadevi. These élites allowed some from modest backgrounds, like the tenant farmer 'Kombur' Venkatesan of Mannargudi and the school teacher Gomathi Shankara Dikshithar in Sermadevi, to play active roles in the local Congress, if they were docile towards their social superiors.[132]

Local notables were prominent in local Congress party organizations in the plains too—e.g. professionals (often landed) in Tiruvannamalai and construction contractors, traders and minor smugglers in Royapuram—but some of modest status could assume autonomous importance too. For instance, the small iron merchant Thangavelu Pillai led the party's Hindu revivalist faction in Dindigul. A group composed mostly of harbour workers and fishermen which left the DMK for Congress under the leadership of the minor publicist Aru. Shankar was somewhat autonomous of the party's dominant trader faction in Royapuram. However, it was the dominant élite faction which had Kamaraj's ear in Dindigul and Royapuram, as elsewhere.[133] Besides, those of modest origins were far more significant in the local DMK leadership in the plains too. The vegetable vendor 'Thakkazhi' Pichai, the SC tannery worker Samadharmam and the unemployed N. Muthu Pillai initiated the formation of the first party branch in Dindigul, while a range of small shopkeepers did so in Tiruvannamalai.[134]

Despite the important roles played by individuals from the lower and intermediate strata in the early DMK, those from ascendant BC groups inhabited the apex of DMK subcultures too—

[131] Interviews: 'Mannai' P. Narayanaswami, P. Venkatesa Solagar (Mannargudi); 'Sithamalli' Somasundaram (Nidamangalam); K. Murugaiyan (Thanjavur); A. K. Subbiah (Perugavazhndan-Sithamalli).

[132] Kombur Venkatesan functioned as the representative of his landlord Moolangudi Gopalakrishna Iyer, and Gomathi Shankara Dikshithar of the Gandhian Brahmin-Vellala landlord/professional faction in Kallidaikurichi and Ambasamudram. Neither could oppose the local élites they represented. Interviews: Kombur Venkatesan, Kakkaji (Mannargudi); A. N. Sivaraman, C. Harihara Subramania Iyer (Madras); S. Thangam Pillai, S. Ananthanarayanan (Kallidaikurichi).

[133] Interviews: K. A. Vasimalai, P. V. Das (Dindigul); Aru. Shankar, V. Ramanibai, Ganesan, Ananthakrishnan, Mayakrishnan (Madras).

[134] Interviews: Samadharmam, K. Angusami, Abdul Samad (Dindigul).

the traders P. A. K. Palaniswami Nadar and 'Lotus' Ramaswami in Royapuram; the sons of mercantile families, 'Mannai' P. Narayanaswami Ontharayar and Ku. Balakrishnan in Mannargudi; the bazaar merchants Pa. U. Shanmugam, Pa. U. Thyagarajan and Era. Dharmalingam in Tiruvannamalai; the restaurant owner Velayudhan and the cotton merchant O. N. Sivagnanam in Dindigul; a small landlord and rice mill owner Dhanakoti Gounder in Tanipadi, and the traders M. S. Sivaswami and R. S. Thangapazham in Tuticorin.[135] Such individuals gained greater social eminence through their role in the DMK's social networks. The poorer individuals who also helped build the early DMK hoped to use their role in these networks, more significant than that of their social equals in Congress, to attain some dignity and wealth. Once the DMK assumed power, patronage was routed through the wealthier and some of the poorer local leaders.

Regional Variations in Partisanship

Tamil Nadu, like most of India, had a system of one-party dominance with shallow participation and a fragmented political opposition through the first post-colonial decade. The Tamil party system became bipolar by 1962 (and has remained so since then—see Table 1.6) because Congress consolidated its support, the communists and the socialists declined and the DMK became the focus of opposition to Congress.[136] While Congress consolidated its support in much of India through the 1950s, the communists and the socialists declined in many states, and a single party became the focus of opposition to Congress earliest in Tamil Nadu.

The DMK grew most rapidly in the northern plains, where it won 14 of its 15 assembly seats in 1957 and 38 of its 50 seats in 1962 (see Tables 1.3A). In the already intensely mobilized Kaveri valley, its electoral growth was more gradual (1 seat in 1957; and

[135] Interviews: P. A. K. Palaniswami, 'Lotus' Ramaswami, P. U. Shanmugam (Madras); B. Neelakantan (Tiruvannamalai); 'Mannai' P. Narayanaswami, Ku. Balakrishnan (Mannargudi); G. Anguswami, Samadharmam, O. N. Sivagnanam (Dindigul); Dhanakoti Gounder (Tanipadi); M. S. Sivaswami (Tuticorin).

[136] Bipolarity arose in West Bengal and Kerala too in the early 1960s due to communist growth and has existed since independence in Punjab and Jammu & Kashmir, where ethnic parties have been Congress's main opponents. It made party competition fiercer, enhancing voter participation everywhere except Jammu & Kashmir (which has had few free elections).

5 in 1962), but its subculture was particularly cohesive (as were those of other parties). So, DMK support proved more durable there than in the north when the party's fortunes declined in the mid-1970s. The party's organization was also strongest in the north and the Kaveri valley.[137] The DMK achieved limited success in the western and southern plains and the Tamiraparani valley until the mid-1960s, winning merely 7 seats in 1962 in these regions which account for 43 per cent of the state's electorate and legislative assembly seats. None of the DMK's victories of 1962 were in the western plains, the Tamiraparani valley or the deep south, which contribute 33 per cent of the seats. The party's share of the popular vote ranged from a high of 35.56 per cent in the northern plains to a low of 8.24 per cent in the deep south.

Communist support was spread even more unevenly by 1962. It was virtually non-existent in the north (2.05 per cent of the popular vote) and insignificant in the southern plains (9.13 per cent). But, the CPI was an important force in parts of the Kaveri valley, western plains and Tamiraparani valley (where it polled 15.17 per cent, 15.24 per cent and 10.09 per cent of the vote respectively). In the Tamiraparani valley, west and deep south where the DMK was weakest, the CPI fared no worse than the DMK until 1962 in the constituencies it contested and had stronger party units. The CPI was weakest where the DMK was strongest (the north), but both parties were strong in the Kaveri valley.

Congress consolidated its strength through the 1950s by reabsorbing small parties which had split from it around 1947, incorporating caste parties which had emerged after independence, and attracting some new voters. It retained its core support in all areas, especially in its early bases in the valleys and the west, and built further support mainly in the southern and western plains, where the DMK was still weak. It remained weakest in the northern plains, its weak spot even before the DMK entered the electoral fray.

The DMK, Caste Solidarity and Migrants

The regional variations in the DMK's success are related to the DMK's varying interactions with pre-existing caste associations and

---

[137] Party branches seem to have been concentrated in these areas, though precise figures are unavailable. It is also said that major party leaders and orators ventured into the other regions infrequently till the early 1960s.

parties. Two Vanniar parties, the Commonweal Party and the Tamil Nadu Toilers' Party, won 25 seats among them in the 1952 elections as Vanniar caste associations had been strong for some decades and party mobilization weak in their ambit, the northern plains.[138] The Forward Bloc, which became a caste party of the Mukkulathor in Tamil Nadu, enjoyed considerable support in areas of Mukkulathor concentration in the southern plains and the Tamiraparani valley in the 1950s and early 1960s.[139]

The prior solidarity of the Vanniars and Mukkulathor proved an obstacle to the DMK where these castes were numerous. In the north, one of the Vanniar parties merged with Congress; while the other, allied with Congress from 1952 to 1959, joined Swatantra upon its formation.[140] These parties enjoyed the support of most Vanniar notables, with whose influence the DMK had to contend. The DMK was successful in the north because it incorporated many Vanniars into its cross-caste social networks, weaning them away from their ties to the notables. While it won over some caste leaders who had been in the Vanniar parties, notably A. Govindaswami, its success was not based primarily on their social influence. The party did not emphasize appeals to particular castes in this area. For instance, seven of the eleven DMK candidates who won in 1957 in areas with large Vanniar populations were not Vanniars. The DMK's attempts to emphasize Vanniar solidarity backfired in Tiruvannamalai in 1962 as it alienated other castes, and the party avoided such an approach thereafter.[141]

[138] Singh & Bose (1988: 45); Interviews: M. P. Subramaniam, K. Ramdas, 'Panruti' S. Ramachandran (Madras); N. C. Ramaswami Gounder (Tandrambattu); Dhanakoti Gounder (Tanipadi); Venugopal Gounder (Tiruvannamalai).

[139] While a faction of the Forward Bloc in Tamil Nadu, with members from different castes, rejoined Congress after doing poorly in the 1952 elections, the other faction was shaped by its charismatic leader, 'Pasumpon' U. Muthuramalinga Thevar, into a caste party. Interviews: K. Nagaimugan, Dr. T. Kannan (Madras).

[140] The Tamil Nadu Toilers' Party later reverted to independent existence without regaining the significance it had in the 1950s.

[141] The DMK leaders and activists were conscious of following such a 'non-casteist' strategy in the Vanniar belt. TH, 2 March 1962; NN, 25 December 1956; Interviews: M. P. Subramaniam, P. U. Shanmugam, 'Pulavar' Govindan,

The DMK tried to compensate for its organizational weakness in the south by appealing to Mukkulathor caste sentiments. To this end, it refrained from taking a position on Tamil Nadu's biggest caste riots of this period, in which many Mukkulathor attacked SCs in large numbers (in 1958) and in which Forward Bloc leaders were implicated.[142] These clumsy manoeuvres did not gain the DMK a significant foothold until later among the Mukkulathor, most of whom remained closely linked to the Forward Bloc, whose leader was averse to the DMK's separatism and critique of religious orthodoxy. The DMK contested in only a few constituencies with high Mukkulathor concentrations in 1957 and remained relatively weak there even in its heyday (1967–72). Although it gained some Mukkulathor support from the 1960s, once the Forward Bloc declined, it thereby alienated other castes in the south. This solidified the alignment of Nadars and SCs in the area, initially behind Congress and later behind the ADMK. Besides, the DMK's use of the caste card was one of the reasons for the party being less cohesive in the south.[143]

Rudolph (1961) identified deracinated migrants as the primary cadre and supporters of the DMK in the northern plains, especially Madras city, in a variant of the view of the atomized individual

---

Era. Sezhiyan, 'Senji' N. Ramachandran, 'Veerapandi' S. Arumugam, N. M. Mani Varma (Madras); S. Murugaiyan, N. Venkatachalam, K. Neelakantan, Venugopal Gounder (Tiruvannamalai).

[142] Annadurai admitted that the party stooped to casteism in Ramanathapuram district, in the Mukkulathor heartland (TH, 2 March 1962). The riots are discussed in TH, 16, 19, 21, 22, 23, 25, 26, 27 September; 1, 2, 4, 5, 6, 8, 12, 13, 14, 27, 29, 30, 31 October; 1, 2, 25 November; 18, 19 December 1957; 13 February 1958; *Mudukulathur Bayangaram* (n.d.).

The state government cracked down on the Mukkulathor after the riots and declared a state of emergency in the area where riots occurred, and the police shot some alleged aggressors dead. While the DMK's SC leader Sathyavani Muthu condemned the riots in the state assembly (TH, 29, 30 October 1957), other party leaders abstained from the vote on the issue. TH, 31 October, 2 November 1957; 13 February 1958; Interview: Sathyavni Muthu (Madras).

[143] Interviews: S. S. Thennarasu, Vai. Gopalswami, K. Nagaimugan, P. H. Pandian (Madras); 'Pathamadai' Paramasivam (Pathamadai); M. S. Sivaswami (Tuticorin); K. Ilamathi, Karuppuswami Pandian, 'Nellai' Buhari, Azhagiya Nambi (Tirunelveli); K. S. Subramaniam (Kallidaikurichi).

as populism's typical adherent. Links between migrants and populism were drawn most elaborately, and refuted most convincingly, regarding early Peronism.[144] Atomized migrants were not significant among the DMK's early supporters. Seasonal migratory workers, who have the least effective social links, were quite insignificant to the DMK's growth. The migrants who were important among the early DMK cadre and supporters belonged to groups which migrated with a range of kinsfolk from their areas of origin. Such a migration strategy helped them establish effective socio-economic ties in their new areas of residence, where they became politically active.[145]

Migration has contributed significantly to population growth in Madras city through this century.[146] Royapuram reflects the history of the city, built by the British in an area formerly occupied by fishing villages. About half of the constituency (Royapuram and Kasimedu), consists of urbanized fishing settlements, whose migrant population is small. The other half, Washermanpet, part of the 'Black Town' of the seventeenth and eighteenth centuries which provided British inhabitants services, has attracted many migrants, as have more recently urbanized areas further north.[147] A caste/occupational association of the locally rooted fishermen, formed in the 1940s, became closely associated with the DMK, though a rival association later supported Congress. So, the DMK acquired considerable support among the fisherman caste which provided some important local party leaders, like N. Jeevarathinam, a harbour worker who became the Deputy Mayor of Madras in 1959, as well as the storm-troopers who provided protection for the party headquarters located in the area.[148] In recognition of this,

[144] Kenworthy (1973), Schoultz (1983: 43–95) and Madsen and Snow (1991) effectively refuted Germani's (1978: 160–97) thesis that migrants were an important source of support for Peron from 1946 to 1955.

[145] Many migrant groups in India maintain strong social bonds and retain significant social efficacy. This was true of the majority of migrants to Madras city in the 1950s and 1960s, when the city industrialized rapidly and saw quick DMK growth. More of the later migrants settled into less secure niches, though even they often retained wide social links. See Nagaraj and Majumdar (1983); TH, 8 March 1983.

[146] Nagaraj & Majumdar (1983).

[147] See Census of India (1951, 1961, 1981), Madras District Handbooks.

[148] The 'fierceness' of the local fishermen is said to have been a reason for locating the party office there. Jeevarathinam later shifted to Congress, but

the DMK has always chosen its local candidate for the state legislative assembly from the fisherman caste.

The Nadar traders, who migrated to Royapuram from Ramanathapuram district from about the 1920s onwards, were the DMK's other major local supporters. They tapped their kin links in the area in their professional and political activities and were among the local party's early benefactors—e.g., P. A. K. Palaniswami Nadar, 'Lotus' Ramaswami and Ganesan, the publisher of the magazine *Thenral*.[149]

Tiruvannamalai, another early DMK stronghold in the northern plains, is a small commercial town which has attracted migrants only from its immediate vicinity and has grown slowly. The DMK's early cadre and support came primarily from the local shopkeepers, mostly Udayars and Muslims rooted in the town; and from the smaller peasants in the vicinity, mainly from the Vanniar and Udayar castes. Immigration was even more limited and migrants similarly unimportant to DMK growth in the Mannargudi area, where the DMK had achieved moderate success by the early 1960s.

The early DK and DMK did rely heavily on migrants in Dindigul, in the southern plains. Two migrant trader groups, Nadars from Tirumangalam town and its vicinity and Chettiars from the nearby village of Kalvarpatti, provided some of the early DK and DMK leaders in the area, and were among the few DMK supporters in the 1950s. The party's roots among these migrants impeded its spread, which did not become considerable until the DMK took power in the state. Thus, excessive reliance on migrants was a recipe for failure, as was a strong emphasis on appeals to particular castes.

Communist Decline: A Closer Look

The communists built their support in the valleys through agitations from the mid-1940s to the mid-1950s, which led to legislation that ended agrarian slavery, provided greater security of tenure to the tenants who were better off, and increased agricultural wages. As a result, many former bonded serfs and tenants became landless

---

failed to take many supporters with him. Interviews: Sathyavani Muthu, Velur Narayanan, 'Kathadi' Kuppuswami, N. Vedachalam (Madras).

[149] Interviews: P. A. K. Palaniswami, 'Lotus' Ramaswami, Ganesan (Madras).

agricultural workers and others became small farmers.[150] Communist support declined among the small farmer class, largely BC, that had emerged in the aftermath of the agitations as the CPI primarily raised the demands of landless workers and insecure tenants, and became closely identified with the SCs in the Kaveri valley, where the party was strongest. Most defectors from the communist coalition gravitated towards the DMK from the late 1950s, and their ranks increased after the DMK assumed power and passed legislation favouring tenants and sub-tenants. By 1962, the DMK had won over many former communist supporters in the larger villages of south-western and northern Mannargudi taluk, which have a higher proportion of secure tenants and the BCs; while it had hardly dented communist dominance in eastern Mannargudi taluk, with a higher proportion of SCs and landless workers.[151]

Communist support declined more rapidly in industrial centres from the mid-1950s onwards, especially in the northern plains where the DMK grew most rapidly. This happened in north Madras, Salem and the smaller industrial towns of North and South Arcot districts. On the contrary, the CPI retained significant support in industrial areas in the west and south (Coimbatore, Tiruchi, Madurai, Dindigul, Ramanathapuram, Tuticorin, Kovilpatti

[150] By 'small farmers', I refer to both freeholders and tenants enjoying secure tenure over sizeable plots of land, who could produce viably for the market, unlike tenants leasing smaller plots on more insecure terms. See Bouton (1985: 183–201), Veerayyan (1980) and Iyer & Vidyasagar (1986).

[151] The share of the SCs and landless workers in the total population is greatest in eastern Mannargudi taluk, less in the south-west and least in the north of the taluk. The DMK gained much of its meagre vote in 1957 (13 per cent) and established its earlier rural party branches in the taluk in villages in the north and south-west (Ullikottai, Paravakottai, Koilvenni, Vaduvur, Nidamangalam, Kuthanallur, Idamelayur and Idakeelayur). The defections from the communists to the DMK increased in the constituency in these areas by 1962, when the DMK relegated the CPI to third place (gaining 26.6 per cent of the vote, while the CPI got 21.5 per cent). Such shifts in these and smaller neighbouring villages like Vadapathimangalam, Vadapathi and Talayamangalam increased after the DMK assumed power. Singh & Bose (1988: 488); Bouton (1985: 201–6); Interviews: K. Murugayyan (Thanjavur), G. Veerayyan (Tiruvarur), A. K. Subbiah (Sithamalli), P. Venkatesa Solagar, P. Thangavelu, N. Govindarajan, 'Ullikottai' Arunachalam (Mannargudi), Soma. Tamilarvan (Nidamangalam).

and Vikramasingapuram), where the DMK remained weak. This further indicates the link between the DMK's growth and the CPI's decline.[152]

The CPI formed the strongest unions in many factories in north Madras through the 1940s, and used these unions as bases from which to build support in poorer residential areas. This was true of the harbour, where many residents of Royapuram work. Along with the formation of party-affiliated associations (*manrams*) in the area through the 1940s, this helped the CPI gain considerable support in Royapuram, where union activists spearheaded the party's successful election campaign of 1952. The AITUC union began to decline in the harbour after a major strike in 1953; and union activists, deterred by repression, became less active in the neighbourhood. This led to a rapid decline in the communist share of the vote in the constituency, from 33.2 per cent in 1952 to 17.6 per cent in 1957 and 14.8 per cent in 1962.[153]

The tendency of some communist union members to vote for other parties was reinforced by the focus of communist organizers on the workplace rather than on residential areas, where many of the DMK's public meetings, debates and plays were staged. While some of the early DK and DMK activists in Royapuram were recruited through the formation of a small union in the harbour by a Justice Party notable, many harbour workers who were DMK activists remained passive members of the AITUC union. However, some of these very workers played major roles in neighbourhood politics. The harbour workers N. Jeevarathinam and 'Kathadi' Kuppuswami led the influential caste association of the locally numerous fishermen; while the SC casual labourer V. S. Anandan actively represented local demands in the Madras Municipal Corporation from the late 1950s, thereby gaining local

---

[152] While the CPI gained between 10 per cent and 35 per cent of the vote in six constituencies in northern industrial areas in 1952 (Washermanpet (Royapuram), Choolai, Perambur, Vellore, Salem and Krishnagiri), by 1962 it could do so only in four (Washermanpet, Gudiyatham, Vellore and Salem II), in all of which its vote share declined. Singh & Bose (1988: 449–61, 472–83).

[153] Singh & Bose (1988: 449, 472); Interviews: A. Srinivasan, 'Nagai' K. Murugesan, V. Ramanibai, 'Russia' Manickam, Manickam, S. C. C. Anthony Pillai (Madras).

influence.[154] Further, the DMK organized party schools in the area for activists, and party leaders frequently visited the locality and addressed meetings because the party headquarters were located there. While Congress maintained its support through this period, the DMK gained support through these activities, its vote share increasing from 28.3 per cent in 1957 to 35.4 per cent in 1962. The CPI candidate in the constituency in 1957 was a Brahmin, fuelling the DMK's non-Brahminist propaganda and helping the party grow at the CPI's expense.[155]

Semi-industrial and plantation workers, who tend more often than industrial workers to live in the same localities, share kin and caste links and a common way of life, remained loyal to the CPI much longer. Party leaders and activists forged close links with such workers and their families, in the tanneries of Dindigul and parts of North Arcot, and on the plantations of Valparai, in stark contrast with their declining presence in everyday life in Royapuram. Most tannery workers and municipal scavengers, among whom communist unions were formed in Dindigul from the late 1940s, were SC Christians and lived in secluded neighbourhoods close to their workplaces. Party leaders shared the workers' coarse food, such as millets and cattle innards, thus overcoming caste barriers. The concentration of worker residences meant that the workers' families shared the repression unleashed on the party and workers during major strikes. These experiences built strong loyalties to the party, which endured through this period and beyond, despite layoffs in the tanneries and a gradual decline in union membership.[156]

PROFILES OF PARTISANSHIP AND
PATTERNS OF CONTENTION

While the DMK's assertive populist character accounts for the groups amongst which the party found greatest support, regionally

[154] Interviews: 'Kathadi' Kuppuswami, V. S. Anandan, Ananthakishnan (Madras).

[155] Singh & Bose (1988: 472); Interviews: N. Vedachalam, P. A K. Palaniswami Nadar, S. V. Sargunam, Nagai K. Murugesan, Manickam (Madras).

[156] Communists continued to dominate the wards where tannery workers and scavengers are concentrated in elections of the 1950s and 1960s. Interviews: V. Madanagopal, S. A. Thangarajan, Charles, A. Chinnaswami, C. K. C. M. Dulkarnine, V. Karuppiah (Dindigul).

varying patterns of contention explain the restriction of DMK's early growth, mainly to the northern plains and the Kaveri valley.

Chapter I indicated the close correlation between ecotype and social structure—the valleys are socially polarized and exhibit considerable overlap between caste and class; while the plains have a less rigid social hierarchy, with a larger proportion of groups of intermediate status, and less overlap between caste and class. Social structure does not predict the geographical spread of DMK support as the DMK was strong in some plains areas (north) and not others (south and west); and in one valley region (Kaveri), but not the other (Tamiraparani). However, it did influence the extent of support in areas where the DMK did strike root—greater in the northern plains, with a high BC and intermediate class population; and lower in the Kaveri valley, with a smaller middle rung in the social hierarchy. It also shaped the social meaning Dravidianism acquired—while it asserted BC autonomy/dominance[157] in the plains, it was more of a voice for the emancipation of subordinate groups in the valleys. The interactions between social structure, prior solidarity and ongoing party competition (the 'social matrix of contention') crucially influenced the profiles of partisanship.

The Plains

Among the plains, broad Congress subcultures had developed before independence in parts of the west (Coimbatore district) and the south (Tirunelveli district) through vigorous anti-colonial agitations. These subcultures included some BC groups that might have otherwise felt an affinity with the DMK. The Kongu Vellalas and Naidus were the dominant groups in agriculture and industry in the west, and largely continued to support Congress.[158] Mobilization by other parties in the western plains was rendered difficult by the social dominance and numerical preponderance of these groups. Only the communists were effective in the industrial belt around Coimbatore city due to their involvement in trade unions. Congress remained dominant elsewhere in the west through the 1950s and 1960s, relying on prior party loyalties and bureaucratic clientelist links. The DMK was weakest and voter participation increased the least in the west during this period.

[157] Autonomy in relation to upper castes; and sometimes, dominance over the SCs.

[158] Arnold (1974).

Even in the less politically active regions in the south (Ramanathapuram district), a strong tendency towards recruitment along caste lines had developed among the three major caste clusters (the Mukkulathor, Nadars and SCs). By the 1940s, this tendency primarily favoured Congress which was the only party significantly active in the area. The tendency towards caste cohesion in politics continued after independence. The major Mukkulathor leader of the period, U. Muthuramalinga Thevar was outmanoeuvred by Kamaraj and left Congress to head the Forward Bloc, which attracted much Mukkulathor support in Ramanathapuram and Madurai districts until the early 1960s. Nadar support for Congress increased even in regions where it was formerly shallow as Kamaraj became the Tamil Congress leader and the Chief Minister.[159]

The situation of the Mukkulathor and the Nadars was conducive to Dravidianist appeals. The Nadar were traditionally toddy-tappers and peasants of low ritual status, much like the barbers (Maruthuvar) and temple servants (Isai Vellalar) who were drawn towards the DK and the DMK as vehicles for emancipation in the Kaveri valley.[160] Some of them had the resources to assert a higher status, having prospered through commerce. The Mukkulathor, a group of warrior/marauder/peasant castes, had exercised domi-nance through repression. Their relative status declined during the colonial period as the British deemed them a 'criminal tribe' and subjected them to close police supervision; and because some of the Nadars, their former social inferiors, had gained in wealth. Thus, in different ways, the Nadars and Mukkulathor had the kind

[159] The 'southern Nadars', inhabiting much of Tirunelveli district, were generally poorer peasants and toddy-tappers and mostly supported Congress before independence. The 'northern Nadars', concentrated in the region spanning much of Ramanathapuram district, southern Madurai district and northern Tirunelveli district, grew more affluent through the nineteenth century. The latter group largely switched from the Justice Party to Congress in the 1940s and 1950s. See Hardgrave (1969) and Arnod (1977, 1988).

[160] These castes occupied the rung just above the SCs. They were not subjected to as much residential seclusion and ritual exclusion as the SCs were, but many forms of dress and behaviour indicative of higher status were denied them—Nadar women, for instance, were required to be bare bodied. They were included among the 'most backward castes' in lists compiled by the state government in 1957 and 1989.

of grievances about varnashrama dharma as embodied in colonial legality that non-Brahminism addressed. While the Nadars largely sought answers within Congress, the Mukkulathor chose to assert caste pride under the leadership of Muthuramalinga Thevar. This left the DMK unable to build effective local networks, and the party's superficial efforts to play the caste game popular in the politics of the region bore no fruit.

Congress enjoyed narrower support in the northern plains before independence, much of it by virtue of traditional clientelist links. Nationalist agitation was restricted to a few Reddiar landlords, town notables and their dependents in Tiruvannamalai.[161] Agitators in Royapuram, such as the militant Kamma Naidu physician, Dr. T. Kannan, became isolated from local politics after independence, and left Congress soon thereafter.[162] The region benefited from the location of many industries and dams, and a major expansion in well irrigation after independence. Industries sprung up during the second and third Five Year Plans in Madras, Salem and around North Arcot; and by the 1970s, North Arcot became the district with the greatest density of wells in India outside the fertile Punjab. But, Congress did not bolster such economic development by building a cohesive subculture or through effective caste appeals. It did try to appeal to the Vanniars, numerous in the area, by absorbing their two caste parties and offering its leaders important positions in the government. But, the Vanniar parties had not built strong social networks or become the focus of caste solidarity, as the Forward Bloc had in the south. The communists did not grow beyond the factories, and declined even there, as discussed earlier. This gave the DMK greater scope to mobilize. Thus, the patterns of prior and ongoing mobilization helped DMK growth in the northern plains, but hindered it in the south and west despite significant similarities in the social structure of these regions.

The Valleys

The Kaveri and Tamiraparani valleys have somewhat similarly polarized societies, with Brahmins enjoying great social and

[161] Interviews: Sivarama Reddiar, T. S. Tirunavukkarasu, Ghaffar, Natesa Pillai (Tiruvannamalai); Venkatachalapathi Chettiar (Tanipadi).

[162] Interviews: Dr. T. Kannan, S. C. C. Anthony Pillai (Madras).

economic power. The caste-class overlap is greater at the top of the social spectrum in the Tamiraparani valley—only the Brahmin and Vellala upper castes have had a long history of substantial landholding. The overlap is greater at the bottom of the spectrum in the Kaveri valley—the majority of landless, once bonded, agricultural workers being SCs. The social structure of both valleys was conducive to an emancipatory interpretation of Dravidianism. This was especially so in the Tamiraparani valley, where the bottom rungs of society contained a more even mix of the SCs and BCs, as Dravidianism took both the BCs and the SCs to be oppressed by Brahminism. Yet, the emancipatory appropriation of Dravidianism emerged only in the Kaveri valley.

Congress was led by the dominant landed classes in both valleys. This meant greater upper caste dominance in the party leadership in the Tamiraparani valley, where landlords were drawn more exclusively from the upper castes. Yet, the party's subculture reached deeper in the Tamiraparani valley than it did in the Kaveri region before independence. It extended to the intermediate strata in the towns and some villages of the Kaveri valley, but activists from these groups mostly acted according to the dictates of the party leadership. In the Tamiraparani valley, the non-Gandhian, especially socialist, factions of the party were strong and independent of the leadership. They mobilized lower status groups, mainly Nadars, more directly through agitations against colonialism and in pursuit of their economic interests. Despite recurrent tensions between the socialists and the Congress mainstream, the socialists remained identified with the Congress subculture.

The CPI gained support primarily among SC bonded workers and tenants before independence in the Kaveri valley. But, its base included more BCs (mainly Mukkulathor) in the Tamiraparani valley. This was facilitated by the lower degree of caste-class overlap at the bottom of society in the Tamiraparani valley. The differences in the nature of the support enjoyed by Congress and the CPI in the two valleys meant that the Dravidianists had a ready niche available among the BCs of intermediate status in the Kaveri valley, but not to the same extent in the Tamiraparani valley. The DK moved to occupy this niche in parts of the Kaveri valley, while it hardly struck root in the Tamiraparani valley before independence. Thus, the interaction of prior solidarity with social structure defined the social space readily available for Dravidianism, and influenced the extent of its early success.

As the levels of political mobilization were higher in the valleys, the partisan subcultures which emerged prior to independence shaped later mobilization more strongly here than it did in the plains. The contrasts in the social bases of the different parties in the two valleys became more stark over time in many respects. The decline in land concentration and agrestic bondage, spurred by agitation and legislation, broadened the class gap between the BCs and the SCs in the Kaveri valley. Until the 1940s, some BC temple servants and tenants shared many aspects of the bondage of the SC manorial serfs/slaves (*pannaiyaatkal*)—obligatory labour, restrictions on mobility and consumption, and subjection to repression.[163] The decline of landlordism led to the growth of a significant small peasantry, mainly among the BCs, while most SCs became landless workers. Concurrently, and partly as a result, the CPI became more exclusively identified with the SCs.

As the extent of land concentration and bondage had been less in the Tamiraparani valley than in the Kaveri valley, the changes wrought by their decline were less dramatic there. Both SCs and BCs were to be found among the landless as well as the newly landed (tenant or owner farmers) from the 1950s in the Tamiraparani valley. Unlike in the Kaveri valley, the CPI retained significant support in this region among the BCs based on its union activities among agricultural tenants and landless agricultural workers, and in the textile mill of Vikramasingapuram.

The socialists split from Congress in 1948 and used the greater independence they thus gained to deepen their support among peasants and artisans in the Tamiraparani valley through a series of agitations. As socialist support declined throughout India and Congress veered closer to socialism, the majority of Tamil Nadu's socialists returned to Congress in 1954. Their close prior identification with the Congress subculture enabled them to bring their supporters back with them into the Congress fold. This consolidated Congress support among the lower and intermediate strata.

---

[163] In some cases, the same term was used to refer to the bonded condition of some BC and SC groups—*adimaik kudikal* (slave clans). See Dharma Kumar (1965) and Bouton (1985).

The prior strength of the Congress and communist subcultures, and their consolidation in the 1950s, continued to marginalize Dravidianism in the Tamiraparani valley.

In contrast with the situation in the Tamiraparani valley, the narrowed identifications of Congress (with landlords) and the communists (with the SCs) in the Kaveri valley expanded the niche available to the Dravidianists.[164] Despite the bitter opposition from the DK, the DMK gained a significant base among the BC peasantry in the Kaveri valley. Some BC peasants who had been propelled towards Congress by the DK's heresies found the DMK a better alternative by the early 1960s, helping the DMK become the second strongest force in the Kaveri valley, as in the northern plains.

Although BCs of small property had the closest affinity with assertive Dravidianism, affinities between ideology and caste clusters did not solely shape the DMK's initial support. Populist ideology and methods of mobilization interacted with the matrix of contention to produce variations in partisanship and in the social meaning attached to the DMK. So, the DMK still attracted only 27.1 per cent of the popular vote in 1962, though the BCs and the intermediate classes have accounted for the majority of the Tamil population through the century.[165] However, the party had taken rapid strides towards its aim of representing plebeian Tamil society, and attained this goal in 1967. The path it took to the fortress exercised a durable influence on its social base and popular image.

[164] Both Congress and the CPI had support extending beyond the landlord and SC groups respectively. But, these groups placed their stamp on the respective local parties, which were popularly viewed in those terms.

[165] Singh & Bose (1988: 45).

V

Assertive Populism and State Power: The Period of DMK Dominance, 1964–76

(Thi. Mu. Ka. oru) naankaam thara katchi thaan—
Naankaam thara makkalin katchi.
(The DMK is indeed a 'fourth rate' party—
A party of people of the fourth rank [the Shudras])
— M. Karunanidhi, second leader of the DMK

Assertive populism helped the DMK build a broad enough coalition, dominated by the intermediate strata, to become Congress's major challenger by the early 1960s. But, the DMK had reached the limits of its purely assertive populist project by then. It altered its appeals over the next decade, enabling it to gain control over the state government in 1967 and retain power for almost a decade.

The DMK added a significant paternalist touch to its primarily assertive populist appeals from about the early 1960s to the early 1970s. It also toned down its ethnic militancy, especially after it assumed power, in moves congruous with its paternalist turn. Not only did party leaders make public a decision they had earlier made in private to abandon the goal of secession, they moved from initiating language agitations to restraining them. These changes helped the party gain support among groups and in regions which had been only peripherally touched by the early assertive populist wave. The DMK regime focused on fulfilling some long-lasting assertive Dravidianist demands in its early years, in keeping with the emphasis of the party's appeals at all times, but also addressed some of the party's recent paternalist promises through its first few years.

Although the DMK did not press its demands regarding national language policy and state autonomy strongly, it moved to reshape public culture in the image of a putative Tamil cultural logic upon assuming power. The slogan '*yengum Tamizh; yethilum Tamizh*' (Tamil everywhere and in everything) inspired attempts to change language policy within the state and more lasting changes in the idiom of official ritual. Along with the increased distribution of patronage to the intermediate strata, the adoption of a plebeian official idiom helped the DMK regime present itself as the plebeian republic of early Dravidianist promise and maintain the loyalty of early supporters.

Autonomous supporters put pressure on the DMK regime to address expectations raised by its promises. The regime did so through increases in the quotas for intermediate castes in education and government employment, an expansion of the range of castes eligible for these quotas, rapid growth in well irrigation, the extension of agricultural loans (particularly to supporters) and minor land reforms. Supporters and others challenged the regime through farmers' associations, and forced concessions regarding the repayment of agricultural loans and the terms of trade between agriculture and industry. While the regime attempted to repress militant trade unions and bring industrial workers under state tutelage, its successes in this respect were limited by the prior strength of non-Dravidianist trade unions and the DMK's belated entry into the trade union field.

The DMK retreated from its relatively brief paternalist gambit to its assertive core from the early 1970s, reemphasizing its demands for state autonomy without reverting to separatism. This shift was closely associated with the formation of the ADMK, which effectively laid claim to the paternalist aspects of Dravidian populism. While the DMK's retreat to assertive populism precipitated the split within the party, the ADMK's challenge urged the parent party to further highlight its assertive character and raise strident nativist appeals. The DMK's shifts, the ADMK's emergence and the repression of ADMK activists made the DMK lose considerable support through the mid-1970s, much of it to the ADMK. While the ADMK gained the initiative thereafter, the emphasis the DMK laid on the assertive strand of the populist project helped it retain its core early support.

The DMK's populist clientelism ensured that it remained the most popular party as long as bureaucratic clientelist pan-Indian parties were its primary opponents. However, the impression grew that many of the regime's assertive populist policies, such as increases in caste quotas, land reforms and easier availability of government loans primarily benefited rising groups, and that too primarily party loyalists. Rice rationing and dry laws, introduced by the early DMK regime, were abandoned later. The visible growth of corruption among party activists seemed a further departure from the party's paternalist promise. The Dravidianist critique of the aloof bureaucratic state began to lose its relevance to the lower strata who gained little from assertive populist clientelism. Yet, the DMK lost support only when another populist party emerged to highlight its betrayal of its paternalist promises and appropriated Dravidianism's paternalist aspects. The ADMK did so very effectively due to the prior paternalist image associated with its leader, MGR.

As appeals against ethnic out-groups were not central to the initial success of the DMK, nativist appeals failed to reinforce the party's base in the face of the ADMK's challenge. The attempts of DMK leaders to gain from highlighting MGR's non-Tamil origins backfired as MGR's status as an immensely popular film star made him a Tamil cultural hero in the public eye.

THE DECLINE OF CONGRESS POWER, 1964–7

Two economic trends, caused by factors lying mainly outside Tamil Nadu, adversely affected Congress's fortunes in the state. Industrial growth declined gradually after 1960 in Tamil Nadu as some basic industries had already been established, the state's capacity for hydel power generation had already been exploited almost to the fullest, and the priorities of the national government shifted to other states.[1] A crisis in food production and distribution which hit India from 1964 to 1967 was particularly grave in Tamil Nadu, affecting even Thanjavur district, the state's rice bowl.[2] The DMK's discourse was especially conducive to addressing the grievances arising from these trends. Many could make sense of the problems they faced in light of the party's claims that the Nehruvian economic strategy was irrelevant to the needs of the middling and lower strata. Further, the DMK responded to this

[1] Tamil Nadu's industrial decline preceded that which beset all of India by a few years, and became more pronounced when the industrial malaise became nation-wide. See MIDS (1988), Frankel (1978).

[2] TH, 28 August, 1 September 1964; 13, 15 December 1966.

conjuncture by promising to reduce the price of rice at ration shops to a little under a tenth of its prevailing price and claimed after assuming power that ministers would work unpaid until this promise was fulfilled.[3] Weakened by two splits through the mid-1960s, the communists were unable to address even economic grievances as effectively at this point. Swatantra's libertarianism could hardly comfort people who hoped for state intervention to ease their plight.

The national government's persistence with its plan to introduce Hindi as the national official language in 1965, despite growing opposition in Tamil Nadu since 1957 and more limited protest in some other non-Hindi-speaking states, also contributed to Congress's electoral decline in Tamil Nadu. While the national government continued to use English in communication with non-Hindi-speaking states, it offered no guarantee that this practice would continue.[4] Some national government departments started issuing circulars solely in Hindi and others required Hindi speakers to use only Hindi for official purposes.[5] These changes and the rejection of proposals to make English an associate language suggested that a complete switch to Hindi would occur soon.[6] The Tamil petty intelligentsia felt it would be placed at a serious competitive disadvantage with its Hindi-speaking counterpart even if those writing recruitment examinations for national government services could use either English or Hindi, but not other Indian languages.[7]

Changes in the state Congress and government also contributed to Congress's electoral decline. Kamaraj relinquished the Chief Minister's post and became the President of the national party in 1964, as part of a plan to revitalize the party organization in response to strong challenges emerging in many regions, including Tamil Nadu. However, the state party and government suffered from the removal of Kamaraj's immediate supervision. M. Bhaktavatsalam, who replaced Kamaraj as the Chief Minister, was unlike his predecessor in many respects—he lacked Kamaraj's

[3] The promise was that three measures of rice would cost a rupee. TH, 10 March 1967; DMK (1967); HT, 28 July 1967.

[4] TH, 7 January 1965.

[5] TH, 21 January; 6, 7 February 1965.

[6] TH, 28 May, 12 September 1962; 15 February, 14 April 1963; 7, 18 January 1965.

[7] TH, 7 January, 2 February 1965.

organizational skill, was from an upper caste (Tondaimandala Vellala) and was known to be corrupt and distrustful of Tamil nationalist opinion. The Tamil Congress's cohesion declined further under his leadership, which symbolized for many Congress's growing distance from the public.

The state government responded to the food crisis by restricting the transport of food grains to help it procure them from farmers for distribution in ration shops at low prices. It imposed these restraints with great severity, harassing even people carrying small amounts of rice for consumption.[8] Nevertheless, many black marketers circumvented the government's levy, rice supplies dwindled and food rationing was close to a breakdown by 1967. The levy on food grains also alienated farmers, who attacked procurement officials in some places.[9] These problems outraged even many Congress sympathizers, especially as less wheat was sent to Tamil Nadu and millets were diverted to other states in the midst of this crisis.[10] The DMK protested the failures in food provision by demonstrating in front of ration shops.

While agreeing that Hindi would eventually be the sole official language of national administration, the state government made the following demands from 1958 to 1963: guarantees of the continued use of English as an official language; the indefinite postponement of a complete shift to Hindi; leaving Hindi instruction optional in non-Hindi-speaking states; and requiring the instruction of another Indian language in Hindi-speaking states.[11] However, Congressmen from Tamil Nadu and Andhra, who primarily pressed for these policy changes, had limited support within the national party and in the parliament. Besides, the Tamil Nadu government gave these demands less importance under Bhaktavatsalam's leadership. Bhaktavatsalam had for long headed the Dakshin Bharat Hindi Prachar Sabha, established under Gandhi's inspiration to promote

[8] TH, 11 February 1967; *Patriot*, 11 March 1967.
[9] TH, 28 August, 1 September 1964; 21 December 1966; IE, 1 March 1967.
[10] TH, 17 November, 13, 21, 23, 24 December 1966; 4 February 1967.
[11] The state government urged that three languages be taught in schools in all states—English, the regional language and another Indian language, not necessarily Hindi. It argued that a reciprocal effort on the part of Hindi speakers to learn another Indian language was required to achieve national integration. TH, 29 December 1957; 4, 7, 17, 18 January 1958; 14 April 1963; 1 December 1964; 1 February 1965.

Hindi competence in South India. Although he demanded the parallel use of English as an official language, the close mental association that he and some other Tamil Congressmen made between Indian nationalism and learning Hindi coloured their response to language demands.[12]

Tamil nationalist feeling grew as the national government remained intransigent regarding the transition to Hindi in 1965. The state government had little effect on national policy and its opposition to the switch to Hindi seemed irresolute to many. Besides, the state government decelerated the introduction of instruction through the medium of Tamil in colleges in 1963, announced that some Hindi instruction would become mandatory in schools by 1964 and opposed efforts to change the state's name from Madras to Tamil Nadu.[13]

Although the DMK had abandoned secession, it maintained that a federal India did not require a single official language; that English could continue to be the medium of communication between states, and between the national and state governments; and so, that Hindi instruction and official communication in Hindi should not be mandated.[14] Swatantra and some other minor parties also proposed the permanent continuation with English as the official language.[15] By the mid-1960s the unconditional opposition to Hindi introduction advocated by these parties was favoured by most Tamils, especially the youth, including many in the Congress subculture.

[12] TH, 23 December 1957; 7 January 1958; 11 January 1965; Interview: C. Subramaniam.

[13] TH, 16 March 1963, 14 April 1963; TI, 3 August 1964.

Madras was the name given to the state's capital city built during colonial rule, and later became the name of the province. As *nadu* connotes country in its modern usage, the name Tamil Nadu has a strong autonomist resonance. The Congress government changed official references to the state in Tamil from 'Madras' to 'Tamil Nadu'; but continued to refer to it as Madras in English, arguing that people in other parts of India were accustomed to this name. The curious situation of the state bearing two names ended only after the DMK assumed power. The capital city similarly bore two names, Madras (in English) and Chennai (in Tamil) from 1967 to 1997.

[14] Annadurai (1963); Maran (1974); TH, 13 February 1958, 3 May 1963, 7 March 1965.

[15] TH, 12, 24 October 1957; 25 February 1965.

Agitations in protest against the switch to Hindi erupted from 1963 onwards. The agitation of 1963–4 was limited to the ceremonial burning of the portions of the Constitution dealing with language policy by DMK activists.[16] However, opposition to Hindi introduction and support for the DMK grew among many not involved in this agitation, especially students. Activists eager to agitate against national language policy gained control over student unions in many of Tamil Nadu's colleges and formed a coordinating body called the Tamil Nadu Students Anti-Hindi Agitation Council.[17] The DMK's call for ceremonial public mourning on 26 January 1965, the date when the switch to Hindi was to occur, evoked a massive response from college and high school students, extending beyond lines of prior partisanship. While the leaders of the student agitation were largely DMK members or sympathizers, they responded more to activist sentiment than to party leaders, who lost control over the agitation's momentum. Agitators hoisted black flags and 'Tamil flags' in many homes and public places, burnt copies of the Constitution and Hindi books, obstructed transport and attacked government offices, and seven activists committed suicide as a mark of protest.[18]

The national and state governments responded with intransigence and repression. The police opened fire on protesters in many locations, killed 66 activists and attacked even peaceful public 'mourning'. Those who burnt the Constitution were disqualified from contesting in local body elections on grounds of 'moral turpitude'. Bhaktavatsalam refused to meet the student leaders to discuss their demands. The repression and intransigence evoked anti-Congress feelings across lines of generation and subculture.[19]

After a fortnight of agitation, Tamil Congressmen felt pressed to respond to some of the demands. The state government demanded a permanent policy of two official languages, Hindi and English, and the two Tamil members of the national cabinet resigned, demanding a constitutional amendment embodying

[16] TH, 15, 21 October, 17 November, 1, 3, 9, 18 December 1963; 9 May, 3 August, 29 October 1964.

[17] Interviews: L. Ganesan, K. Kalimuthu, N. 'Senji' Ramachandran, Durai Murugan, Balasubramaniam, K. Raja Mohammad (Madras).

[18] TH, 10, 21, 23, 25, 26, 27, 30, 31 January; 2, 6, 9, 11, 13, 14, 15 February; 24 March 1965.

[19] TH, 22, 23, 24, 25, 27, 30 January; 1, 2, 15 February 1965.

Nehru's earlier assurance that Hindi instruction would not be mandated in non-Hindi areas until people in these areas were willing to accept this.[20] In the meantime, DMK leaders grew concerned that continued violence would restrict their gains in popularity, and retained sufficient influence over the agitation's major leaders to end the agitation.[21] The Tamil Congress abandoned its opposition to national government policy once the agitation ended, and the two national cabinet members who had resigned resumed their posts without extracting significant concessions.[22]

As the agitation of 1965 ended without a negotiated settlement, language policy remained unsatisfactory to Tamil nationalist opinion. The national government frequently diluted provisions for the continued official use of English, leading to periodic agitations until 1969.[23] The agitations attracted broad support primarily because of popular concerns regarding the impact of language policy on the job prospects of Tamils, although some agitators were moved by less material concerns. Despite the profuse glorification of the Tamil language during these agitations, most students were indifferent to exploratory shifts to instruction through Tamil in colleges, and some actively opposed this policy as education in English was considered more prestigious and improved one's job prospects more.[24] The main concern of the agitators and their

[20] TH, 1, 11, 21 February 1965; Subramaniam (1978); Interview: C. Subramaniam (Madras).

[21] Annadurai's call for an end to the agitation was resented by many agitators and party members, and the student leaders complied only with reluctance. The agitations continued for some days in regions where the DMK had not been strong for long. TH, 6, 9, 11, 13, 14 February; 7, 8, 10, 12, 15, 16, 24 March 1965; TI, 7 March 1965; Statesman, 23 March, 2 July 1965; Interviews: L. Ganesan, K. Kalimuthu (Madras).

[22] TH, 1, 11, 17, 20, 22 February; 23 March; 15, 17, 21 April; 3, 9, 21 June 1965.

[23] TH, 3, 7, 19, 26 July, 6, 11, 18 Agusut 1965; 28 January, 13 April, 29 August, 23, 24 September 1966; 26 January, 5, 6 October, 17, 22, 23, 24 December 1967, 26 February 1968; TI, 2 July 1966; 29 February, 3 March 1968; Statesman, 28 December 1967; Tribune, 24 February 1968; Patriot, 28 January 1969.

[24] TH, 16 March 1963; 13, 14, 19 December 1970; 17 March 1971; TI, 3 August 1964, 29 January 1971; NH, 14 December 1970; IE, 17 December 1970, 20 January 1971; FPJ, 18 January 1971.

supporters was to retain English in education and national government administration; not to shift to Tamil in education within the state. But, the petty intelligentsia also hoped for more job openings within the state.

The language agitations extended across the state, and were strongest in some old Congress strongholds like Madurai, Tirunelveli and Coimbatore (in the southern and western plains and Tamiraparani valley). These agitations and the sentiments they aroused helped DMK growth in these regions, where Congress nevertheless remained stronger than elsewhere. The DMK gained from these agitations even while tempering their tide because the agitators drew their main inspiration from the party's discourse. Besides, most leaders of the agitation joined a new generation of second-rung DMK leaders.[25] However, the Congress regime's failures in food distribution were ultimately more costly than its unpopular positions on language demands.

Language militancy was popular only when it was associated with populism. Thus, Swatantra gained limited support though it opposed Hindi as much as the DMK did in the mid-1960s because its libertarianism was unattractive, its elitism obvious and its organization weak.[26] Other parties supporting the agitations (the state unit of the Muslim League and the Tamil Arasu Kazhagam) were fringe parties. The pan-Indianism of the communists and their wariness of ethnic sentiments made their support for the anti-Hindi agitations half-hearted.

Although the support for Congress had declined, party leaders had lost sufficient touch with public opinion to be overconfident about the 1967 elections, which Kamaraj predicted Congress would win easily. The Speaker of the legislative assembly, S. Chellapandian, showed little concern even in an election year for farmers in his constituency (Sermadevi) who demanded the early release of water for the crops from the Kannadian channel to help them reverse

---

[25] For example, K. Kalimuthu, Pe. Srinivasan, K. Raja Mohammad, L. Ganesan, Durai Murugan, Vai. Gopalswami. The first five were state cabinet ministers through the 1970s and 1980s (the first three joined the ADMK at some point) and Gopalswami became a parliamentarian and later the MDMK's leader.

[26] Vai. Gopalswami, a leader of the agitation, was initially with Swantantra, but quickly saw that the future lay with the DMK.

the poor agricultural trends of the last two years.[27] Both Kamaraj and Chellapandian lost their assembly seats, the former to a leader of the language agitations. Chellapandian polled little in the areas around Gopalsamudram and Melaseval fed by water from the Kannadian channel, as Congress lost power in 1967.

DMK GROWTH AND ITS PROFILE, 1964–7

The major problems the state government faced in the mid-1960s were not only relevant to the DMK's early supporters. The DMK augmented its support outside its core bases from the mid-1960s onwards as its paternalist and ethnic appeals suggested it would address these problems more effectively than Congress had.

Growth Among the Upper Strata

English educated professionals were drawn predominantly from the upper castes until independence. Although the caste profile of this group became more heterogeneous after independence, many from the intermediate castes who were educated in the medium of English began to assume the cultural outlook of upper caste professionals. To attract the professional élite, the DMK moved to alter its image as an opponent of the upper strata. Party leaders placed greater emphasis on some discursive changes initiated with the birth of the party—the focus on language use more than caste as the basis for conceiving the political community and the acceptance of Brahmins as fellows Tamils.[28] Party orators and activists internalized these changes more than they had in the DMK's early years.

These efforts of the DMK were aided by the party's growing association with Swatantra and its Brahmin leader, Rajaji, after Rajaji left Congress and started opposing the introduction of Hindi

[27] Kamaraj boasted during the 1967 election campaign 'paduththukkutte jeyppom' (We'll win lying down). Chellapandian told the farmers who approached him: 'Thanneer en pocketle illai' (The water is not in my pocket). The DMK popularized a response to this statement in the locality: 'Vote enga pocketle illai' (The votes are not in our pockets either). Interviews: S. Chellapandian, P. Azhagiya Nambi (Tirunelveli); S. Thangam Pillai (Kallidaikurichi); D. S. A. Sivaprakasam (Mukkoodal); Thangam Pillai (1975).

[28] See Annadurai (1986b, vol. 11); NN, 2 February, 14 April 1962; 5 May, 13 August 1964; 3 August, 24 October 1967.

as the sole official language in 1957.[29] Although the DMK and Swatantra failed to forge an electoral alliance for the 1962 elections, the two parties avoided direct contests in most constituencies.[30] They grew closer as the tempo of the anti-Hindi agitations increased and Congress's popularity declined, and were electoral allies from 1964 to 1970.[31]

Rajaji used his stature as the state's most respected Brahmin politician to help alter the DMK's image. He argued that the DMK had outgrown the casteism it had inherited from the DK, much as it had abandoned secessionism.[32] He directed these arguments particularly at Brahmins during the 1967 election campaign, reminding them of the DK's tacit alliance with Congress.[33] This helped disarm the suspicions that many from the upper strata had about the DMK.

These changes in the DMK's image led to increased support from the professional and commercial middle classes through the 1960s. The interests of the former group were threatened by the proposed introduction of Hindi as India's sole official language, in resisting which the DMK played a central role. Besides, the food distribution problems affected all but the most affluent by 1966.

Although the DMK had been strong in Tiruvannamalai since the late 1950s, it was able to recruit college educated youth and win municipal council seats in middle class wards only after 1962.[34] While party campaigners had been chased away from many middle class homes during the 1957 elections in areas of DMK weakness

[29] NN, 12 October, 11, 13 December 1957, 1 September 1958; TH, 12, 24 October 1957, 1, 8 February 1958, 12 September 1962.

[30] TH, 3, 16 February 1962.

[31] NN, 24 January 1958; TH, 1 February 1958, 1 September 1962, 28 February 1966; 5 October, 18 November 1970; *Tribune*, 26 November 1970; FPJ, 30 December 1970.

[32] TH, 16 February, 1 September 1962; 3 February 1967.

[33] Rajaji then advised Brahmins to hold their sacred threads in one hand, say 'Down with Congress; Down with Kamaraj,' and vote for the DMK with the other hand, emphasizing such statements in areas with large Brahmin populations such as Kallidaikurichi and Mylapore. Interviews: K. S. Ramanujam, Dr. Sowrirajan, H. V. Hande (Madras); Thangam Pillai (Kallidaikurichi); D. S. A. Sivaprakasam (Mukkoodal); TH, 9 January 1966.

[34] Interviews: N. Venkatachalam, S. Murugaiyan, Kumaraswamy, Azizullah (Tiruvannamalai).

like Dindigul and Mannargudi town, the party won seats after 1964 in wards comprising the central streets of Mannargudi, largely inhabited by the landed upper castes, and Dindigul's middle class residential localities.[35] Even in the inhospitable Tamiraparani valley, the DMK found increasing support among educated Vellala youth in the small towns of Ambasamudram, Sermadevi, Gopalsamudram and Melaseval.[36]

Dravidianism for the Lower Strata

The DMK also grew through the 1960s among the SCs, lower classes and women mainly due to its increasing adoption of paternalist appeals. It targeted the erosion of standards of living due to inflation, starting with a major agitation protesting inflationary trends in 1962.[37] As rice supplies dwindled through the mid-1960s, the party organized scattered demonstrations in front of ration shops and promised before the 1967 elections to reduce rice prices and extend food rationing beyond urban areas.[38] It also advocated dry laws, favoured by many in Indian society, especially women affected by the expense and domestic violence resulting from male drinking.

A crucial component of the DMK's paternalist turn was the growing popularity of MGR as a movie actor and his increasing political influence (discussed in greater detail in Chapter VI).[39] MGR, who played heroic roles in Tamil films from 1947 until the early 1980s, joined the DMK in 1953 and made his films media of political appeal. He consistently projected an image of a protector of the weak, which assumed reality in the imagination of his growing legion of fans, drawn predominantly from the lower strata and women. While projecting the paternalist aspect of Dravidian populism, MGR's films did not refer much to ethnic themes. So,

[35] Interviews: 'Mannai' P. Narayanaswami, Ku. Balakrishnan, Siva. Rajamanickam, Nadanam (Mannargudi); K. Anguswami, Abdul Samad, Samadharmam, Raju Naidu, Dhanaswami (Dindigul).

[36] Interviews: Shanmugam Pillai (Ambasamudram); K. S. Subramanian (Kallidaikurichi); 'Pathamadai' Paramasivam (Pathamadai); Sivan Pandian (Sermadevi).

[37] TH, 20, 21, 24, 27 July, 17 August 1962; NN, 17–31 July, 1–10 August 1962.

[38] DMK (1967); TH, 10 March 1967.

[39] Also see Dickey (1933a), Pandian (1992).

MGR was not tainted in the popular eye with association with backward caste or Tamil chauvinism, and could appeal to Indian nationalists and many marginal to early Dravidianist discourse— the upper castes, SCs and non-Tamil speakers.

MGR became one of the two most popular actors in Tamil films by about 1954, his popularity as an actor began to translate into political support especially from 1958 (when the first film he directed was released) and he became an important DMK election campaigner from the early 1960s. The MGR fan clubs, which sprang up, promoted MGR's films, helped in DMK election campaigns and became informally affiliated with the party.[40]

MGR's role was crucial to DMK growth among groups and in areas the party's assertive populism had not effectively reached. The decisive nature of his electoral impact was first noticed during the DMK's success in the important 1963 by-election in Tiruvannamalai.[41] In Royapuram, where some of the earliest fan clubs were established, his appeal solidified DMK support among fishermen and increased it among the SCs and Anglo-Indians.[42] In Dindigul, it helped the DMK diminish the control Congress and the communists exercised over Saurashtra speaking weavers and Christian SC municipal sweepers.[43] MGR's electoral impact was especially dramatic in the 1967 elections as he was recovering from a life-threatening injury. The outpouring of sympathy contributed to the highest voter turnout ever recorded in Tamil Nadu (76.6 per cent) and the DMK's first electoral victory.

While assertive populism reduced the influence of traditional clientelist bonds on the voting choices of the intermediate strata in the 1950s and 1960s, the DMK's paternalist turn and MGR's

[40] Interviews: R. M. Veerappan, Madhusoodhanan (Madras); M. Manimaran (Mannargudi); S. S. Mani (Thanjavur); P. Ilamathi, M. M. Mohideen (Tirunelveli); Sivanath Babu (Dindigul); Khaleel Pasha (Tiruvannamalai).

[41] Interviews: P. U. Shanmugam (Madras); E. Va. Velu, Avur Ramalingam, N. Venkatachalam (Tiruvannamalai); V. A. Krishnan, Janardhanam, Vijayakumar (Vettavalam); K. P. Kannan (Kilpennathur).

[42] The growth of support among fishermen was aided by the release of films in which MGR played the roles of a boatman (*Padakotti*—The Boatman) and one who fights for the rights of fishermen (*Meenava Nanban*—Friend of the Fisherman). Interviews: Vannai Mu. Pandian, Madhusoodhanan, N. Vedachalam, Arumugaswami, V. S. Anandan (Madras).

[43] Interviews: Sivanath Babu, Samadharmam, C. Srinivasan, Rangarajan, Charles (Dindigul).

influence played the same role for women and many from the lower strata. Notably, the voting decisions of many women became independent of the judgement of family patriarchs. The growing support of fishermen, SCs and Anglo-Indians moved the DMK from a strong second position in 1957 and 1962 to the first place in 1967 and thereafter in Royapuram. DMK support increased in the SC area of Kilnathur in Tiruvannamalai, enabling the party to contest Congress's hold on town politics.[44] However, the DMK's appeal remained restricted among SCs in southern regions like Sermadevi, where the party was closely associated with the belligerence of some Mukkulathor and in Thanjavur district, where communist influence over the SCs remained strong.[45]

How the DMK Forged a Link with Muslims

The DMK also grew through the 1960s among Muslims, who constitute 5.2 per cent of Tamil Nadu's population. It did not acquire comparable support from Christians who it did not specifically target and claim as significant components of its vision of political community, though they are slightly more numerous (5.8 per cent of the state's population). The DK drew some Muslim support as its criticism of the polytheist and animistic features of Hindu belief and its opposition to idol worship and caste dominance were compatible with Islamic precept; and Periar sometimes urged people to embrace Islam or Buddhism if they could not do without the consolations of faith as these religions lacked the features of Hinduism he detested most.[46] Annadurai acquired an image as a friend of Muslims even before the DMK was formed when he called for an end to minor attacks on Muslims after Gandhi's assassination in 1948.[47] In the appeals it directed at Muslims, the DMK argued that its vision of community and deity was compatible with the Islamic view of a god without form or

[44] Interviews: Santhanam, S. Murugaiyan, Kumaraswami, Murugan, Veeraraghavan, N. Venkatachalam (Tiruvannamalai).

[45] Interviews: 'Pathamadai' Paramasivam (Pathamadai), Shanmugam Pillai (Ambasamudram), Buhari (Tirunelveli), Ku. Ve. Lakshmanan (Veeravanallur), Ma. Su. Muthu Kutty (Mukkoodal), Ullikottai Arunachalam, P. Venkatesa Solagar, N. Govindarajan (Mannargudi).

[46] Interviews: K. Veeramani (Madras), T. M. Peer Mohammad (Kallidaikurichi).

[47] This was especially effective in Tiruvannamalai and the neighbouring village of Avur as Congress members instigated the riots there.

attributes. Muslims, even those that spoke Dakhni Urdu rather than Tamil at home, were attracted to the DMK's stance on language policy because the choice of a Sanskritized Hindi as the national language over a Hindustani with greater Persian influence was part of the marginalization of Muslims in dominant constructions of Indian nationhood.[48]

Social changes occurring among Tamil Nadu's Muslims made them more receptive to the DMK's appeals to a Tamil community. Tamil Nadu's Muslims shifted increasingly after decolonization from Arabic instruction in parochial *madrassas* to education in Tamil in secular schools, which opened better job opportunities. As the Koran was translated into Tamil in the 1960s, many Muslims who were educated then and later ceased to think that the Koran represented god's word only in its Arabic version. These changes made them more receptive to the ongoing Tamil nationalist wave. Many Tamil Muslims felt they could find an equal place for themselves in the DMK's vision of community without abandoning their specifically Muslim mores, unlike in most conceptions of Indian identity.[49]

Despite these factors, most Tamil Muslim notables favoured Congress, as did their religious brethren in much of India, after the formation of Pakistan led to the banning of the Muslim League and left Indian Muslims vulnerable. But, the Muslim League was revived in the late 1950s, and both the DMK and the League began to gain significant Muslim support in the northern plains. The two parties dominated the Muslim wards of Gorimedu in Tiruvannamalai from the early 1960s.[50] The DMK also gained some early Muslim support in the Kaveri valley among traders (in parts of Mannargudi and Nagaipattinam taluks) and *beedi* workers (in Tiruchi district).[51]

[48] Native speakers of Dakhni Urdu, concentrated in northern Tamil Nadu and comprising 1.8 per cent of the state's population, mostly speak Tamil fluently outside their homes.

[49] A minority of DMK oriented Muslims take Tamil identity to mean an alteration of the markers of Muslim identity or a rejection of the political relevance of religious identity—e.g. a DMK legislator who changed his name from Shamsuddin (a name with Arabic roots) to Kathiravan, a Tamil name suggestive of DMK's electoral symbol.

[50] Interviews: Azizullah, Malik, Sattar, Qutubuddin, Ghaffar (Tiruvannamalai).

[51] Karunanidhi (1986); Interviews: S. S. Nathan (Nidamangalam), Samad (Kuthanallur).

The DMK became more closely associated with Muslims because it was allied with the Muslim League from 1962 to 1974. This alliance was close enough that the two party organizations became virtually indistinguishable by the mid-1960s in areas like Begumpur (a Muslim locality in Dindigul). Many Muslim Leaguers developed loyalties to the DMK also, and some joined the DMK when the alliance between the two parties ended. (Similar sentiments led to a split in the Muslim League in Tamil Nadu in 1989 when party leaders allied themselves with Congress). The growth of Tamil revivalism increased Muslim support for the DMK even in the party's areas of weakness through the 1960s. The solid support of Muslims helped the DMK become the second strongest party in Dindigul by 1967 and the strongest one in northern towns with significant Muslim populations like Vaniyambadi, Ambur, Tiruvannamalai and Tirupathur.[52]

Despite the many discursive and strategic shifts the DMK had initiated, Annadurai highlighted his claims to continuity with early Dravidianism by visiting Periar to request his blessings immediately after the DMK's electoral victory in the 1967 elections was announced, and stating that he owed his success to Periar's inspiration.[53] After this meeting between the two leaders, the first since the DMK's formation, the DK allied itself with the DMK.

THE INTEGRATION OF ASSERTIVE AND PATERNALIST POPULISM: THE EARLY YEARS OF DMK RULE

Having risen to power by effectively using populist and ethnic appeals, the DMK pursued and highlighted policies which addressed some of the expectations aroused by those appeals. Policies reflected both the paternalist and assertive sides of Dravidian populism in the DMK regime's early years.

Paternalism and Policy

While the Congress regime had focused on long-term industrialization, the DMK prioritized short-gestation industrial projects,

---

[52] Interviews: Abdul Latheef, Rahman Khan, Sadiq Pasha (Madras); Oomer Shah, Abdul Samad, Abdul Razack (Dindigul); Annamalai Gounder, Marappan (Tirupathur); Buhari (Tirunelveli).

[53] Ramanujam (1971); Iinterviews: K. Veeramani (Madras), A. M. Muthuswami (Tiruvannamalai).

from which benefits would flow quickly.[54] The DMK government attempted to implement its promises regarding the provision of wage goods, especially rice. It sealed the border with Kerala to prevent food grain smuggling, and initially reduced the price of rationed rice to one rupee a measure in the two largest cities of Madras and Coimbatore.[55] Although the regime got no closer to fulfilling its promise of providing three measures of rice per rupee, even this step reduced rice prices to a third of their previous level.[56] As the national government provided only Rs 50 million to support the subsidy and did not heed demands to increase the allotment of rice to Tamil Nadu from the national pool, the scheme could not be extended to the other parts of the state.[57] Although the cheap rice scheme applied to only 3.2 million people, about 7 per cent of the state's population, it signalled the regime's commitment to improving the lives of the lower strata. While Congress demanded the extension of the scheme to the rest of the state and Congress-O (one of the two Congress offshoots after the party split in 1969) criticized the inadequate implementation of the DMK's promises regarding rice subsidies, these claims rang hollow in light of the policies of the earlier Congress regime and the constraints imposed by national government grants.[58]

The provision of cheap public housing, along with the rice subsidies, strengthened the DMK's base among the urban poor. A slum clearance board was established and priority given to relocating dwellers of thatched huts in Madras city in concrete tenements. While the Congress government had built such apartments for 8,900 families between 1956 and 1967, the DMK regime did so for over 10,000 families in its first four years.[59] This however represented a very small proportion of Madras city's slum dwellers,

[54] Such priorities were strictly maintained until 1969 and more loosely thereafter, except for projects already approved during Congress rule. TH, 24 February 1967; TS, 30 May 1968; TA (1969).

[55] TH, 9 March, 3 May 1967; TI, 22 June 1967; *Statesman*, 24 October 1967.

[56] TH, 16 May 1967; *Patriot*, 18 May 1967.

[57] It was estimated that a further Rs 170 million was needed if the scheme was to cover all areas (mostly urban) with food rationing, which had 12.3 million inhabitants (about 30 per cent of the state's population); and Rs 250 million more to extend the scheme to the entire state. TI, 22 June 1967; *Statesman*, 19 June, 24 October 1967; HT, 15 April 1969.

[58] NH, 3 August 1968; IE, 26 February 1971

[59] NH, 7 January 1971; Arangannal (1975); De Wit (1988).

who accounted for about a third of the city's population.[60] The quality of the housing was often so poor that the occupants' lives did not improve considerably. Yet, the scheme changed the urban landscape noticeably and was given much publicity, especially in the government news programmes which precede the screening of films in movie theatres. Its location in the DMK's old bases in the city helped consolidate support. The accommodation of many fishermen and SCs in public tenements in Royapuram was among the reasons the DMK retained its hold on this constituency until the end of the 1980s.[61]

The DMK regime addressed the concerns of poor and middling peasants by introducing a tiered approach to the levy of food grains for public distribution. It exempted peasants owning less than an acre of land from the levy and left those owning one to ten acres with some surplus, but levied the entire marketable surplus from farmers with over ten acres.[62] All dry land and peasants owning under an acre of wet land were exempted from land revenue, and agrarian tenants and sub-tenants given greater security of tenure if they could register their status.[63] These measures conformed to the demands the DMK adopted in 1965, nudged by its communist allies, and helped consolidate its small peasant base.[64] But, they were not effectively implemented, partly because the DMK had not built peasant organizations. The party formed a farmers' wing only in the 1980s, after a wave of farmers' agitations, but this organization had little corporate presence and organized perfunctory demonstrations to press agrarian demands raised by party leaders. So, the legislation providing security of tenure for sub-tenants was not followed up by the systematic registration of sub-tenants, countering the pressure of superior right holders, contrary to the experience under communist-led governments in Kerala and West Bengal.[65] As a result, it was primarily some DMK supporters who benefited from the policy, particularly in Thanjavur district where peasant organizations have always been strongest.[66]

[60] See Ramani (1985), Arangannal (1975).
[61] Interviews: V. S. Anandan, Era. Manoharan, Radhakrishnan.
[62] TH, 24 March 1967.
[63] TI, 22 June 1967, 24 June 1968; NH, 20 March 1967.
[64] NN, 3, 5, 7 July 1965; DMK (1967); TH, 24 March 1967.
[65] See Herring (1983), Nossiter (1988).
[66] Kamaraj complained about the favour shown to DMK supporters in this

The DMK regime introduced dry laws and party leaders spoke about temperance in increasingly paternalist tones, claiming that illiteracy prevents people from distinguishing between drinking and getting drunk, and promising to retain dry laws until 70 per cent of the state's population was literate.[67] In the same paternalist vein, the DMK abolished horse racing to 'curtail vice', i.e. gambling.[68] Within a year of assuming power, the DMK government nationalized bus routes longer than 75 miles and waived tuition fees for poor students of all castes in the pre-university and pre-technical courses.[69] Prosperity Brigades were formed in all districts, composed of young DMK activists, which contributed an hour's voluntary labour daily for noticeable public projects such as desilting temple tanks.[70]

After the Congress split in 1969, the DMK allied itself with Congress-R, the offshoot led by Indira Gandhi, from 1969 to 1972. This associated the DMK with Indira Gandhi's promises to end poverty through extensive welfare policies, especially during the 1971 elections, further bolstering the DMK's paternalist image.

Assertive Populist Policies

While the DMK regime addressed many paternalist expectations through its first two years, its agenda remained assertive populist in emphasis as did the core of its coalition. The regime established a ministry for Backward Classes Welfare, making Tamil Nadu the first Indian state to do so.[71] It also appointed a state Backward Classes Commission and increased the BC quota in educational institutions and government employment from 25 per cent to 31 per cent based on the Commission's recommendations. It made

---

regard. TH, 21 February 1970; Interviews: A. K. Subbiah (Sithamalli); Ullikottai Arunachalam, N. Govindarajan (Mannargudi).

[67] TH, 9 April 1967.

[68] TH, 25 February 1967.

[69] The tuition fee exemption initially applied to students in pre-university courses from families earning less than Rs 1,500 per year. The income limit was later raised to Rs 1,860 and the scheme extended to students in pre-technical courses in polytechnic institutes. TH, 25 February, 18 May 1967; TI, 22 June 1967, 24 June 1968; TS, 19 March 1968.

[70] TI, 22 June 1967.

[71] ABP, 20 February 1971; SC Welfare Ministries existed in other states too.

a range of new caste groups, mostly more affluent, eligible for these quotas, increasing the estimated share in the population of groups officially recognized as BCs from 41 per cent to 51 per cent.[72] SC converts to Christianity and Islam, and Dakhni Urdu speaking Muslims were made eligible for the BC quotas by 1974, helping the DMK maintain considerable support among Muslims even after its alliance with the Muslim League ended.[73]

Many policies favoured rising agrarian strata, mostly of BC origin. The DMK regime exempted farmers owning five to twelve acres of land from agricultural income taxes. The simultaneous exemption of all dry land from land taxes benefited 4.5 million farmers, from both the lower and middle agrarian strata.[74] The ceiling on land ownership per individual was reduced from thirty to fifteen standard acres in 1970; and that for a family from sixty to forty, and later to thirty, standard acres in 1972.[75] The least secure sub-tenants lacked the social capability to benefit from these and earlier land reforms, but tenant farmers leasing considerable land were enriched as a result, especially in the valleys where large landholders were already selling their land as absentee landlordism was becoming unviable. Many BC tenant farmers in the Mannargudi and Sermadevi areas bought the land they tilled, and some prospered enough to become money-lenders.[76]

The DMK regime's agrarian policies urged the shift of some small and middling freeholders and tenant farmers, mainly BCs but also some SCs, from the communists to the DMK in southern Mannargudi taluk, the scene of Tamil Nadu's earliest communist-led peasant agitations. The state's most durable communist base eroded and the DMK won in Mannargudi for the first time in 1971. Reflecting the outlook of ascendant tenant farmers, a small faction within the CPI welcomed the DMK regime's agrarian policies and

[72] TH, 16 March 1973, 10 January 1974; Government of Tamil Nadu, Backward Classes Commission (1974–5).

[73] *Motherland*, 26 July 1971; *Statesman*, 25 October 1971; TH, 10 January 1974, 25 July 1975.

[74] IE, 28 June 1967; TI, 22 June 1967.

[75] TH, 27 February 1970; 2 March, 12 August 1972; 21 May 1975.

[76] See Bouton (1985) and Gough (1989); Interviews: A. Nallasivan, G. Veerayyan (Madras); N. Govindarajan, P. Venkatesa Solagar (Mannargudi); A. K. Subbiah (Sithamalli); Soma. Tamilarvan (Nidamangalam); S. Thangam Pillai (Kallidaikurichi).

in 1972 formed the Tamil Nadu Communist Party, which was aligned with the DMK and joined the latter party in 1977.[77]

DMK rule saw a major expansion in well and tank irrigation in areas not fed by canals, especially in the northern plains, the primary site of early DMK growth. In the first two years of the DMK regime's existence, 21,000 water pumps were given electric connections, a trend which continued thereafter.[78] This gave a boost to commercial agriculture, the growth in peanut farming in the DMK bases in Tiruvannamalai and Chengam taluks being an instance.[79] The construction contracts associated with these schemes were allocated to party supporters and used to attract wealthy farmers into the party. For instance, N. C. Ramaswami Gounder, a minor Vanniar caste leader and astute political entrepreneur in Chengam taluk, was lured to the DMK by big contracts to build roads and water tanks, and brought with him the votes of many kinsfolk and dependents.[80]

The DMK government did not implement national government legislation regarding urban property ceilings, reflecting the DMK's growth among prosperous traders and industrialists.[81] Besides, it was in Madras and other cities that DMK leaders constructed palatial houses as they enjoyed the benefits of rule.

The clientelist aspect of DMK policies lay both in the targeting of key support groups and in the distribution of patronage through the channels of the party subculture. People within the subculture, especially those with prior social influence, got the lion's share of the benefits, although those beyond the fold could also share in

[77]This faction was led by Manali Kandaswami and A. K. Subbiah, middling peasants who had been important local leaders for decades. Kandaswami claimed that the DMK regime had achieved more with the stroke of a pen than decades of communist agitations had. His eloquence did not bring him the material rewards said to have been promised, but Karunanidhi helped Subbiah celebrate his daughter's wedding in considerable style. Interviews: A. K. Subbiah (Sithamalli); Ullikottai Arunachalam, N. Govindarajan, Nadanam (Mannargudi).

[78] HT, 3 January 1969; Kurien (1981); MIDS (1988).

[79] Harriss (1982); Interviews: R. Renu, S. Murugaiyan, Veeraraghavan (Tiruvannamalai).

[80] Interviews: N. C. Ramaswami Gounder, Ganapathi (Tandrambattu); Sahadeva Gounder (Edathanoor); Venkatachalapathi Chettiar (Tanipadi).

[81] *Tribune*, 3 May 1972.

benefits by dint of merit or through bribes. Bribes often had to be supplemented by appropriate party contacts to ensure access to patronage under the DMK regime. This rule tended to govern the redistribution of land rights and the allocation of caste quotas, especially recruitment to the lower ranks of government officialdom. Thus, ruling party loyalists filled the lower echelons of such government departments as the Electricity Board, the offices of government cooperatives and local government bodies, and the police force.[82]

The state government also adopted policies related to the specifically Dravidianist cast of its assertive populism. Following the Dravidianist critique of upper caste control over ritual legitimation, it imposed greater government control over temple trustee boards, to which it appointed many local DMK leaders, giving BCs a greater share in ritually generated honour.[83] The state legislature also passed bills permitting individuals of all castes to become temple priests and enabling non-Hindus to enter temples. Although both bills were overturned by the courts, this did not restrict the DMK's political gains from these steps.[84] While these moves aimed to Dravidianize sacred spaces, the removal of idols and pictures of deities from government offices desanctified the administrative spaces Dravidianism had occupied.[85]

Assertive Populist Rule and Associational Life

Although the DMK did not promote party-affiliated occupational and caste associations before it assumed power, it did so among some social groups after 1967, to shape mobilization in tune with its populist agenda. It also transacted with independent interest groups whose autonomy posed limited threats to its agenda and electoral base, but contained those impelled by visions incompatible with assertive populism. The flexibility of the regime's strategies and the prior strength of civil society meant that a primarily assertive populist policy agenda coexisted with considerable social pluralism. This can be seen in the experiences of farmers'

[82] TH, 7 November 1972, 17 February 1977; *Statesman*, 28 June 1978.
[83] TH, 24 September 1970; Presler (1987).
[84] TH. 17 September, 21 October 1969; 3 March 1970; 26 July 1972; *Motherland*, 17 December 1973.
[85] TH, 18 July, 8 August 1968.

associations, caste associations, and unions of industrial and agricultural workers.

Farmers' Associations: Richer farmers were able to counter the DMK regime's efforts to isolate them from middling farmers through policies favouring the latter. They formed a strong farmers' association in Coimbatore district, the biggest centre of the Green Revolution in Tamil Nadu, and demanded that electricity charges for water pumps be made independent of the extent of land owned by the individual. Two landlords owning 900 and 600 acres of land respectively were among the association's major leaders.[86]

When electricity charges were raised from 10.8 paise to 12 paise per unit in 1972, the association launched a big agitation, gaining the support of smaller farmers too. The agitational methods (blocking transport with bullock carts) and the police violence which the agitators encountered set the patterns followed by more extensive farmer agitations elsewhere in India from the late 1970s onwards.[87] After a month of violent confrontation, a settlement was reached which maintained preferences for small and middling farmers and set the tone for periodic government concessions to mobilized farmers.[88] The DMK initially felt threatened by the association, but lacked the organizational means and inclination to mobilize smaller farmers independently to break the association's coalition.[89] Congress-O and other parties supported the farmers' agitations, but did not thereby gain much electoral support as they too lacked farmers' organizations.[90] However, the association's attempts to turn into a political party failed because of its inability to present a broad agenda and the prior strength of political parties.[91] So, the growth of farmers' associations and the partial

[86] HT, 19 June, 4 July 1970; TH, 20 June 1970, 11 August 1972; Gurusamy (1993).

[87] HT, 20 June, 6, 9 July 1972; HS, 13 July 1972; TH, 7 July, 11 August 1972; NH, 6 July 1972; TI, 14 July 1972; *Patriot*, 23 July 1972.

[88] *Patriot*, 23 July 1972.

[89] DMK activists tried initially to intimidate some association leaders. TH, 18 March 1971.

[90] HT, 20 June 1972; HS, 13 July 1972.

[91] TI, 20 February 1971; Interviews: Sivaswamy (Thondamuthur); R. Renu (Tiruvannamalai).

satisfaction of their demands did not diminish the DMK's electoral support much. Following the logic of their strategy while they were in the opposition, DMK leaders transacted with those autonomous associations which did not threaten their electoral base.

Caste Associations: As caste mobility was a central Dravidianist tenet, the DMK regime transacted more willingly and closely from the outset with caste associations than it did with the more recently formed farmers' associations. It consulted caste association leaders in the formulation and implementation of caste quotas, and gave these leaders influence over appointments to fill these quotas in return for their electoral support. Besides, DMK leaders maintained contacts with associations of their castes. Yet, the party and the associations jealously guarded their autonomy.[92] The DMK leadership disbanded most caste associations informally affiliated with the party after assuming power as these associations, unlike the MGR fan clubs, did not generate much electoral support and association members were more loyal to the party than to the leaders of these associations. It cracked down quickly on associations the loyalty of whose leaders it suspected (e.g. the Depressed Classes Human Rights Society, an SC association), but allowed others to exist longer (e.g. the *Kongu Nanbar Manram*, a Kongu Vellala Gounder association).[93]

Although the DMK appealed to caste loyalties, we saw that it resisted the official recognition of distinct caste groups. So, particular megacaste clusters remained important bases of political solidarity amidst Dravidianist dominance, even while religious affiliations became less politically salient. As a result, Dravidianist dominance did not inhibit caste clashes as effectively as it curtailed violence along religious lines. But, the caste clashes were generally restricted to the local pockets in which particular megacastes were concentrated. As the aggregation of megacaste demands posed problems, the activities of different caste associations were only loosely coordinated. This prevented these associations from curtailing Dravidianist electoral support, at least until the PMK emerged in 1989.

[92]Interviews: S. 'Panruti' Ramachandran, S. D. Somasundaram, Kovai Sezhiyan, K. Raghavanandam, K. Nagaimugan, Subramaniam (Madras).
[93]TH, 29 October 1970; HT, 5 November 1970; Sathyavani Muthu (1981); Interviews: Sathyavani Muthu, O. P. Raman, Kovai Sezhiyan (Madras).

Industrial Unions: Hoping that its alliance with the DMK from 1965 to 1969 would help it mobilize industrial workers without facing repression, the CPI-M launched a mobilizing wave after the DMK assumed power, leading to strikes in the major industrial centres of Madras, Coimbatore and Madurai. Communist unions grew, attracting many DMK supporters, including Madras harbour workers residing in Royapuram.[94]

DMK leaders, who had tolerated party supporters joining communist unions before they assumed power, were now concerned that the growing strength of these unions would affect industrial growth. So, they initiated the formation of pro-DMK unions in factories experiencing unrest and merged them in 1970 into a federation of unions formally affiliated with the party, the *Thozhilaalar Munnetra Kazhagam* (the Federation for the Progress of Labour—LPF).[95] As the LPF was formed primarily to restrict communist unions, all early LPF unions were formed in factories with some communist strength.[96] The LPF and other moderate unions (INTUC and some unions without party affiliation) raised lower wage demands than the communists and other militant unionists did. The state government facilitated settlements between the moderate unions and managements, aiding LPF growth and helping contain militant unions, which were repressed for good measure. As favourable government mediation was crucial to LPF growth, these unions declined rapidly after the DMK lost power in 1976.

Militant unions were repressed and LPF unions simultaneously formed in many factories where industrial disputes broke out. When communist and other unions led a strike in 1971–2 in the Simpson's factory in Madras, for instance, the state government declared it an essential service and brutally repressed strikers and union leaders, although the national government opposed this

[94]TH, 15 July 1965, 12 February 1967, 10 December 1968, 5 January 1969; HT, 9 November 1967, 4 July 1970; TI, 24 November 1967, 31 May 1968; *Tribune,* 29 February 1968; TS, 30 May 1968; *Patriot,* 15 January 1969, 26 February 1970; *Statesman,* 21 January 1969. Interviews: A. Srinivasan, S. S. C. Anthony Pillai, Tha. Pandian, Radhakrishnan (Madras).

[95] HT, 8 April 1968; *Patriot,* 22 February 1970; *Statesman,* 30 April 1970. Interviews: 'Murasoli' Maran, Kuppuswami (Madras).

[96] Soon after the LPF was formed, it claimed 120,000 members in unions in 167 factories, all of which had communist unions. *Tribune,* 29 May 1970.

course. An LPF union was formed in this factory which enjoyed some support while the DMK ruled.[97] Similar measures were used during strikes in many other factories in Madras, in textile mills in Coimbatore and Madurai, in mines in Neyveli, on plantations in Valparai, in tanneries in Dindigul and around North Arcot district, and among electricity board workers around the state.[98] Strikers were repressed more harshly than during the last decade of Congress rule—union leaders were imprisoned using the Maintenance of Internal Security Act, the police fired on strikers in many locations and striking workers were permanently replaced by prisoners at a dairy farm.[99]

Agricultural Labour Unions: Strikes also erupted among CPI-M led agricultural workers in East Thanjavur district (Kaveri valley) between 1967 to 1969 around demands for higher wages and in opposition to the reduced employment of unionized workers due to the use of tractors and seasonal migrant workers during harvests.[100] They pitted landless workers, mostly the SCs, against the BC and upper caste landholders, organized in the Paddy Producers' Association. The landholders gained the support of some of their caste brethren who worked for a wage, as well as of migrant workers, Congress-O and the DMK.[101] Clashes occurred in connection with the strikes (especially between communist and DMK activists), and the land-grab agitation which the CPI conducted in central Thanjavur district. Many were killed in these clashes, the murder of forty-two SC women and children in the

---

[97] IE, 3 January 1972; HT, 3 January 1972; NH, 6 January 1972; interviews: Kuppuswami, K. Raghavanandam, Kuchelar, A. Srinivasan (Madras).

[98] TH, 10, 13 January, 20 March 1968; 1 May, 5 August 1970; 29 June, 8 August 1971; 3, 4, 8, 12, 29 January 1972; *Tribune*, 29 May 1970; *Patriot*, 19 July, 14 August 1970; IE, 3 January 1972; HT, 3 January 1972; Interviews: Kuppuswamy, G. Viswanathan, A. Nallasivan, K. T. K. Thangamani, P. Manickam (Madras); K. Ramani (Coimbatore); M. Basheer Ahmed, S. A. Thangarajan, Ramaswami, Charles (Dindigul).

[99] TH, 10 January 1968, 8 August 1971; *Tribune*, 29 May 1970; *Patriot*, 19 July, 14 August 1970.

[100] *Statesman*, 8 October 1967; TS, 24 January 1969; TH, 18 August 1968, 1, 2, 17 January, 1, 24 July 1969; Veerayyan (1980); Interviews: G. Veerayyan (Madras); K. Murugaiyan (Thanjavur); A. Natarajan (Kumbakonam); N. Govindarajan (Mannargudi); Soma. Tamilarvan (Nidamangalam).

[101] TH, 27 December 1968; 1, 24 July 1969.

village of Kilavenmani being the most glaring instance.[102] Faced with the threat that communists would regain support in this conjuncture, the DMK formed agricultural labour unions in parts of east Thanjavur district which, along with previously existing DK unions, confronted the communists. These DMK unions existed in parts of Tiruvarur and Nagaipattinam taluks, primarily attracting BC peasants and agricultural workers. When the communist agrarian agitations subsided, and the DK complained that the DMK unions were attracting support away from the DK rather than the communists, the DMK leaders disbanded their agricultural labour unions.[103]

The DMK regime's response to associations which challenged its policies depended on the relationship that the vision animating specific associations bore to assertive populism. It accommodated farmers' associations and caste associations, but repressed militant trade unions of industrial and agricultural labour; and promoted party-affiliated associations and encouraged other associations amenable to state tutelage to compete with the unions alone. The farmers' and caste associations were led by the kind of propertied and upwardly mobile strata which occupied the apex of Dravidianist subcultures, and their demands for subsidies and preferential policies were closely linked to an assertive populist outlook. Communist mobilization, on the other hand, was impelled by visions at odds with populist approaches to promoting upward mobility among intermediate and lower status groups. While the communists demanded only higher wages and benefits, and greater security in employment and land tenure at this point, the DMK leaders were wary of the directions the communists might take if they grew stronger.

The regime's different responses to associations did not depend on their level of militancy, the extent of violence they used, or how far their activities were legally permissible, as the farmers' associations were comparable to the militant trade unions in these respects. Its repression of militant unions weakened threats to the

[102] TH, 17 November, 27 December 1968, 7 June, 9 August 1970; IE, 22, 30 September, 4, 8, 16, 17 November 1968.
[103] Interviews: K. Veeramani (Madras); 'Thaazhai' Mu. Karunanidhi (Thaazhai); S. S. Batcha (Nagaipattinam); N. Govindarajan (Mannargudi); A. K. Subbiah (Sithamalli); V. Subramaniam, K. Marimuthu (Tiruvarur); T. Govindarajan (Kumbakonam).

populist agenda without eliminating communist unions or electoral support altogether. Civic life continued to draw its inspiration from diverse ideological sources, but was disciplined in such a way that policies could thereafter bear a populist stamp. This shows the compatibility of populist dominance with social pluralism; as well as the limits of social pluralism—for the policy agenda got insulated from some visions inspiring civic life even while diverse outlooks found room for articulation.

THE RETREAT FROM PATERNALISM

The paternalist aspects of the DMK's populism waned after Karunanidhi became the party leader, upon Annadurai's demise in 1969. The DMK retreated from paternalism because of growing fiscal constraints and changes in the style and priorities of party leaders. This laid bare once again the DMK's assertive populist core, particularly during the party's second term in office (1971–6), leading to an erosion in support through the 1970s.

Karunanidhi and Assertive Populism

The careers and rhetoric of Annadurai and Karunanidhi were such that the former could more readily project a paternalist image and appeal to the upper strata and those not nurtured in Dravidianist subcultures. Annadurai was more given to moderation and compromise and built Dravidianism's ideological bridges with both Indian nationalism and with the Brahmins. He was from a higher caste than was Karunanidhi, maintained greater contacts with social élites, was better educated and far more fluent in English, and more active in national politics.[104] So, the title 'thennattu Gandhi' (the Gandhi of the southern country), which Dravidianists sometimes used to refer to him, did not seem incongruous despite early Dravidianist opposition to Gandhi.[105]

In contrast with Annadurai, Karunanidhi revelled in confrontations with the police during the DMK's ascent and used shrill invective against opponents, even those within his party.[106] He had

[104] While Annadurai led the DMK parliamentary party between 1962 and 1967, Karunanidhi was never a member of the national parliament.

[105] Annadurai also wrote a pamphlet extolling Gandhi (Annadurai, 1985f).

[106] Karunanidhi (1986, 1988) himself contrasts his confrontational style with Annadurai's.

two wives, was reputed to employ prostitutes, and wrote novels and short stories which verged at times on the pornographic.[107] He wore his lower caste status as a badge of Dravidian authenticity and seemed at times to justify the coarse elements of party culture as natural in a plebeian party. Karunanidhi's style was altogether poor raw material from which to sculpt a paternal image. Public opinion polls conducted in Tamil Nadu (by the Statistics Department, Madras Christian College) show that Karunanidhi has, since the 1970s, consistently been the state politician to whom the largest number have been strongly opposed, though he has also been the state's second most popular politician through much of this period (and at times the most popular one). Since the 1980s, Karunanidhi has tried to alter his image, aware of the problems it caused, but with limited effect.

The Abandonment of Paternalist Policies

The significant paternalist policies adopted during the first two years of DMK rule were abandoned between 1969 and 1971. These policies were difficult to sustain without substantial grants from the national government due to the limited fiscal powers of state governments. The national government was disinclined to so favour the DMK regime even when the ruling Congress-R was allied with the DMK. As Karunanidhi was less committed to paternalist policies than Annadurai had been, he abandoned them in the face of budgetary constraints. By contrast, when faced with similar constraints in the 1980s, the ADMK regime would choose to maintain more ambitious paternalist policies at the cost of allocations for industry and infrastructure.

The first major step away from paternalism was a reduction in rice subsidies in the two largest cities in 1970.[108] The national government initially provided Rs 50 million to fund the cheap rice scheme, but rejected demands for further monetary grants and greater rice allotments to Tamil Nadu to help sustain the scheme.[109]

---

[107] Kannadasan (1972), an account clearly coloured by personal antagonism towards Karunanidhi, nevertheless reflects Karunanidhi's public image. The public was more willing to forgive Annadurai's affairs and fondness for gambling due to his dignified public bearing.

[108] TH, 9 January 1970.

[109] HT, 15 April 1969.

Rice production within the state was also affected by the conversion of considerable land from rice to sugar cultivation to use loopholes in the land ceiling laws, and the decline of productivity in the Kaveri valley, the state's rice bowl, as water supply became less reliable and soil fertility declined.[110] This led to the abandonment of the cheap rice scheme. While the front led by Congress-O failed to embarrass the DMK on this score in the 1971 elections, the ADMK later capitalized on the abandonment of such paternalist policies.

The next crucial step away from paternalism was the repeal of dry laws in August 1971. The state government demanded compensation from the national government for the revenue foregone due to the dry laws, as the division of taxation powers between the state and national governments made liquor production and consumption among the major potential sources of state government revenue. As the national government refused to compensate states with dry laws, the DMK regime abandoned these laws in 1971 to ease revenue constraints.[111] Although it conducted a campaign to publicize the virtues of the dry laws and the national government's role in forcing their abandonment, the DMK was stripped of the Gandhian garb it had taken to sporting.[112] Alcohol consumption increased considerably, especially hurting the poor and women.

The identification of the DMK with the emergent BCs became stronger, further alienating the upper and lower strata. It became increasingly evident that the extension of the BC quotas to more affluent castes impeded the access of poorer individuals and less privileged BCs, despite the increase in the overall BC quota.[113] The funds allocated by the national government for SC Welfare were used to benefit both the BCs and the SCs, thus reducing the amount spent on SCs. The police seemed to pursue complaints regarding the practice of untouchability with diminished interest. Sathyavani Muthu, the DMK's major SC leader, already relegated to the sidelines in factional battles, publicized these aspects of the DMK regime's treatment of the SCs. This led to her expulsion from the

[110] *Tribune*, 29 December 1968; Kurien (1981); Gough (1989).
[111] TH, 16 March, 17 September 1969; 20 June 1971.
[112] TH, 16 August 1971.
[113] TH, 10 January 1974; Interviews: A. Sattanathan, K. Nagaimugan, Subramaniam (Madras).

party in 1974.[114] While the share of the BCs in the state cabinet did not increase during Annadurai's Chief Ministership, it did so appreciably under Karunanidhi, as shown in Table 5.1 (in which UC denotes upper caste).

TABLE 5.1   Caste Composition of Representative Cabinets

Year	Chief Minister	UC	BC	SC	Other
1952	Rajagopalachari	2	3	1	1
1957	Kamaraj	2	3	1	2
1967	Annadurai	2	3	1	2
1971	Karunanidhi	1	5	1	1
1974	Karunanidhi	2	5	1	1

The decline in the DMK's popularity due to its retreat from paternalism was enhanced by the growth and increasing openness of corruption and nepotism among party functionaries, ministers, legislators and members of public boards and local bodies. Party officials were frequently seen seeking favours in government offices and extricating activists and kinsfolk from legal problems in police stations. It became known that bribes had accompanied the barter of rice for electric power from Kerala in 1972, evoking sharp outrage as food supplies were then limited and rice prices were rising.[115] Even measures that were once popular seemed to have served ulterior purposes. For instance, the Prosperity Brigades were used to divert government funds to the ruling party.[116]

The former Chief Secretary (the state's chief bureaucrat) and various leaders who left the DMK were among those who charged party leaders with corrupt practices.[117] When party activists occupying executive posts complained of political interference, they were divested of their posts and subjected to police

[114] Sathyavani Muthu said that the DMK government had utilized only Rs 25 million for SC/ST welfare, of the Rs 85 million allocated for this purpose. TH, 29 October 1970; HT, 5 November 1970, 9 May 1974, 6 December 1975; FPJ, 5, 6 May 1974; ABP, 6 May 1974; *Statesman*, 6 May 1974; IE, 7 May 1974; Sathyavani Muthu (1981); Interview: Sathyavani Muthu (Madras).

[115] TH, IE, *Patriot*, 4 April 1975; TI, 7 April 1975; Interview: G. Viswanathan (Madras).

[116] NH, April 1976.

[117] *Motherland*, 21 July 1972; TI, 3 May 1973; HT, 9 December 1974.

harassment.[118] The state government responded brazenly to allegations of corruption. It argued that the national government had no right to investigate complaints against it and passed a bill empowering committees composed of state government officials, obviously open to executive pressure, to do so.[119] However, as criticism increased and losses in by-elections made the erosion of support evident, the DMK's General Council ordered party members to stop exerting their influence over the distribution of essential commodities, thereby implicitly admitting that such practices had been rampant.[120] A commission of inquiry instituted by the national government after the dismissal of the DMK ministry in 1976 considered as many as 23,000 complaints of corruption and administrative malpractice against Karunanidhi and many of his ministers, and found many of the charges valid.[121]

The DMK's popularity suffered its sharpest blow when MGR, irked at not being made a minister and at Karunanidhi's attempts to undermine his popularity, raised corruption charges against party leaders in 1972, leading to his expulsion from the party.[122] The ADMK, which MGR formed after his expulsion, compiled a list of corruption charges against the DMK leadership, aided by the ally it found in the CPI, and conducted rallies throughout the state demanding an enquiry into these charges and the dismissal of the DMK ministry.[123] The new party focused its criticism of the DMK on the betrayal of paternalist promises, shown in the abandonment of the cheap rice scheme and dry laws, and the growth of corruption.[124] Paternalist attitudes towards the provision of rice

[118] For instance S. K. Sambandam, the President of the Handloom Weavers' Cooperative Society, was removed from this post, suspended from the party and assaulted by the police. *Statesman*, 7 August 1970; HT, 2 December 1970; *Patriot*, 3 December 1970.

[119] *Patriot*, 14 February 1973.

[120] TH, HT, 17 June 1973; NH, 20 June 1973.

[121] TI, 8 March, 14, 15 May 1976; *Statesman*, 4, 17 May 1976; HT, 4 February 1976, 20 January 1977; TH, 15 May 1976.

[122] *Statesman*, 10, 11, 20 October 1972; NH, 12, 17 October 1972; *Motherland*, 12 October 1972; *Tribune*, 12 October 1972; HS, 12 October 1972; HT, 13, 28 October 1972; TI, 17, 18 October 1972.

[123] TI, 11 January 1973.

[124] TI, 11 January 1973, 4 April 1975; IE, 27 April 1973, 4 April 1975; TH, 4 April 1975.

and liquor, on which the DMK had capitalized earlier, now led to an erosion of support for the party. Many found the complaints against the DMK more credible when the party's own former popular vote-getter began to voice them. The DMK's attempts to restrict the damage by reintroducing dry laws in 1974 came too late, for the party had lost its paternalist appeal by then, and with it, the ability to dominate Tamil politics.[125]

ETHNIC DEMANDS AND DMK RULE

Many party activists, anti-Hindi agitators and the Tamil revivalist petty intelligentsia expected the DMK to fulfil some of its language demands upon assuming power. While the DMK regime adopted both symbolic and substantive measures to address these hopes, the expectations were only partially fulfilled due to the constraints imposed by federal rule, the profile of opinion within Tamil Nadu and the priorities of party leaders, which did not coincide fully with those of some ethnic militants.

The DMK lost support because it did not fulfil some of its populist promises, but did not pay similarly for failing to pursue its ethnic demands vigorously. Those disappointed by the DMK's abandonment of its paternalist promises found a viable alternative in the ADMK. But, Tamil ethnic militants found that parties attempting to outflank the DMK on ethnic demands drew limited support.[126] Ethnic militants could either stay in the DMK, hoping for propitious moments to urge the party towards greater militancy, or lose access to power and all influence over policy by leaving the party, and most took the former option.[127] So, policies concerning ethnic demands affected cadre loyalty and mass support much less than populist policies did. Barnett's understanding of the DMK as a cultural nationalist party misled her regarding the flank

[125] TH, 23 August 1974.

[126] The DK, *Naam Thamizhar* (We are Tamils), the Tamil Arasu Kazhagam, Swatantra and the Tamil Nadu Kamaraj Congress were minor parties of this kind. They were allied with or part of the DMK at different points, further reducing the electoral cost the DMK had to pay for moderation on Tamil ethnic demands.

[127] Some shifted to the ADMK after 1972, but this was due to this party's obvious popularity rather than its stand on ethnic issues, which was more moderate than the DMK's.

on which the party was most vulnerable (the populist, not the ethnic flank).[128]

Two parties, the MDMK and the PMK, adopted more militant ethnic positions than the DMK and gained greater electoral support in the late 1980s and 1990s than their militant predecessors had. They were able to do so because the growth of the Sri Lankan Tamil secessionist movement slightly widened the niche for ethnic militancy in Tamil Nadu, and because they linked Tamil ethnic militancy to other issues—the MDMK to the revitalization of assertive populism and the PMK to backward casteism. Even these parties have drawn far less support than the DMK, the ADMK and Congress.

Language Policy

The DMK regime declared at the outset that it would press the national government for a constitutional amendment for the retention of English as an official language, but Hindi instruction continued in Tamil Nadu's schools on an optional basis.[129] Several symbolic changes were introduced to compensate for the lack of immediate substantive change in language policy. Anti-Hindi agitators (whom the government likened to anti-colonial agitators) were released from prison, official references to the state in both English and Tamil were changed to Tamil Nadu/Tamizhagam and the government slogan rendered in Tamil rather than Sanskrit.[130] State government functions began with a song to 'Mother Tamil' rather than a prayer song, a Tamil appellation was used to refer to the national radio station in Tamil language programmes and a World Tamil conference celebrated with pomp in Madras.[131] Prayers in Tamil began in temples and names were officially

[128] See Barnett (1976: 242–8).

[129] TH, 9, 29 March 1967.

[130] TH, 17, 21 March, 16 April 1967; 18 August 1968. This slogan, drawn from Hindu scripture, was translated into Tamil but not changed. Symbolic assertions of Tamil pride were no longer necessarily connected to a rejection of high Hinduism.

[131] The DMK regime turned the conference, planned even while Congress was in power, into a celebration of Dravidianist power. The statues erected then and later of Tamil poets and scholars included one of Annadurai. TH, 31 December 1967, 3 January 1968; HT, 28 August, 14, 16 September 1970; FPJ, 16 September 1970; NH, 27 September 1970.

rendered with the pure Tamil prefixes, *Thiruvaalar* and *Thirumathi* rather than the Sanskritic *Shri* and *Shrimathi*.[132]

A parliamentary amendment to the Official Languages Act provided for the continued official use of English by the national government, but fell far short of Tamil demands. It made knowledge of Hindi sufficient for recruitment to national government employment and a prerequisite for promotion (though not recruitment), introduced government service recruitment examinations in Hindi but no other Indian language, made Hindi instruction compulsory in non-Hindi speaking areas and did not require Hindi speakers to learn any other language. These provisions angered most Tamils, including Congressmen.[133] Although the DMK regime urged students not to agitate, promising to use its power to ensure changes in national language policy, agitations broke out and agitators raided *Hindi Prachar Sabhas* and picketed Hindi films.[134] In response to the unrest, the state government ended Hindi instruction in all schools receiving aid from it, suspended a national student service organization in which commands were given in Hindi and briefly suspended the screening of Hindi films.[135]

The battles over national language policy ended in a stalemate by 1969. While the 'Nehru assurance' that Hindi and English would together serve as official languages until people in the non-Hindi states decided otherwise was not given statutory form, the national government has continued to use English for official purposes. Hindi instruction has been limited in Tamil Nadu since then, although it is no longer barred in schools. Public opinion in Tamil Nadu, in flux at the peak of the language agitations, settled into an unenthusiastic acceptance of this stalemate. Although DMK leaders were dissatisfied with the stalemate, they restrained militants from agitating further as they realized that public opinion had

[132] The Dalmiapuram train station was also renamed, as the DMK had demanded for long. TH, 8, 28 December 1969.

[133] TH, 17 December 1967.

[134] TH, 11, 22–24 December 1967, 26 February 1968; *Tribune*, 24 February 1968; TI, 29 February, 3 March 1968; IE, 28 February 1968.

[135] Only some national government schools and schools run by religious minorities were allowed to continue Hindi instruction. TH, 24, 26 January, 31 March, 28 May 1968; TI, 3 March 1968; *Tribune*, 7 June, 3 January, 13 September 1969.

changed and were concerned that the national government might dismiss the DMK regime if agitations exploded again.

Language agitations thus petered out after 1969 as popular support declined and the student agitators had not built the organizational resources needed to sustain themselves as an independent political force.[136] The student militants bartered their allegiance in return for access to the DMK's organizational resources and did not entertain the possibility of building an alternative party when DMK leaders restrained their militancy.[137] Swatantra supported the agitations more enthusiastically in the late 1960s, but its weak organization and the dominance of affluent libertarian élites in its leadership rendered it a poor refuge for militants shaped by Dravidian populism.[138]

Having settled for a stalemate in national language policy, the DMK regime tried to realize its aims more fully within the state. It passed a bill in 1970 to make Tamil the sole medium of instruction in schools and increase its usage as a medium of instruction in colleges.[139] This policy was never fully implemented because it faced student opposition from the outset. The DMK regime found, as its Congress predecessor had in 1963, that the preferences of students regarding medium of instruction were set more by job prospects than by cultural nationalism. Opting for education in the Tamil medium was risky as most private employers offering high paying jobs conducted their business operations in English and recruitment examinations for national government services were conducted only in English and Hindi. Although the state government announced that it would give Tamil medium graduates preference in recruitment and force private firms to employ such graduates, it seemed unlikely that private employers would bow to such pressure.[140] The move to change the medium of instruction was especially unpopular as it was introduced when unemployment was rising.

[136] *Patriot*, 28 January 1969; TH, 24 February 1970; TI, 5 March 1970.
[137] Interviews: L. Ganesan, T. K. Ponnuvelu, K. Kalimuthu, N. 'Senji' Ramachandran, Vai. Gopalswami.
[138] TH, 23 December 1967.
[139] TH, 24 January, 15 December 1968; 13, 14, 19, 21 December 1970; NH, 14 December 1970; IE, 17 December 1970.
[140] TH, 1 August, 4 November, 19, 23 December 1970.

The DMK lost the monopoly it had enjoyed of the streets for at least a decade, as its rallies to promote Tamil medium education were overshadowed by student protest against the policy. Congress-O and Swatantra actively supported the protests, leading to Congress-O supplanting the DMK briefly as the dominant force in many college student unions.[141] Concerned about possible adverse electoral consequences, the DMK abandoned the move towards education in the Tamil medium on the advice of an expert panel just prior to the 1971 elections.[142] Militant language politics, which had dominated the streets when the DMK assumed power, had ceased to be electorally effective within four years.

Autonomism

Secessionism, officially abandoned by the DMK in 1963, resurfaced periodically in the rhetoric of party activists and student militants. Secessionist statements were heard during the anti-Hindi agitations, between 1965 and 1969, after the birth of Bangla Desh in 1972 and at other points.[143] Some DMK legislators asserted their desire for secession in the state assembly on several occasions after 1963, and a few times even after their party assumed power.[144] Some student anti-Hindi agitators highlighted their demand for secession by burning Indian flags and hoisting presumed Tamil flags, and a group of them once confronted Annadurai in 1968 and demanded that he immediately declare the creation of a separate Tamil Nadu.[145] Periar too revived his secessionist demands between 1971 and 1973 (the last two years of his life).[146] The DMK regime contained such pressures by underlining the demands for greater

[141] TH, 23 November, 13, 14, 21 December 1970, 11 January 1971.

[142] TH, 23 December 1970, 16 January, 17 March 1971; FPJ, 18 January 1971; TI, 19 January 1971; IE, 20 January 1971.

[143] *Tribune*, 24 February 1968, 11 March 1972; TH, 26 February 1968, 13 February 1972; TI, 29 February 1968; *Patriot*, 28 January 1969; *Statesman*, 22 January, 16 February 1972.

[144] See for instance HT, 3 February 1964; TH, 9 March 1969.

[145] TH, 26 February 1968; *Tribune*, 24 February 1968; Ramanujam (1971).

[146] *Patriot*, 19 October 1971; *Statesman*, 22 January 1972; TH, 19 October 1973; HT, 25, 29 May 1973; *Motherland*, 17 December 1973; *Tribune*, 18 December 1973.

state autonomy that the party had been raising since abandoning secessionism.[147]

Upon assuming power, the DMK regime demanded that the national government reconsider the structure of federalism, a demand supported by other non-Congress state governments, especially those ruled by the communists. These parties conducted joint pro-autonomy conferences.[148] The DMK regime appointed a commission on centre-state relations, which recommended that state governments be given full responsibility for all issues except defence, foreign affairs, communications, currency and interstate relations. The state government and the DMK adopted these demands with minor changes and passed a resolution in the state assembly endorsing this position.[149] They repeatedly demanded greater control over industrial licensing to arrest the industrial decline in the state.[150] While a minority government ruled India from 1969 to 1971, the DMK suggested that representatives of the state governments rule India in a coalition.[151] It also highlighted its autonomism by demanding a separate state flag.[152] However, it was entirely unsuccessful in altering the trend towards the greater concentration of power in the hands of the national government during Indira Gandhi's rule.

The DMK failed to effect significant changes in national language policy and the federal framework primarily because the state government had limited leverage over national policy, and also

[147] Annadurai (1963); Maran (1974); Chittibabu (1975); TI, 27 October 1963; HT, 4 November 1963; *Patriot*, 4 November 1963; *Statesman*, 4 November 1963; NH, 14 July 1964.

[148] TH, 28 March 1967, 13 September 1970; IE, 7 April 1967; Interview: 'Murasoli' Maran (Madras).

[149] Centre-State Relations Committee (1971); Maran (1974); HS, 12 April 1972; TH, 22 May 1972, 21 April 1974; ABP, 23 May 1972; *Motherland*, 3, 21 May 1972.

[150] TI, 30 July 1971.

[151] HT, 3 March 1970; *Patriot*, 3 March 1970.

Karunanidhi summarized the DMK's position on federalism in the slogan, '*Maththiyil Koottaatchi; maanilaththil suyaatchi.*' While the second part of the couplet means autonomy in the states, the first part may be taken to mean either federal rule or rule by coalition at the centre. The latter twist was given to the slogan in 1970, although it is the former meaning that was more often imputed. See Karunanidhi (1986).

[152] TH, 15, 24, 27 August 1970; 13 March 1975.

because (despite its rhetoric) it considered these priorities second-ary. The DMK's priorities in this regard were revealed by the choices it made when the split within Congress left the Congress-R-led national government dependent on DMK support from 1969 to 1971. Not only did the DMK not push whole-heartedly for changes in national language policy and federalism then, it even opposed a parliamentary initiative to curb the national government's powers because Congress-O sponsored the initiative.[153] The con-stitutional amendment that the DMK proposed embodying Nehru's assurance on language policy was defeated in parliament in 1970 due to Congress-R's opposition. Although Congress-O abstained from voting on the resolution, the DMK continued to support Congress-R, claiming that it was more progressive than Congress-O.[154] The DMK's preference for Congress-R over Congress-O was clearly not due to the two parties' positions on language policy and state autonomy, but because Congress-R shared more of the DMK's populist features and posed less of a challenge to the DMK in Tamil Nadu. At times, the DMK's populism determined even its allies at the national level more than its ethnic aspirations did.

The DMK's autonomist rhetoric became more strident by 1975, in response to competition from the more moderate ADMK and rumours that the state government might be dismissed on charges of corruption.[155] But, the threat of dismissal also made DMK leaders wary of offending the national government, thus tempering their rhetoric. So eager was the DMK to placate the national government that it refused to join a front of opposition parties less than a month before its ministry was dismissed.[156] Even after the ministry was dismissed in January 1976, Karunanidhi offered to help defuse popular protest and supported the social programmes implemented during the emergency.[157] The DMK leaders were clearly more concerned by 1975–6 about the prospect of losing power and being

---

[153] *Patriot*, 6 November 1970.

[154] TH, 24 February 1970; TI, 5 March 1970.

[155] TH, 26 November 1974; 6, 25 March, 12, 16 August, 21 November 1975.

[156] TH, 26 November 1974, 2, 6, 7, 8, 11, 12, 13, 25, 30 March, 12, 16 August, 21 November, 27, 31 December 1975, 2 January 1976; TI, 26 December 1975, 2 January 1976; HT, 31 December 1975.

[157] Karunanidhi supported Sanjay Gandhi's five-point plan and took the CPI to task for not doing so. HT, 19 February, 28 December 1976.

indicted for corruption than about state autonomy, which was irrelevant to them unless they remained in power.

The Failure of Nativism

Some assertive Dravidianist appeals had a nativist potential, which was never quite realized. Certain demographic features of Tamil Nadu made the success of nativism unlikely. Tamil speakers account for 84.5 per cent of the state's population and most of the state's other inhabitants are culturally indigenized (their ancestors having moved to Tamil speaking areas centuries back) and are generally regarded as 'Tamils'. More recent migrants, who tend to be more distinct in their language use, probably constitute under 5 per cent of the state's population. Malayalis (1.4 per cent of the population, from the neighbouring state of Kerala) are the largest such language group and were the primary targets of the only significant nativist move in Tamil Nadu's politics.[158]

These demographic features did not predetermine the failure of nativism, however. Culturally indigenized migrants could also have been deemed outsiders, much as European anti-Semitism did. Periar's calls for expelling Brahmins appeared to be in such a vein, but served primarily to highlight Periar's anti-élite appeals rather than to inspire *pogroms* against Brahmins.

The potential for nativism appeared strong during three phases of the DMK's history—in connection with the campaigns against the alleged economic dominance of the north in the 1950s, in response to nativist attacks against Tamils in the western state of Maharashtra in the late 1960s, and in response to the ADMK's formation and rapid growth in the early 1970s. During the first phase, local non-Tamil industrialists, traders and money-lenders were sometimes vilified, but they and their properties were not attacked.

The second phase of potential Dravidianist nativism was triggered by attacks launched by the *Shiv Sena* (Shiva's Army) on South Indian migrants in Bombay in the late 1960s. The DMK regime, which had just assumed power in Tamil Nadu, demanded that the national government and the government of Maharashtra protect Tamils residing in the area.[159] Some DMK and DK activists

[158] Department of Statistics (1987: 62).
[159] FPJ, 18 April 1968; TI, 31 May 1968.

formed a 'Tamil army', aiming to retaliate against Tamil Nadu's 'North Indian' residents. This group, whose activities were primarily restricted to Madurai district, had a shadowy existence from 1968 to 1972. It picketed shops and institutions run by non-Tamils, but the scope and violence of its activities were limited, and its significance lay other than in opposing North Indians.[160]

Although Malayalis were among the victims of the Shiv Sena's attacks in Bombay in response to which the Tamil army was formed, the posters of the latter group demanded the expulsion of Malayalis from Tamil Nadu. The assertion of nativist belligerence turned against the state's largest group of recent and linguistically distinct migrants, towards whom diffuse resentments already existed. Even after the Tamil army was nominally disbanded under pressure from the party leadership, its members were active in violence against political opponents, especially ADMK activists.[161]

The third phase saw the DMK leaders attempting to counter the ADMK's growing challenge by highlighting their Tamil militancy. DMK ideologues claimed during this phase that MGR's Malayali origins made him unlikely to press the language and caste demands they considered central to the Dravidian community's interests. They claimed that MGR's rise to the Chief Ministership would make Tamil Nadu's government indistinguishable from Kerala's, and Karunanidhi declared in the legislature: 'We will not allow two Keralas in South India.'[162]

The *Tamizhar Paathukaappu Peravai* (Forum for the Protection of Tamils) was launched in 1974, with the proclaimed aim of

[160] The group assumed different names in posters—the *Tamizhar Padai, Tamil Sena* (both meaning the Tamil army), We Tamils and the Tamils' Party. Although its convenors, 'Madurai' S. Muthu and S. S. Thennarasu, claimed that it was a wing of the DMK, Annadurai denied this. Karunanidhi said that it was also formed to respond to the paramilitary activities of the Hindu revivalist *Rashtriya Swayamsevak Sangh* (RSS). TH, 2 October 1967, 15, 16 April 1968, 9 March 1969; TI, 31 May 1968; HT, 3 October 1967, 15 March 1968, 17 June 1970, 26 February 1971; *Dawn*, 5 October 1967.

[161] HT, 17 June 1970, 12 May 1973; *Statesman*, 17 July 1972; TH, 5 August 1972, 15 May 1973; *Patriot*, 26 April 1973; Interviews: S. S. Thennarasu, Qadir Shah (Madras); Manimaran, O. N. Sivagnanam, Oomer Shah, K. Anguswami, C. Srinivasan, Sivanath Babu (Dindigul).

[162] Some DMK General Council members opposed these moves on the grounds that they were contrary to Annadurai's identification with all South Indians. TI, 27 March 1974; Interview: S. 'Panruti' Ramachandran (Madras).

230 NARENDRA SUBRAMANIAN

protecting Tamils from the threat of Malayali dominance. As with the Tamil army, it was composed of DMK activists, although Karunanidhi disavowed its links to the DMK.[163] This group, armed with knives, cycle chains and soda bottles, attacked some establishments owned by Malayalis, but primarily targeted ADMK activists, theatres screening films of MGR, and advertisements for these films.[164] Karunanidhi backed the Peravai's nativist cast by promising massive quotas for Tamils and those settled in Tamil Nadu for over fifteen years in the state government (80 per cent) and private employment (60 per cent),[165] which were never instituted. Many non-Tamil residents of Tamil Nadu felt threatened by the DMK's nativist rhetoric, though the violence which accompanied it was mostly directed at ADMK activists, most of whom were Tamils. There were no systematic physical attacks against non-Tamils, but it is well known (though difficult to systematically document) that some Malayalis faced discrimination in admission to colleges and recruitment to state government employment when the DMK's nativism was at its peak.

These efforts of the DMK to halt the ADMK's growth failed. Anti-Malayali feelings were not decisive in the political choices of many and the DMK's nativist claims were too transparent a veil for attacks directed at MGR.[166] The rhetoric of DMK leaders seemed especially disingenuous as these leaders had lionized MGR and benefited from his appeal until the eve of his expulsion from the DMK. The DMK's flirtation with anti-Malayali chauvinism

[163] P. K. Muthuramalingam, the Peravai's president, later said that Karunanidhi had instigated the organization's activities, confirming what informed observers already knew. Like the Tamil army, the Peravai was supported by a group from the DK called the *Sakthi Sena*, led by the actor M. R. Radha, who had tried to kill MGR in 1967 in a private dispute. ABP, 2 August 1974; HT, 28 January 1977; TI, 20 July 1974.

[164] NH, 19 June 1974; Interviews: Vannai Mu. Pandian, Madhusoodhanan, Kapada Raje, Mari, Dayalan, K. V. Raman, Sethu, Das (Madras); K. R. Venkatesan, Khaleel Pasha, E. Va. Velu (Tiruvannamalai); Sivanath Babu, Maya Thevar, Oomer Shah, Manimaran, C. Srinivasan (Dindigul).

[165] TH, 28 May, 18, 28 July, 6 August 1974; FPJ, 9 July 1974.

[166] Even the DMK activists involved in the anti-Malayali rhetoric and violence did not take the nativism too seriously. Peravai members granted that there were no Malayali shops to attack in Royapuram. Interviews: Kapada Raje, Mari, Dayalan, Sethu, K. V. Raman (Madras).

and the accompanying violence only earned it unpopularity. No further attempts were made to resurrect nativism after the miserable failure of this venture.[167]

The DMK's nativist gambit failed as the notion of ethnicity that the party's mobilization had instilled at a mass level was related more to cultural practices than to blood ties. This notion was linked to 'doing Tamil', not merely with 'being Tamil', to paraphrase Barth. Barth argued that in rural Pakistan Pashtoons' recognition of individuals as belonging to their ethnic group was not merely based on their 'being Pashto', i.e. speaking the Pashto language and being the descendants of Pashto speakers; but also based on 'doing Pashto', i.e. following a range of customs common to traditional rural Pashtoons. Dravidianism revalued plebeian Tamil cultural practices ('doing Tamil') in reaction to their devaluation by British colonial ideology and marginalization in most versions of pan-Indian nationalism. In so doing, it placed many Tamil speakers at the margins of the popular Tamil community—e.g. those who used a Sanskritic idiom or who were part of pan-Indianist subcultures.

Dravidianist ideologues extolled important figures in Tamil popular culture who helped define the putative identity and ambitions of the Tamil community. Although of Malayali origin, MGR was foremost among these figures as he was culturally indigenized, a popular voice of the DMK, and closely associated with the way many ordinary Tamils imagined their conditions of existence and their social horizons. So, MGR fell within the ambit of the conception of Tamil ethnicity promoted by the DMK, and even party activists and those nurtured in the assertive populist subculture were not convinced by the nativist critique of MGR.[168]

The definition of ethnicity promoted by the Dravidian parties alluded to essentialized constructions of ethnicity. However, the prejudices inherent to these constructions do not necessarily provoke extensive violent hostility towards ethnic out-groups. The

[167] Chastened by his failure, Karunanidhi learnt Malayalam in the late 1980s, as part of his attempts to alter his image.

[168] Many Malayali members of the DMK were not bothered by the party's anti-Malayali rhetoric of 1972–6 as they took it to be just a means to attack MGR. They had, after all, been accepted within the DMK subculture precisely because they were culturally indigenized migrants. Interviews: Sundar (Madras); Krishnan, Velu Nair (Nidamangalam).

popular notions of ethnicity resulting from Dravidianist mobilization did not exclude individuals from the political community by virtue of their social origins. This was possible because the identities posited by Dravidianism were layered, alluding to such diverse categories as caste and language use, status and power, with different markers being accorded priority in different contexts. Migrants were admissible into this vision of political community if they adopted the norms of plebeian Tamil culture. The conception of popular culture operative for such purposes was only loosely shaped by revivalist notions, and relied substantially on the norms and idioms of everyday life. Such a vision undoubtedly marginalized those who preferred other norms. In response to Dravidianist dominance, some of these individuals strategically adopted a 'Tamil' idiom in public interactions without changing their forms of speech and ways of living at home (e.g. many Brahmins who attained adulthood from the 1970s onwards). Such strategic changes in self-presentation created some emotional anguish in some of them, but not in others.

The ADMK's paternalist populism accepted migrants even more readily than assertive Dravidianism did as it was more moderate in its orientation towards ethnic issues and explicitly incorporated its notion of Tamil ethnicity within a pan-Indian identity. So, it attracted the 'others' of early Dravidianism in much larger numbers than the DMK had. So, although ethnic parties have dominated Tamil politics since the 1970s, the ADMK, the most popular party through much of this period, has been led by two leaders of non-Tamil/non-Dravidian origin, MGR and subsequently his former lover, J. Jayalalitha, who is both non-Tamil (Kannadika) and Brahmin. As Jayalalitha, like MGR, was raised in Tamil Nadu, was an actress in Tamil films and was fluent in the plebeian Tamil of popular oratory, her claims to 'doing Tamil' could not be disputed either, and were not.

PARTY INSTITUTIONS AND PARTY COMPETITION DURING DMK RULE

The DMK as a Ruling Party

The DMK party organization underwent changes through this period associated with its abandonment of secession, the end of the major language agitations, the party's assumption of power and the increased concentration of power in the hands of Karunanidhi after he became the party leader. Its focus on electoral considerations increased after the battles for Dravida Nadu and against Hindi had ended. The assumption of power made the distribution of patronage more central to the party's contact with society. The increasing concentration of power in Karunanidhi's hands restricted debate within the party and drained some substance from the continuing democratic procedures, such as inner-party elections. Despite these changes, activists retained a sense, though weakened, of an ideological purpose which the party embodied, and the party retained a significant social presence.

These related changes began by the early 1960s, and their effects were fully evident by the early 1970s. After the DMK abandoned secession, party schools ceased to function and the outlook of activists and orators were shaped by more informal processes of political socialization. Nevertheless, the ideological fervour of activists remained strong initially as leaders suggested that the retreat from secession was merely temporary and tactical, and the major anti-Hindi agitations gripped the state. This began to change as party leaders focussed on containing the agitations from 1965 and on retaining power after 1967. However, the DMK's strident assertions of autonomy after the ADMK's emergence and retention of its early core base helped the DMK's subculture retain some coherence.

Annadurai (unlike Periar) did not designate a successor, preferring to let the party decide that democratically.[169] However, his actions suggest that he might have preferred V. R. Nedunchezhian, a college educated Vellala with a knowledge of Dravidianist mythohistory, who was a ponderous orator and remained aloof from activists. Nedunchezhian was one of the five so-called founding leaders of the party (while Karunanidhi was not), and was the Assistant General Secretary through the first six years of the party's existence. As Annadurai wished to cultivate leadership capacities among his lieutenants, he ceded the General Secretary's post to Nedunchezhian from 1955 to 1960. After Annadurai resumed the post in 1960, Nedunchezhian was given the important posts of Propaganda Secretary (1960–1) and Chairman of the General

[169] NIP, 12 February 1969; Ramanujam (1971); Chittibabu (1975).

Council (1961–9). Nedunchezhian led the DMK legislative party when Annadurai had lost his seat in the legislature (1962–7), occupied the second spot in the cabinet while Annadurai was the Chief Minister, assumed Annadurai's most important portfolio while Annadurai underwent treatment for cancer and was the acting Chief Minister immediately after Annadurai's death.[170]

While Nedunchezhian appeared to enjoy Annadurai's favour, Karunanidhi displayed the greatest skill in building the party, raising funds, conducting election campaigns and directing agitations.[171] His important role in these activities earned him greater significance within the party from the mid-1950s onwards and helped him to build a faction loyal to him which reached down to the party's roots and extended across the state.[172] E. V. K. Sampath, Periar's nephew and another major DMK leader in the 1950s, attempted to challenge Karunanidhi's growing influence. As Sampath's faction did not reach below the level of the district leadership, Karunanidhi outwitted him, leading to his departure from the party in 1961. Annadurai intervened in such factional struggles only when they seriously threatened party cohesion. By the 1960s, Karunanidhi was the party Treasurer and more directly involved than Annadurai in the routine activities of party building and election campaigns.[173]

Of Karunanidhi's potential rivals, K. Anbazhagan, a former university professor, shared some of Nedunchezhian's weaknesses; and K. A. Mathiazhagan, weakened by his close association with the Sampath faction, had factional support comparable to Karunanidhi's only in his home district of Coimbatore. Thus, Karunanidhi's supporters won the crucial District Secretary's post

[170] IE, 11 September 1968; Patriot, 7 February 1969; TH, 28, 30 January, 13 July 1969; HT, 13 July 1969; NH, 13 July 1969; Interviews: V. R. Nedunchezhian, Era. Sezhiyan (Madras).

[171] Karunanidhi began his rise to prominence within the party by playing important roles in the Kallakudi agitation of 1953 and the Nangavaram agitation of 1957.

[172] Karunanidhi was the leader, other than Annadurai, whose activities were given greatest coverage in party newspapers from the mid-1950s onwards. The distribution network for his newspaper, Murasoli, was his faction's initial base, which soon became much broader.

[173] Karunanidhi (1986, 1987); Barnett (1976); Interviews: K. A. Krishnaswamy, S. 'Panruti' Ramachandran, Sulochana Sampath (Madras).

in all but one district in inner-party elections in 1968.[174] Aware
of Karunanidhi's significance for the party, Annadurai supported
him when his tussles with Sampath, and later, Mathiazhagan, came
to a head.[175] When a contest to succeed Annadurai seemed likely
between Karunanidhi and Nedunchezhian, 300 of the 383 members
of the General Council pledged their support to Karunanidhi. As
Nedunchezhian could count on the support of no more than 30
of these members, he withdrew from the contest, leaving
Karunanidhi in charge of the government and the party.[176] MGR
was associated with Karunanidhi for long, and gave him valuable
support in the factional struggles of the 1960s.

Upon assuming the leadership, Karunanidhi further undermined the power of potential state-level opponents, and his
dominance over the party became entrenched after the DMK's
grand triumph in the 1971 elections. The few weak efforts some
made thereafter to challenge his leadership or some crucial policies
were easily defeated.[177] As a result, debates on policy and strategy
effectively ended in the party's Executive and General Councils
and within the cabinet. Those who demanded a change in the
leadership gained inadequate support even when Karunanidhi's
position was at its weakest during the emergency. They were
expelled from the party and some of them were assaulted.[178]

[174] TH, 13, 14 August 1968; *Tribune*, 5 September 1968; *Statesman*,
5 October 1968; HT, 3 November 1968.

[175] *Statesman*, 11 June 1968; TH, 13 June 1968; Karunanidhi (1986);
Interviews: K. A. Krishnaswamy, S. 'Panruti' Ramachandran.

[176] A compromise was reached, making Karunanidhi the party President
and Nedunchezhian the General Secretary. HT, FPJ, *Statesman*, 10 February
1969; *Patriot*, 5 August 1969; *Tribune*, 21 February, 8 August 1969; TH, 10,
26 April, 12, 13, 16, 26, 27, 28 July 1969; HT, NH, 13 July 1969; NH, 27 July
1969; TI, 28 July 1969.

[177] Nedunchezhian accepted Karunanidhi's leadership, MGR (then
Karunanidhi's supporter) became the Treasurer, and Mathiazhagan and
Sathyavani Muthu were defeated in inner-party elections in 1969. Karunanidhi
inducted many of his supporters into the cabinet in 1969 and 1971. The DMK
Executive Committee supported Karunanidhi against criticisms levelled by
Mathiazhagan and Anbazhagan, and Mathiazhagan and some other ministers
were sacked on the charges of corruption in 1970. TI, 28 July 1969; *Patriot*,
16 March 1969, 9 October 1970; HT, 5 November 1970; TH, 16 February,
16, 26, 28 July 1969, 10 September 1970.

[178] HT, 11, 13, 18 February, 4 April, 7 October 1976; IE, 3, 13 April 1976;
Patriot, TI, 3 April, 7, 15 July 1976; TH, IE, HT, ABP, 4 July 1976; ABP,

The factional battles leading to Karunanidhi's dominance diminished solidarity among party activists. These rivalries were particularly intense in the southern districts, where the party organization had always been weakest. In Tirunelveli district, where party rivals had assassinated a district secretary as early as 1956, the elections for the district secretary's post in 1968 were attended by violence, vote-buying and overt caste appeals. S. B. Adithyan, a newspaper tycoon whom Karunanidhi lured into the party with the bait of the assembly Speaker's post, bribed district council members to vote for Karunanidhi's favoured candidate, Rathnavel Pandian. As activists arrived at the polling site armed with knives, the police had to intervene to ensure peaceful polling. When Rathnavel Pandian's opponent, M. S. Sivaswami, became the municipal chairman of Tuticorin later, a rival DMK activist committed suicide in protest.[179] Although such fierce rivalry diminished party cohesion, many who lost factional battles continued to view the DMK as the vehicle of a larger Dravidianist project, and remained in the party until the ADMK's birth or even later. They did not neglect or disrupt election campaigns as Congress dissidents frequently did.

Local DMK leaders and party activists resorted increasingly to violence to enforce their will, the activities of the Tamil army, the Prosperity Brigade and the Tamizhar Paathukaappu Peravai being particularly noticeable examples. Even if they bore no formal titles, gangs of toughs became parts of the party's repertoire everywhere. While groups composed of fishermen and casual labour ruled the roost in Royapuram, a gang primarily comprising truck and rickshaw drivers roved Mannargudi town especially during elections.[180] However, this did not significantly increase social violence in these areas—Royapuram was always crime-ridden and Congress had long been cosy with petty smugglers; and Mannargudi had witnessed violent confrontations between communist agricultural

---

5 July 1976; Karunanidhi (1987); Interviews: S. 'Panruti' Ramachandran, K. A. Krishnaswamy (Madras).

[179] TH, 13, 15 August 1968, 14 May 1969; Chittibabu (1975); Karunanidhi (1986); Interviews: M. S. Sivaswami (Tuticorin), Vai. Gopalswami, P. H. Pandian, G. R. Edmund (Madras), Vallimuthu (Kovilpatti).

[180] Interviews: Madhusoodhanan, R. T. Seethapathi, Kapada Raje (Madras); Ku. Balakrishnan, Siva. Rajamanickam, M. Manimaran (Mannargudi).

workers and thugs recruited by pro-Congress landlords since the 1940s. It did in Dindigul, where the strong arm tactics of the DMK town secretary Pon. Srinivasan were backed by the district secretary, Madurai S. Muthu, a convener of the Tamil army.[181] The police seldom restrained the violence of DMK activists as local party bosses and legislators usually cowed zealous police officials into passivity with threats of transfer or suspension.

The DMK's violence reached its peak when the birth and growth of the ADMK severely threatened the party's base. The ADMK's rallies and election meetings were attacked by DMK activists, sometimes along with the police, and Congress-O activists were also targeted by the mid-1970s.[182] DMK activists primarily used knives, cycle chains and soda bottles during this violent period, rather than the machine guns and bombs introduced into political contention elsewhere in India by the 1980s.

Although party cohesion declined, the path Karunanidhi took to power meant that he could not afford to damage party institutions too much. Karunanidhi was not a leader with considerable charisma and owed his support both within and outside the party to his occupying the apex of the party machine, whose viability he therefore had to maintain. District Secretaries and other local bosses were important figures who mediated party-society transactions, especially the distribution of patronage, and ensured activist loyalty. Karunanidhi could not override their authority indiscriminately without paying a price.[183] So, the DMK retained some organizational pluralism and close contact with society despite the concentration of power in the leader's hands, contrary to Congress's experience under Indira Gandhi's leadership and later.

Congress: A Decade of Decline

Congress underwent both electoral and organizational decline during the DMK's first two terms in power. Its electoral decline

---

[181] Interviews: S. Kaverimaniam, P. T. R. Palanivel Rajan (Madurai); Oomer Shah, Manimaran, O. N. Sivagnanam, Maya Thevar, Qadir Shah, Sivanath Babu, K. Anguswami, Samadharmam, Chandran, Raju Naidu (Dindigul).

[182] HT, 2 December 1975.

[183] Thus, while Karunanidhi could easily remove a state-level leader like Mathiazhagan, he retracted his efforts to remove the Tiruchi district boss, Anbil Dharmalingam. *Statesman*, 29 August 1972.

began in 1967, predating its organizational decline, which became pronounced only after the ADMK was formed in 1972.

Factionalism increased within Congress between the party's defeat in Tamil Nadu in 1967 and the split within the party at the national level in 1969, hindering a clear strategic focus. C. Subramaniam became the President of the state Congress Committee after the party lost power in 1967 and tried to renew the party's appeal by emphasizing the national government's new populist programmes associated with Indira Gandhi and the Green Revolution he had helped pilot while he was a central minister.[184] Tensions between Subramaniam and Kamaraj dated back at least to the 1950s when the former had been Rajaji's follower and had challenged the latter unsuccessfully for the Chief Ministership after Rajaji was ousted from that post. Subramaniam not only sought to give Kamaraj's personality less significance in party appeals, he also distanced himself from such legacies of the period when Kamaraj directed the state party as an emphasis on backward caste appeals and collaboration with the DK.[185]

Kamaraj resisted Subramaniam's strategy effectively as his faction was much stronger than Subramaniam's. He thwarted Subramaniam's efforts to form a party youth wing, which he felt would become a base for opposing him. Moreover, his faction dominated the National Students' Tamil Progressive Committee, formed to oppose the anti-Hindi agitations, and the Tamil Nadu Congress Socialist Forum.[186] The rivalry between the two factions reached its peak when they came to blows at the state committee office.[187] The bitter factional battle prevented party leaders from effectively presenting their criticism of the DMK regime's growing corruption and the two-language policy for the state.[188] When Congress split in late 1969, it freed the two new parties to pursue more effective strategies in the state.[189]

[184] TH, 28 December 1967; HT, 3 June 1968; *Patriot*, 26 August 1968.

[185] TH, 31 December 1967; HT, 3 June 1968; Subramaniam (1993).

[186] TH, 11 September 1967; HT, 3 June 1968; TI, 30 June 1969; NH, 11 July 1969.

[187] *Patriot*, 7 September 1968, 6 June 1969; HT, 14 October 1969.

[188] TH, 11 September, 31 December 1967; IE, 4 January 1968; TI, 31 May 1968; *Patriot*, 22 June 1968; NH, 18 November 1969.

[189] TI, 11 December 1969, 2 January 1970; Interviews: C. Subramaniam, G. Karuppiah Moopanar, P. Nedumaran (Madras).

Congress-O inherited the lion's share of the party organization in all states after the split, particularly in Tamil Nadu. Further, only two of the parent party's fifty legislators joined the Congress-R initially, although the number soon increased to eight.[190] The state Congress-O, led by the popular Kamaraj, attracted many effective organizers loyal to him, and a group of former Dravidianists led by E. V. K. Sampath. The state Congress-R leaders, on the other hand, either lacked mass appeal (e.g. C. Subramaniam, Mohan Kumaramangalam) or had a record of corruption and repression (e.g. Bhaktavatsalam, T. T. Krishnamachari).[191] Congress-O inherited most of the parent party's popular support too. While Congress-R was devastated in the village panchayat elections of 1970, gaining a mere 7 per cent of the votes and 3 per cent of the seats, Congress-O was a close second to the DMK in the state, even marginally outdoing the DMK in parts of the west, south and the Kaveri.[192]

Congress-O promised a return to propriety, and criticized the DMK regime's corruption, its abandonment of the cheap rice scheme and its promotion of college education in the medium of Tamil.[193] Prior to the 1971 elections, Kamaraj also called attention to the slippering of idols at a DK conference which, he claimed, enjoyed the DMK government's protection.[194] The criticism of the DMK's corruption had limited effect as many were either sceptical of the charges or remembered the corruption of the earlier Congress regime and felt that populist clientelism at least distributed patronage more widely than Congress's machine politics did. The demand for the extension of rice rationing echoed hollow in light of the Congress regime's earlier performance, as did the critique of the DK after Congress's long alliance with it. Besides,

---

[190] TI, 11 February 1970; *Statesman*, 4 May 1970.

[191] C. Subramaniam was an effective administrator who held many important cabinet portfolios in the state (1952–63) and national governments (1963–7, 1971–7, 1979), but had poor contacts with activists and supporters. Mohan Kumaramangalam, the scion of a major landlord family who organized communist unions in the 1940s, maintained so little contact with the state thereafter that he had lost all fluency in Tamil by the 1970s. Krishnamachari had been dismissed from the union cabinet on corruption charges.

[192] TH, 5, 6 August 1970; *Tribune*, 7 August 1970.

[193] *Sthaapanak Kaangirasu Therthal Veliyeedu* (1971); IE, 26 February 1971.

[194] *Motherland*, 19 February 1971; Ryerson (1988).

rice supplies were plentiful again before the next elections. Although the opposition to the DMK's state language policy drew considerable student support and revived Congress-O strength in student unions, the DMK restricted its losses by abandoning the shift to instruction purely in the medium of Tamil just before the 1971 elections.[195]

Repelled by the DMK's agrarian reforms, corruption and support for Congress-R, which it associated with big government, Swatantra shifted its support to Congress-O, which it considered more conservative than Congress-R on socio-economic issues at the national level.[196] Rajaji urged industrialists and the upper castes to support Congress-O, in the same tones in which he had asked them to vote for the DMK in 1967, but found he had changed sides once too often. Although it retained considerable organizational strength, Congress-O was no more successful in appealing directly to the intermediate and lower strata than the parent Congress party had been. Its theme of reinstating propriety connoted to voters a return to the élite paternalism and bureaucratic clientelism of which most of them were tired. Only parties better attuned to the mass sentiments shaped by a generation of populist mobilization could outwit assertive populism, which rolled to a decisive victory in the 1971 elections, though Congress-O continued to attract as much as 35 per cent of the vote.[197]

The state Congress-R's weakness led Indira Gandhi to sacrifice the party's prospects in the state to the end of solidifying its position at the centre. Over the objections of the state Congress-R, she struck a bargain with the DMK which allowed Congress-R to contest 10 parliamentary seats, but no assembly seats.[198] So, when Indira Gandhi's populist appeal was at its peak, it was not presented as an option at the state level to the Tamil electorate.

[195] TH, 13, 14, 21 December 1970.
[196] TS, 30 May 1968; *Tribune*, 21 February 1969, 26 November 1970; TH, 5, 21 October, 18 November 1970, 26 February 1971; FPJ, 30 December 1970.
[197] Singh & Bose (1988: 43).
[198] *Statesman*, 29 January 1971; TI, 19 January 1971; *Patriot*, 20 January, 2, 6, 21 February 1971; HT, 21 January 1971; TH, 31 January, 1, 5, 7 Februry 1971; IE, 1 February 1971; Ramanujam (1971); Karunanidhi (1987); Interviews: C. Subramaniam, A. Chengalvorayan (Madras); T. S. Tirunavukkarasu, A. S. Ravindran (Tiruvannamalai).

Congress-O's state unit reconsidered its strategy after its defeat in the 1971 elections. At various points in the 1970s, Kamaraj and most other party leaders favoured a merger with Congress-R, which continued to rule at the centre, as they wished to present a unified opposition to the DMK, and hoped for the assistance of the national government in this task. But, Congress-O's national leaders were overwhelmingly against reunification, and the state unit preferred to wait for their consent.[199] Merger was also hindered by divided opinion within Congress-R.[200] The discussions about a merger led no further than an alliance between the two parties in the elections to the Pondicherry assembly in 1972.[201] While the undivided Congress was paralyzed by factionalism between 1967 and 1969 and Congress-R enjoyed little support in the state for some years after the party split, Congress-O was disoriented by the indecision on merger which persisted from 1971 to 1976.

The birth and growth of the ADMK in the meantime placed the Congress parties at the margins of the primary political struggle in the state, between the DMK and the ADMK. Congress-R welcomed the formation of the ADMK, and was allied with it in some of the by-elections of the mid-1970s.[202] But, Congress-O regarded the ADMK as merely another incarnation of cheap Dravidianist politics and claimed that the ADMK leaders were themselves fully involved in the corruption they criticized. Wary of losing support to the ADMK, it stayed aloof from the party, while opposing the repression set loose on it.[203] The different attitudes which the two Congress offshoots adopted to the ADMK also arrested moves to reunify Congress. However, the prospect of repression which came with the abolition of civil rights in

[199] A small group led by Sampath shifted to Congress-R as early as 1971. TH, 22 September 1971; *Statesman,* 3 June 1971; TI, 13 March 1972.

[200] IE, 13 December 1971, 6, 22 May 1972; HT, 3 April, 21 May 1972; *Statesman*, 3 April 1972.

[201] AT, 20 February, 28 March 1972; *Mortherland*, 13 March 1972.

[202] *Patriot*, 17 March 1973; FPJ, 19 March 1973; TH, 1 July 1973; *Motherland*, 3 July 1973; *Statesman*, 10 December 1973.

[203] Kamaraj's terse response to the ADMK's formation was '*irandum ore kuttaiyil ooriya mattai*' (Literally, both are fronds which have soaked in the same pond). IE, 14 March 1973; *Patriot*, 17 March 1973; HT, 26 June 1975.

1975 rendered merger with the ruling Congress-R doubly attractive to some Congress-O members. Soon after Kamaraj's death in October 1975, about half of the state Congress-O activists joined Congress-R, while the other half preferred to oppose Indira Gandhi's suppression of democracy.[204]

Strengthened by the entry of half of the state Congress-O, Congress-R conducted an intense mobilization campaign while the emergency shielded it from all opposition, hoping to attract support with the so-called twenty-point and five-point programmes, which had strong populist features.[205] The growth in the party's membership during this period was largely fictive, although some did shift to Congress-R from other parties to avoid repression.[206] What remained of the state's Congress-O converted itself into the state unit of the Janata party, which won the national elections after the emergency in 1977.

Unlike in most of India, Congress-R was stronger in Tamil Nadu in 1977 than it had been in 1971. The authoritarian phase had not been widely unpopular in the state because only opposition party activists were repressed and the DMK regime's dismissal through this period was greeted with considerable relief. Further, Congress-R had been strengthened by the entry of a large chunk of the Congress-O. Nevertheless, 1977 was not a propitious time to gain support for Indira Gandhi's populism anywhere in India. While Congress-O had polled 35 per cent of the vote in the state in 1971, the Congress and Janata parties together gained 37 per cent of the vote in 1977. But in 1977, former Congress/Congress-O voters were either divided between the two equally strong Congress offshoots or shifted to the ADMK, which they considered

[204] There is some evidence that Kamaraj favoured the merger at the time of his death, although it was effected only after he died. TI, 2, 19, 24 January, 14 February 1976; HT, 3, 14 January, 5, 11, 15, 18 February 1976; TH, 2 January, 11, 17 February 1976; *Patriot*, 20 January 1976; IE, 11 February 1976; NH, 17 February 1976; *Statesman*, 15, 17 February 1976; Interviews: P. Nedumarn, G. Karuppiah Moopanar (Madras).

[205] HT, 26 April, 12 July 1976; TH, 13 May 1976, 12 January 1977; ABP, 12 July 1976; TI, 2 January 1977; IE, 15 November 1976.

[206] Congress-R claimed to have registered 500,000 members in thirteen weeks! Not only were these figures most probably inflated, many who joined the party during the emergency did so to save their skins and left soon after the return of democratic rule. ABP, 12 July 1976; TI, 2 January 1977.

a more viable alternative to the DMK.[207] With the 1977 elections, the Congress offshoots had ceased to be viable contenders for power in Tamil Nadu. The weaknesses of these two parties helped the DMK recoup some of its losses of the mid-1970s in the 1977 polls and become the second strongest party.

Paternalist Dravidianism Blossoms[208]

Despite MGR's significance in attracting voters to the DMK, Annadurai had given MGR no formal party posts and did not include him in his cabinet, on the argument that MGR was fully occupied with his movie career. Annadurai was probably also wary of encouraging MGR's political ambitions. As Karunanidhi was not the undisputed party leader that Annadurai had been, he was more wary of potential competitors, none more popular than MGR. MGR had crucially helped Karunanidhi in intra-party factional battles and in piloting the party to its biggest electoral victory in 1971. So, he felt that Karunanidhi was more beholden to him than Annadurai had been and expected an important cabinet portfolio after the 1971 elections. He was dissatisfied with the post of party treasurer that he was given, which proved largely nominal as Karunanidhi controlled party finances.

Soon after the 1971 elections, Karunanidhi attempted to under-mine MGR's base, although MGR had issued no overt challenge. While Karunanidhi was able to effectively undercut other party leaders, MGR's appeal and base were too strong. Attempting to turn the party into his patrimony, Karunanidhi induced his son Mu. Ka. Muthu to act in films he scripted in 1972 and sculpted his movie *persona* to resemble MGR's. The plots of Muthu's films drew obviously on themes associated with MGR, Muthu imitated MGR's gestures in his films and Muthu Fan Clubs were formed by Karunanidhi loyalists to rival those of MGR.[209] DMK leaders exerted pressure on some MGR fan clubs to convert themselves

---

[207] After party competition became bipolarized in 1962, more voters have tended to vote for a party which they consider a viable contender, even if it is not their first preference. This hastened the electoral decline of Congress and minor parties.

[208] Chapter VI provides a fuller account of the ADMK's early history.

[209] Muthu's first film, *Pillaiyo Pillai* (Oh, What a Son!) was released in September 1972. *Patriot*, 27 September 1972; *Statesman*, 12 October 1972.

into Muthu fan clubs, using financial inducements and police repression. The MGR fan clubs took to the streets in protest and the secretaries of eight hundred of his fan clubs threatened to disaffiliate their clubs from the DMK, forcing Karunanidhi to disband the Muthu clubs.[210] Although Karunanidhi backed down, MGR felt that the ground was shaky under his feet and found the moment (late 1972) a propitious one to challenge Karunanidhi due to the DMK's increasing unpopularity.

MGR demanded that he be given control over the party finances and, in his capacity as the party treasurer, asked for explantations of discrepancies in the party accounts. As his demand went unheeded, he criticized the growth of corruption in party ranks and challenged ministers and legislators to disclose the assets of their families and close relatives.[211] In response to this challenge, the DMK executive committee, packed with Karunanidhi's loyalists, expelled MGR from the party.[212]

MGR's expulsion created a major upsurge of agitations, primarily involving young men. The MGR clubs used this upsurge to convert themselves into branches of the ADMK, leading MGR to formally announce the formation of a new party.[213] Only 5 per cent to 10 per cent of the DMK members and leaders shifted at the outset to the ADMK, whose personnel was composed predominantly of fan club members, some defectors from pan-Indian parties and individuals newly entering politics.[214]

The ADMK initially had a much weaker party organization than Congress-O. Yet, it succeeded better in tapping resentments against the DMK regime because the ADMK's paternalist populism

[210] Karunanidhi used this occasion to demand that MGR merge his clubs with the DMK or disband them. MGR was expelled from the DMK before a tussle could develop over this issue. *Patriot*, 27 September 1972; TH, 2 October 1972; TI, *Tribune*, 2 October 1972; *Statesman*, 14 October 1972; HT, 28 October 1972; Interviews: R. M. Veerappan, K. A. Krishnaswamy, Velur Narayanan, 'Vannai' Mu. Pandian, Madhusoodhanan (Madras).

[211] TH, 30 September, 9 October 1972; *Statesman*, 10, 12, 15 October 1972; HT, 13 October 1972; TI, 18 October 1972.

[212] *Statesman*, 11 October 1972; TH, 11 October 1972.

[213] TH, 18, 19, 21, 22, 24, 26, 27, 29, 30 October, 3, 14 November 1972; TI, 18, 20 October 1972.

[214] TI, 18, 20 October 1972; TH, 19, 21, 27 October 1972; Interviews: R. M. Veerappan, K. A. Krishnaswamy, S. D. Somasundaram (Madras).

better addressed the disenchantment of masses whose political sentiments had been predominantly shaped by populist appeals than Congress-O's tune of a return to propriety could. Although Congress-R used paternalist populist appeals, it had little corporate substance in Tamil society in the early 1970s and did not present itself as a contender for power in the state in this crucial period of realignment, preferring often to form electoral alliances with the Dravidian parties.

The ADMK's emergence reshaped party competition and forced all other parties to alter their strategies. The DMK focused its attention thereafter on the containment and repression of the ADMK. Differing attitudes towards the ADMK arrested moves to reunify the Tamil Congress party for four years and induced a minor split within the CPI. The ADMK's rise also hastened Swatantra's disappearance.

The ADMK's success in appropriating the paternalist strand of Dravidian populism, and experience of leading agitations against the DMK regime and withstanding its repression strengthened the party's organization through its first few years. So, the ADMK had a stronger social presence and could count on more activist loyalty than the Congress offshoots could by the mid-1970s. When the first state assembly elections after the party's birth were held in 1977, it had laid a secure foundation for a decade of dominance. As the DMK's assertive populist subculture proved more durable in decline than the shallower Congress subculture, it was the DMK, and not the Congress offshoots, which offered the ADMK its main opposition thereafter. Indeed, the DMK even returned to power— first when the ADMK split after MGR's death, and then again when Jayalalitha squandered a lot of the support she had inherited from MGR.

VI

The Efflorescence of Paternalist Populism: The ADMK

Naan aanaiyittaal, adhu nadanthuvittaal,
Intha yezhaigal vedhanai padamaattaar.

(If I were to command, if my wish became true
These poor people will no longer suffer.)

Ninaththathai nadaththiye mudippavan naan naan
Thunichchalai manaththile valarththavan naan naan
Yennidam mayakkam kondavar pazhakkam
Inrum yenrum thevai yenru solladi thangam

(I am one who realizes his will,
Resolve has grown in my mind,
Dear girl, say you need the company
Of those I entrance, today and always.)

— Lyrics of songs from films of M. G. Ramachandran,
ADMK's founding leader

The experience of the ADMK elaborated fully for the first time the paternalist features of Dravidian populism. The ADMK grew dramatically through the mid-1970s, gained power in Tamil Nadu in the next general elections in 1977 and retained power until MGR's death a decade later. It succeeded because of its paternalist appeals and the policies it pursued upon achieving power, which addressed some of the expectations raised by these appeals. Its policies regarding the supply of food and liquor helped fulfil the expectations of core supporters like the poor and women. Other policies, such as those regarding preferential quotas and agrarian subsides, reflected a willingness to accommodate some demands of the intermediate strata. This mix of policies helped the ADMK gradually expand its base through its decade in power.

The ADMK's flexible strategy in power and more consistent response to the different kinds of expectations generated by populist mobilization stands in contrast to the DMK's retreat to an almost exclusively assertive focus in the 1970s. This helped the ADMK stay in power longer than the DMK had. The party lost power briefly (1988–91) when it split after MGR's death, but regained its former support and more after regrouping in 1989 under Jayalalitha's leadership. So, it returned to power in 1991, and lost substantial support only from the mid-1990s onwards as Jayalalitha blatantly violated pluralist norms. Even in decline, the DMK retained the loyalty of most groups it had attracted with its assertive populism and ethnic militancy at least until the formation of the PMK in 1989 and the MDMK in 1994.

CELLULOID IMAGES AND PATERNALIST POLITICS: MGR'S FILM AND POLITICAL CAREER UNTIL 1972

MGR had imprinted in the popular Tamil imagination an image of himself as an exemplar of paternalist populist values well before the formation of the ADMK. He achieved this primarily by consistently playing in his films the roles of champions of the oppressed, who promote the rights of the weak and defend women's honour. MGR also undertook many well publicized actions which reinforced his image, in the minds of his growing legion of fans, as one who supported and fully empathized with the poor. While he was in the DMK, MGR successfully used this altruistic image to gain support for his party. Yet, his message, and the paternalist subculture it inspired, remained autonomous of the party leadership, helping MGR take his supporters with him when he left the DMK. As MGR appealed to groups beyond the assertive subculture, he was able to broaden his political support once, with the formation of the ADMK, he had distanced himself fully from the DMK's ethnic militancy.[1]

MGR was born in a white collar professional Malayali family that was impoverished by the death of MGR's father while MGR was still a baby. The town of Kumbakonam, where his family lived through much of his childhood, is located in the most intricately stratified part of Tamil Nadu, in the Kaveri valley.[2] MGR's early

[1] For discussions of MGR's career, see Government of Tamil Nadu (1977), Jagathrakshakan (1986), Pandian (1992), Dickey (1993a).

[2] Bouton (1985) indicates the intricately stratified pattern of landholding and land tenure and the close correspondence between land control and caste status in the area around Kumbakonam.

experience urged people to accept claims that he intimately understood the plight of the poor and helped him depict the typical signs of dominance in Tamil society. Yet, his position as a Malayali from a formerly white collar family placed him somewhat beyond the pale of the caste and class jealousies central to plebeian Tamil society. This helped him portray himself as a paternal arbiter of such jealousies.

His family's poverty led MGR to take up a theatre and film career while he was still a boy. He played minor roles in films through the 1930s, but grew to the status of a star by 1947, as India underwent decolonization. The dominant political wave of Indian nationalism influenced him at the time, and he became an insignificant Congress member in the 1940s, and remained so until 1953. MGR gained increasing popularity and became the most popular of the triumvirate of male actors who dominated Tamil films from the 1950s to the mid-1970s.[3]

MGR came in contact with many Dravidianists, who were beginning to play major roles in artistic fields just as he became a prominent actor. He met Annadurai and became closely associated with Karunanidhi, who was the script writer for three of his early major films and collaborated with him extensively for the next two decades. Karunanidhi helped bring MGR over to the DMK from Congress by 1953.[4] With this began two decades of association between the party and the actor, which despite being mutually beneficial, was fraught with tensions.

The Hero's Voice: The Paternalist Discourse of MGR's Films

Until the formation of the ADMK, MGR primarily addressed his public through his films. After he became an important star, he played a significant role in shaping the films in which he acted—their themes, the roles he played, the dialogues and songs, and sometimes even the cinematography and editing. The discursive

[3] The other two major actors of the times were 'Sivaji' Ganesan and 'Gemini' Ganesan. The latter faded from the film scene by the late 1960s. See Aranthai Narayanan (1981).

[4] Karunanidhi was the assistant script writer for the first film in which MGR was the hero, *Rajakumari*, released in 1947, and the main script writer for others released in 1950. Karunanidhi (1986: 140–1), Aranthai Narayanan (1981: 369–84), Thandavan (1987: 48); Interview: R. M. Veerappan (Madras).

strategies employed in his films provide a clue to his impact on popular political culture.

MGR's films adopted a paternalist discourse, which implicitly defined notions of the popular interest and projected MGR as the typical altruistic hero who promoted this interest. The protection of the poor and the weak was central to this vision of the popular interest. If the poor and the weak were to be protected, women, referred to as the *thaaikulam* (community of mothers), were regarded as preeminently weak and so especially worthy of protection. Besides, the protection of the chastity and well-being of women was considered essential to the maintenance of community norms. This struck deep chords in Tamil culture.[5] As the dichotomous perception of women, as mothers or whores, is common in Indian society, the equation of women with mothers served two purposes. It promised women that they would be treated as mothers, with reverence rather than violence; while implicitly addressing male anxieties about uncontrolled female sexuality as women did behave like 'mothers' in MGR's films. While older women repaid the hero's protection with boundless affection and gratitude, the attraction which young women felt for the hero (and nobody else) was rendered honourable by the hero's virtues.[6]

The altruistic hero who helped establish paternalist norms in MGR's films was either from plebeian ranks or a wealthy person whose empathy with the poor led him to adopt some of their mores. MGR invariably played the role of this hero.[7] The audience

---

[5] Pandian (1987) discusses the relationship between chastity and bounty in Tamil cultural traditions.

[6] Kakkar (1989) discusses images of women and sexuality in Indian culture and literature. The centrality of notions of motherhood and femininity in MGR's films is evident from some of their titles themselves: *Thaaikkuppin Thaaram* (The Wife Comes After the Mother), *Thaai Sollai Thattaadhey* (Don't Disobey Your Mother), *Thaayaik Kaatha Thanaiyan* (The Son Who Protected His Mother), *Deivaththai* (Divine Mother), *Thaayin Madiyil* (On Mother's Lap), *Kanniththai* (Virgin Mother), *Thaaikku Thalaimakan* (A Mother's First/ Special Son), *Kudiyiruntha Koil* (The Temple Which Housed Me), *Annamitta Kai* (The Hand That Fed You), *Oruthaai Makkal* (Children of One Mother), *En Thangai* (My Sister).

[7] The titles of many of MGR's films highlight the altruism of the characters—e.g. *Oorukku Uzhaippavan* (He Who Works For the People),

could read either heroic type into MGR's own experience as he was once poor, but had subsequently gained considerable wealth and glamour. The hero typically defeated wealthy and exploitative villains by appropriating important sources of élite power and using considerable pugilistic and fencing skills. His victory led to the moral transformation of the villains, who did not lose their wealth but agreed to use it benevolently.[8]

MGR also played a second role in some films, that of a good natured but weak man. The audience was invited to identify with both figures, the hero who successfully confronted villains, as well as the weak individual (perhaps representing their more pedestrian selves), whose good intentions the hero helped realize. The hero urged people to gain education, reject superstition and shun alcohol, rather than resorting to direct action, to solve their problems. It is the hero who acted as the people's representative to correct injustice.

The roles MGR played ranged across the spectrum of occupational and caste groups in plebeian Tamil society. MGR played roles such as those of a peasant, an industrial worker, a rickshaw puller, a fisherman, a hunter, a boatman and an office clerk, or a champion of such occupational groups. The caste status of the characters he played also varied greatly. The culturally indigenized Malayali liminal to Tamil society could wear any social mask with conviction.[9] MGR also acted as dispossessed princes who regained their kingdoms to establish a moral order, social bandits, mythic

---

Aayiraththil Oruvan (A Man in a Million), *Urimakkural* (A Voice for Our Rights), *Engal Thangam* (Our Beloved), *Enga Veettu Pillai* (The Child of Our House), *En Kadamai* (My Duty), *Meenava Nanban* (A Friend of the Fisherman).

[8] The song beginning *'Ninaiththathai nadaththiye mudippavan naan naan'* (I am one who realizes His will) in the film *Nam Naadu* states explicitly the ability of MGR-as-hero to realize his ambitions in almost all his films. It inspired the title of a later film, *Ninaiththathai Mudippavan* (He Who Realizes His Will).

[9] See *Vivasaayee* (The Peasant), *Vettaikkaaran* (The Hunter), *Thozhilaali* (Worker), *Kalangarai Vilakkam* (The Lighthouse), *Nam Naadu* (Our Country), *Rikshaakkaaran* (The Rickshaw Puller), *Pattikkaattu Ponnaiya* (Ponnaiya the Hillbilly), *Enga Veettu Pillai* (The Child of Our House), *Uzhaikkum Karangal* (Hands That Toil), *Padakotti* (The Boatman), *Meenava Nanban* (The Friend of the Fisherman).

warrior-kings and heroic deities of lower caste groups.[10] As his role in the DMK became more significant, the roles MGR chose to play in films were drawn more from everyday society and less from religious or historical mythology. The range of roles MGR played elicited the empathy of many who found their life situations reflected in these roles. But, in a choice which appeared significant later, he did not ever play the role of a Tamil Muslim.[11]

MGR's films dealt with a variety of popular demands, including the provision of homestead land, food and clothing, protection from usury, prevention of the dismissal of workers, higher wages, lower prices, the formation of workers' cooperatives, the introduction of temperance through education and dry laws, and an end to violence against women and the poor. These needs were always fulfilled in the films without the enforced redistribution of property, a quintessential part of the populist project. While malevolent élites eventually recognized the validity of just norms, benevolent patriarchs shared their wealth with the poor.[12] Fans were invited to regard the fulfillment of various popular demands in the movies as promises that policies addressing these demands would be central to the political agenda of MGR and those associated with him.

Some of MGR's films depicted how the hero would like to reshape the world, especially those in which MGR acted as dispossessed kings who eventually enthrone justice, including the first one MGR himself directed (*Naadodi Mannan*—The Nomad King). Such films contrasted strikingly in spirit with the title of one of Annadurai's polemical tracts, *Yellorum Innaattu Mannar* (All Are Kings in This Land), which expressed the DMK's assertive

[10] See *Naadodi Mannan* (The Nomad King), *Maduraiyai Meetta Sundarapandian* (Sundarapandian, Madurai's Saviour), *Raajaa Desingu* (King Desingu), *Vikramadityan* (a historical king), *Abhimanyu* (an epic warrior), *Sarvaathikaari* (The Dictator), *Malaikkallan* (The Mountain Bandit), *Alibabavum Naarppathu Thirudarkalum* (Ali Baba and the Forty Thieves), *Baghdad Thirudan* (The Bandit of Baghdad), *Madurai Veeran* (The Hero of Madurai).

[11] He did play the roles of characters from Arabic myths, which sufficed to induce many Muslims to identify themselves with him.

[12] A popular song beginning '*Naan Aanai Ittaal, Athu Nadanthu Vittal, Intha Yezhaikal Vedanai Padamaattar*' (If I Were To Command, and My Commands Were Realized, These Poor People will No Longer Suffer) in the film *Enga Veetu Pillai* explicitly stated that the hero would alleviate suffering without expropriating property. These lyrics inspired the title of a later MGR film—*Naan Aaanaiyittaal* (If I Were to Command).

core. There is a strong suggestion that the solutions for social problems offered at the end of MGR's films will endure. If this resembles the image of a thousand-year *Reich*, the faces beaming in happiness at the end of the films also resemble Nazi representations of stolid Aryan serenity.[13]

MGR played consistently virtuous roles, in contrast with his major film rival, 'Sivaji' Ganesan, who often played the roles of immoral or weak characters (e.g. thieves, alcoholics, womanizers, illiterates). MGR played up this contrast between 'Sivaji' Ganesan and himself. When Sivaji Ganesan played the role of a thief in a movie released in 1961, MGR countered that very year with a film entitled *Thirudaathey* (Don't Steal). The rivalry between the two actors assumed sharp political significance as 'Sivaji' Ganesan joined Congress in the early 1950s, just when MGR shifted to the DMK.

MGR reinforced the benevolent image projected in his films through sporadic acts of donorship, especially at times of distress for the poor. He periodically distributed goods which fulfilled basic needs, like clothes, slippers and utensils, and contributed in money and kind when huts were destroyed by tidal waves or hurricanes. MGR usually handed out these articles himself or distributed them through his supporters, to ensure that he was acknowledged as the source of the gifts. He supplemented philanthropy with frequent dramatic gestures such as hugging poor old women during public events, which reinforced his film image of filial devotion to a 'community of mothers'. When the ADMK assumed power, the promises implicit in MGR's films were revivified for supporters, tapping the emotive power of the empathy of movie audiences to generate support for policies.

The Thrill of the Action: The Experience of the Audience[14]

Although characters other than the hero were not galvanized into action in MGR's films, the experience of watching these films mobilized many in the audience. It aroused many of them to

[13] The film titles *Inrupol Yenrum Vaazhga* (Live Hereafter as You are Today) and *Sirithu Vaazha Vendum* (Live With a Smile) reflect these features of MGR's discourse, as do a film and an autobiographical sketch, both of which were entitled *Naan Yen Piranthen* (What I was Born to Achieve). See Ramachandran (1971).

[14] The field work for this section should ideally have included participant observation of movie audiences and conversations with some of them just after

ecstatic empathy with the hero, much as Nazi cinema did with its enthusiasts,[15] to attend MGR's public meetings in large numbers, to form fan clubs which publicized MGR's films and deeds, and to campaign and vote for what they regarded as 'MGR's party'. Young men committed suicide at times in grief when their hero was seriously ill,[16] and women shed some of their habitual restraints and defied the strictures of family patriarchs to catch a glimpse in the flesh of their ideal image of a lover or son.[17]

The response of MGR's fans to his films highlights the nature of the controlled mobilization which paternalist populism effected. While the leader articulated and addressed the needs of supporters on his own initiative, supporters mobilized to praise the leader and urge others to admire him as they did. In forging such a link between the leader and his supporters, paternalism encouraged supporters to adopt an ambidextrous stance—passive in pressing

---

they had watched the films. Dickey (1933b) uses such methods to some extent, but her account is not informed by an adequate appreciation of the political context framing the experience of movie audiences. I could not adopt such methods due to time and resource constraints, and because MGR had died before I commenced my field work and had withdrawn from cinema over a decade earlier. So, I interviewed fans well after they had watched the films they discussed.

[15] When MGR's films were screened, the applause was always loudest when his name appeared in the credits, when he first appeared on screen and when he performed heroic feats. Sontag (1980) discusses the social psychology of Nazi art, including cinema.

[16] The rash of suicides was particularly great at three points when MGR's death seemed likely—1967, when he was recovering from a bullet wound; 1984, when he suffered from kidney failure; and 1987, when he died. The first two occasions coincided with election campaigns. These elections were strongly influenced by the state of MGR's health—voter participation peaked and MGR's party won resoundingly in both instances.

[17] Two anecdotes illustrate the fervent affection many women had for MGR. When MGR passed through a Madras suburb in an open jeep, a proper middle-aged housewife went running after his jeep, oblivious to her saree having come undone. Another woman kept a nocturnal outdoor vigil along with her young baby, awaiting MGR's arrival for a public meeting. When her husband berated her later for exposing the child to the elements, she cut off her *thaali* (the necklace tied during most Hindu weddings) and walked out on him. Jeyakanthan (1986) satirizes the imagined affective bond between MGR and his female enthusiasts.

their demands, but active in empowering the leader who represented these demands.[18] The tensions in this discursive strategy
were especially strong in Tamil Nadu, where many groups were
mobilized around somewhat definite notions of interest, independent of political parties.

MGR's paternalist discourse struck a chord among many groups
in Tamil society as it addressed their pressing needs. To the extent
that these groups had not been previously mobilized and lacked
clear visions of how to fulfil their needs, they tended to accept how
this discourse defined their interests. But, to the extent that they
had already formed notions of interest and were even rudimenta-
rily organized to pursue these interests, they tended to reappropriate
paternalism. To do so, they had to follow some of paternalism's
strictures, to appeal to the leader and the party as the source of
their benefits, even if they pressed for solutions rather different
from what the party intended.

MGR especially attracted people from the lower strata and
women of all but the uppermost strata, particularly in rural areas
and smaller towns. His coalition was narrower in areas where these
groups had already been mobilized behind other political conceptions—the SCs of the Kaveri valley were largely aligned with the
communists, and even many BC lower class groups and women
of the northern plains were attuned to more assertive variants of
populism. MGR's films were by far the most popular in villages
and small to medium-sized towns from the mid-1950s onwards, but
rivalled 'Sivaji' Ganesan's films in metropolitan areas only by the
mid-1960s, aided by the organized efforts of the MGR fan clubs.
Among the bigger cities, they were least popular in the 1950s in
areas where the lower strata were well mobilized—in the two
biggest industrial centres, Madras and Coimbatore, and a Kaveri
valley town, Thanjavur.[19]

There was a clear affinity between MGR's discourse and the
lower strata and women. MGR directed his appeals towards these
groups precisely because he considered them most likely to

[18] Peron represents the closest, though imperfect, parallel to the intense
link MGR forged with his supporters. See Madsen & Snow (1991).

[19] No systematic film distribution figures are available as much of the
distribution has been decentralized. But, this trend was clearly indicated by
various people associated with the film industry. Interviews: R. M. Veerappan,
'Sivaji' Ganesan, 'Tiruvarur' Thangarasu, 'Murasoli' Maran.

respond to paternalist appeals. These groups were numerous and were also the least mobilized groups in Tamil society, incapable of achieving many of their demands purely by virtue of their social power. Acting directly against dominant groups in pursuit of their aspirations could well have invited attacks they could not resist. The promise of the intervention of a benevolent and powerful hero, as a political force, to fulfil their needs was thus attractive to them.[20] Such promises might also have been more credible as they did not involve major changes in property rights, which would have evoked the resistance of dominant strata.

Alternative political projects had failed to galvanize the lower strata and women in great numbers, especially in rural areas.[21] This was linked to the means of communication and mobilization employed by the parties which piloted these projects, and the foci of their promises. Congress did not mobilize large numbers outside the valleys and the western plains, and linked itself often to traditional clientelist networks, from which women and the poor gained only limited benefits. The communists had managed to effectively mobilize the lower strata only in the valleys. The methods of communication DMK leaders employed—alliterative oratory, pulp literature, the newspaper and conversations in talk shops—readily reached only the politically literate, who were also the ones most likely to respond to the party's linguistic revivalism. The benefits the DMK promised, such as expanded caste quotas, were also most likely to benefit men of intermediate and rising strata. Congress regimes had already granted the SCs quotas at the national level and in all states; and even among the BCs, the women and the poor were least likely to gain sufficient education to benefit from these quotas. Women and the poor were more inclined towards the non-literate world of the movie-house and the promises of a paternalist hero to deliver benefits for which they need not compete. The alliance of women and the poor behind the MGR banner was that much easier as the majority of women in the work force were propertyless (a much greater proportion than among men), and both they and housewives shared with poor men the inability to control many of the basic circumstances of their lives.

[20] The social outlook of core MGR supporters was thus similar to that Marx attributed to French peasant supporters of Louis Napoleon. See Marx (1977).

[21] The assertive DMK of course represented a political project different from MGR's.

Relative literacy levels corresponded closely with the social profile and geographical distribution of MGR's supporters, as the above argument would lead one to expect. Literacy has been significantly lower among women, the poor and in rural areas since independence, and the gap has not diminished. If the disparity between men and women (58.26 per cent and 34.99 per cent) and between urban and rural areas (63.45 per cent and 38.56 per cent) is significant, that between urban men and rural women is immense (72.5 per cent and 25.8 per cent). Illiteracy is also much greater among the lower-paid occupational categories. Madras, where MGR gained great popularity latest, is also the most literate city in Tamil Nadu (68.4 per cent).[22]

Other factors also influenced the bonding of women with MGR, and assertive populism's relative failure in attracting women. Firstly, literacy figures understate the disparity between the sexes in politically relevant literacy. This is because men, especially in urban areas, have the opportunity to tarry in public spaces where they may have newspapers read out to them or participate in political discussion, even if they are illiterate. Women have been marginal to the popular culture of the streets and the talk shops, in which assertive demands for caste mobility and reconstruction of identity through linguistic revivalism gained dominance. This culture was associated with alcohol, violence and the construction of women as whores, forces from which women most desired protection.[23] Women were also most sensitive to the basic issues MGR raised—the availability of food and water, as they are home-makers; and temperance, as excessive male drinking constricts their family budgets and often leads to violence against them.[24]

[22] Department of Statistics (1987: 36–8), MIDS (1988: 262, 264).

[23] Novels, short stories and film scripts written by DMK leaders like Annadurai and Karunanidhi did propagate notions of reverence for woman-as-mother (e.g. the film *Manohara*, scripted by Karunanidhi). But, these rhetorical flourishes coexisted with the greater use of the woman-as-whore motif. Besides, the behaviour of leaders like Karunanidhi, who is reputed to employ prostitutes, and many of their followers associated the DMK primarily with the woman-as-whore motif in the public eye.

[24] Yearly opinion polls conducted by the Statistics Department of the Madras Christian College after 1968 show that between 80 per cent and 90 per cent of women of all income groups have consistently supported dry laws and the subsidized provision of rice, while the figures for men have been significantly lower and have fluctuated more.

For most women, assertive attempts at claiming greater entitlements were likely to leave them open to allegations of failing to play their appropriate gender roles, and perhaps violence. By being fans and followers of MGR, women sought a measure of dignity and relief from the difficulties and drabness of everyday life while simultaneously conforming to patriarchal definitions of femininity. While patriarchal control denied women access to public spaces where they may freely mingle with men, it permitted them to go to the movie theatre, with their families or their women friends. At the movie theatre, they could consort with the beloved hero in the imagination, identifying with MGR's various heroines whose attraction towards him was ratified by his virtue. The intensity of this identification meant that support was readily transferred after MGR's death to Jayalalitha, who was one of MGR's popular screen heroines through the 1960s and the early 1970s.[25] The sexual overtones of the ecstatic bond with the leader were far clearer than in the Nazi case. The identification of male fans with MGR was also partly with the access his heroism gave him to the hearts and bodies of attractive women, many of them of upper status groups.[26] Not surprisingly, MGR's public meetings were typically attended with much sensual tension, as people shoved their way to the front to catch a clearer glimpse of him.

While the discourse of MGR's films and aspects of the situation of women and the lower strata common to developing societies facilitated the growth of a broad popular subculture surrounding MGR, certain features of the uneven development of Tamil Nadu further aided this process. The state is the most densely urbanized in India and electricity was introduced into its villages relatively

[25] The ADMK temporarily split in 1988–9 into two factions, led by MGR's wife (V. N. Janaki) and Jayalalitha. V. N. Janaki had acted as MGR's heroine in just one movie released in 1951, which had faded in the public imagination by then, while Jayalalitha had played such roles well into the 1970s. In an informal survey I conducted in ten state assembly constituencies before the 1989 elections, I found that, of former ADMK supporters, a significantly higher proportion of women than of men supported the Jayalalitha faction.
[26] In many of MGR's films, the character he plays is involved with princesses (e.g. *Raajakumari, Marudhanaattu Ilavarasi, Chakravarthi Thirumagal, Arasilankumari, Rani Samyuktha*) or with other women of wealth and status (e.g. *Mandhiri Kumari, Rathna Kumari, Kalai Arasi, Koduthuvaithaval, Periya Idaththuppen, Panakkaara Kudumbam*).

early. This enabled cinema theatres to sprout more widely than in other Indian states. A little under a half of them are temporary structures (called touring theatres), which are moved to different locations in smaller towns and villages, to facilitate access for rural people.[27]

Despite such development, poverty levels were relatively high in Tamil Nadu—40.45 per cent in 1983, towards the end of MGR's life, and slightly higher when MGR's star was on the rise, according to one estimate.[28] A higher proportion of the work force was, and continues to be in the job categories most prone to poverty (casual labour and the unemployed) in Tamil Nadu than in India as a whole. The incidence of poverty and insecure employment for low wages is especially high among women.[29] These factors lent women and the poor a greater affinity with paternalist populism, made paternalist populism's potential coalition broader and made it easier to build an alliance between women and poor men in Tamil Nadu. Further, films were readily accessible to these groups as cinema tickets are quite cheap in India.

The Enthusiasts Congregate: The Fan Clubs

From the mid-1950s onwards, fan clubs emerged from the loosely knit popular subculture growing around MGR. Similar clubs were begun by fans of some other major film actors, notably Congress's 'Sivaji' Ganesan. But, MGR's clubs were far more numerous and active, as MGR was a more popular actor and enthusiasm for him was more closely associated with a distinctive social vision. Individual fans, mostly young men from the lower and intermediate strata, formed these clubs on their own initiative, thereby gaining minor social recognition. These clubs became talk shops,

[27] Department of Statistics (1987: 26).

[28] It was 44.1 per cent in 1961–2. 20.18 million people are estimated to have been poor in 1983, and 15.16 million in 1961–2. MIDS (1988: 85, 86).

[29] Among rural workers, 40.9 per cent of the men and 49.6 per cent of the women are casual labourers in Tamil Nadu, compared with 28.6 per cent and 34.4 per cent respectively at the all India level. The share of casual labour in the urban work force is 22.3 per cent for men and 34 per cent for women in Tamil Nadu, compared to 14.7 per cent among men and 27.3 per cent among women throughout India. While the urban unemployment rate is 14.96 per cent among men and 17.34 per cent among women in Tamil Nadu, the figures are 9.2 per cent and 12.1 per cent respectively in India. MIDS (1988: 55–78).

much like those central to the assertive populist subculture. The exclusively male and predominantly young composition of the clubs lent them the air of a street-corner gang.

The activities of the clubs and the outlook of their members centred around MGR's public *persona*, rather than the DMK's assertive populism and ethno-nationalism. While most club members supported the DMK, they did so only from loyalty to MGR, and a significant minority supported other parties. The clubs publicized and praised MGR's films and celebrated their success. They also publicized MGR's sporadic acts of donorship and repeated the same act in their localities in 'MGR's name'. This helped build an image of MGR as a donor disproportionate to the extent of his donations. Club membership brought with it material benefits—members often bought large numbers of tickets for MGR's films in advance and scalped them at much higher prices. While MGR contributed funds to some of these clubs, especially when they participated in election campaigns, resources also flowed in the opposite direction. For instance, the clubs once raised over Rs 2 million to help MGR pay his income tax arrears.[30]

Although MGR was most popular in smaller towns and the countryside, the fan clubs grew earliest and were most extensive in the densely populated modest residential areas in major cities, especially in slums. They mushroomed most rapidly after 1958, when MGR's most popular film of the pre-ADMK era (*Naadodi Mannan*—The Nomad King) was released, and competition intensified with 'Sivaji' Ganesan's fan clubs. They became constituent units of a state-wide organization, formed in 1961, which directed their activities towards aiding the growth of MGR's popularity in big cities, where it had been relatively low. Club activities brought MGR's growing metropolitan appeal to the attention of cinema theatre owners and helped MGR's films match the success of 'Sivaji' Ganesan's films in big cities by the mid-1960s.[31] The coordination of the activities of fan clubs also enhanced their political significance as it helped mobilize club members to campaign for the DMK before the elections of the 1960s and early 1970s.

[30] IE, 24 July 1977.
[31] MGR's films were thereafter released in as many big theatres in the centre of cities and in middle class residential localities as were 'Sivaji' Ganesan's films.

After the DMK assumed power in 1967, the clubs became more important in party activities. They became a refuge for party dissidents who had lost inner-party elections and factional battles at the village, ward, town, *panchayat* union or taluk levels. By the eve of the ADMK's formation, MGR's fan clubs claimed a membership of 300,000 while the DMK claimed 600,000 members.[32]

Among Karunanidhi's subtle moves to undermine MGR's political significance after the 1971 elections were efforts to undermine the fan clubs' autonomy and loyalty to MGR, and the clubs were the first to voice their opposition to these moves. When the confrontation between Karunanidhi and MGR led to MGR's expulsion from the DMK, the fan clubs helped mobilize the popular indignation. Further, many clubs spontaneously converted themselves into ADMK party branches, urging MGR to formally announce the new party's formation, in a course he had not foreseen until then.[33]

Stardust and Ballot Box: MGR and the DMK

Realizing MGR's popular appeal, DMK leaders and publicists projected him as a representative of the DMK and its message. They gave him honorific titles and party journals publicized MGR's films and their success, further augmenting MGR's popularity. Upon Annadurai's urging, R. M. Veerappan, a party member, became the manager of MGR's film career and finances, bringing the party closer to MGR's film *persona*.[34]

The success MGR enjoyed in his film career promoted the DMK's growth in many ways. MGR's films included shots and short stretches of dialogue alluding to the DMK, its flag, its

[32] *Tribune*, 12 October 1972.

[33] NH, *Statesman*, 12 October 1972; *Statesman*, TH, TI, 13 October 1972; TH, 16, 19, 30 October 1972; TI, 16, 17, 18, 20, 21 October 1972; IE, 18 October 1972; *Motherland*, 22 October 1972; Interviews: R. M. Veerappan, S. D. Somasundaram, Velur Narayanan, K. A. Krishnaswamy, 'Vannai' Mu. Pandian, Madhusoodhanan (Madras); M. Manimaran, S. Gnanasekaran (Mannargudi); P. Ilamathi, M. M. Mohideen (Tirunelveli); Radha (Veeravanallur); Sivanath Babu (Dindigul); Khaleel Pasha, K. R. Venkatesan, E. Va. Velu (Tiruvannamalai).

[34] Thandavan (1987: 49); Interview: R. M. Veerappan.

electoral symbol or its leader, Annadurai.[35] These flourishes, combined with the portrayal of corrupt or aloof political élites in MGR's films, associated MGR's image with the DMK and against Congress's bureaucratic clientelism. These aspects of MGR's films, the activities of the fan clubs and MGR's active role in DMK election campaigns ensured that admiration for MGR would translate into increased electoral support for the DMK.[36]

We saw earlier that MGR's appeal was a crucial component of the paternalist garb which the DMK assumed through the 1960s. It helped the DMK grow among groups and in areas which the party's assertive populism had not effectively reached. The DMK polled heavily even in some villages where most people were unfamiliar with the name of the party and its leader, but were already devoted to MGR.[37] Although many were drawn to MGR by the 1960s even in regions dominated by other parties, only some of them voted for the DMK due to the strength of the subcultures of other parties or aversion from the DMK's assertive features. In these regions, attraction towards MGR translated into votes more effectively after the ADMK's formation, rapidly in the southern and western plains and more gradually in the Kaveri and the Tamiraparani valleys.

Although the DMK benefited in many ways from MGR's support, the extent of MGR's popularity and the autonomy of the subculture associated with him made party leaders wary of his ambition. Although MGR never challenged Annadurai's leadership, Annadurai was embarrassed by the greater attention that crowds at public meetings gave to MGR than to those like him who had a higher rank in the party. The speeches of leaders tended

[35] The image of a rising sun and portraits of Annadurai were shown in many of MGR's films. The allusions to the party were most sustained in the film *Kaanchi Thalaivan* (The Leader from Kanchi—Annadurai's hometown) and the song which referred to Annadurai as the '*thennaattu Gandhi*' (the Gandhi of the south).

[36] In recognition of MGR's impact on voting, Annadurai said of him: '*muhaththaik kaanbiththaal paththaayiram vottu; vaayaith thiranthaal paththu latcha vottu*' (If he shows his face, we get ten thousand votes; if he opens his mouth, we get a million votes).

[37] During the 1962 and 1967 elections campaigns, DMK activists found that many people in poorer villages in the southern plains had not heard of the DMK, only of 'MGR's party'. Interviews: K. Anbazhagan, K. Arivazhagan, Velur Narayanan (Madras).

to be disturbed when large sections of the crowd stirred upon MGR's arrival or left after his departure. So, Annadurai decreed at one point that MGR should always be the last speaker at the public meetings and party conferences that MGR addressed.

To the tensions between the political ambitions of DMK leaders and MGR were added the tensions between the assertive populist core of the DMK and MGR's paternalist populism. Both tensions grew with the DMK's accession to power and the demise of Annadurai in 1969. Not only was Karunanidhi far more jealous of MGR's independent influence than Annadurai had been, the DMK regime also shed much of its paternalist features after Annadurai's death. MGR felt the need to distance himself from these moves as they were contrary to the spirit of his appeals. Being put in charge of a campaign to mollify public indignation at the abandonment of dry laws could only have been an embarrassment for one who had advocated temperance for long.[38] Besides, the DMK's reversion to a purely assertive posture provided MGR an opening to split the party's coalition. The autonomous paternalist subculture and fan clubs which had grown around him provided MGR the social and organizational base on which to build the ADMK.

THE EMERGENCE AND RAPID GROWTH OF THE ADMK, 1972–7

The ADMK was formed and grew rapidly after MGR's expulsion from the DMK in 1972. It recruited over a million members (2 per cent of the state's population) within the first two months of its existence and won every by-election conducted between 1973 and 1977. The party clearly enjoyed great popularity from its inception, although it assumed power in the state only five years after its formation, when the next state assembly elections were held.[39]

[38] TH, 16 August 1971.

[39] The ADMK's performance in the by-elections conducted in this period overstate the party's strength as these elections were held in areas of historic DMK weakness—Dindigul (southern plains), Coimbatore (western plains) and Pondicherry, a Tamil speaking region formerly colonized by France, which is ruled directly by the national government. HT, 30 October 1972; TH, 30 October, 7 November 1972; TI, 31 October 1972; Statesman, 27 November 1972.

The prior existence of a paternalist subculture surrounding MGR helped his party gain considerable support. Aspects of the conjuncture in which the ADMK was formed facilitated this process. The profile of prior voter alignments and changes in the fortunes of the DMK and Congress were conducive to the growth of a broad paternalist populist alternative. The demands which led to MGR's expulsion from the DMK, and the DMK's response to the ADMK's challenge with repression and a renewed emphasis on its assertive populism and ethnic militancy, further helped the ADMK associate itself fruitfully with paternalism.

If the DMK's support had always been strongest among the intermediate strata and groups nurtured on assertive populist notions, this was particularly so by 1972. The party was rapidly losing the paternalist appeal it had acquired through the 1960s due to the policy changes discussed earlier and its growing association with *arriviste* groups, corruption and violence. The DMK's already tattered paternalist veil was cast aside after MGR's expulsion. Congress had a shallow subculture all along in the Tamil plains. Although it gained significant electoral support among the lower strata for over two decades, this support was primarily built on élite paternalist appeals and patronage distribution through traditional and bureaucratic clientelist channels. The loosely incorporated lower strata were particularly receptive to alternative appeals by the early 1970s as Congress had split, with its major offshoot in the state disoriented after two successive electoral defeats and the minor offshoot insignificant in state politics. So, it proved particularly easy for the ADMK to attract the typical supporters of paternalist populism.

While the factional battles between Karunanidhi and MGR did not solely concern policy priorities, MGR chose to emphasize his criticism of growing corruption when he challenged the party leadership. After MGR was suspended and subsequently expelled from the party, he also criticized the DMK regime's abandonment of paternalist policies like the cheap rice scheme and dry laws, and clearly distanced himself from the DMK's ethnic militancy, separatism and autonomism.[40] Along with the CPI with which it allied itself, the ADMK compiled a list of corruption charges against the DMK leaders, and conducted rallies throughout the

[40] HT, 25 October 1972; *Statesman*, 22, 27 November 1972; TH, 6, 26 January 1973, 13 March 1974.

state demanding both an inquiry into these charges by a non-partisan commission to be appointed by the national government, and the DMK ministry's subsequent dismissal.[41] As these positions of the ADMK addressed pressing concerns, especially among groups outside the assertive core of the DMK coalition, the ADMK became the primary voice of popular dissatisfaction with the state government. The contrast between the assertive and paternalist emphases of the two major Dravidian parties' appeals was highlighted by the close association of the leaders of the two parties with the alternative variants of populism.

The DMK regime responded to the ADMK's criticisms with denials of the charges, attempts to evade an investigation of these charges by the national government and repression of the ADMK.[42] The repression was accompanied by a strident nativist stance, meant to discredit MGR by highlighting his non-Tamil origins.[43] As we saw earlier, nativism evoked little positive popular response and, along with the DMK's resort to repression, alienated people from the DMK further and aroused sympathy for the ADMK.[44]

The ADMK's Early Ideological Postures

Soon after forming the ADMK, MGR began to define the party's positions on the ideological and policy questions which had been central to Tamil politics. On the one hand, ADMK leaders stressed

[41] TI, 11 January 1973.

[42] It introduced legislation enabling it to act on allegations of criminal misconduct against public officials. This seemed intended to diminish the authority of the national parliament in this regard so that an inquiry committee favourable to the DMK leaders could be appointed. Further, the relevant bill excluded the solicitation and acceptance of bribes from its definition of criminal misconduct. TH, 13, 17 February, 31 March, 15, 21 August 1973; Patriot, 14 February 1973.

[43] The anti-Malayali propaganda began just five days after MGR was expelled from the DMK, even before the ADMK was formed. TI, 16 October 1972.

[44] Soon after MGR's suspension from the DMK, Raghavan Mampally, a Malayali member of the DMK's General Council, urged Malayali DMK members to support MGR. While the DMK's nativism solidified support for the ADMK among Malayalis, this was of marginal electoral significance as Malayalis account for merely 1.4 per cent of Tamil Nadu's population. TH, 15 October 1972; HT, 28 October 1972; Department of Statistics (1987: 62).

continuity with Dravidian movement ideology, which they rhetorically associated with the DK and the DMK under Annadurai.
On the other, they distinguished themselves from the specifically
assertive aspects of Dravidian populism, which they associated
with Karunanidhi and the post-Annadurai DMK. The tensions in
this ambidextrous rhetorical move did not become evident until
the ADMK assumed power, but the party was able to resolve the
tensions between the paternalist and assertive aspects of its populist
appeal more effectively than the DMK had.

In claiming continuity with the history of the movement, MGR
followed Annadurai's ploy when he formed the DMK. This claim
was highlighted by the party's name, which included the name of
the parent party and its founder, and the party's flag—which was
composed by adding a white stripe and Annadurai's portrait to the
red and black of the DMK flag. It was aimed at former DMK
supporters disenchanted with the DMK's abandonment of paternalist promises and other recent changes in the party. Even the
symbols of continuity highlighted the ADMK's specifically paternalist character—the white stripe in the party flag signified that
social justice would be pursued without resort to militant means,
and the inclusion of Annadurai's portrait in the flag followed the
paternalist definition of the party with reference to a leader.[45]

As the DMK regime was in disrepute at the time of the split
and MGR expected his primary source of support to lie beyond
the assertive populist coalition, he sharply distinguished the ADMK
from the assertive, militant and exclusionary aspects of the DMK's
appeals. He indicated that he had never favoured anti-Brahminism
and that the ADMK would oppose ethnic exclusion on grounds
of caste or language.[46] Further, he disavowed secessionism, which
he promised to repress were he to come to power, as well as
strident autonomism. He distanced the ADMK from the Tamil
revivalist slant which the DMK's language policy had assumed,
saying that the question of the medium of instruction would be
left for educationists, teachers and students to determine.[47] As it
was rumoured that regional parties would be banned during the

---

[45] TI, 29 October 1972; Interviews: K. A. Krishnaswamy, Velur Narayanan
(Madras).

[46] HT, 25 October 1972.

[47] ADMK leaders claimed that Annadurai did not favour anti-Brahminism,
by selectively referring to Annadurai's later career, and that he never raised

emergency, MGR even changed the party's name to the All India Anna Dravida Munnetra Kazhagam (AIADMK), to emphasize the party's acceptance of pan-Indian nationalism.[48] The party retained this name thereafter, although it was incongruous with its exclusively regional support base.[49] These gestures were lent greater effect as the DMK heightened its nativist and autonomist demands just after the ADMK was formed. They helped the ADMK gain considerable support from those who both accepted pan-Indian nationalism and took pride in their Tamil identity.

The ADMK's combination of paternalist populism and moderate Tamil nationalism, congruous with MGR's appeals before the ADMK's formation, filled the political vacuum resulting from the changing fortunes of the DMK and the Congress parties. This ideological package became closely associated with the ADMK, although the party also accommodated some assertive populist demands after it assumed power.

White-Hot Mobilization: The Formative Phase

The early years of the ADMK's existence were attended by the mobilization of groups which had played a limited political role until then, growing protest and some violent conflict with DMK activists and the police. The agitations were comparable in scale to the strongest anti-Hindi agitations of 1965 and 1968. Even before the formation of the ADMK, MGR's expulsion from the DMK brought large crowds of protesters into the streets in all of Tamil Nadu's towns. This state of spontaneous mobilization persisted

---

demands for state autonomy, though he did so until his death without using the term *maanila suyaatchi* (state autonomy). *Statesman*, 27 November 1972; TH, 6, 26 January 1973, 13 March 1974, ABP, 13, 18 March 1975; HT, 6 April 1975, 22 November 1977; NH, 22 November 1977.

[48] A small faction opposed this move, which it considered contrary to Annadurai's Tamil/South Indian nationalism, as well as MGR's command to party members to tattoo the party flag on their arms, which it said was contrary to Periar's rationalism. It left the party, only to return within two years. TH, 12, 15 September 1976; HT, 22 September 1977; Interviews: 'Kovai' Sezhiyan, G. Viswanathan (Madras).

[49] Both the DMK and the ADMK enjoyed substantial support only within Tamil Nadu and in other regions with large numbers of Tamil speakers, along the state's borders and in the cities of Bangalore and Bombay.

through the first months of the party's existence, despite repression of a level which was high by the standards of Tamil Nadu's political history. Such widespread mobilization by the ADMK occurred in spurts thereafter, especially during by-election campaigns, until freedom of association was curtailed throughout India in 1975. Although the upsurge was led by former DMK dissidents and MGR fan club members, the crowds were primarily composed of youth with little prior political experience. School and college students, the unemployed, and urban and rural casual labour formed the main active components of these crowds which, unlike those of the language agitations, also had a sizeable but relatively passive female component.[50]

Protesters engaged in large demonstrations on the streets and in front of government offices, forced the closure of shops and other businesses, conducted processions to the houses of DMK legislators and parliamentarians to demand their resignation, and attacked vehicles and some DMK leaders.[51] When groups like the Tamizhar Paathukaappu Peravai tried to coerce cinema theatre owners and managers, with the DMK regime's support, into stopping the screening of MGR's films, large crowds appeared to support or pressure theatre managers to screen the films.[52] Some of the ADMK's early rallies in Madras were larger than any previously seen in Tamil Nadu, and dissuaded the DMK from launching counter-rallies.[53] The major demands raised then were for an end

[50] NH, 12 October 1972; TH, 13, 15, 16, 19, 21, 27 October 1972, 8 February 1973; TI, 13, 18, 20, 27, 31 October 1972; *Statesman*, 12, 13, 14, 15 October 1972; HS, 12 October 1972; *Tribune*, 16 October, 13 November 1972.

[51] NH, 12 October 1972; *Statesman*, 12, 13, 15 October, 26, 27 November 1972; TH, 13, 15, 16, 19, 21, 27 October, 12, 16 November 1972; TI, 13, 20 October 1972; HS, 12 October 1972; NH, 14 October 1972; *Tribune*, 13 November 1972; HT, 11, 25 November 1972; *Patriot*, 22 November 1972.

[52] The confrontations between DMK and ADMK activists were especially dramatic and violent during the screening of the film '*Netru, Inru, Naalai*'. TI, 18, 27 October 1972; *Statesman*, 14 October 1972; Interviews: R. M. Veerappan, S. D. Somasundaram, 'Vannai' Mu. Pandian, Madhusoodhanan, Das (Madras); Khaleel Pasha, K. R. Venkatesan (Tiruvannamalai); Sivanath Babu, C. Srinivasan, Jeyaseelan (Dindigul); Radha (Veeravanallur); 'Kooniyur' Madasami (Sermadevi).

[53] HT, 11 November 1972; TH, 12 November 1972; Interviews: R. M. Veerappan, K. A. Krishnaswamy, S. Madhavan, J. C. D. Prabhakaran (Madras).

to corruption, the reimposition of dry laws, the containment of inflation and a return to cheap rice rationing. These demands, central to the paternalist outlook, were combined with local issues such as famine relief for weavers in Madurai and Chinnaalapatti (near Dindigul) and restraints on offshore trawlers in Royapuram.[54]

The early phase of ADMK mobilization ended with the first by-election which the party contested, held in Dindigul seven months after the party was formed. The ADMK billed this election a referendum on DMK rule, and faced concerted DMK campaigning and police repression. The entire state cabinet campaigned in the constituency and Karunanidhi tried to augment the party's limited support among the SCs by granting Rs 1.3 million for the purchase of cows in local SC villages during the campaign, and by highlighting his son's recent marriage to an SC woman.[55] The district secretary forced shopkeepers to contribute money to the DMK campaign, into which government officials were recruited. Both the DMK and the ADMK brought very many activists into Dindigul from around the state to campaign against and confront each other. DMK toughs attacked activists of other parties, primarily of the ADMK, killing an ADMK town secretary. The police joined in the violence and arrested 400 ADMK activists, but not a single DMK member. Despite the violence and a paucity of funds, the ADMK managed a spectacular victory, beating the other parties handily in all six segments of the Dindigul parliamentary constituency, and Congress-O relegated the DMK to the third place.[56] Although the results of this election overstated the ADMK's strength and the DMK's weakness, as the DMK was always rather weak in Dindigul, it changed the tone of state politics. The

[54] Interviews: V. P. Balasubramaniam (Dindigul), N. Vedachalam, Mathivanan, Madhusoodhanan (Madras).

[55] Karunanidhi's initiation of this marriage proposal was associated with a seamy story of adultery. HT, 12 May 1973; TI, 19 May 1973; Interview: O. P. Raman (Madras).

[56] Patriot, 26 April 1973; HT, 12 May 1973; TH, 15 May 1973; NH, Motherland, 21 May 1973; HT, TH, 22 May 1973; Interviews: O. N. Sivagnanam, Maya Thevar, Manimaran, K. Anguswami, Samadharmam, V. S. Lakshmanan, Abdul Samad, Oomer Shah, Sivanath Babu, C. Srinivasan, V. P. Balasubramaniam, S. A. Thangarajan, Ramaswami (Dindigul); S. Madhavan, O. P. Raman, Qadir Shah (Madras).

DMK remained on the defensive throughout its three remaining years in power.

Party Organization and Support

The MGR fan clubs and some DMK branches initially converted themselves into ADMK branches, providing the framework for the party organization. Some dissident DMK leaders who had lost factional battles joined the ADMK soon after its formation.[57] Those who had been close to MGR, like his film finance manager R. M. Veerappan, became important figures in the new party. Further, the bulk of the student wing of the DMK shifted to the ADMK, providing it some of its major early organizers, like S. D. Somasundaram and Azhagu Tirunavukkarasu. But, only a minor proportion of the district- and local-level leaders and members of the DMK shifted to the ADMK in the early years of the latter party's existence.[58]

The early leaders of the local ADMK branches were the main fan club organizers, most of whom were not DMK party officials and thus not centrally involved in the DMK's patronage networks. They could therefore credibly criticize the DMK's corruption. In Royapuram, the ADMK was led initially by 'Vannai' Mu. Pandian, who had formed one of the earliest MGR fan clubs in 1957. In Tiruvannamalai, the early leaders were Khaleel Pasha, a tailor's apprentice, and K. R. Venkatesan, a small shopowner, who organized the fan clubs. Similarly, N. Manimaran and Sivanath Babu, the town fan club secretaries, led the ADMK in Mannargudi and Dindigul respectively. Such local leaders remained most fiercely loyal to MGR, but some of them were marginalized by more socially influential individuals or defectors from the DMK once the ADMK assumed power.

Assertive Dravidianism had reshaped public culture in such a way that individuals from outside the Tamil speaking caste Hindu

[57] Among the prominent DMK leaders to join the ADMK early on were K. A. Mathiazhagan (one of the DMK's five founding leaders), K. A. Krishnaswamy, 'Nanjil' Manoharan, T. K. Srinivasan, Vallimuthu and Thillai Villalan. TH, 30 September, 21, 22 October, 14 November, 3 December 1972; HS, 16 December 1972; NH, 17 October 1972; Interview: K. A. Krishnaswamy (Madras).

[58] TI, 18, 20 October 1972; Interviews: R. M. Veerappan, S. D. Somasundaram, L. Ganesan, Balasubramaniam (Madras); Azhagu Tirunavukkarasu (Idamelayur).

core of Tamil society, as conceived by it, had ceased to play a major political role even in Congress by the 1960s.[59] Such individuals regained significance with the ADMK's emergence. While H. V. Hande, a Kannadika Brahmin who had been with the Swatantra party, and G. R. Edmund, a Christian from the fisherman caste, became state-level ADMK leaders, the likes of the Marwari merchant Pavan Kumar, the son of a Tiruvannamalai town Congress leader, and the Saurashtra speaking mechanical goods shopowner Sivanath Babu and the Telugu speaking former Congress student activist Gopalakrishnan in Dindigul became local leaders. Along with MGR's new emphasis on his insignificant past as a Congress member,[60] the ADMK's moderate ethnic appeals attracted many from early Dravidianism's out-groups and aided the recruitment of many nurtured in pan-Indianist subcultures. The party gained considerable support from the outset from Christians in Dindigul and Sermadevi, Saurashtra speaking weavers in Dindigul town, Telugu speaking Reddiar landlords in Tiruvannamalai, and Anglo-Indians in Royapuram, and somewhat later, from Brahmins around the state.

While women played only a secondary role in the party, the significance of female support for the ADMK was reflected in the existence of a strong women's wing to the party. The women's wing was stronger and more active in organizing the party's public meetings and in election campaigns than the women's wings of any other party in the state.[61]

Those drawn into politics by the ADMK's early mobilization swelled the party's ranks rapidly. The membership was composed primarily of the lower strata typically attracted to paternalist populism. Pre-existing rivalries between the lower and intermediate strata were played out in terms of alignments behind the paternalist and assertive brands of populism in many areas. Some local DMK leaders had bought trawlers in the Royapuram area, benefiting from generous loans granted during DMK rule and conflicts arose between them and artisanal fishermen. The latter rallied behind the ADMK banner, joined by the casual labour in

[59] The communist parties and Swatantra were the only exceptions to this trend by then.

[60] TH, 6, 26 January, 13 March 1974.

[61] Interviews: Alamelu Appadurai, B. Valarmathi, Sathyavani Muthu (Madras).

the area, especially the SCs.[62] Similarly, in the Sirumalai hills and the neighbouring dry villages on the outskirts of Dindigul town, landless SCs rallied behind the ADMK, while the largely BC proprietor peasants were with the DMK, and the biggest land-holder and contractor in the area was the town Congress leader, Ponniah Ravuthar.[63] Political alignments followed lines of strati-fication less once the ADMK broadened its coalition after assuming power.

The differences in the social backgrounds of DMK and ADMK activists are reflected by the different media the two parties primarily used for propaganda. While the DMK appealed primarily through journals to activists habituated to reading, the ADMK appealed through films to activists who were predominantly not politically literate. The DMK leaders published a wide range of journals, but the ADMK did not have a party organ through significant periods. The newspaper *Thennagam*, published by some prominent defectors from the DMK, was adopted as the party organ, and replaced later by *Anna*, which had a fitful existence.[64]

The ADMK retained the signs of its spontaneous emergence around a charismatic leader. It was always looser in its structure and more unsystematic in its activities than the DMK, although it had a greater social presence than the non-populist parties. The leader was the source of all authority within the party and local party functionaries owed their positions to those above them in the party hierarchy. Strict rules did not govern the formation of party branches and the selection of office-bearers. While MGR, and later Jayalalitha, often recognized local leaders with strong support among activists, sycophancy and loyalty to the leader were crucial for survival. Even important leaders proudly proclaimed that they were mere zeroes who required MGR to provide the 'one', which when placed ahead of a string of zeroes gives them value at the

[62] Interviews: 'Vannai' Mu. Pandian, Madhusoodhanan, Das, Kapada Raje, Veeranathan (Madras); Bavinck (1977).

[63] Interviews: C. Srinivasan, V. S. Lakshmanan, Jeyaseelan, Gopalakrishnan (Dindigul).

[64] ADMK activists grant that their cadre do not read regularly, making newspapers a poor medium through which to publicize party activities and directives. Interviews: K. A. Krishnaswamy, Velur Narayanan, Sathyavani Muthu (Madras); Gnanasundaram, Gnanasekharan (Mannargudi); C. Srinivasan, Gopalakrishnan (Dindigul).

polling booths. Activists were often lax in voter registration and election campaigning, in the belief that it was primarily MGR's name that delivered the vote. Despite the claims to continuity with Dravidian movement history, it was good form for party orators to declare that MGR was the only leader they ever recognized, not Periar or Annadurai. The role of former DMK leaders in the parent party did not ensure them significance within the ADMK.[65] No serious challenges emerged to MGR's leadership and, after the succession battle was over, to Jayalalitha's. As the leader's charisma motivated mass support, all attempts to split the party failed during MGR's lifetime, contrary to the DK's and the DMK's experiences.[66]

While the ADMK's paternalist populist character made charisma central to authority within the party, the leader's charisma was ultimately founded on being an exemplar of the paternalist outlook. Although authority within the party emanated from the leader, supporters could appropriate party ideology in diverse ways with the collusion of local party leaders, much as in the DMK. Such appropriation was generally possible if it could be legitimized with reference to the particular nature of the party's populist appeals. While the leader could appoint or remove all party functionaries at will, he did not wish to prevent the appropriation of ADMK appeals by the squatters and artisanal fishermen of Royapuram in their conflicts with police bulldozers and trawlers as his charisma rested on his image as a champion of such demands. The role of populist appeal in generating and maintaining support introduced some accountability even though the leader apparently enjoyed absolute power.

Responses of Other Parties to Paternalist Populism

As the ADMK captured the political initiative, all other parties had to alter their strategies in light of this development or lose support.

[65] Mathiazhagan realized this during his brief tenure in the ADMK.

[66] The ADMK underwent minor splits in 1976 and 1984. Finding themselves in the wilderness, the dissenters returned to the party after a few years in both cases. TH, 12 November 1976, 24 January 1977, 4, 6 September 1984; TI, 2 September 1984; *Statesman*, 4 September 1984; Interviews: 'Kovai' Sezhiyan, G. Viswanathan, S. D. Somasundaram (Madras); Azhagu Tirunavukkarasu (Idamelayur).

The DMK and the CPI altered their approaches most, Congress-R and the CPI-M less, and Congress-O the least. Partly due to this, it was Congress-O that lost the most support when voters realigned themselves after the ADMK's emergence. However, the ADMK also benefited at the expense of other parties.

We saw that the DMK reacted to the ADMK's criticisms with a heightened emphasis on its assertive populism, ethnic militancy and autonomism. Karunanidhi claimed that MGR and Congress-R leaders were involved in a conspiracy to destabilize the DMK's pro-BC regime, motivated by ethnic prejudice. His play for the support of the intermediate and rising strata was reinforced by an increase in the BC quota from 25 per cent to 31 per cent, and an expansion in the list of groups eligible for the BC quotas. When the ADMK's growth seemed inexorable, Karunanidhi appealed to Congress-O in desperation, saying he would prefer Kamaraj to MGR as the Chief Minister, as the former was a Tamil.[67] The DMK regime launched physical attacks on ADMK activists and pro-ADMK students, denied loans to known ADMK supporters and tried to nationalize cinema theatres, to hamper the screening of MGR's films.[68] It also tried to defend its record on corruption, reintroduced dry laws and abolished horse racing, in ineffective steps to regain its paternalist appeal.[69] While its repression and nativism were counter-productive, the DMK's return to its assertive moorings might have been its best response to the ADMK's growth as the DMK was incapable of outflanking MGR on paternalist grounds. This move restricted the erosion of support from the core of the DMK's assertive populist coalition.

The CPI responded most favourably to the ADMK upon its creation, hoping to tap the popular resentment against the DMK. M. Kalyanasundaram, one of its leaders, and Mohan Kumaramangalam, a former communist who had become a minister in the national cabinet, colluded closely with MGR after the latter's expulsion from the DMK. They encouraged MGR to form a new party and stay aloof from Congress-O, and joined him in compiling a list of charges of corruption and misuse of power

---

[67] *Tribune*, 14 November 1972; HT, 22 November 1972.
[68] TH, 12 January, 8, 20, 21 February, 23, 27 March 1973.
[69] TH, 6, 19, 20, 27 June, 1 September, 20 December 1973; 23 August 1974; *Patriot*, 3 September 1974.

against the DMK regime. These charges, presented to the national government, were used to dismiss the state government some years later.[70] The CPI helped the ADMK's early activists organize the unrest generated by MGR's expulsion from the DMK and actively participated in the early ADMK-led agitations.[71] Although the CPI thereby restricted its loss of support to the ADMK, it did not gain at the DMK's expense. Besides, the party's alliance with the ADMK provoked a minor internal split, weakening the party in its strongholds in Thanjavur district.[72]

The CPI-M was more guarded in its response to the ADMK. While endorsing the ADMK's campaign against corruption and supporting ADMK candidates in some by-elections, it did not join all of the ADMK's agitations and made its support contingent on the ADMK staying aloof from Congress-R. The party was united in this attitude and lost less support than the CPI did through the mid-1970s.[73]

Congress-R responded somewhat favourably to the ADMK as the perception had grown within the party that its alliance with the DMK for the 1971 polls had hindered its prospects in the state. While not allying fully with the ADMK, it maintained contacts with the party and encouraged its criticisms of DMK corruption. Congress-R hoped thereby to gain at the expense of both Dravidian parties.[74]

Kamaraj argued that ADMK leaders were as involved as the DMK leaders in corruption, ethnic chauvinism and populist gimmicks. He maintained that the split within the DMK was merely over the sharing of the loot and urged his party organ to

[70] TH, 16, 24 October, 7, 13 November, 5 December 1972, 21 August 1973; Patriot, 14 February 1973; IE, 2 October 1979.

[71] Interviews: P. Manickam, K. T. K. Thangamani, A. Srinivasan (Madras).

[72] TH, 5, 6, 11 July 1973; TI, 13 March 1972; Interviews: A. K. Subbiah (Sithamalli), Ambikapathi (Mannargudi).

[73] TI, 13 November 1972; Statesman, 23, 26 November, 10 December 1972; TH, 5 December 1972; Interview: A. Nallasivan (Madras).

[74] Congress-R leaders suggested a poll alliance with the ADMK at one point, and DMK leaders claimed that the national government encouraged MGR's opposition to the DMK by easing the pressure that had been put on him to pay his tax arrears and clear his cloudy record on foreign exchange transactions. Statesman, 5 December 1972; Patriot, 17 March 1973; FPJ, 19 March 1973; HT, 14 January 1976.

restrict its reportage of the ADMK's activities, wary of losing much of the anti-DMK vote to the ADMK. Congress-O tried unsuccessfully to attract disaffected DMK legislators and maintained its opposition to the ADMK until it merged with the Janata party in 1977.[75]

Congress-O's stance restricted its contact with the popular mobilization against the DMK regime. Besides, the differing attitudes towards the ADMK adopted by the two Congress parties arrested moves to merge the state units of these parties for at least four years. The view that only a reunified Congress party could defeat the DMK was gaining support within both Congress parties after the 1971 elections. Differing attitudes towards the ADMK, along with opposition within the Congress-R state unit and the national Congress-O, delayed such a reunification, which could have merged Indira Gandhi's paternalist populist appeals with a strong organization.[76] Such a merger did not happen until the ADMK had already redrawn the Tamil political map. As it occurred during the emergency, only about half of the Congress-O shifted to Congress-R in the state. The other half joined the Janata party, leaving the pan-Indian forces still divided.[77] The timing of the shift from Congress-O to Congress-R created the perception that it was motivated more by a desire to avoid repression than to promote a pan-Indian alternative to Dravidianism.

The strategic shifts which the ADMK forced upon other parties were a measure of its significance, and further aided its success at their expense.

---

[75] HS, 12 October 1972; *Motherland*, 9 November 1972; ABP, 12 November 1972; *Statesman*, 5, 10 December 1972; TH, 9 January, 8 May 1973; IE, 14 March 1973; HT, 26 June 1975; Jeyakanthan (1973); Interviews: G. Karuppiah Moopanar, M. P. Subramaniam, P. Nedumaran, V. Ramani Bai (Madras).

[76] *Statesman*, 3 June 1971; TH, 22 September 1971, 13 March 1972, 26 August, 15, 16, 18 November 1973; IE, 13 December 1971; 6, 22 May 1972; TI, 13 March 1972; HT, 3 April, 21 May 1972; *Patriot*, 17 March 1973.

[77] TH, 3 December 1975, 2 January, 11, 17 February 1976; TI, 2, 19, 24 January, 14 February 1976; HT, 3, 14, January, 5, 11, 15, 16, 18 February, 26 April 1976; *Patriot*, 20 January 1976; IE, 11 February 1976; *Statesman*, 15, 17 February 1976; NH, 17 February 1976; Interviews: G. Karuppiah Moopanar, 'Sivaji' Ganesan, P. Nedumaran (Madras).

THE ONSET OF DRAVIDIANIST DOMINANCE

The ADMK, the DMK and the Congress Parties

The ADMK's ideological position lay roughly between those associated with the DMK and the Congress parties. The ADMK shared the DMK's populist character, but not its assertive emphasis. It adopted the paternalism of the Congress parties, but did not share their élite orientation and bureaucratic clientelism. While the ADMK alluded to ethnic identity, it distanced itself from the exclusionary, separatist and militant features of the DMK's appeals. It embraced pan-Indian nationalism, but made it a secondary aspect of its appeals, unlike the Congress parties. Further, paternalist populism was more central to the ADMK than to Congress-R, and the party's social presence was greater than that of either Congress offshoot by the mid-1970s. The intermediate position occupied by the ADMK helped it draw considerable support from both parties that previously dominated Tamil politics.

The ADMK gained support more from former Congress voters than from former DMK voters for four reasons. First, the Congress subculture was shallower and less cohesive than the assertive populist subculture, and so more vulnerable to alternative appeals. Most of those who shifted from the DMK to the ADMK had supported the DMK due to their admiration for MGR rather than because they were part of the assertive subculture. Second, groups with the greatest affinity with paternalist populism, the lower strata and women, had been predominantly aligned with the Congress offshoots until the ADMK emerged. These groups had been linked to the Congress subculture mainly through the mediation of social élites, but felt a more direct link with the ADMK due to MGR's prior image as their benefactor and the more significant role that people from the lower strata found in the ADMK party organization. Third, many nurtured in the pan-Indianism of the Congress tradition considered the Congress offshoots no longer electorally viable and found the ADMK a tolerable alternative to the DMK. Fourth, many former Congress supporters from the upper strata dismayed by the erosion of social deference due to the growth of assertive populism felt that the ADMK's paternalism would threaten their dominance less.

As the ADMK grew primarily at their expense, pan-Indian parties could not consistently attract over 20 per cent of the popular vote on their own steam after 1972.[78] The ADMK augmented its support by dispensing patronage after it assumed power.

The Social Geography of Partisanship After the Rise of the ADMK

As many voters were already aligned with other parties when the ADMK emerged, the depth and social profiles of pre-existing subcultures affected the ADMK's growth. The geographical variations in partisanship since the ADMK's birth show the durable impact of prior subcultures.

The ADMK, the DMK and Congress offshoots have been the state's most significant parties since the ADMK's formation. The dominant Congress offshoot has been allied with a Dravidian party in all the general elections of this period except those of 1977 and 1989.[79] As the ADMK's support declined due to a temporary split in 1989, the results of the 1977 state assembly elections best indicate the extent and geographical dispersal of support for the major parties after the ADMK's emergence. Four parties gained over 15 per cent of the vote in the 1977 elections, and none of them were allied with each other. The 1980 poll results are particularly misleading as the alliance during those elections between the DMK and Congress brought together parties whose social and geographical bases were quite different, alienating many who had tended to

[78] While Congress polled over 20 per cent of the vote in the 1980, 1984 and 1989 elections, it gained most of its votes in 1980 and 1984 due to its alliance with one of the Dravidian parties. It gained at the ADMK's expense in 1989 because the ADMK was temporarily divided, but polled barely over 20 per cent of the vote even then. My claim is borne out by the poor performance of the pan-Indian parties in the 1977 elections and in by-elections which they contested without an alliance with a Dravidian party through the 1980s and 1990s.

[79] A Congress offshoot has significantly outdistanced the others in all general elections conducted through this period except the one in 1977. The offshoot which polled most votes was Congress-O until 1976, Congress-I from 1980 onwards and the Tamil Maanila Congress (TMC) in the 1996 elections. Congress-R and Janata polled approximately equal proportions of the vote in 1977. The TMC probably owed much of its vote in 1996 to its alliance with the DMK.

support either party. As the social and geographical bases of the
ADMK and Congress have been rather similar, the results of the
1984 elections, in which these parties were allied, are more useful.[80]
So, the succeeding analysis relies primarily on the 1977 election
results, with some reference to the results of 1984 and 1989.

The social matrix of contention helps capture the social and
geographical profile of partisanship. Prior partisanship, especially
the depth of pre-existing subcultures, predicts partisanship better
than social structure does. Although the ADMK's paternalist
populism has been most popular among the lower and upper strata,
its support has not been greater in the stratified valleys, where these
groups have a larger share in the population, that in the plains
regions, where the intermediate strata are more numerous. The
ADMK gained early and significant strength in one valley
(Tamiraparani) and not the other (Kaveri); and in two of the plains
regions (south and west), but not the other (north). Although the
party's support increased through its years in power, it remained
relatively stronger in its early bastions—the western and southern
plains, and the Tamiraparani valley. These were the regions where
Congress electoral dominance was most pronounced during the
bureaucratic clientelist period, and where the DMK was weak
early on and lost greatest support from the mid-1970s to the late
1980s.

The above pattern of partisanship was seen in all the elections
of the last two decades except the ones in 1980. Tables 1.3 B, 1.3
C and 1.3 D illustrate this pattern. Indeed, a comparison of Tables
1.3 A and 1.3 B shows that the relative share of the vote accruing
to the ADMK and the DMK in 1977 broadly resembles the pattern
of vote distribution between Congress and the DMK in 1962, when
the DMK began to mount its assertive challenge. The areas of
relative DMK strength (the northern plains and the Kaveri valley)
and weakness (the southern and western plains, and the Tamiraparani

[80] The ADMK was allied with Congress-I in the 1991 and 1996 elections
also. The DMK performed poorly in the former elections as it was unfairly
blamed for the assassination of Rajiv Gandhi during the election campaign.
The ADMK polled much less than it customarily does in 1996 due to popular
aversion to Jaylalitha's blatant corruption and violation of pluralism. It
remains unclear whether the ADMK will recover from its current problems.
So, neither the 1991 nor 1996 election results indicate the usual profile of
support well.

valley) were the same in both elections, although the expansion of the DMK's clientelist networks during its years in power made its support less unevenly dispersed in the later election.

The depth and cohesion of past subcultures explain some features of the electoral outcomes after the ADMK's emergence better than past electoral strength does. Congress lost support most rapidly in regions where its subculture was shallow, even if it might have enjoyed considerable traditional clientelist support in some of these areas. Major Congress offshoots contested two elections (1977 and 1989) without the aid of a Dravidian party in the era of Dravidianist dominance. While they polled 31.74 per cent of the vote in 1977 and 18.5 per cent in 1989 in the north-east, where the Congress subculture had been shallowest, they polled 43.04 per cent and 30.01 per cent respectively in the Tamiraparani valley, where the Congress subculture had been deepest.[81] Congress's electoral decline was more rapid in Dindigul, where it was once electorally dominant despite having a somewhat shallow subculture, than in Tiruvannamalai, where it had been electorally weaker in its heyday than in Dindigul, but had a deeper subculture.

The DMK retained greatest support in the regions where its subculture was broadest. Thus, it gained a higher proportion of the vote in 1977 in the Kaveri valley, where its subculture was broadest, than in the northern plains, where its earlier electoral strength was greatest. This pattern of vote distribution was the result of the ADMK gaining the support of most groups whose loyalty was not already firmly pegged to other parties. The ADMK also made minor inroads into the subcultures of other parties, especially after it attained power.

In the southern plains, where the subcultures of all parties were relatively shallow, the ADMK grew fastest and attained its most dominant position. It was here that the ADMK had its pocket boroughs where MGR and other major leaders tended to contest. Dindigul is a prime example of this trend, having provided the ADMK its first electoral victory, by a landslide, within a few months of the party's emergence. The ADMK or its ally won every election in this constituency decisively until disunity led to defeat

---

[81] Both Congress-R and Janata were major offshoots in 1977, but only Congress-I was in 1989. The figures refer to the vote shares of the alliances, including some minor parties, led by major Congress offshoots.

in 1989. This party was especially dominant in the rural sections of the constituency, largely beyond the pale of the Congress and communist subcultures, winning in every rural polling booth in 1977, 1980 and 1984.[82] The shift from Congress to the ADMK was greatest in villages where Congress's electoral strength had been primarily based on traditional clientelism, and those where the ADMK had allied itself with subaltern opposition to repression and exclusion.[83] Even in Dindigul town, the ADMK was most successful among groups that had not been closely incorporated by any party, such as the *arriviste* middle classes living in the new residential localities in the western parts of the town, and groups whose specific demands it had taken up (e.g. weavers).[84] The pattern was similar in the western plains, although the ADMK's growth was less rapid and spectacular here than in the southern plains as the Congress and communist subcultures had some depth in some pockets in the west.

In the Tamiraparani valley, Congress had a deep subculture and the communists had some strength, but assertive populism was a limited force. So, the ADMK gained considerable support, but not

[82] The Congress subculture was stronger in the bigger villages of Thadicombu and Agaram. The ADMK was commensurately weaker there. The establishment of a small mill in Thadicombu also helped the communists and the DMK gain some strength there in the 1980s as their unions were stronger than the ADMK's. Even in 1989, the combined vote of the two ADMK factions was greater than that of the other parties in all but one rural polling booth. Booth-wise elections results for Dindigul, 1977, 1984, 1989; Interviews: Gopalakrishnan, C. Srinivasan, V. S. Lakshmanan, Charles (Dindigul).

[83] The Sirumalai hills, where the plantation owner and Congress leader Ponniah Ravuthar dictated much of the vote in the 1950s, and the villages surrounding Sukkampatti, dominated by the landlord and former Congress legislator Rangaswami Reddiar, belong to the first category. The villages of Kallipatti, Alakkuvarpatti and Irandellaiparai, where local ADMK activists opposed the practice of untouchability, helping SCs gain direct access to their burial grounds, are in the second category. These were among the villages of greatest ADMK strength in Dindigul panchayat union. Interviews: Rangaswami Reddiar, V. S. Lakshmanan, Gopalakrishnan, C. Srinivasan, Jeyaseelan (Dindigul).

[84] Weavers were attracted by the agitation the ADMK conducted on their behalf in 1974, when rising yarn prices found them in distress. Interviews: Sivanath Babu, Gopalakrishnan, V. P. Balasubramaniam (Dindigul).

the degree of dominance it enjoyed in the southern and much of the western plains. It won every election in Sermadevi until 1996, but Congress was a close second until the local ADMK legislator's effective pork-barrel politics augmented ADMK support through its decade in power. Congress retained greatest strength in the bigger towns of Kallidaikurichi and Ambasamudram where its Gandhian wing had been active in nationalist agitations and social work, and among the weavers, peasants and brown sugar makers in the dry villages of the Kadayam and Pappakkudi panchayat unions, whose agitations had been led by socialists who subsequently merged with Congress.[85] The DMK retained some support among the Mukkulathor whose social ascent it had promoted, and the communists among the tenant farmers and mill workers they had organized.

The ADMK increasingly made inroads into caste-based Nadar and SC support for Congress, partly because P. H. Pandian, the local legislator for over a decade, restrained the violence of some Mukkulathor farmers and cattle-rustlers. It grew strongest in the smaller towns and villages irrigated by the Kannadian channel as P. H. Pandian used his powers, as the state assembly's Deputy Speaker and later Speaker in the 1980s, to ensure that his constituency would be favoured with much of the water from the channel.[86] Further, the initiation of many minor public works in the constituency helped the ADMK grow steadily during MGR's rule.[87]

[85] Congress polled most in these pockets in 1977. Interviews: C. Hariharasubramania Iyer, V. Rathnasabapathi, S. Thangam Pillai, S. Ananthanarayanan, K. S. Rajagopal, Gajendra Thevar, Sankaralinga Adaviyar, Subbiah Adaviyar, P. H. Pandian, 'Pathamadai' Paramasivam.

[86] This made for a contrast with the record of Chellapandian, the local Congress legislator of the 1960s. While Chellapandian had also been the assembly Speaker, a Congress leader with greater factional strength, K. T. Kosalram, directed water from the Kannadian channel to areas he represented, in Srivaikuntam taluk. Both water supply and ADMK support increased during ADMK rule in Melaseval (Chellapandian's village), Tiruppudaimarudur (the village of the former DMK District Secretary, Rathnavel Pandian), Gopalsamudram, Sermadevi and Kallidaikurichi. Interviews: P. H. Pandian, S. Ananthanarayanan, 'Kooniyur' Madaswami, Sivan Pandian, S. Sethuramasubramaniam.

[87] P. H. Pandian even gained the ADMK's minor faction its sole assembly seat of the 1989 elections in Sermadevi.

The depth of the DMK's subculture in the northern plains restricted the ADMK's growth, as evidenced by the electoral histories of Royapuram and Tiruvannamalai. While the DMK won all but one election in Royapuram after 1967, it lost in Tiruvannamalai only when the ADMK and Congress joined forces in 1984 and 1991. The early growth and depth of the assertive subculture in Royapuram ensured continued DMK strength. But, the paternalist subculture was also strong' in the constituency, which had about sixty MGR fan clubs by the early 1970s. So, the ADMK attracted consistent support from many fishermen, SCs and casual workers, some of whom had been MGR loyalists since the 1960s, and others of whom shifted later to the ADMK from Congress, with which they had been but loosely aligned. With some of the merchants in the area joining the ADMK bandwagon after it assumed power, the party was a close second in Royapuram in all but the 1991 elections, which it won.[88]

The ADMK was weaker in Tiruvannamalai than in Royapuram as the Congress subculture was broader in the former constituency, while the assertive populist subculture was equally strong in the two places. Further, more influential local notables remained loyal to Congress in Tiruvannamalai than in Royapuram and enjoyed the reputation of being good patrons, and their clients' voting decisions were influenced by this reputation even through the 1970s.

The constraints to ADMK growth were even greater in the Kaveri valley, where the subcultures of Congress, the communists, the DMK and the DK were vigorous. In Mannargudi, the ADMK has only been one of many strong parties, winning only when allied with one of the other major local forces. It grew only after the systematic direction of patronage towards local landless SC agricultural workers weakened the bonds between this group and the communists, and the use of activist and police muscle countered the threats of violence which the communists had used to ensure the loyalty of their supporters.[89]

[88] Interviews: 'Vannai' Mu. Pandian Madhusoodhanan, Das, Arumugasami (Madras).

[89] Interviews: M. Mahalingam (Adichapuram-Nemmeli), P. Thangavelu (Mannargudi).

THE AGENDA OF PATERNALIST POPULISM: THE ADMK IN POWER

The paternalist promises implicit in MGR's films and the demands of the ADMK while in the opposition, influenced the party's policy agenda after it assumed power in 1977. However, the paternalist populist coalition was not broad enough to ensure electoral triumph. Further, many segments of the assertive coalition were well organized to press their demands. So, the ADMK regime also addressed many of the latter coalition's demands while retaining its predominantly paternalist emphasis. As it addressed the expectations it aroused more consistently than the DMK had, it enhanced its support through its ten years in power (1977–88), unlike the DMK regime, whose support had eroded badly within its the first six years.

Four factors helped the ADMK regime succeed more than its predecessor. First, the agenda of paternalist populism dispersed benefits more widely than that of assertive populism. Second, the greater strength of MGR's prior paternalist image meant that the distribution of benefits generated more support. Third, the first two factors made many voters more willing to excuse corruption during the ADMK's rule. Fourth, the ADMK regime managed some of the fiscal problems which frequently accompany populist policies more effectively than the DMK regime had, although at the cost of neglecting industrial development.

PATERNALISM AND POLICY

The ADMK regime's policies regarding the supply of food and alcohol were most important in addressing paternalist promises regarding the cheap provision of wage goods. Other policies were also consistent with the party's paternalist orientation—housing provision, pension schemes, unemployment doles, an abortive attempt to change the basis of preferential policies, the writing off of unpaid agricultural loans and the pattern of agrarian subsidies. These policies were combined in such a way that they paid their way over time, while maintaining support for the regime.

In keeping with MGR's advocacy of temperance, the ADMK regime introduced dry laws soon after assuming power.[90] The

[90] TH, 1 July 1977.

conditions for issuing liquor consumption permits were tightened, reinforcing measures adopted during the emergency. Government employees were barred unconditionally from drinking and the penalties for illicit liquor distillation and bootlegging were increased. A police cell was established to identify and punish government officials who sabotaged dry laws, and posters were put up in major cities urging people to report violations of these laws. By the end of the ADMK's first term in office in 1980, a three month term of rigorous imprisonment and a fine of Rs 3,000 were mandated for those who so much as smelt of liquor; and 300,000 people were charged with the violation of dry laws. While a limited amount of alcohol could still be produced, the excise duty on it was increased, and the Indian government was requested to introduce a dry belt of 25 km around the borders of the state.[91]

While these policies effectively addressed the paternalist coalition, they caused a considerable fall in tax revenue. This led the ADMK regime to relax dry laws in the early 1980s, in a reprise of the earlier DMK administration's moves.[92] The regime reversed its course so rapidly that by 1981 it had auctioned off as many as 15,000 licenses for the production and sale of liquor. ADMK activists acquired a number of these lucrative licenses and got big payoffs in granting them to others. Alcohol production became the fastest growing industry in the state through the early 1980s, growing at an annual rate of 20 per cent, and the taxation of alcohol production and sale became the state government's largest source of revenue.[93] MGR attempted to gloss over the contradiction between these policies and the party's promises. He dismissed the Excise and Revenue minister who initiated the policy changes, claimed that the intended aim was to curb illicit liquor distillation and vaguely promised to reimpose dry laws.[94]

[91] TH, 5 May, 9 June, 16, 26 July, 1, 5, 8 August 1977, 8 January 1978, 16 November 1983; *Statesman*, 31 July 1977, 9 February 1980, 1 August 1984; HT, 26 September 1978.

[92] TH, 8 August 1977; HT, 25 January 1980, 15 June 1981; TI, 7 April 1980; IE, 9 September 1981; *Statesman*, 13 August 1981.

[93] *Statesman*, 13 August 1981, 1 August 1984.

[94] IE, 9 March 1981; *Statesman*, 1 August 1984; Interview: S. D. Somasundaram.

The abandonment of dry laws in the face of fiscal burdens was widely unpopular, especially among women and poorer groups.[95] To offset the damage to its paternalist image, the ADMK regime introduced a free lunch scheme in 1982.[96] This scheme initially covered six million children between the ages of two and nine who were attending public schools and child-care centres, numbering six million. By 1984 it was extended to children in the first ten grades of school, non-school going children under the age of fifteen, pensioners, military veterans and destitute widows. The number of beneficiaries increased to over eight million by 1985 and to twelve million (a fifth of the state's population) by 1986. About 200,000 people were employed to implement the scheme, many of them destitute widows and SCs, who were given preference in hiring.[97] A study commissioned by the UNDP showed that this scheme had an appreciable effect on children's health. Further, school enrollments increased after the scheme was introduced, although they overstate the effect on education as many children came to school only at lunch time.[98]

Although the fiscal feasibility of the lunch scheme was questioned by many, it was widely popular, especially among women and the poor.[99] As choices regarding sharing food are an important means through which status is affirmed, the arrangement for members of all castes to eat together was a potent symbol of their equal recognition as citizens. The scheme was called the 'Chief Minister's Nutritious Noon Meal Scheme' and publicized with photographs of MGR sharing a meal with some children on the day the scheme was inaugurated. It was highlighted in news programmes produced by the state government, which were screened prior to all feature films in movie theatres. Further, government propaganda films about the lunch scheme and other policies linked them to promises implicit in MGR's films. Shots from MGR's films in which the hero provides food for the hungry were spliced with documentary footage of children eating their free lunches, for instance.

[95] Madras Christian College (MCC) Yearly Opinion Polls, 1981–4.

[96] Harriss (1986); TH, 1, 2, July 1982; *Statesman*, 25 August 1982.

[97] *Statesman*, 25 August 1982; *Tribune*, 17 April 1984; TH, 14 September, 3 October 1984, 18 May 1985.

[98] TH, 11 September 1984, 18 May 1985; Harriss (1986).

[99] MCC Opinion Polls, 1983–8.

The popularity of the lunch scheme more than compensated for the abandonment of the dry laws, and the revenue generated from the latter move helped fund the expensive lunch scheme. While the revenue from taxing and licensing the production and sale of alcohol was around Rs 2 billion per year through the mid-1980s, the amount spent on the lunch scheme was just a little under that figure.[100] ADMK leaders and activists gained kickbacks in implementing the lunch scheme, by influencing hiring and the contracts given to supply groceries.

By promoting the growth of liquor production, the ADMK regime created a base to sustain and expand the ambitious lunch scheme. It maintained its budgetary commitment to the scheme, unlike the Andhra Pradesh government, which abandoned a similar programme based on the Tamil example. So popular was the lunch scheme that the DMK, initially critical of its fiscal feasibility and the corruption associated with it, felt compelled to augment it when it returned to power in 1989, but gained little support as a result because it was MGR who had initiated the scheme.[101]

The lunches were supplemented by other steps to improve food supply—increases in the number of ration shops and in the amount of subsidized rice to which low- and middle-income earners were eligible.[102] The new ration shops were opened in rural areas, contrary to the urban focus of the DMK's rationing schemes. The DMK regime's scheme to provide slum dwellers permanent housing was extended beyond Madras to smaller towns and villages. These moves and the village self-sufficiency scheme, which provided the rural poor social infrastructure and loans, were also consonant with the paternalism of the ADMK's appeals and addressed the party's social base.[103] So were other policies which were announced with much fanfare, but hardly implemented— pensions and provision of free rice for destitute farm workers,

[100] *Statesman*, 1 August 1984; TH, 18 May 1985.

[101] In criticizing the corruption associated with the scheme initially, some DMK orators claimed that the poor women employed as cooks in connection with the scheme had suddenly grown fat. Such blunders did not help the DMK regain a paternal image. Interview: 'Pulavar' K. Govindan.

[102] TH, 16, 25 July 1977; IE, 27 August 1984.

[103] TH, 16 November 1983, 7 May 1984, 9 January 1986.

doles of Rs 50 per month for unemployed high school graduates and of Re 1 per day for those below the poverty line, and a promise that at least one person in every family would be given employment.[104]

The ADMK regime could distribute goods more widely than its predecessor had as it dispensed less lumpy goods—for instance, lunches and small loans, rather than land or jobs. Not only was patronage distributed to non-ADMK supporters, such groups were sometimes especially favoured to help win them over, quite in contrast to the way the DMK regime had allocated caste quotas. The SC communist strongholds in East Thanjavur district gained a larger share of the funds distributed in connection with the village self-sufficiency scheme. It was ADMK activists, rather than bureaucrats, who distributed such benefits, and that too mainly during election campaigns, showing that the aim was to gain electoral support.[105] Such a disbursal of benefits, without regard to current partisanship, was clientelist to the extent that it was aimed at cultivating future loyalty, and succeeded in doing so to a significant extent.

This approach of the ADMK regime succeeded more than the efforts of the DMK regime had in making inroads into communist support among SC agricultural workers in eastern Mannargudi taluk. The bits of homestead and agricultural land that the DMK regime had offered some communist defectors could of necessity be given only to a few village leaders. By marking them as people who had been bought over, it undermined their ability to command support. This happened to the local SC communist veteran, A. K. Subbiah, who brought with him to the DMK only a few communist supporters, primarily those who had experienced some upward social mobility.[106]

The patronage extended by the ADMK regime appeared to be aimed at social development, rather than to be a part of a political bargain, although such a bargain was implicit. While many SC caste

[104] *Statesman*, 13 May 1980; HT, 7 March 1982; TH, 17, 26 August 1980, 16 November 1983; IE, 27 August 1984.

[105] TH, 28 December 1983; Interviews: N. Govindarajan, Gnanasekharan, Manimaran, Gnanasundaram, P. Thangavelu (Mannargudi); Mahalingam (Adichapuram-Nemmeli).

[106] Interviews: 'Ullikottari' Arunachalam, N. Govindarajan, Ku. Balakrishnan (Mannargudi), A. K. Subbiah (Sithamalli).

elders who had helped maintain loyalty to the communists were enticed into the ADMK with lucre, this brought them no odium as many other local SCs also gained benefits. Further, many local ADMK leaders from the SCs were regarded as having joined the ADMK from conviction, not due to opportunism. M. Mahalingam, the son of an SC communist village leader in eastern Mannargudi taluk, who began his political career in the ADMK while he was a student and rose to the status of a parliamentarian, is a good example.[107] Due to the efforts of such activists and judicious patronage distribution, the ADMK attracted more SC communist supporters than the DMK had in Mannargudi, including many who remained landless agricultural workers.

Congress's sustained strength in the Tamiraparani valley in the 1970s helped the ADMK legislator from Sermadevi bargain for funds and favours for his constituency. We saw that he increased river water supply and built social infrastructure in villages where Congress was strong until the 1970s, helping the ADMK augment its support in these regions. These efforts evoked support all the more effectively as the benefits were not made explicitly contingent on supporting the ruling party.

The wider non-partisan distribution of patronage coexisted well both with MGR's Bonapartist tendencies and with the growth of corruption in the ADMK's lower echelons. MGR cultivated a group of bureaucrats, especially police officials, who provided him information and helped control society independent of the party, as well as spy on his political lieutenants, of whom he was suspicious. Bureaucrats were likely to play such a role only if the channels of recruitment into government employment, especially at the higher levels, were more distinct from the ruling party's subculture than they had been during DMK rule. The greater discretion the leader enjoys in a paternalist party helped MGR insulate government recruitment somewhat from the party subculture. MGR's reliance on bureaucrats to direct the course of policy became stronger during his last term in office, when his powers of speech were impaired by a stroke, and the ADMK was in some disarray due to intense factional struggles.[108]

[107] Interviews: M. Mahalingam (Nemmeli—Adichapuram), V. Rangaraj (Kottur).
[108] The information which the police supplied about the activities of some ministers that contained the slightest suggestion of disloyalty led MGR to

Corruption seeped further down the lines of command in the ruling party during ADMK rule, a trend common through much of India over the last two decades. This occurred primarily after the ADMK's first truncated term in office (1977–80), during which the ruling party had a relatively clean record, and found itself as a result with limited campaign funds for the next elections. As lower-level DMK cadre did not share much in the bribes when their party ruled, they dispensed favours primarily in view of their social contacts, which were strongest within the party subculture. As the ethos changed through the 1970s to give ADMK activists a greater share of the bribes by the time their party attained power, the political loyalties of individuals became less relevant to them than the payoffs they received in dispensing patronage. The homes of the cadre of the two Dravidian parties reflect these differences in their fates. While many DMK activists and local leaders still lived in modest homes in the early 1990s, only local ADMK leaders who had lost their significance within the party by the 1980s made few visible material gains through their party's periods in power.

The policies of the ADMK regime ensured it widespread support, while simultaneously giving rise to a system of corruption somewhat unfettered by party loyalties. The regime of political rents was presided over by a leader whose charisma led supporters to dissociate him from the corruption, although his cut was reputed to be the largest. The wide distribution of benefits without obvious regard to partisanship made many willing to tolerate the visible corruption of activists. Corruption and democratic legitimacy coexisted comfortably.

PATERNALIST POPULISM AND SOCIAL PLURALISM

Of the ADMK regime's paternalist policy initiatives which favoured less organized groups, some came into conflict with already mobilized interests. The regime abandoned some of these policies in the face of protest without giving up its focus on paternalist populism and the lower strata. It was initially more obdurate on some other issues, thereby temporarily alienating some organized industrial workers and white collar workers. However, it often accommodated these groups, always peripheral to its coalition, in

---

invite these ministers to his palatial home, only to have them roughed up. Such anecdotes were related by officials who insisted on anonymity.

other contexts. Policies regarding caste quotas, agrarian subsidies and industrial relations illustrate how the ADMK regime augmented its primarily paternalist coalition while maintaining social pluralism.

Caste Quotas and the Caste Associations

Support for the poor was always more crucial to the ADMK's appeals than was the promotion of BC interests. Indeed, caste was not central to the ADMK's conception of the popular interest in the way that it was for assertive Dravidianism. MGR was somewhat sympathetic to the criticism that BC quotas had predominantly benefited the upwardly mobile groups among these castes, rather than the poor. So, he announced in 1979 that caste would be supplemented by income as a criterion for the quotas for the so-called 'other backward classes'. Only those BCs whose families earned under Rs 9,000 a year were to be eligible for the quotas.[109] Although this revision in the basis of access to preferential quotas was a departure from the practice of the previous six decades, MGR introduced it without prior consultation with his cabinet.[110] It was a risky manoeuvre as most groups which would benefit from this move were poorly organized, while the interests it attacked had long been organized in strong caste associations.

The caste associations took to the streets in concerted protest against the change in preferential policies, and were considerably strengthened in the process, as many who had taken the BC quotas for granted and preferred to ride free until then hastened to join and finance the associations. As a sacred cow of assertive Dravidianism was under attack, the DK and the DMK lent their strident voices to the protest, hoping to split the ADMK's base. Organizations emerged to coordinate the activities of caste associations during these agitations, and continued to play this role thereafter. A clear divide also emerged in the process between the associations of the BCs of lower status and those of higher status.

The Janata party lost control over the national government at this stage. Congress-I allied itself with the DMK in the ensuing parliamentary elections as the DMK offered to let it contest more

[109] However, caste was to remain the sole basis for eligibility for the SC quotas.
[110] HT, 25 January 1980; Interviews: R. M. Veerappan, S. 'Panruti' Ramachandran, S. D. Somasundaram, Sathyavani Muthu (Madras).

seats than the ADMK did. Tamil Nadu favoured the Congress-DMK alliance overwhelmingly in these elections, in keeping with its sustained preference since the early 1970s for Indira Gandhi's rule at the centre. This created the impression that support for ADMK rule in the state had declined as the party had performed far better in the 1977 parliamentary elections, in alliance with Congress-I, and the 1977 state assembly elections, in alliance with some minor parties. The ADMK's success in subsequent state elections strongly suggests that no such decline had occurred. However, the strength of the agitations that the associations were conducting at the time led MGR to suspect that the ADMK's popularity had indeed declined and that his paternalist remoulding of preferential policies was an important reason for this decline. So, MGR not only reinstated caste as the sole basis of the 'other backward class' preferences, but also increased the BC quota from 31 per cent to 50 per cent, in a sudden *volte face*.[111]

Congress-I regained control over the national government in the 1980 elections, and dismissed the state government, claiming that the ADMK has lost its popular support. However, the ADMK won handily in the assembly elections which followed, with the support of some minor parties, over the same Congress–DMK front which had vanquished it a few months earlier in the parliamentary polls. The difference in the outcomes of the two elections of 1980 in Tamil Nadu showed that the electorate had taken account of the very different patterns of party competition at the state and national levels and adopted different voting strategies at those two levels, as it would in other Indian states later. The majority of Tamil voters favoured Congress rule at the centre in all post-colonial elections until 1996, and that of the ADMK in the state between the ADMK's formation and MGR's death. Yet, the results of the two elections of 1980 created the impression that preferential policies were a crucial voting issue, dissuading subsequent state governments from altering the entrenched position of caste as the sole basis for preferential quotas. Even groups complaining that rising strata benefited disproportionately from the existing quotas pressed for separate quotas for the less privileged BCs, rather than the use of income as a basis of eligibility for preferences, in Tamil Nadu.

[111] Radhakrishnan (1989); TH, IE, HT, 25 January 1980.

The ADMK regime's quick change of course on preferential policies signalled to the intermediate and rising strata that the regime was likely to accommodate typical assertive populist demands if they were backed by sufficient mass mobilization. Indeed, MGR transacted more closely with caste associations through the 1980s than the DMK regime had. These associations retained influence over the allocation of BC quotas and those of some of the less privileged BCs launched militant challenges to the ADMK regime and its successors.

Even the agitations which took place during ADMK rule threatened the DMK's coalition more than that of the ADMK. The lower BCs, whose associations launched the more militant agitations, associated the existing BC quotas with the assertive Dravidianist vision of the BCs as a homogeneous group. The ADMK's paternalist populism appeared to these groups more in tune with their demand for a greater share for the lower BCs. This was especially true of the Vanniar, the largest megacaste of the northern plains, amongst which the DMK had gained considerable support through the 1960s and 1970s. A new Vanniar association emerged in the 1980s around demands for a separate quota for the Vanniar, whose gains from the BC quotas were neither commensurate to their numbers nor to their role in Dravidianist subcultures. It launched violent agitations through the 1980s and effected a breach in the DMK's base of the northern plains when it called for a boycott of the 1989 assembly elections, and formed the PMK later in 1989 to represent the lower BCs. Not only was the 1989 poll boycott successful in some pockets, but the PMK attracted over 3 per cent of the vote in 1991 and 1996, concentrated in the northern plains.[112] The emergence of a party on the basis of the Vanniar caste association restricted the violence the latter engaged in. Localized caste clashes continued under ADMK rule, however, following the earlier pattern.

The DMK eventually responded to the Vanniar association's demands by introducing a separate quota for the so-called 'most backward castes' and 'denotified communities' (which had been deemed criminal tribes in the colonial period). But, it did so too late, after the Vanniar association had become an independent political force, with the effective 1989 poll boycott.

[112] Interviews: K. Ramdas, Subramaniam, 'Panruti' S. Ramachandran (Madras).

Farmers' Associations

Farmers' associations, led by rich farmers to press for better terms of trade for agriculture, had attained significant strength in Tamil Nadu by the early 1970s, before they did in other parts of India. We saw that they spearheaded violent agitations under DMK rule. Like the caste associations, they grew in strength during the tenure of the ADMK regime and made it cater to strata beyond the core of its coalition. By the early 1980s, such farmer mobilization was widespread in many regions of India, as was the willingness of governments to accommodate their demands.[113]

Major farmers' agitations and tax revolts arose in Tamil Nadu in 1978 and 1981, and smaller ones thereafter, over demands for increase in the rice procurement prices set by the government and in subsidies for fertilizers and other inputs; for reductions in the power tariff for water pumps, in crop cesses and other agrarian levies; and in opposition to government efforts to confiscate the property of loan defaulters. They occurred in all areas of extensive well-irrigated commercial agriculture, not just in the northern plains where many proprietor farmers supported the DMK, but also in parts of the western and southern plains, which were the ADMK's strongholds.[114] The strength of these agitations and the regime's inability to placate the more militant farmers' associations seemed a threat to ADMK support at one point. The threat seemed greater as the DMK supported the agitation and formed a farmers' wing of the party, to maintain contact with the farmers' associations and increase its support among the intermediate and rising agrarian strata.[115] Despite the violent confrontations that ensued between the police and farmer agitators, the ADMK regime adroitly split the base of the farmers' associations and managed to restrict its electoral losses.

The ADMK regime responded to the agitation of 1978 by decreasing power tariffs and interest rates on agrarian loans, and increasing paddy procurement prices to levels higher than those recommended by the national government.[116] Yet, the militant

[113] See T. Brass (1994).
[114] TH, 10, 11, 17 April 1978; TI, 13, 17 April 1978; *Statesman*, 10 April 1978; HT, *Tribune*, 11, 12 April 1978; Gurusamy (1993).
[115] TH, 29 December 1977, 5 March 1979; NH, HT, 11 April 1978.
[116] NH, TH, 11 April 1978.

associations continued to agitate and disrupt traffic, and attacked the police in many regions. Although further concessions ended this protest phase, the militant associations retained the support of most farmers, and initiated further agitations and tax revolts by the end of 1980 over similar demands.[117] Their strength was sufficient to urge the Prime Minister to initiate negotiations with them.

Embittered by its confrontations with the ADMK regime, the strongest association opposed the ADMK in the 1980 parliamentary elections, supporting the DMK in the legislative assembly elections and Congress in the parliamentary elections.[118] It was however unable to determine the voting decisions of many supporters, underwent several splits, and declined thereafter. The prior pattern of Dravidianist mobilization and the ADMK regime's selectively accommodative response to the agitations helped the regime weather the challenges the farmers' associations posed. The strong party allegiances to which Dravidianist mobilization had given rise limited the ability of interest groups to determine voting decisions. This was especially so once the major farmers' association converted itself into an electoral party in 1982. As supporters of the Dravidian parties could pursue many demands through associations without changing their party loyalties, interest groups were likely to induce changes in voting preferences only if one of the major parties was unreceptive to their demands.

The ADMK regime did not grant the demand of the Vanniar caste association for a separate quota for its caste, and the DMK was initially hostile to demands for tiers within the BC quota. So, the Vanniar association could induce many of its members to abandon the Dravidian parties and vote for the PMK instead. On the contrary, the ADMK regime effectively accommodated some of the demands of the farmers' associations. The Vanniar association more successfully became an independent political force also because it organized around ethnic appeals that were similar to those of the Dravidianists in some respects, while the farmers' associations relied purely on the bonds forged by material interests.

---

[117] TH, NH, HT, *Statesman*, 10–13 April, 27 May 1978; TH, 14, 20, 24 April, 6 July 1978, 8 May 1981; TI, 14 June 1978, 3, 12 November 1980; IE, 1 January 1981; Gurusamy (1993: 55–119).

[118] IE, 9 May 1980; Interviews: Sivaswami (Thondamuthur), R. Renu, Murugan (Tiruvannamalai).

Not only did the ADMK regime accommodate various farmer demands from the outset, it also divided the associations' coalition by granting greater concessions to smaller farmers, among whom it always enjoyed greater support. Tiered tariffs were introduced in 1978, lower for smaller than for bigger farmers.[119] The regime thus maintained its paternalist emphasis even while conceding the demands of richer farmers. This helped it retain the loyalty of party supporters who had joined the agitations, as well as gain further support among smaller farmers. The regime was better able to split the base of the farmers' associations as the farmer leaders opposed the preferences for smaller farmers. Although the earlier DMK regime had also given smaller farmers preferences, the ADMK regime more effectively created a rift between the smaller and more prosperous farmers because of its prior affinity with the lower strata and its use of less repression against farmer agitators.[120] It was the DMK and the communist parties, rather than the ADMK, which lost some support among farmers as a result of the agitations in the areas surrounding Tiruvannamalai and Dindigul respectively.

The newer farmers' associations of western and north-western India, unlike those in Tamil Nadu, retained their strength and gained independent political influence because parties were weaker in these regions before the rise of farmer unrest, the governments of these states were unable to split the farmer coalitions as effectively as the ADMK regime did, and these associations combined appeals to an agrarian community with appeals to an intermediate caste coalition. The decline in farmer militancy in Tamil Nadu did not end the growth of agrarian subsidies. The associations were contained only because the ADMK regime and its successors continued to hand out subsidies, often of a tiered nature, to preclude a return to agitations. Power was supplied free to small farmers and hut dwellers by 1984 and loan recovery

---

[119] TH, NH, 11, 20 April 1978; *Statesman*, 27 May 1978.

[120] While 24,329 agitators were arrested in 1972, fewer than 3,000 were in 1978. Besides, the police used less violence during the 1978 and 1981 agitations, and the army played a more limited role, although these agitations were as strong and more widespread than the one of 1972. While the police killed about 50 agitators in 1972, they killed none in the agitations which took place during ADMK rule. TH, 7 July 1972, 20 April 1978; NH, HT, 6, 9 July 1972.

became increasingly lax, especially from poorer farmers.[121] The farmers paid a long-term cost, however, as the decline in revenue meant that well-digging and water pump installation decreased from the rapid rates of the 1970s.[122]

Trade Unions

While many farmers and members of intermediate castes supported the ADMK, the majority of industrial and white collar workers supported the DMK or the communists at the onset of ADMK rule.[123] Trade unions of diverse affiliations had considerable strength among industrial workers, mainly in larger firms, and among many white collar government employees. The organized strength of these groups and their prior alignment behind other parties made them likely threats to a paternalist regime inclined to give other interests priority. So, the ADMK regime's responses to the demands of these groups were oriented to bringing them under its tutelage, but these efforts were only partially successful.

The ADMK regime began a frontal attack on trade union militancy within a year of assuming power. It banned strikes in 1978, empowered itself to arrest strikers and unionists in a wide range of services it deemed essential, and vowed to end all agitations within three months. The Central Reserve Police Force was stationed permanently in major industrial areas to aid employers facing worker militancy.[124] Such measures were used to attack militant unions, especially those led by communists and the DMK, and urge workers towards moderate unions like the INTUC and those floated by the ADMK, which were more willing to accept government mediation and terms favourable to employers. The police were particularly violent in suppressing strikes in bicycle, automobile and textile factories, and in the Madras harbour.[125]

[121] IE, 27 August 1984.

[122] MIDS (1988).

[123] The only significant exceptions were the upper castes, SCs and Christians.

[124] Although the 'essential services' ordinance was repealed due to trade union pressure later in the year, it was revived again in 1980. TH, 19 July, 29 October 1978; ABP, 17 May, 19 July 1978; Statesman, 25 July 1978; HT, 10 February 1981.

[125] TH, 27 October 1977, 19 July, 19 October 1978; Statesman, 25 July 1978; IE, 10 January 1981; HT, 1 February 1982; Interviews: A. Srinivasan,

The ADMK regime dealt more severely than its predecessor had with strikes by government employees, especially those launched by transport workers, school and college teachers, and the lower ranks of the government office staff (called 'non-gazetted officers').[126] While militant party-affiliated unions were repressed in the private sector, even initiatives by moderate unions without party affiliation were not tolerated in the public sector. Middle class sentiments were particularly offended when a large number of teachers, many of them women, were jailed for long periods in the mid-1980s when they demanded revisions in their salaries, which had not been adjusted to keep pace with inflation for almost a decade.[127]

The repression of militant trade unions considerably weakened communist- and DMK-affiliated unions in some industries, especially in transport and textiles. But, the ADMK unions did not themselves make major gains. Even those that gained some support lost much of it while the ADMK was out of power between 1988 and 1991, only to regain it when the ADMK returned to power. The DMK-affiliated LPF unions were not weakened to a comparable degree when their party was out of power. Unions unaffiliated with parties grew in some sectors during ADMK rule. The regime's unresponsiveness to the demands of government employees led to the unionization of some government employees for the first time, notably school teachers and the police.

Despite the ADMK's limited success in the trade union field, laws empowering the government to mediate in industrial disputes and measures for labour welfare (the latter only partially implemented) helped the regime bring more organized workers under government tutelage.[128] The government mediated industrial disputes more frequently under ADMK rule and often applied pressure on both workers and employers to accept the settlements it suggested. It refused to intercede on behalf of workers when unions reneged on government-mediated agreements, and forced

---

A. Nallasivan, Kuppuswami (Madras); K. Ramani (Coimbatore); Ananthakrishnan (Vikramasingapuram).

[126] TH, 11 June 1977, 8 September 1979; *Patriot*, 2 October 1977; *Statesman*, 28 June 1978.

[127] See Radhakrishna (1985).

[128] TH, 16 November 1983.

employers to negotiate with workers during lockouts by threatening to remove police protection for factories.[129] Workers often shifted to moderate unions which accepted government mediation during prolonged confrontations with obdurate managements, reducing strikes and other challenges to the government's industrial policy.[130]

Even in cases in which the government repressed strikes, it remained open to reconciliation with workers by granting some of their demands. Many dismissed strikers at the T. I. Cycles factory and in the police force were later reinstated when they gave assurances of 'good behaviour' and the wage demands of white collar government employees were partially satisfied after their strike wave was over.[131] However, such concessions were granted not when the unions raised their demands, but as a gesture of the regime's magnanimity after the strikes had been broken. Such an approach weakened unions without entirely alienating workers from the regime. The ADMK did not make major electoral gains as a result, however, as many workers left militant unions for tactical reasons without changing their voting behaviour.

The paternalist regime thus managed to contain trade union militancy without entirely undermining pluralism, by using limited and selective repression while offering some inducements for accommodation. It transacted willingly with interest groups such as farmers' associations and caste associations, whose demands did not threaten the apparent social consensus underwritten by Dravidianism. It was more wary in dealing with groups which it considered greater threats, either in its role as an employer—thus, the intolerance of strikes among government employees; or in its role as the guarantor of the social order—thus, the repression of communist unions. As the ADMK repressed these groups more than its predecessor had, it also attracted them less.

Dissent and Social Control

The ADMK regime was especially intolerant of explicitly political threats. It passed legislation to help suppress political dissent,

[129] TH, 27 October 1977; *Tribune*, 17 April 1984.
[130] TH, 2 August 1984; Interviews: K. Raghavanandam, Palani, A. Nallasivan, A. Srinivasan, S. C. C. Anthony Pillai, Kuppuswami, Kuchelar (Madras).
[131] TH, 27 October 1977, 13 February 1986; NH, 9 June 1981.

whether expressed in the press, by publicists and political parties, or in the form of minor armed revolts. It used a bill to ban 'scurrilous writing' to briefly jail some journalists who criticized some of its policies, and another bill banning films critical of legislators to curtail the screening of films scripted by Karunanidhi.[132] The government suppressed the report of an official committee investigating the mysterious death of a bureaucrat, in which some ADMK leaders were alleged to have been involved, and DMK leaders were harassed when they released sections of the report.[133] Attempts were also made to restrict protest by requiring political parties to pay for damage to property resulting from the agitations they led.[134]

The regime strengthened provisions for the preventive detention of criminals and protesters.[135] MGR created a niche in the police force, occupied by trusted officials, which oversaw the politically sensitive aspects of social control. The police acquired sophisticated equipment, such as armed helicopters, which it used to hunt down non-parliamentary communist groups which became active in some of the state's poorest regions.[136] Greater repression was employed against such groups, most clearly opposed to the Dravidianist social consensus, than Tamil Nadu had seen since the crackdown on the CPI in the early post-colonial years. Many activists were killed and tortured, and methods to wreck the nervous systems of prisoners, later used more widely in other parts of India, were first tried in Tamil Nadu.[137] Such repressive methods, used mainly against left-wing extremists when MGR ruled, were extended to forces closer to the political mainstream during Jayalalitha's rule (1991–6), contributing to the ADMK's downfall in the 1996 elections. Although the inclinations of paternalist populism towards social control were tempered by the prior strength of social pluralism, civil rights were abridged when

---

[132] TH, 27 September 1981, 5, 7 April, 14 May 1987; *Statesman*, 25 August 1982, 25 June 1983; HT, 12 June 1983.

[133] HT, 1 February 1981; TH, 10 May, 26 November 1981.

[134] *Statesman*, 13 September 1981; IE, 27 September 1981.

[135] TI, 11 January 1982; IE, 17 December 1982; *Statesman*, 14 February 1983.

[136] TH, 2 May 1984.

[137] IE, 16 August 1980, 25 August 1981; *Statesman*, 23 June 1983.

MGR's government faced radical challenges and when Jayalalitha's felt beleaguered.

PATERNALIST POPULISM AND ETHNICITY

Due to its disinclination towards ethnic militancy and the lessons it learnt from the earlier failures of the DMK's strident autonomism and nativism, the ADMK regime did not initiate mobilization on language and caste demands. But, it responded to such demands when they arose and sometimes pre-empted them. The ADMK's methods of mobilization and policies restricted conflicts with the national government and provided more space for non-Tamils, the upper castes and, to some extent, the SCs than the DMK's did. But, they did not inhibit intolerance towards non-Hindus as effectively as the DMK's approach did, and were no better in containing caste conflict.

Tamil Nationalism and ADMK Rule

We saw that a somewhat stable equilibrium had been reached in national language policy by the late 1960s. On the one hand, Hindi came into use along with English as an official language at the national level, and the national government avoided formally committing itself to continue using English permanently. On the other, attempts to replace English entirely with Hindi were stalled, and Hindi played a marginal role in education and official communication within Tamil Nadu. The minor moves which the proponents of 'Hindi only' at the national level have subsequently made to supplant English have invariably evoked Tamil nationalist denunciation, often leading to their retraction. The ADMK joined the Tamil nationalist chorus on such occasions, even pre-empting it at times.

Language grievances were voiced when particular central government departments announced that knowledge of Hindi was necessary for recruitment or promotion, despite the parliament not having adopted resolutions to this effect, and when such departments sent circulars in Hindi to the Tamil Nadu government.[138] As the television spread beyond the Indian metropoles to all other parts of the country through the late 1970s and early 1980s, Tamil

[138] For examples, see *Tribune*, 9 February 1983; TH, 21 September, 16 October 1986.

nationalists complained of subtle Hindi imposition because much of the programming in the government-controlled channels was in Hindi. The ADMK regime echoed such complaints, using former stalwarts of the language agitations as spokesmen. It also made adherence to the existing equilibrium regarding language policy a condition for supporting various governments in power at the centre.[139]

The ADMK opposed the DMK's autonomist demands from the outset, maintaining that they were irrelevant if relations between the state and central governments were satisfactory. When it voiced autonomist demands, these pertained only to the limited devolution of specific powers to the states, in contrast with the DMK's position that the states should have authority over all issues except defence, communications, currency and foreign relations.[140] The ADMK was keen to maintain good relations with whichever party ruled at the centre, and tended to support this party through much of its decade in power.[141] Besides, MGR slew a few Dravidianist sacred cows in outlawing attempts to mourn in public the anniversaries of Indian independence, India's birth as a republic, and Gandhi's birthday.[142] The ADMK regime continued to observe the Tamil nationalist official rituals which the DMK had introduced, but introduced no new ones. It however made some symbolic cultural revivalist gestures, such as establishing a university for Tamil research and holding a World Tamil Conference on a grander scale than the DMK regime had done, to supplement MGR's image as a patron with that of a patriarch of ethnic pride.

The Sri Lankan Tamil Militancy and the Dravidianists

The growth of ethnic conflict in Sri Lanka and the resulting flow of large numbers of Sri Lankan Tamil refugees and militants into

[139] TH, 12 June 1978, 7 May 1985; ABP, 12 June 1978; *Statesman*, 4 November 1978, 27 July 1979; *Tribune*, 9 February 1983; Interviews: K. Kalimuthu, Pe. Srinivasan (Madras).

[140] TH, 8 July 1977; NH, 22 November 1977, 9 June 1981; HT, 22 November 1977; *Statesman*, 4 November 1978, 27 July 1979; *Patriot*, 13 December 1984; Interviews: 'Murasoli' Maran, S. Madhavan, Sathyavani Muthu (Madras).

[141] Indeed, when Janata lost power in 1979, MGR forthrightly said that he would support any party which could form a stable government. HT, 17, 18 July 1979.

[142] TH, 2 April 1982.

Tamil Nadu in the 1980s once again lent Tamil ethnicity a sharp salience.[143] Although only some intellectuals in Tamil Nadu were concerned about ethnic relations in Sri Lanka before the 1980s, news of attacks against Tamils in Sri Lanka, especially the anecdotes of refugees, aroused much popular sympathy in the state from 1983 onwards. The DMK, which had for long raised the issue of discrimination and attacks against Sri Lankan Tamils without making it a central concern, demanded Indian military intervention to protect Sri Lankan Tamils and to help militant groups in their quest for secession after the violence against Sri Lankan Tamils escalated in 1983.[144] Many activists of the DK, the DMK and smaller Tamil parties built close links with Sri Lankan Tamil militant groups and conducted an extensive drive throughout Tamil Nadu to build public awareness and support for their cause. The DMK made its demand for the protection of the civil rights of Sri Lankan Tamils and its support for the secessionist movement major planks of its election platform of 1984.[145]

The ADMK regime, which had allowed the discussion of ethnic relations in Sri Lanka in the state assembly only due to DMK pressure in 1977, began to associate itself with the agitations in solidarity with Sri Lankan Tamils from 1981. By giving government support to agitations organized by the coalition of groups allied with the DMK, it limited the DMK's propaganda gains from its support of the Sri Lankan Tamil militants. The state government ordered the stoppage of most trains and some buses during these agitations to avoid the embarrassment of having to arrest agitators who stopped the traffic. The national government aided these efforts through this period, when the ADMK was allied with the ruling Congress party, as it too wished to stem the growth of ethnic militancy in Tamil Nadu and the DMK's potential resurgence.[146] The ADMK also aided some Sri Lankan Tamil guerilla groups. As the ruling party, it could dispense far more patronage

[143] See Palanithurai & Mohanasundaram (1993).

[144] TH, 25 August 1977, 5, 13, 19 September 1981, 7 August 1983; *Statesman*, 25 August 1977, 12, 16, 23 September, 5 October 1981, 15 August 1983; *Patriot*, 2 October 1977; IE, 27 September 1981; NH, 2 August 1983; TI, 15 August 1983.

[145] DMK (1984); *Patriot*, 13 December 1984; Interviews: 'Murasoli' Maran, Vai. Gopalswami, L. Ganesan, P. Nedumaran, K. Veeramani (Madras).

[146] NH, 2 August 1983; TH, 7 August 1983.

than the DMK and smaller militant Tamil nationalist parties could, and so won the major Sri Lankan Tamil guerilla group, the Liberation Tigers of Tamil Eelam (LTTE), over to its side through the mid-1980s. MGR required the LTTE to refuse the DMK's aid if it was to receive his, and the LTTE complied. The ADMK did not, however, officially support the demand for secession from Sri Lanka and cracked down on calls to provide armed support to the secessionist movement.[147]

Although it did not mobilize people much regarding the Sri Lankan ethnic conflict, the ADMK regime did enough to satisfy some Tamil nationalists and forestall potential electoral losses. It was aided by the limits to the empathy which India's Tamils felt with Sri Lankan Tamils due to over a millennium of different historical experiences.[148] So, the Sri Lankan ethnic conflict was not a critical voting issue for most of Tamil Nadu's electorate and irredentism appealed to very few. The DMK's efforts to mobilize and gain from public sentiments regarding the Sri Lankan conflict were more than overshadowed by the wave of sympathy which arose in response to MGR's critical illness during the 1984 election campaign. The ADMK won its most decisive triumph of the MGR era, as voters flocked to the polling booths with an enthusiasm seen only when the DMK unseated Congress from the state government in 1967.

Popular sympathy for the Sri Lankan Tamils declined thereafter in stages in Tamil Nadu. Sympathy declined because the guerilla groups engaged in fratricidal battles, their violence spilled over sometimes into Tamil Nadu which they used as a refuge through

---

[147] ADMK leaders previously associated with language agitations struck more militant postures at times, especially Kalimuthu whom MGR authorized to direct militant statements both towards the national government and those Tamil voters more sympathetic to the Sri Lankan Tamils. TI, 16 April 1983; IE, 25 October 1983; Interview: K. Kalimuthu (Madras).

[148] The ancestors of the majority of the so-called 'Sri Lankan Tamils', who reside in the northern and eastern parts of the island, have lived there for over a millennium. Migration from India has continued over the years, and the ancestors of Tamil speaking tea plantation workers living in central Sri Lanka ('Indian Tamils') migrated from India less than a century back. However, the secessionist movement has primarily been based among the former group, which also contributed to most of the refugee influx of the 1980s. See Tambiah (1986).

much of the 1980s, the Indian army's intervention in Sri Lanka led to its engaging the LTTE on the battlefield (1987–9), and LTTE activists assassinated Rajiv Gandhi in 1991. The DMK gained some support, however, by virtue of championing the cause of the Sri Lankan Tamils, especially in the southern plains where most of the refugees stayed. This broadened the party's base somewhat, increased the ethnic militancy of some of its activists and reinforced the party's image as a vehicle of assertive Dravidianism.

The LTTE revived its links with some DMK activists after the ADMK withdrew its support when it engaged Indian troops in battle. These links had an adverse effect on the DMK's performance in the 1991 polls, held in the aftermath of Rajiv Gandhi's assassination. The DMK's support for the LTTE (albeit conditional), the concerted efforts of the ADMK and Congress to associate the DMK with Rajiv Gandhi's assassination and the widespread outrage at the assassination led to the DMK's worst electoral performance since 1957. But, the assassination did not remain a crucial popular concern for long, and opinion polls indicated that the DMK had more than recovered its losses by 1993.[149]

The resurgence of ethnic militancy within a part of the assertive populist subculture contributed to a split within the DMK in 1994. Many second-rung DMK leaders and activists had come to regard Karunanidhi and his loyalists as more intent on maximizing electoral support and maintaining their control over the party than on pursuing central aspects of the assertive Dravidianist agenda. Some of them felt that major DMK leaders had compromised their stand on the Sri Lankan conflict and others were upset by the rift between party leaders and some of the lower BC associations. Yet others disliked the retention of most of the bribes among the top leaders during the DMK's brief return to power from 1989 to 1991. Such activists and others considered Karunanidhi's efforts to promote his youngest son, Mu. Ka. Stalin, as his successor out of tune with the assertive vision of the activist as the author of the populist project.

Vai. Gopalswami, who had his political baptism during the language agitations of the 1960s and rose to prominence within the DMK through close association with Sri Lankan Tamil militancy,

---

[149] IT, 1 April 1993.

became a rallying figure for many disgruntled DMK members. Much as he had during his confrontation with MGR in 1972, Karunanidhi responded to a perceived challenge with bitter recriminations and expelled Gopalswami from the party in 1993, precipitating the MDMK's formation. The MDMK immediately attracted a larger section of the second-rung DMK leadership, including as many as nine district secretaries, than the ADMK had in 1972. But, as there was no autonomous subculture loyal to MDMK leaders, unlike the case with MGR when he was in the DMK, the MDMK attracted far less popular support. By-elections conducted in May 1994 suggested that the MDMK had greater strength than the DMK in the western plains.[150] However, opposition to Jayalalitha's attacks on pluralist norms became the main concern of many voters in the next state assembly elections of 1996, leading them to back the DMK as the party most likely to outdo the ADMK. So, the MDMK gained a mere 5.7 per cent and the PMK 3.8 per cent of the vote in these polls. These results reflect no widespread resurgence of Tamil ethnic militancy. The militant postures the MDMK and the PMK have struck seem more likely to underscore their claims to revitalize assertive populism than to promote a sharply exclusionary or irredentist politics.

Caste and the ADMK

The DMK's vision of the BCs as a homogeneous group failed to recognize the distinct identities of particular megacastes and their mutual jealousies, voiced by caste associations. The ADMK's paternalist populism was not similarly predisposed against recognizing particular caste clusters. In this respect, it was closer to the DK's vision of the Dravidian community as an aggregate of megacastes than the DMK was. The associations of the lower BCs complained that assertive populism had become the vehicle solely of the rising strata, a view compatible with the ADMK's paternalist gambit which split the DMK coalition. So, the Vanniar association was more hostile to the DMK than to the ADMK.

After it abandoned its efforts to modify the basis of preferential policies in 1980, the ADMK regime transacted more closely with caste associations than the DMK regime had, thereby keeping its

[150] The MDMK outpolled the DMK in Perundurai (western plains). *Frontline*, 15 June, 1 July 1994.

finger on the social pulse. ADMK leaders mediated their party's transactions with associations of their megacastes, whose demands they used to augment their factional strength. These transactions were closer with some BC associations, which have had consider-able mass support, than with SC associations, largely based among the thin SC white collar stratum which emerged partly due to caste preferences.[151]

The government lent SC associations and SC parties its ear too. But, its welfare policies were more important in incorporating poorer SCs, who constitute the majority of their castes and a major source of ADMK support. The SCs were given priority in recruitment to implement the lunch scheme, and as beneficiaries of housing schemes, cooperative loans, and other welfare policies, and the share allocated to SCs was given wide publicity.[152] Further, the police force responded more often to complaints against the practice of untouchability than it had under earlier regimes. However, these measures were too scattered to have a significant effect on the situation of SCs throughout the state. Besides, the ADMK regime neither prevented attacks against SCs, launched by some BC groups and Hindu revivalists during its rule, nor responded to SC concerns in the aftermath of these attacks. Indeed, local ADMK leaders instigated some of these attacks.[153] As these conflicts were local in scope, the ADMK regime's inaction in these contexts did not undermine the perception among many SCs around Tamil Nadu that this regime was their benefactor.

Red, Black and Saffron: The ADMK and Hindu Revivalism

Major DMK leaders like Annadurai and Karunanidhi seemed to retain their atheism even after they split from the DK, although

[151] Interviews: K. Nagaimugan, Subramaniam, Moorthy, Bhim Rao, Seppan (Madras).

[152] *Statesman*, 13 May 1980; HT, 7 March 1982; TH, 14 September, 3 October 1984; Sathyavani Muthu (1981); Interview: Sathyavani Muthu (Madras).

[153] The ADMK regime was particularly unresponsive after major clashes between Vanniars and SCs in Villupuram, and between Mukkulathor and SCs in Ramnad, Puliangudi and Vasudevanallur. Hindu revivalists were also involved in the last case. HT, IE, 27, 28, 29 July 1978; TH, 29, 30, 31 July,

they made conciliatory gestures towards non-Sanskritic religious practices and transacted with non-Brahmin religious institutions. MGR, on the other hand, was always religious, acted as deities in his films and was open to Sanskritic culture and Brahminical religiosity. In keeping with these attitudes of MGR's, the ADMK regime made no legislative changes based on the Dravidianist critique of Brahminical Hinduism comparable with the DMK regime's legalization of Self Respect weddings. It transacted more closely with Brahmin religious institutions than the DMK regime had, and its ministers patronized both established and newly risen religious figures. As many of the latter religious figures have adopted rituals that involve less caste-based exclusion than those in older Tamil temples, the ADMK's association with these figures reinforced its plebeian image.

Nevertheless, novel forms of popular Hindu religiosity have a closer affinity with revivalist visions of an integral Hindu community, symbolized by the saffron garb many of their adherents sport, than with Dravidianism. In a greater departure from earlier Dravidianist practice than on language and caste issues, the ADMK showed some sympathies with Hindu revivalism. Paternalist populism contained the potential of Dravidianist appeals to disrupt stability and pluralism more fully than assertive populism had. However, assertive populism more effectively contained the growth of Hindu revivalism, the largest exclusionary political force in Indian politics. While it was conciliatory towards Hindu revivalists, the ADMK did not systematically promote animosity between religious groups. So, violence against non-Hindus has been relatively low in Tamil Nadu so far, despite having increased since the early 1980s.

The role of Hindu revivalists in opposing Indira Gandhi's authoritarian practices and their share of power in the national government in the late 1970s helped them grow slowly thereafter even in their regions of historic weakness. Hindu revivalists gained a foothold in Tamil Nadu as early as 1960 through their association with the construction of a monument to honour Swami Vivekananda, a religious figure they claimed as a forebear, in

3, 10, 11, 14, 25, 26 August, 18, 22 September 1978; TI, 29 July, 2 August 1978, 23 June 1982; *Statesman*, 29 July 1978; HT, 13 April 1981; IE, HT, 13 June 1982; *Tribune*, 1 July 1982.

Kanyakumari, at the tip of peninsular India. While they gave Kanyakumari increased importance in their vision of India's sacred geography thereafter, they gained significant support in pockets of Tamil Nadu only after the conversion of a group of SCs to Islam in 1981, in the village of Meenakshipuram in the southern plains. Both Hindu revivalist organizations and Hindu religious institutions responded to these conversions by raising the cry that Hinduism was endangered by the influx of 'Muslim money' from the Persian gulf, which they claimed had influenced the conversions. They hastened to appeal to SCs in the region, while also threatening them with violence, to closely incorporate them into the Hindu fold whose margins they have so far occupied.[154]

The conversions of Meenakshipuram led to a wave of Hindu revivalist mobilization concentrated in the two southernmost Tamil districts, Kanyakumari and Tirunelveli. Hindu revivalist organizations like the Rashtriya Swayamsevak Sangh (RSS) and the Vishwa Hindu Parishad (VHP) become more active, and promoted local organizations which made limited attempts to adapt Hindu revivalist appeals, initially forged in the cultural crucible of northern and western India, to Tamil culture. They instigated attacks against Christians, Muslims and SCs in some pockets and cultivated antagonism between religious groups in others.[155]

The ADMK regime regarded Hindu revivalist organizations as neither important threats nor major allies as these organizations became electorally significant only in a few state assembly constituencies in the southern plains. It responded ineffectively to the violent incidents in which these organizations were involved. MGR said that the RSS had as much of a right to promote Hindu interests as the Muslim League had to promote Muslim interests.[156] In so doing, he disregarded crucial differences between the two organizations—while the RSS gives its members paramilitary training which they have used in sparking scattered violence in Tamil Nadu since the early 1980s, the Muslim League is an electoral party which has provoked little unrest after decolonization despite

---

[154] Subramanian (1997); Mujahid (1989); TH, 4 July 1981; IE, 13 July 1981, 13 June 1982; HT, 13 June 1982; TI, 23 June 1982; *Tribune*, 1 July 1982.

[155] IE, HT, 13 June 1982; TI, 23 June 1982; *Tribune*, 1 July 1982; TH, 14, 15 February 1983.

[156] HT, 10 December 1979; *Tribune*, 22 February 1984.

having enjoyed some strength in the state since the early 1960s. The ADMK regime's tacit support helped the growth of Hindu revivalism, which nevertheless remains weakest in Tamil Nadu.

The ADMK's attitude towards Hindu revivalism has not changed much after MGR's death. After the BJP made major electoral advances in 1991, the ADMK began supporting Hindu revivalist demands to construct a Hindu temple in Ayodhya without advocating the destruction of the mosque which stood there, and ended its alliance with Congress. When the BJP gained fewer seats in the state assembly elections of 1993–5, the ADMK distanced itself from the BJP and renewed its alliance with Congress. It later allied itself with the BJP, when that party's prospects seemed brighter in 1998, and subsequently cooperated with the BJP (though not smoothly) as part of a BJP-led coalition government at the centre through 1998–9. These shifts in the ADMK's choice of allies have been in keeping with the ADMK's tendency to forge links with whichever party appears strongest in national politics.[157]

The agenda of paternalist populism represented emergent groups differently from that of assertive populism. It distributed very divisible forms of patronage which addressed the basic needs of the lower strata. This form of clientelism enabled the distribution of benefits to a larger number than assertive populism did. The cost of wider distribution was that the benefits were more meagre and improved the life prospects of beneficiaries less.

Assertive populist patronage strengthened the economic position of many from the intermediate strata through policies such as the caste quotas in education and government jobs, enabled such individuals to sustain themselves without continued dependence on patronage and helped some of them gain considerable social power. The lunches which paternalist populism dispensed benefited the lower strata in ways that assertive populist patronage did not, improving the health and perhaps the life expectancy and educational attainments of many children from these strata. But, such schemes reached the lower strata without altering their marginality. The ADMK regime redistributed property and changed the

---

[157] Its calculations went awry in this regard in the 1996 elections, in which its ally, Congress, was unseated from power in Delhi.

profile of income distribution less than the DMK regime did. Nevertheless, paternalist populism gave the lower strata benefits they would not have received unless development strategies were pursued that would have change their life prospects more fundamentally.

The two variants of populism had different consequences for social pluralism. Assertive populism urged cadre and supporters to regard the benefits they received as the fruits of their own political endeavour, and gave them more autonomy to challenge regimes to grant their demands, or to shift their political allegiances if they were dissatisfied. Many DMK supporters remained loyal to their party nevertheless, at least until the 1980s, because some of those who gained from the assertive populist project felt beholden to the party, while the larger number who did not hoped that their turn might come next. Moreover, assertive populism shaped their identities too ineluctably for them to consider political alternatives. The ongoing attempts of the PMK and the MDMK to revitalize assertive populism are not oriented towards fundamentally changing the political horizons of such groups.

Unlike assertive populism, paternalist populism encouraged cadre and supporters to consider the leader's beneficence the reason for the benefits they received. It gave cadre and supporters less autonomy, and altered the distribution of social power less than assertive populism did. This made it a more effective clientelist strategy, which reproduced clients' dependence on patronage, thus enhancing the likelihood that clients would continue to flock to the paternalist banner. It did not, however, reduce all supporters to a mendicant posture as many of them had the social capability to appropriate paternalist discourse for their ends. Some of them acquired these capabilities while mobilizing in praise of the hero who piloted the paternalist project.

VII

Conclusion

The book posed the following three related questions: (1) *How* can *pluralist democracy be preserved under conditions of high ethnic mobilization when accommodative compacts between states and ethnic élites prove inadequate to the task?* (2) *Under what conditions does populism temper the potential of ethnicity to provoke disintegrative social conflict, and instead promote pluralist democracy?* (3) *When is populism likely to attain sustained success in semi-industrialized societies and aid the representation of emergent social groups?* By examining the course of the Dravidian parties and their impact on Tamil society, the study shows that organizational pluralism can channel ethnic and populist forces towards promoting stability, social pluralism and the increased representation of emergent groups within a democratic system. Social pluralism and increased representation are desirable ends, and stability is too, if it is achieved along with such desirable ends.[1] The work suggests some responses, from citizens as well as states, to the growth of ethnic and populist politics which might help reinforce stability, and preserve and strengthen pluralist democracy.

ORGANIZATIONAL PLURALISM AND THE CONTAINMENT OF ETHNIC INTOLERANCE

At its outset, the Dravidian movement placed Tamil speaking intermediate Hindu castes at the core of its vision of political community and relegated other groups to its margins, to varying degrees. This vision, combined with the movement's opposition to Hinduism, the religion of much of Tamil Nadu's population, and its demand for secession could have provoked violent conflict and led to the establishment of an exclusionary political order. Moreover, the early mass Dravidianist organizations, the Self Respect Association and the DK, highlighted their appeals through

---

[1] Otherwise, stability might help entrench an unjust social order, and in such circumstances, some instability might be necessary to promote just ends.

demonstrative acts of heresy. While many of these actions attacked religious orthodoxy (e.g. idol breaking), others aimed at post-colonial political orthodoxy (e.g. burning copies of the section of the Indian constitution guaranteeing freedom of religious belief and practice). As the religious sentiments of many Tamils are strong and the constitutional guarantee for freedom of religious belief and practice is an important cornerstone of tolerance in India's multi-religious society, the heresies of the early Dravidianists had considerable potential to disrupt stability and undermine tolerance.

The politics of heresy could produce alienation effects, akin to the impact which Brechtian theatre aimed to produce. Periar hoped, as Brecht had, to shock Tamil society into insight regarding caste-based domination and its legitimation in the Hindu scriptures and epics. But, the DK's mobilizing strategy evoked far more popular antagonism than support and was inimical to building broad coalitions, a shortcoming reflected in the party's rejection of electoral politics. Besides, the DK deployed ethnic appeals directly derived from colonial knowledge, relied heavily on the support of non-Brahmin notables and supported the colonial state. So, its attempts to link ethnic appeals to a populist discourse did not inspire widespread mass mobilization. The party remained a vehicle of protest, rather than change, and lagged well behind the Indian nationalists in the late colonial period.

Indian independence brought with it universal franchise and federalism. These change precipitated a strategic reorientation on the part of the Dravidianists, which was brewing through the 1940s. The DMK, which split from the DK, redirected mass Dravidianism from a politics of heresy to a politics of community. Central to this change was the fuller incorporation of early Dravidianism's essentialized ethnic categories within a populist discourse, which inspired the mobilization of a broad coalition spanning the intermediate and lower strata. The populist turn was effected in such a way that ethnic notions highlighted the norms of middling status groups as central to the political community without promoting intolerance and ethnic violence.

While the DMK provoked limited conflict within Tamil society, it collided repeatedly with the Indian government during language agitations until the late 1960s. These agitations were associated with some violence, but far less than that generated by ethnic mobili-zation in many other parts of India. They subsided from the 1970s onwards and the ethnic militancy of DMK activists declined. The DMK's ethnic militancy declined gradually from the late 1950s to the mid-1970s. Among the crucial steps in this process were the abandonment of secessionism in secret by the party leaders, the disbanding of the party schools in which separatist ideology was inculcated in activists and orators, the public disavowal of secession when the Indian government moved to ban secessionists from holding elected office, partial victory in language agitations, the formation of the ADMK and the defeat of the DMK's subsequent nativist moves.

Organizational pluralism crucially enabled Dravidianism's populist turn, the subsequent emergence of diverse populisms and the benign consequences of these changes. The populist outlook was able to grow within the womb of the DK from the late 1930s to the late 1940s although Periar harped on exclusionary ethnic appeals. The leaders of the DK faction which later formed the DMK developed and articulated their alternative strategic emphasis, attuned to impending decolonization, in independent journals and the DK's youth organization, which they dominated. They were able to ply their alternative line within movement fora, to Periar's discomfiture. They ensured changes in the DK's formal organizational structure and, unlike Periar, welcomed Indian independence. Despite these disagreements, this faction was strong enough to urge Periar to acknowledge its leader, Annadurai, as his designated successor at times.

It was not only cadre autonomy but also supporter autonomy and leadership flexibility which enabled the DMK to take the steps it did. The material interests of many core DMK supporters were not directly linked to secessionism and language demands. This was more true of small property owners than of the petty intelligentsia. Nevertheless, small property owners found in ethnic militancy an expression of opposition to the bureaucratic clientelism of Congress, to whose subcultures they were peripheral in many regions. The DMK's rhetorical claim that the Congress way was not the Tamil way helped reinforce a sense among core supporters from such groups that the DMK was rooted in their outlook and represented a coherent alternative to Congress. These supporters had some autonomy to orient local party strategies in accordance with their vision of the party's mission.

By the late 1950s, many DMK leaders realized that secession was not a priority for most party supporters and that commitment to it hindered further growth. This led them to abandon secession in private, in the belief that demands for autonomy would serve the same symbolic purpose that secessionism earlier had. As the majority of supporters were not strongly committed to secession, the DMK could abandon secessionism when the Indian government moved to curb separatism in 1963, without losing appreciable support even within the core of the assertive populist subculture.

The DMK's retreat from ethnic militancy from the mid-1960s onwards was associated with the emergence of a paternalist strand to Dravidian populism. While Annadurai used paternalist appeals, Dravidianism's paternalist face was primarily associated with MGR. The political sentiments of MGR's fans were shaped by MGR's films, in which ethnic appeals played a limited role. So, many of these fans, and others attracted by the paternalist garb which the DMK assumed through the 1960s, were wary of the party using violence to press ethnic demands or striking strident autonomist postures. MGR's fan clubs inhabited an autonomous space within the DMK fold, loyal primarily to MGR and only by association to the party. The autonomy of the paternalist populist subculture urged DMK leaders to be sensitive to the sentiments of its paternalist clientele. So, they tried to restrain language agitations from the mid-1960s onwards by indicating that they were on the verge of coming to power in the state and promising that they would use the state government's powers to fulfil the agitators' main demands or press the Indian government to do so.

The autonomy of the paternalist subculture meant that members of this subculture could revolt against the party if the party failed to fulfil the expectations aroused by paternalist appeals. MGR was able to use the DMK regime's abandonment of many of its paternalist promises to split the DMK and to found the ADMK in 1972. The new party was shaped in a paternalist mould, and used ethnic appeals to augment its prestige and that of its leader rather than to mobilize protest. So, its formation and growth, partly at the DMK's expense, diminished ethnic stridency. The attempts of DMK leaders to discredit the ADMK through nativism failed miserably as party supporters had not been nurtured on anti-immigrant attitudes, and the DMK lost its pride of place in Tamil politics to its moderate offshoot. The failure of nativism and the

ADMK's success over the next decade urged the DMK leaders to tone down their ethnic demands further. Even the growth of the secessionist Tamil guerilla movement in Sri Lanka did not entirely reverse this process.

DRAVIDIANISM AND HINDU REVIVALISM

A contrast between the Dravidianist experience and the course of Hindu revivalism highlights the significance of organizational pluralism. Hindu revivalism constructed visions of Hindu tradition by appropriating Hindu epics and scriptures partly in light of the norms of the landholding and mercantile castes of northern and western India, its core supporters. It considered only those who accord Indian soil sacred significance, following such a 'Hindu tradition', truly Hindu/Indian, regardless of their citizenship, religious practices and how censuses record their religious affiliations. Other Indians were said to lack a cultural bond with the nation, making their patriotism unreliable. This has justified the demonization of adherents of religions of foreign advent, particularly Muslims, and the instigation of violence against them through different phases of the movement's history.

The absence of organizational pluralism within the Hindu revivalist fold has impeded the emergence of movement offshoots compatible with social pluralism. Hindu revivalist organizations are hierarchical in structure, with leaders nominating lower-level office holders and commanding complete activist loyalty. As activists and core supporters are rigidly socialized into accepting central aspects of the movement's vision, not many of them are likely to support more tolerant offshoots. Although many movement organizations have emerged, they have not differed significantly in their visions of political community or competed with one another for cadre or popular support. Rather, they have formed an interlinked network, referred to as a family, and played mutually complementary roles. While the Vishwa Hindu Parishad (VHP) has spearheaded violent agitations, the BJP has contested elections and the RSS has trained leaders of the other organizations and coordinated their activities loosely. Although the BJP has assumed relatively moderate postures when leaders expected this to be electorally rewarding, its close links with the RSS and the participation of its activists in all major instances of Hindu revivalist violence show that the BJP has not pursued a distinct and more inclusive long-term strategy. The formation of the Hindu revivalist subculture along these lines has prevented the emergence of tolerant movement offshoots even though such organizations might have drawn significant support, especially when existing movement organizations were in disrepute (e.g. after Gandhi's assassination in 1948 and after the destruction of a medieval mosque, the *Babri Masjid*, in 1992).[2]

Not only did Dravidianism develop in a direction contrary to that of Hindu revivalism, it also inhibited Hindu revivalist growth in Tamil Nadu, for which there was considerable potential as the vast majority of the state's inhabitants are Hindus. This curtailed a major potential source of intolerance and violence.

The links between prior partisanship and the pockets of Tamil Nadu in which Hindu revivalism has grown to some extent since the 1980s clarifies Dravidianism's role in containing Hindu revivalism. Hindu revivalists have grown strongest and won their only seats in the state legislative assembly in Kanyakumari district, the only part of Tamil Nadu not dominated by the Dravidian parties over the last two decades.[3] Besides, Hindu revivalism has grown most in areas such as Dindigul and Sermadevi, which Congress and the ADMK have dominated, but has not gained a foothold in pockets of sustained DMK strength like Tiruvannamalai and Mannargudi.[4]

The religious composition of the population has not influenced the diverse outcomes. Dindigul, Sermadevi, Tiruvannamalai and Mannargudi constituencies have significant and roughly comparable

[2] See Jaffrelot (1996), Basu et al. (1993), Thapar (1989), Andersen & Damle (1987).

[3] Kanyakumari district is in some respects beyond the pale of Tamil Nadu's political culture. It was not part of Madras Presidency, which contained most Tamil speaking regions from colonial times to 1956. The pattern of political competition there is closer to that in Kerala, which it adjoins, than to Tamil Nadu's. Pan-Indian parties have been dominant and the DMK so weak that it typically contests only in some of the district's constituencies. The ADMK has attracted considerable support, however, especially along the coast. Hindu revivalist growth in Kanyakumari district is partly an extension of trends in Kerala. The Hindu revivalists won one legislative assembly seat from the district in 1984 and in 1996, and have performed well in other constituencies there from 1984 onwards.

[4] However, not all areas of Congress and ADMK strength have experienced Hindu revivalist growth.

concentrations of Muslims, and Christians too are numerous in some of them. The history of ethnic relations prior to the growth of assertive Dravidianism has also not had a clear effect. Tiruvannamalai experienced a significant Hindu-Muslim riot in 1948, but Dindigul has not experienced one. Further, some local Congress leaders were also members of the revivalist Hindu Mahasabha in both towns and made some anti-Muslim appeals in the late colonial and immediate post-colonial periods. This suggests that the formation of deep assertive populist subcultures has been crucial to curbing Hindu revivalist growth in Tamil Nadu, and that the weakness of such subcultures in some pockets has left room for the recent growth of these forces there.

If prior partisanship has influenced receptivity to Hindu revivalism, this cannot be traced to the explicit content of party appeals or to the ethnic composition of support bases. The ADMK did not systematically appeal against non-Hindus anywhere in the state and only some Congress members did so, and that too to a limited extent. Both parties have drawn significant support from non-Hindus. Yet, the DMK influenced local society in ways that inhibited Hindu revivalist growth, while Congress and the ADMK did not, at least to a comparable extent. The difference lay in the extent to which these parties regarded non-Hindus, particularly Muslims (the focus of Hindu revivalist ire), as an integral part of their vision of the political community and in how far partisan subcultures embodied cooperative social contacts among the adherents of different religions. While the DMK scored highly on both counts, the ADMK fared poorly and Congress even worse. These differences between the DMK, on the one hand, and Congress and the ADMK, on the other, affected the long-term prospects for tolerance between religious communities and thus the pattern of recent Hindu revivalist growth in Tamil Nadu. The sentiments which underlay the Hindu-Muslim riot of 1948 in Tiruvannamalai were counteracted by decades of assertive populist mobilization, which built cooperative links between the Muslims and the intermediate Hindu castes. Thus, Hindu revivalist organizations were unable to grow there and in Mannargudi. On the contrary, these organizations grew by inducing ethnic hostilities during religious festivals and local body elections in Dindigul and Sermadevi in the 1980s and 1990s, although such antagonism was limited in the past.

If the ADMK did not inhibit Hindu revivalism to the degree the DMK did, does the ADMK represent a departure from Dravidian movement traditions, as assertive Dravidianists claim? The ADMK appears far removed from heretical Dravidianism in its enthusiastic embrace of Hindu religiosity, tolerance of its exclusionary political deployment and ambivalence about caste as a basis for imagining the political community. However, there are continuities between the DK's vision and the ADMK's position on Hindu revivalism.

Despite Periar's critique of religion and Hinduism, a section of Tamil Hindus (BCs) occupied the core of Periar's vision of the Dravidian community, while other Hindus and non-Hindus were relegated to the margins. Besides, Periar viewed his movement as primarily engaged in an effort to reform Tamil Nadu's Hindu society. These features of the early Dravidianist vision made it possible to find common ground with Hindu revivalism. This did not happen in Dravidianism's earlier phases as the norms the assertive Dravidianists upheld were entirely at variance with those promoted by the Hindu revivalists. The rejection of Brahminical Hinduism, of Sanskritic culture and of the cultural homogeneity of India, and the associated celebration of the autonomous elements in the culture of the intermediate Tamil castes distanced assertive Dravidianists considerably from Hindu revivalist efforts to construct a Hindu/Indian nation on the basis of upper caste and Sanskritic norms. Indeed, assertive Dravidianism attracted some of the groups which flocked to the Hindu revivalist banner in other parts of India partly by upholding those regional variants of Hinduism associated with the intermediate castes. As the ADMK was not averse to Sanskritic culture and upper caste mores, it was not hostile to Hindu revivalism, thus realizing a potential implicit in aspects of early constructions of Dravidian identity for the coexistence of Dravidianism and Hindu revivalism.

POPULISM, PLURALISM AND REPRESENTATION

Due to their organizational pluralism, the Dravidian parties embraced populism in ways that not only contained the intolerant potential of ethnicity, but also promoted social pluralism, the increased representation of emergent groups and the stabilization of democracy amidst growing mass mobilization.

The DMK and the ADMK absorbed the social networks among socially capable strata into their subcultures, rather than seeking to sever the independent social links of supporters to ensure loyalty to the party. Further, the layered conceptions of a popular community they deployed alluded to many social categories, lending party appeals flexibility. So, groups that were numerically preponderant or socially decisive within party subcultures could, to some extent, interpret party appeals and shape local party strategies in tune with their interests and prior orientations. Besides, supporters could pursue their demands through independent channels while remaining loyal to the party. The high levels of mobilization outside the party system before the onset of Dravidianist mobilization aided the emergence of cadre and supporter autonomy, and urged leaders to adopt flexible strategies and tolerate autonomy within the party fold.

The Dravidian parties outdid Congress because they mobilized emergent groups, rather than aggregating already mobilized interests. Even the ADMK's paternalist appeals, which urged supporters to praise and empower the leader, were deployed to mobilize people for this purpose. As mobilization was crucial to their electoral success, the Dravidian parties could not afford to demobilize supporters too much even after they had attained power. Thus, supporters could autonomously appropriate not only the DMK's assertive appeals, which beckoned people to action, but also the ADMK's paternalist appeals, which apparently required them only to await the leader's beneficence. While assertive populism aided the upward mobility of the more resourceful of the small shopkeepers, middling peasants and petty intellectuals it mobilized, urban squatters and artisanal fishermen used paternalist promises of protecting the poor to defend their meagre belongings. Supporters of both the major Dravidian parties joined trade unions more militant than those of the Dravidianists, as well as the agitations conducted by farmers' associations and caste associations which challenged Dravidianist regimes.

As Dravidianist mobilization promoted considerable autonomous associational activity, it introduced some accountability. The pressure from mobilized supporters and the competitive threat that each Dravidian party posed to the other constrained Dravidianist regimes to deliver on some of their promises. So, the immediate demands of emergent strata gained greater representation in the policy agenda than they had during Congress's bureaucratic clientelist rule in Tamil Nadu. The DMK increased the quotas for intermediate and lower castes in 1971 and the ADMK introduced its free lunch scheme in 1982 to satisfy supporters' expectations. Independent associations forced the Dravidianist regimes to grant other concessions. Pressure from some caste associations urged the DMK to expand the range of groups eligible for caste quotas in 1974, while more aggressive agitations forced the ADMK to abandon attempts to supplement caste with income as a criterion of eligibility for preferential quotas in 1980s, and pushed the DMK to introduce more tiers in the quota system in 1989.[5] Periodic farmers' agitations induced the Dravidianist regimes to increase subsidies and write off agrarian loans. The wave of mobilization accompanying the ADMK's birth forced the DMK regime to reimpose dry laws, while the ADMK could abandon dry laws only by placating paternalist sentiments through its lunch scheme.

The assertive and paternalist strands of Dravidian populism mobilized somewhat distinct coalitions. As neither coalition was sufficiently large to ensure a party electoral victory, regimes had to address some of the demands of both to retain power. The ADMK combined an expansion of intermediate caste quotas with the more paternalist emphasis of its policies. The first DMK regime abandoned its paternalist promises to subsidize rice prices, maintain dry laws and curtail corruption, and paid for it at the hustings. When the DMK returned to power thirteen years later, it appeared to have learnt its lesson, as it improved the quality of the food offered in the free lunch scheme, in addition to altering the caste quotas. Policies addressed some of the interests of a wide range of intermediate and lower strata, albeit in a piecemeal fashion.

Populist regimes addressed some needs of the emergent strata, but did not optimally improve the life prospects of these groups. They increased entitlements at the expense of long-term economic

---

[5] 50 per cent of government jobs and seats in colleges were reserved for the BCs from 1980 to 1989. The DMK regime apportioned 20 per cent for the castes deemed 'most backward' and the so-called 'denotified communities', which had been considered criminal tribes during colonial rule, and set the share of the other BCs at 30 per cent. The STs were given a separate 1 per cent quota, while the 18 per cent shared until then by the SCs and STs was reserved for the SCs alone thereafter. The successor ADMK regime modified these policies slightly in the 1990s.

growth and impeded basic changes in property rights. Either the promotion of economic growth or the redistribution of property might have improved the economic situation of the lower and intermediate strata in a self-sustaining way, without resort to continuous government subsidies. While well irrigation increased rapidly through the 1970s, satisfying the Dravidianists' farmer clientele, less attention was paid to industrial growth through this period. The practice of frequently writing off agricultural loans under pressure restricted the government's capacity to maintain the pace of well digging and rural electrification. Limited reforms in land tenancy laws and legislation giving the state an increased role in the mediation of industrial disputes reduced support for militant industrial and agricultural unions, thus diminishing pressure for far-reaching changes in property rights.

Dravidianism broadened avenues for upward mobility without changing property distribution much. It thereby limited popular challenges to the basic interests of the dominant strata while the emergent strata became more politically active and felt an increased degree of political efficacy. Dravidian populism maintained stability and social pluralism by effectively presenting the rule of property as the plebeian republic towards which Periar once gestured. So, rapid mass mobilization was attended by limited ethnic and class conflict, and so placed few stresses on representative democracy. Populism maintained stability and democracy in a sustained fashion only because it accorded many from the lower and intermediate strata considerable autonomy, expanded clientelist networks to give some individuals from these groups access to prosperity and altered the idioms of legitimation so that some of them could attain higher status.

The restrictive and benign consequences of Dravidian populism were closely interlinked. The constraints on the autonomy of activists and supporters were conducive to stability as they lent the Dravidian parties coherence and durability. These constraints inhibited pressure for substantial property redistribution, in keeping with the preferred economic agenda of Dravidianist leaders. Such effects of Dravidianist success and rule indicate some of the advantages of pluralist democracy, such as the diffusion of conflict and the restriction of intolerance. But, they also highlight the limits of pluralist democracy, for pluralist democracy proved compatible with significant restraints on citizens' autonomy and the policy agenda.

Autonomous spaces became constricted within the ADMK fold and the ADMK regime repressed centrist political opponents harshly under Jayalalitha's leadership. These changes affected the popularity of the ADMK, leading to its resounding electoral defeat in 1996. But, it was the DMK, rather than a pan-Indian party, which gained from the ADMK's debacle, reflecting populism's continued dominance. The DMK made these electoral gains although a faction left the party in 1993 to revitalize assertive populism, showing the continued vigour of cadre autonomy. This split in the DMK and the ADMK's subsequent reverses confirm that Dravidianist mobilization shaped mass politics in ways that constrain leaders from departing too much from the ethos binding their party's subculture and punish rulers who blatantly attack social pluralism. These recent changes suggest that social pluralism is likely to endure in Tamil Nadu unless organizational pluralism declines drastically in all major parties.

THE POLITICS OF COMMUNITY AND THE PROSPECTS FOR PLURALIST DEMOCRACY: THE LESSONS

The sustained dominance of the Dravidian parties is part of a global trend of the growth of the politics of community. The study indicates some reasons for this trend, and points to ways in which the politics of community might be reconciled with pluralist democracy.

In India, post-colonial official nationalism demanded loyalty to the state and to secularism, equating the latter with an absence of ethnic chauvinism and with the state acting as a neutral arbiter of the claims of different religious and other ethnic groups. Its cultural component was kept thin, partly to ensure the inclusion of all of India's culturally diverse inhabitants.[6] Many post-colonial states in multicultural societies adopted similar discourses, for allowing an emphasis on specific cultural symbols carried the risk of alienating many of their citizens.

The success of most secular post-colonial nation-building projects was limited by the distance between their culturally thin discourses and the outlook of many from the lower and intermediate strata.

[6] See Chatterjee (1986), Madan (1987) and Smith (1963).

This was all the more so as secularism and civic nationalism reached former colonies in a foreign idiom with which only some élites were conversant, and the development strategies pursued in most of these societies provided limited benefits to many individuals from the lower and intermediate strata.[7] These conditions characterized India, particularly during the bureaucratic clientelist period. So, the post-colonial Indian state's nation-building project and the pan-Indian parties which claimed allegiance to secularism failed to strike deep roots in many regions.

Parties employing culturally thicker appeals to community often used methods of mobilization which reached deeper down into post-colonial societies. Such methods were particularly fruitful where such forces tapped the prior solidarity of socially capable groups (e.g. pre-revolutionary Iran, Algeria in the late 1980s and early 1990s, parts of India over the last generation). They crucially aided the growth of ethnic parties in India (see Table 1.1).

Most ethnic forces have disrupted stability and pluralism in India, as elsewhere. This account of a notable exception to this trend identifies the emergence and continuity of organizational pluralism as the crucial reason for a more benign outcome. While the study does not predict that we will see such outcomes more often, it offers grounds to hope that such a political course might be replicated in other multicultural semi-industrialized societies.

The study shows that organizational pluralism can help build broad support in culturally diverse semi-industrialized societies. A contrast between the patterns of Dravidianist and Hindu revivalist growth illustrates this claim. While the ethnic notions deployed by mass Dravidianist organizations have restricted their potential ambit to Tamil Nadu, Hindu revivalists have aimed for success throughout India as Hindus account for the majority of the population in most of the country. When viewed in light of the potential ambit of the two movements, the Dravidian parties have enjoyed much broader and more sustained support than Hindu revivalist parties have.[8] While the Dravidian parties have been dominant among all groups and in all regions of Tamil Nadu since the 1970s, Hindu revivalist support has been concentrated in northern and western India, though it has grown recently to some

---

[7] See Juergensmeyer (1993).

[8] Hindu revivalist parties have however enjoyed greater aggregate support around India than the Dravidian parties have.

extent in other regions too. As Table 7.1 shows, the disparities have
been great in the electoral support that Hindu revivalist parties
have drawn in northern and western India, on the one hand, and
southern and eastern India, on the other. Moreover, Hindu
revivalists have not been as dominant in any state as the Dravidianists
have been in Tamil Nadu because the former have acquired
substantial and sustained support only among the upper and upper-
middle Hindu castes even in their bastions.

TABLE 7.1   Indian Parliamentary Elections: Hindu Revivalists'
Electoral Performance in Regions of India Share of Valid Vote
(percentage-wise)

Year	North & West[a]	South & East[b]	India
1952	8.6	2.4	5.9
1957	11.3	1.7	7.2
1962	12.8	0.9	7.7
1967	15.4	1.4	9.4
1971	15.9	1.0	7.4
1977[c]	—	—	—
1980[d]	—	—	—
1984	14.5	1.0	7.5
1989	19.3	1.8	11.6
1991	31.1	10.2	21.0
1996	32.9	8.9	21.4

Notes: [a] 'North & West' includes the states of Maharashtra, Gujarat, Rajasthan,
Himachal Pradesh, Jammu & Kashmir, Punjab, Haryana, Uttar Pradesh,
Bihar, Madhya Pradesh and Delhi.
   [b] 'South & East' includes the states of Tamil Nadu, Kerala, Karnataka, Goa,
Andhra Pradesh, Orissa, Bengal, Assam, Meghalaya, Manipur, Nagaland,
Sikkim, Mizoram, Tripura, and Arunachal Pradesh, and the union territories
of Pondicherry, Lakshadweep, Andaman and Nicobar Islands, Daman and
Diu, and Dadra and Nagar Haveli.
   [c] The main Hindu revivalist party, the Bharatiya Jan Sangh, merged with
some pan-Indian parties to form the Janata party in 1977 and remained in this
party until after the 1980 elections. So, the figures for pan-Indian and Hindu
revivalist parties cannot be distinguished for 1977 and 1980.
   [d] See footnote c.

The flexibility of the Dravidian parties regarding their strategy
and goals, and the contrasting rigidity of the Hindu revivalist
organizations are important reasons for the different levels of

electoral success these forces achieved. The DMK's early support was concentrated among the intermediate strata of the northern plains and the Kaveri valley, partly because intermediate castes occupied the core of the early Dravidianist vision. Yet, the emergence of a paternalist variant of Dravidian populism aided Dravidianism's growth among other groups and in other parts of Tamil Nadu. Hindu revivalism has not grown to a comparable extent beyond the cultural mould in which it was initially formed, the culture of the upper and upper-middle castes of northern and western India. Recent attempts to spread beyond this niche have only met with partial success as ideologically distinct movement factions and offshoots have not emerged and the initial appeals have not been altered sufficiently to gain substantial support in other cultural niches. The efforts of the Hindu revivalists to modify their appeals in southern and eastern India are regarded with suspicion by many in these areas as the agenda that the Hindu revivalist organizations pursue at the national level has not changed correspondingly.

The greater success which has at times rewarded strategic flexibility might urge more ethnic forces to adopt tolerant paths in culturally diverse semi-industrialized societies. The rich cultural variation and intricate stratification of many such societies makes it necessary for parties to appeal to a wide range of groups if they are to achieve considerable success. The flexible deployment of ethnic appeals can help achieve this end in such societies. Autonomous spaces have to emerge within ethnic organizations, however, if these organizations are to respond to such incentives to become more flexible regarding their goals, rather than their tactics alone.

The possibility of the flexible and tolerant articulation of ethnicity is more significant due to the declining ability of states to govern effectively amidst rapid political mobilization around idioms foreign to official discourse, and the diminished appeal of secularism and civic nationalism. These trends make it less likely that accommodative compacts between states and ethnic élites, combined with the reassertion of secular motifs, will contain ethnicity's malignant potential. The latter are the approaches that the Indian state has haltingly followed, with rapidly diminishing success, to stem the growing tide of violent ethnic conflict. The Indian state has not adhered to even these approaches consistently, tending to opportunistically encourage ethnic extremists at times and to resort too readily to repression, and has exacerbated ethnic conflict in the process. However, the study indicates that the deeper reasons for the state's inability to contain ethnic conflict lie in the limitations of the state's secularist strategies of social control, rather than the state's failure to adhere to such strategies.

GUIDELINES FOR CITIZENCRAFT: AN AGENDA FOR THE FUTURE

The study suggests that attempts to nurture culturally rooted, yet tolerant, visions of community, and to urge more exclusionary visions in tolerant directions are more likely to promote social pluralism than the approaches advocated by most pan-Indian secularists and followed, albeit rather inconsistently, by the Indian state. For instance, social forces propagating tolerant conceptions of cultural identity are more likely to curb the growth of violent religious revivalism than are those that assert culturally vacuous notions of Indian citizenship. Thus, Hindu revivalism and the violence attendant upon its spread have been more successfully curtailed in Tamil Nadu than in states ruled by pan-Indian parties. The state's focus on secularism and pan-Indian nationalism has impeded it from reaching out to some ethnic conceptions which could have been tolerantly expressed. The consequences of this failure were not grave in Tamil Nadu as the primary ethnic parties moved in a tolerant direction, although the national government did not accommodate many of their demands. But, they were disastrous in Punjab, where Sikh political élites raised demands compatible with pluralism in the 1970s, and the state's refusal to accommodate these demands as they were raised on the basis of religious identity contributed to a turn towards secessionist violence in the 1980s.

To urge emerging ethnic forces to adopt tolerant paths, citizens committed to tolerance must mobilize autonomously of states and parties, even while engaging with these institutions. They need to engage with states, to the extent that states are powerful actors;[9] and with some ethnic parties and movements, for they cannot otherwise urge them towards tolerance. In doing the latter, they have to exercise their informed judgement regarding which ethnic

[9] So, there is less need for this in parts of Central Africa, where states have either collapsed or exercise little effective control over society.

forces can indeed be directed towards pluralism, and which are implacable foes of tolerance. In India, the Dravidian parties, the moderate factions of the Akali Dal, the *Asom Gana Parishad* (AGP), the two Telugu Desam parties and many Kashmiri nationalist organizations are among the forces in the former category; while the Hindu revivalist organizations, the Islamist militant outfits in Kashmir and most of the Sikh militant groups are in the latter category. Some of the ethnic militant groups in north-eastern India are relatively new (e.g. the Bodo groups, though not the Naga and Mizo ones), and could move in either direction, depending on how their interaction with the state and society change. It is necessary for citizens committed to pluralist democracy to engage with states and ethnic forces so that states and other forces are constrained from repressing initiatives to reinforce pluralist democracy, and the emergence of states and more parties inclined to foster such initiatives is facilitated.[10]

If such initiatives are to promote pluralist democracy in societies embroiled in ethnic violence, they should mobilize citizens who favour tolerance in an effective and sustained manner. Although opinion polls conducted after some recent ethnic conflagrations in India attest to the breadth of the desire for tolerance, this desire has been effectively mobilized only during moments of heightened crisis. After Hindu revivalists demolished the Babri Masjid in 1992 and incited ethnic riots in many parts of India thereafter, many voluntary associations sprang up in urban India to restore peace.[11] It is noteworthy that many of these organizations were formed around calls for peace and tolerance, rather than in favour of secularism. These organizations effectively contained conflict in some regions. For instance, their concerted action defeated the attempts of the Hindu revivalists to replicate in Delhi the widespread violence they incited earlier in Bombay. These actions of voluntary associations were far more successful than the ban which the Indian government introduced, and enforced only partially, on some religious revivalist organizations from 1993 to 1995. Such popular mobilization is far more likely to reinforce pluralism than

---

[10] This discussion draws on accounts of state-civil society interactions in Harbeson, Rothchild & Chazan (1994) and Bratton (1994).

[11] IT, 15 March 1993.

the irresolute actions of governments whose efforts at social control are popularly perceived to be bankrupt.

Many of the voluntary associations forged in the fires that erupted over the Babri Masjid's demolition became inactive after a few months, when the crisis appeared to have receded. Some voters and parties coordinated their opposition to Hindu revivalism to a greater extent in the first set of state elections held after the Babri Masjid was demolished, thereby displacing the BJP from power in four North Indian states in 1993. However, the BJP's share of the popular vote declined only in three of these four states in these elections and returned to its levels of 1991 in subsequent state elections, and increased further in the national elections of 1996 and 1998. Besides, the BJP's share of the popular vote (20.1 per cent in 1991; 20.7 per cent in 1996) translated into an increasing share of parliamentary seats (120 in 1991; 161 in 1996) under the first-past-the-post rules due to Congress's continuing electoral decline, the regional concentration of the BJP's support and the fragmented nature of alternatives to these two parties.[12] These trends are likely to continue, although the BJP's electoral support may not increase rapidly because of the party's somewhat slow entry into new social niches. The BJP led a multi-party coalition ruling the country in 1998–9, and rules some states and shares power in others in its regions of strength. A taste of power and electoral incentives have not led to long-term changes in the BJP's goals and strategy. This is only one indication that the threat of ethnic chauvinism is growing stronger in India. Associations committed to tolerance need to achieve a more consistent level of activity and coordinate their efforts more closely to counter this threat effectively.

Popular mobilization is more likely to contain strong forces promoting ethnic chauvinism if it represents diverse visions which share a commitment to pluralism. If a politics of autonomy is to radically challenge a politics of exclusion, it cannot itself exclude forces which pose alternatives to the state's development strategies and official visions of nationhood. Even internally pluralistic organizations such as the Dravidian parties inhibited radical challenges to the existing structure of property rights because the propertied played dominant roles in local subcultures, and upward

---

[12] *Frontline*, 14 June 1996, pp 22–4.

mobility was central to the outlook of these parties. While such organizations helped restrict ethnic chauvinism, they opposed intolerant forces resolutely only if their interests and those of their most influential supporters were at stake. The DMK opposed the growth of Hindu revivalism, seeing in it a potential threat to its future support even in Tamil Nadu. But, the ADMK, which relies less on opposing upper caste Hinduism and North Indian political culture, has coexisted with Hindu revivalism until recently rather than seeking to stem its growth. The struggle for tolerance will attain fuller success only if organizations less constrained by the interests of dominant or upwardly mobile groups play an important role in it. Political parties aiming for electoral success need to appeal to such groups in semi-industrialized societies. Besides, if particular parties play the leading roles in efforts to preserve tolerance, the ideologies and characteristic social bases of these parties are likely to alienate many opposed to ethnic chauvinism.[13] So, these efforts will be more successful if parties do not initiate and place their stamp on them, even while participating in them.

Popular efforts towards pluralist ends are more likely to succeed if the state fosters the growth of the organizations involved in them, even if some of these organizations pose alternatives to the state's strategies for development and social control. Wary of the autonomous visions animating some of these organizations, the Indian government has given them insufficient encouragement and impeded some of their activities. So, the struggle for tolerance in India requires a struggle for a state that fosters a wide range of social forces mobilizing to maintain pluralism. As clientelism intrinsically involves some restraints on autonomy, such a state would have to be piloted not by political forces which replace one form of clientelism with another, but rather by ones oriented to helping society realize more fully and autonomously the ends for which it gets mobilized. The emergence of such a state is crucial if a vision

---

[13] Of the major parties which oppose Hindu revivalism, the Janata Dal and the communist parties rely heavily on secularist motifs; while the Janata Dal, the Samajwadi Party and the Rashtriya Janata Dal are associated with particular caste clusters, whose prospects they promoted at the expense of other groups. So, many who favour tolerance are wary of initiatives dominated by these parties.

of nationhood in terms of the fruitful coexistence of India's diverse, yet partially overlapping cultures, is to become a guiding force of social policy, rather than a platitude mouthed by governing élites. Efforts to defend and deepen India's democracy over the next generation will be intimately linked to attempts to build a state which fosters social pluralism.

Classified Bibliography

GOVERNMENT DOCUMENTS AND COMPILATIONS
THEREFROM

Arangannal, R. (ed.) (1975), *Slums in Madras City*, Tamil Nadu Slum Clearance Board, Government of Tamil Nadu, Madras.

Backward Classes Commission (1974–5), *Report of the Commission*, Government of Tamil Nadu, Madras.

———— (1985a), *Majority Members' Recommendation*, Government of Tamil Nadu, Madras.

———— (1985b), *Chairman's Recommendation*, Government of Tamil Nadu, Madras.

Baliga, B. S. (1971), *Thanjavur District Gazetteer*, Tamil Nadu Government Press, Madras.

Census of India (1991, 1961, 1971, 1981, 1991), Volumes pertaining to Tamil Nadu State, Office of Registrar General, Delhi.

Centre–State Relations Committee (1971), *Report*, Government of Tamil Nadu, Madras.

Department of Statistics (1987), *Statistical Handbook of Tamil Nadu, 1986*, Tamil Nadu Government Press, Madras.

———— (1994), *Statistical Hand Book of Tamil Nadu, 1993*, Tamil Nadu Government Press, Madras.

Government of Tamil Nadu (1977), *MGR: The Chief Minister of Tamil Nadu*, Madras.

Government of Tamil Nadu Public (Elections) Department (1989), Data Diskettes on Tamil Nadu Elections, 1952–84, prepared by Pallavan Transport Corporation Consulting Agency, Madras.

Muthiah, S. (1987), (compiled), *A Social and Economic Atlas of India*, Oxford University Press, Delhi.

National Informatics Centre (1996), *Figures Pertaining to the Eleventh National Parliamentary Elections*, 1996, Planning Commission, Government of India, Delhi.

Press Information Bureau (1996), *Figures Pertaining to the Eleventh State Assembly Elections, Tamil Nadu, 1996*, Government of Tamil Nadu, Madras.

Singh, V. B. and S. Bose (1984), *Data Handbook on Indian Elections, 1952–80*, Oxford University Press, Delhi.

———— (1988), *State Elections in India: Data Handbook on Vidhan Sabha Elections, 1952–85*, vol. V, Sage, Delhi.

MATERIAL IN ENGLISH ON TAMIL NADU

Appadurai, A. (1981), *Worship and Conflict Under Colonial Rule: A South Indian Case*, Cambridge University Press.

Appadurai, A. (1983), 'The Puzzling Status of Brahman Temple Priests in Hindu India', *South Asian Anthropologist*, vol. 4, no. 1.

Appadurai, A. and C. Breckenridge (1976), 'The South Indian Temple: Authority, Honor and Redistribution', *Contributions to Indian Sociology*, vol. 10, no. 2, pp 187–211.

Arnold, D. (1974), 'The Gounders and the Congress: Political Recruitment in South India, 1920–7', *South Asia*, no. 4 (October), pp. 1–20.

———— (1977), *The Congress in Tamilnad: Nationalist Politics in South India, 1910–37*, Australian National University Monographs on South Asia, no. 1, Manohar, Delhi.

———— (1988), 'Quit India in Madras: Hiatus or Climacteric?', in G. Pandey (ed.), *The Indian Nation in 1942*, K. P. Bagchi and Co., Calcutta.

Baker, C. J. and D. Washbrook (1975) *South India: Political Institutions and Political Change 1880–1940*, Macmillan, Delhi.

Baker, C. J. (1976), *The Politics of South India, 1920–37*, Cambridge University Press.

———— (1977), 'Leading up to Periyar: The Early Career of E. V. Rama Swami Naicker', in B. N. Pandey (ed.), *Leadership in South Asia*, Vikas, Delhi, pp 503–34.

———— (1984), *An Indian Rural Economy, 1880–1955: The Tamil Nad Countryside*, Oxford University Press, Delhi.

Barnett, M. R. (1975), 'Cultural Nationalist Electoral Politics in Tamil Nadu, South India', in Myron Weiner and John O. Field (eds), *Electoral Politics in the Indian States*, Manohar, Delhi.

———— (1976), *The Politics of Cultural Nationalism in South India*, Princeton University Press.

Bavinck, M. (1997), 'Changing Balance of Power at Sea: Motorisation of Artisanal Fishing Craft', *Economic and Political Weekly*, vol. XXXII, no. 5 (February), pp 198–200.

Beteille, A. (1965), *Caste, Class and Power: Changing Patterns of Stratification in a Tanjore Village*, University of California Press.

Bhaskaran, T. (1984), *The Message Bearers*, Cre-A, Madras.

Bouton, M. (1985), *Radical Agrarian Politics in South India*, Princeton University Press.

Caldwell, R. (1982), *A Comparative Grammar of the South Indian Family of Languages*, Tirumakal Nilayam, Madras.

Champakalakshmi, R. (1981), 'Peasant, State and Society in Medieval South India', *Indian Economic and Social History Review*, vol. XVIII, nos 3 & 4, pp 411–26.

Dickey, S. (1993a), 'The Politics of Adulation: Cinema and the Production of Politicians in South India', *The Journal of Asian Studies*, vol. 52, no. 2 (May), pp 340–72.

———— (1993b), *Cinema and the Urban Poor in South India*, Cambridge University Press.

Dirks, N. B. (1987), *The Hollow Crown: Ethnohistory of an Indian Kingdom*, Cambridge University Press.

Dumont, L. (1986), *A South Indian Subcaste: Social Organization and Religion of the Pramalai Kallar*, Oxford University Press.

Gandhi, R. (1978), *The Rajaji Story: A Warrior from the South*, Bharathan Publishers, Madras.

Gough, K. (1989), *Rural Change in Southeast India: 1950s to 1980s*, Oxford University Press, Delhi.

Guhan, S. (1981), *A Primer on Poverty: India and Tamil Nadu*, Madras Institute of Development Studies.

———— (1983), *Growth, Inequalities and Poverty in Tamil Nadu*, Madras Institute of Development Studies.

Gurusamy, S. (1993), *Peasant Politics in the South: A Socio-Political Analysis of a Pressure Group*, Kanishka, Delhi.

Hardgrave, R. L. (1969), *The Nadars of Tamil Nadu: The Political Culture of a Community in Change*, University of California Press.

———— (1979), *Essays in the Political Sociology of South India*, Usha Publishers, Delhi.

Harriss, B. (1981), *The Behaviour of Farm Product Prices in Tamil Nadu: An Investigation into the Demands of the Farmers' Movement*, Madras Institute of Development Studies.

———— (1986), *Meals and Noon Meals in South India: Food and Nutrition Policy in the Rural Food Economy of Tamil Nadu State*, Madras.

Harris, J. (1982), *Capitalism and Peasant Farming: Agrarian Structure and Ideology in Northern Tamil Nadu*, Oxford University Press.

Irschick, E. F. (1969), *Politics and Social Conflict in South India: The Non-Brahman Movement and Tamil Separatism, 1916–29*, University of California Press.

———— (1986), *Tamil Revivalism in the 1930s*, Cre-A, Madras.

Iyer, G. and R. Vidyasagar (1986), 'Agrarian Struggles in Tamil Nadu', in A. R. Desai (ed.), *Agrarian Struggles in India After Independence*, Oxford University Press, Delhi.

Jagathrakshakan, S. (1986), *The Political Career of MGR*, Madras.

Kurien, C. T. (1981), *Dynamics of Rural Transformation: A Study of Tamil Nadu 1950–75*, Orient Longman, Delhi.

Ludden, D. (1978), 'Who Really Ruled Madras Presidency?', *Indian Economic & Social History Review*, vol. XV, no. 4, pp 517–19.
———— (1985), *Peasant History in South India*, Princeton University Press.
Madras Christian College (MCC), *Yearly Opinion Polls 1968–94* (Mimeos and Press Releases).
Madras Institute of Development Studies (MIDS) (1988), *Tamil Nadu Economy: Performance and Issues*, Oxford University Press, Delhi.
Mangalamurugesan (n.d.), N. K., *The Self Respect Movement in Tamil Nadu, 1920–40*, Koodal, Madurai.
Mencher, J. (1978), *Agriculture and Social Structure in Tamil Nadu: Past Origins, Present Transformations and Future Prospects*, Allied Publishers, Bombay.
Mines, M. (1984), *The Warrior Merchants: Textiles, Trade, and Territory in South India*, Cambridge University Press, New York.
Mohan Ram (1968), *Hindi Against India: The Meaning of DMK*, Rachna Prakashan, New Delhi.
Mujahid, A. M. (1989), *Conversion to Islam: Untouchables' Strategy for Protest in India*, Anima Books, Chambersburg, Pa.
Nagaraj, K. and S. Majumdar (1983), *Process of Migration: An Analysis of Sample Migrants in Madras Urban Agglomeration*, Madras Institute of Development Studies Working Paper.
Nambi Arooran, K. (1980), *Tamil Renaissance and Dravidian Nationalism, 1905–44*, Koodal, Madurai.
Palanithurai, G. and K. Mohanasundaram (1993), *Dynamics of Tamil Nadu Politics in Sri Lankan Ethnicity*, Northern Book Centre, Delhi.
Pandian, J. (1987), *Caste, Nationalism and Ethnicity: An Interpretation of Tamil Cultural History and Social Order*, Popular Prakashan, Bombay.
Pandian, M. S. S. (1992), *The Image Trap: M. G. Ramchandran in Film and Politics*, Sage, Delhi.
Parthasarthi, R. (1982), *K. Kamaraj*, Ministry of Information and Broadcasting, New Delhi.
Presler, F. (1987), *Religion Under Bureaucracy: Policy and Administration for Hindu Temples in South India*, Cambridge University Press.
Radhakrishna, M. (1985), 'Ruthless Response to Teachers' Agitation', *Economic and Political Weekly*, vol. XX, nos 51 & 52 (December 21–8), pp 2245–6.
Radhakrishnan, P. (1989), 'Reservations and Backward Classes in Madras Presidency', Working Paper, Madras Institute of Development Studies.
Rajagopal, I. (1985), *The Tryanny of Caste: The Non-Brahman Movement and Political Development in South India*, Vikas, Delhi.
Ramanathan, S. (1966), 'Self-Respect Movement', in *Kuttooci Guruswami Ninaivu Malar* (Kuttooci Guruswamy Commemoration Volume), Madras.

Ramani, R. (1985), 'Slums of Madras City', Working Paper, Madras Institute of Development Studies.

Ramanujam, K. S. (1971), *Challenge and Response: An Intimate Report of Tamil Nadu Politics, 1967–71*, Sundara Prachuralayam, Madras.

Ramaswami Naicker (1983a), *Why Brahmins Hate Reservation*, Arivukkadal Achagam, Madras.

——— (1983b), *Declaration of War on Brahminism*, Arivukkadal Achagam, Madras.

——— (1983c), *Self-Respect Marriages*, Arivukkadal Achagam, Madras.

——— (1983d), *Rationalist Thinking*, Arivukkadal Achagam, Madras.

——— (1983e), *March Towards Peace, Prosperity and Progress*, Arivukkadal Achagam, Madras.

Ramaswamy, E. A. (1988), *Worker Consciousness and Trade Union Response*, Oxford University Press, Delhi.

Ramaswamy, S. (1993), 'En/Gendering Language: The Poetics of Tamil Identity', *Comparative Studies in Society and History*, vol. 35, no. 4 (October), pp 683–725.

Rudolph, L. I (1961), 'Urban Life and Populist Radicalism: Dravidian Politics in Madras', *Journal of Asian Studies*, vol. 20, May.

Ryerson, C. (1988), *Regionalism and Religion: The Tamil Renaissance and Popular Hinduism*, Christian Literature Society, Bangalore.

Saraswati, S. (1974), *Minorities in Madras State: Group Interests in Modern Politics*, Impex India, Delhi.

Sesha Iyengar, T. R. (1925), *The Ancient Dravidians*, Tamil University Publishing House, Madras.

Spratt, P. (1970), *DMK in Power*, Nachiketa, Bombay.

Stein, B. (ed.) (1975), *Essays on South India*, University of Hawaii Press.

——— (1980), *Peasant, State and Society in Medieval South India*, Oxford University Press.

Subramaniam, C. (1993), *Hand of Destiny: Memoirs*, Bharatiya Vidya Bhavan, Bombay.

Subramanian, A. (1997), 'Competing Visions of Sustainable Development: Local Fisheries in Tamil Nadu', unpublished paper presented at South Asian Studies Conference, Madison, Wisconsin, USA (October).

Subrahmanian, N. (1989), *The Brahmin in the Tamil Country*, Ennes Publications, Madurai.

Suntharalingam, R. (1974), *Politics and Nationalist Awakening in South India, 1852–91*, University of Arizona Press.

Thandavan, R. (1987), *All India Anna Dravida Munnetra Kazhagam: Political Dynamics in Tamil Nadu*, Tamil Nadu Academy of Political Science, Madras.

Thurston, E. (1975), *Castes and Tribes of Southern India*, 7 vols, Cosmo Publications, Delhi.

Vaidyanathan, A. (1986), 'Agricultural Development and Rural Poverty', Working Paper, Madras Institute of Development Studies.

Venkatesh Athreya, B., G. Djurfeldt and S. Lindberg (1990), *Barriers Broken: Production Relations and Agrarian Change in Tamil Nadu*, Sage, Delhi.

Visswanathan, E. Sa. (1983), *The Political Career of E. V. Ramasami Naicker: A Study in the Politics of Tamil Nadu, 1920–49*, Ravi & Vasanth Publishing, Madras.

Washbrook, D. A. (1976), *The Emergence of Provincial Politics: The Madras Presidency, 1870–1920*, Cambridge University Press.

———— (1985), 'Modern South Indian Political History: An Interpretation' in R. E. Frykenberg and P. Kolenda (eds), *Studies of South India: An Anthology of Recent Research and Scholarship*, New Era Publishing, Madras.

———— (1989), 'Caste, Class and Dominance in Modern Tamil Nadu: Non-Brahminism, Dravidianism and Tamil Nationalism', in F. Frankel and M. S. A. Rao (eds), *Dominance and State Power in Modern India*, vol. I, Oxford University Press.

Zvelebil, K. (1973), *The Smile of Murugan: On Tamil Literature of South India*, E. J. Brill Press, Leiden.

MATERIAL IN TAMIL

Aadalarasan, Thanjai (1986), *Thanthai Periyarum Thaazthappattorum* (Periar and the Untouchables), KD Press.

Anaimuthu, Ve. (1974), *Periyar E. Ve. Ra. Cintanaikal* (The Thoughts of Periyar EVR), vol. 1–3, Cintanaiyalar Kazhagam, Tiruchirapalli.

Annadurai, C. N. (1963), *Nanbarkalukku Anna* (Anna to His Friends), Bharathi Pathippakam, Madras.

———— (1985a), *Aariya Maayai* (Aryan Mystification), Dravida Pannai, Trichy.

———— (1985b), *Arappor* (The Righteous Battle for Justice), Paari, Madras.

———— (1985c), *Viduthalai Por* (The Battle for Liberation), Paari, Madras.

———— (1985d), *1858–1948*, Paari, Madras.

———— (1985e), *Panaththottam* (The Garden of Money), Paari, Madras.

———— (1985f), *Ulagap Periyar Gandhi* (Gandhi—A Great Man of the World), Paari, Madras.

———— (1986a), *Thee Paravattum* (Let the Fire Spread), Bharathi, Madras.

———— (1986b), *Thambikku Annavin Kadithankal* (Anna's Letters to His Younger Brothers—Letters from 'Dravida Nadu'), Paari, Madras.

———— (1986c), *Zamin, Inam Ozhippu* (Abolition of Zamins and Inams), Paari, Madras.

———— (1986d), *Rangon Radha* (Novel), Paari, Madras.

———— (1986e), *Or Iravu* (One Night—Novel), Paari, Madras.

———— (1986f), *Paarvathi, B. A.* (Novel), Paari, Madras.

———— (1986g), *Velaikkari* (Servant Woman—Novel), Paari, Madras.

Aranthai Narayanan (1981), *Tamizh Sinimavin Kathai* (The Story of the Tamil Cinema), New Century Book House, Madras.

Azhagarasan, Tha. (1985), *Indhi Ethirppu Varalaru* (The History of Anti-Hindi Agitations), Valanarasu Press, Madras.

Chinnasami (1993), *Anna: Oru Sariththiram* (Anna: A Biography), Madras.

Chittibabu, C. (1975), *Thi. Mu. Ka. Varalaaru, 1949–67* (A History of the DMK, 1949–67), DMK Arivagam, Madras.

D.M.K. (Dravida Munnetra Kazhagam) (1957, 1962, 1967, 1971, 1977, 1980, 1984, 1989), *Therthal Veliyeedu* (Election Manifestoes), Madras.

Ilanchezhian, Ma. (1986), *Tamizhan Toduththa Por: Mudhal Indhi Ethirppu Poratta Varalaru* (The Battle Waged by the Tamil: An Account of the First Anti-Hindi Agitation), Periar Self Respect Organisation, Madras.

Iraiyan, A. (1981), *Suyamariyathai Sudarolikal* (Major Figures of the Self Respect Movement), Arivukkadal Achagam, Madras.

Jeyakanthan, Tha. (1973), *Or Ilakkiyavaathiyin Araciyal Anubavankal* (The Political Experiences of a Litterateur), Madras.

———— (1986), *Sinimaavukkup Pona Siththaal* (A Construction Worker at the Movies), Madras.

Kannadasan, Kavignar (1972), *Vanavaasam* (Life in the Jungle—a defector's account of his experiences in the DMK), Paari, Madras.

Karunanidhi, Mu. (1985), *Ore Raththam* (Novel), Paari, Madras.

———— (1986), *Nenjukku Neethi* (Justice for the Heart—A Political Autobiography), vol. I-II, Paari, Madras.

———— (1987), *Kalaignarin Kadithangal* (The Letters of Kalaignar—Karunanidhi's editorials in *Murasoli*), Paari, Madras.

———— (1988), *Aaru Mathak Kadunkaaval* (Six Months of Rigourous Imprisonment), Paari, Madras.

Kuttooci Guruswami Ninaivu Malar (1966), (Kuttoci Guruswami Commemoration Volume), Madras.

Maraimalaiyan, A. (1967), *Perarignar Annavin Peruvazhvu* (The Great Life of Anna the Wise), Madras.

Maran, Murasoli (1962), *Yen Vendum Inba Dravidam?* (Why We Need Sweet Dravida Nadu), Madras.

———— (1974), *Maanila Suyatchi* (State Autonomy), Madras.

Parthasarathi, T. M. (1961), *Thi. Mu. Ka. Varalaaru* (History of the DMK), Paari Nilayam, Madras.

Ponneelan (1974), *Jeevaavin Vaazhkkai Varalaaru* (Biography of P. Jeevanandam), New Century Book House, Madras.

Ramachandran, M. G. (1971), 'Naan Yen Piranthen?' (What I was Born to Achieve), *Ananda Vikatan*, part 69, 1 August.

Ramamurthi, P. (1983), *Ariya Mayaiya? Dravida Mayaiya? Viduthalaipporum Dravida Iyakkamum* (Aryan Mystification or Dravidian Illusion? The Freedom Struggle and the Dravidian Movement), Pazhaniyappa Bros., Madras.

Ramanathan, S. (1967), 'Periyar Iyakkam' (Periar's Movement), *Periyar's 89th Birthday Commemoration Souvenir*, Madras.

Ramaswami Naicker, E. V. (1937), *Indhiya Oru Nationa?* (Is India a Nation?), Pakutharivu Pathippakam, Madras.

———— (1947), *Ina Izhivu Ozhiya Islame Nanmarunthu* (Islam Alone is the Right Remedy for Communal Degradation), Pakutharivu Pathippakam, Madras.

———— (1949), *Arivin Yellai* (The Bounds of Knowledge: An Anthology of Periar's Writings), Viduthalai Press, Madras.

———— (1975), *Suyamariyathai Iyakkaththai Thotruviththathen?* (Why was the Self Respect Movement Founded?), Arivukkadal Achagam, Madras.

———— (1982a), *Needhi Kettathu Yaaraal?* (Who Subverted Justice?), Arivukkadal Achagam, Madras.

———— (1982b), *Samudhaya Seerthiruththam* (Social Reform), Arivukkadal Achagam, Madras.

———— (1982c), *Dravida Thozhilalar Kazhagam Yen?* (Why the Dravidian Workers Federation?), Arivukkadal Achagam, Madras.

———— (1983f), *Thanthai Periyar Avarkalin Ilangai Perurai* (Periar's Speech in Sri Lanka), Arivukkadal Achagam, Madras.

———— (1984a), *Materialism Allathu Prakrithivaatham* (Materialism), Arivukkadal Achagam, Madras.

———— (1984b), *Thanthai Periyar Avarkalin Kudanthai Perurai* (Periar's Speech at Kumbakonam), Arivukkadal Achagam, Madras.

———— (1985a), *Kadavul Oru Karppanaiye* (God is But a Myth), Arivukkadal Achagam, Madras.

———— (1985b), *Manu Needhi: Oru Kulaththukku Oru Needhi* (Manu's Laws: Different Rules for Each Caste), Arivukkadal Achagam, Madras.

———— (1985c), *Purattu, Imaalaya Purattu* (Himalayan Obfuscation), Arivukkadal Achagam, Madras.

———— (1987a), *Indhu Madha Pandikaikal* (Hindu Festivals), Arivukkadal Achagam, Madras.

———— (1987b), *Ramayana Paaththirangal* (Characters in the Ramayana), Arivukkadal Achagam, Madras.

———— (1987c), *Theendamaiyai Ozhiththathu Yar?* (Who Abolished Untouchability?), Arivukkadal Achagam, Madras.

———— (1987d), *Thanthai Periyarin Iruthi Perurai* (Periar's Last Speech), 19 December 1973, Arivukkadal Achagam, Madras.

———— (1987e), *Theendaamai: Vaikom Iyakka Varalaaru* (Untouchability: An Account of the Vaikom Agitation), Arivukkadal Achagam, Madras.

———— (1987f), *Inivarum Ulagam* (The World in the Future), Pakutharivu Pathipakkam, Madras.

———— (1987g), *Thathuva Vilakkam* (Exposition of Principles), Pakutharivu Pathipakkam, Madras.

———— (1987h), *Pon Mozhikal* (Wise Sayings), Pakutharivu Pathipakkam, Madras.

———— (1987i), *Ramayana Kurippukal* (Notes on the Ramayana), Pakutharivu Pathipakkam, Madras.

———— (1987j), *Pen Yen Adimaianaal?* (Why Was Woman Enslaved?), Pakutharivu Pathipakkam, Madras.

Sathyavani Muthu (1981), *Yenathu Poraattam* (My Struggle), Sezhiyan, Madras.

Selvaraji, Kazhinjoor (ed.) (1986), *Ezhuththulaka Mannan Kuththooci Guruswami Sinthanaikal* (Thoughts of the Great Writer, Kuththooci Guruswami), 2 vols, Madras.

Sithambaranar, Sami (1983), *Thamizhar Thalaivar* (Leader of the Tamils), Erode, Madras.

Sivagnanam, Ma. Po., *Tamizh Naattil Viduthalaipporin Varalaru* (A History of the Freedom Struggle in Tamil Nadu), 2 vols, Paari Nilayam, Madras.

———— (1986), *Tamizhagam Thonriya Veera Varalaaru* (The Brave History of the Birth of Tamil Nadu), Paari, Madras.

Somayajulu, N. (1982), *Tirunelveli Maavattathil Viduthalaippor* (The Freedom Struggle in Tirunelveli District), VOC Press, Tuticorin.

Sthaapanak Kaangirasu Therthal Veliyeedu (1971), (Congress-O Election Manifesto), Madras.

Subbiah, Rama (1985), *Naanum En Diravada Iyakka Ninaivukalum* (Me and My Memories of the Dravidian Movement), Kanimuthu Pathippakam, Madras.

Suddhanandha Bharathi, Yogi Sri, *Viravilakku Va. Ve. Su. Iyer* (Va. Ve. Su. Iyer—Biography).

Thangam Pillai, S. (1975), *Kannadiyan Kaalvay Neerpaaychchal* (Irrigation from the Kannadian Channel), Ambasamudram.

Veeramani, K. (1985), *Diravida Iyakkam: Unmai Varalaaru* (The Dravidian Movement: The True History), Arivukkadal Achagam, Madras.

Veerayyan, Ko. (1980), *Tamizh Naattil Vivasaayigal Poraattam* (Peasant Struggles in Tamil Nadu), Theekkathir Press, Madurai.

OTHER MATERIAL ON INDIA IN ENGLISH

Ambedkar, B. R. (1945), *What Congress and Gandhi Have Done to the Untouchables*, Thacker & Co., Bombay.

Anderson, W. and S. Damle (1987), *The Brotherhood in Saffron: The Rashtriya Swayamsevak Sangh and Hindu Revivalism*, Westview, Boulder, Colorado.

Baruah, S. (1986), 'Immigration, Ethnic Conflict and Political Turmoil—Assam, 1979–85', *Asian Survey*, vol. 26 (November), pp 1184–206.

————— (1994), 'Ethnic Conflict as State-Society Struggle: The Poetics and Politics of Assamese Micro-Nationalism', *Modern Asian Studies*, vol. 28 (July), pp 649–71.

Basham, A. L. (1959), *The Wonder that was India: A Survey of the Culture of the Indian Sub-continent Before the Coming of the Muslims*, Grove Press, New York.

Basu, T., P. K. Datta, S. Sarkar, T. Sarkar and S. Sen (1993), *Khaki Shorts and Saffron Flags: A Critique of the Hindu Right*, Orient Longman, New Delhi.

Beteille, A. (1974), *Studies in Agrarian Social Structure*, Oxford University Press, Delhi.

Blackburn, S. H. and A. K. Ramanujam (eds) (1986), *Another Harmony: New Essays on the Folklore of India*, Oxford University Press.

Brass, T. (1994), 'Introduction: The New Farmers' Movements in India', *Journal of Peasant Studies*, vol. 21, nos 3–4 (April–July), pp 3–26.

Chatterjee, P. (1986), *Nationalist Thought and the Colonial World: A Derivative Discourse?*, Zed, London.

Dasgupata, J. (1970), *Language Conflict and National Development; Group Politics and National Language Policy in India*, University of California Press.

Derrett, J. D. M. (1963), *Introduction to Modern Hindu Law*, Oxford University Press.

————— (1968), *Religion, Law and the State in India*, Faber, London.

DeWit, J. (1988), 'Slum Clearance and Housing Construction in Bombay and Madras' (mimeo).

Dharma Kumar (1965), *Land and Caste in South India: Agricultural Labour in the Madras Presidency During the Nineteenth Century*, Cambridge University Press.

Diehl, A. (1978), *Periyar E. V. Ramaswami: A Study of the Influence of Personality in Contemporary South India*, B. I. Publications, Delhi.

Dumont, L. (1970), *Homo Hierarchicus: An Essay on the Caste System*, University of Chicago Press.

————— (1971), *Religion, Politics and History of India; Collected Papers in Indian Sociology*, Mouton, Paris.

————— (1983), *Affinity as a Value: Marriage Alliance in South India, With Comparative Essays on Australia*, University of Chicago Press.

Fic, V. M. (1969), *Peaceful Transition to Communism in India: The Strategy of the Communist Party*, Nachiketa, Bombay.

————— (1970), *Kerala, Yenan of India: Rise of Communist Power, 1937 to 1969*, Nachiketa, Bombay.

Fickett, L. P. (1976), *The Major Socialist Parties of India: A Study in Leftist Fragmentation*, Maxwell School of Citizenship & Politics, Syracuse.

Franda, M. (1971), *Radical Politics in West Bengal*, M. I. T. Press.

Frankel, F. R. (1978), *India's Political Economy, 1947–77: The Grandual Revolution*, Princeton University Press.

Galanter, M. (1984), *Competing Equalities: Law and the Backward Classes in India*, Oxford University Press, Delhi.

———— (1989), *Law and Society in Modern India*, Oxford University Press, New York.

Gandhi, M. K. (1946), *Hind Swaraj or Indian Home Rule*, Navajivan Publishing House, Ahmedabad.

———— (1950), *Hindu Dharma*, Navajivan Publishing House, Ahmedabad.

Ganguly, S. (1997), *The Crisis in Kashmir: Portents of War, Hopes of Peace*, Cambridge University Press.

Herring, R. (1983), *Land to the Tiller: The Political Economy of Agrarian Reform in South Asia*, Yale University Press.

Jaffrelot, C. (1996), *The Hindu Nationalist Movement in India*, Columbia University Press, New York.

Jalal, A. (1995), *Democracy and Authoritarianism in South Asia: A Comparative and Historical Perspective*, Cambridge University Press.

Jeffrey, R. (1976), *The Decline of Nayar Dominance: Society and Politics in Travancore, 1847–1908*, University of Sussex Press.

Jones, K. (1989), *Socio-Religious Reform Movements in British India*, Cambridge University Press.

Kakkar, S. (1989), *Intimate Relations: Exploring Indian Sexuality*, Viking, New Delhi.

Kohli, A. (1990), *Democracy and Discontent: India's Growing Crisis of Governability*, Cambridge University Press.

———— (1997), 'Can Democracies Accommodate Ethnic Nationalism: The Rise and Decline of Self Determination Movements', *The Journal of Asian Studies*, vol. 56, no. 2 (May), pp 325–44.

Low, D. A. (ed.) (1977), *Congress and the Raj: Facets of the Indian Struggle, 1917–47*, Arnold-Heinemann, London.

Madan, T. N. (1987), 'Secularism in its Place', *The Journal of Asian Studies*, vol. 46, no. 4, pp 747–59.

Mohan Ram (1969), *Indian Communism: Split Within a Split*, Vikas, Delhi.

Nehru, J. (1989a), *The Discovery of India*, Oxford University Press, Delhi.

———— (1989b), *Glimpses of World History*, Oxford University Press, Delhi.

Nossiter, T. J. (1982), *Communism in Kerala*, Oxford University Press, Delhi.

———— (1988), *Marxist State Governments in India*, F. Pinter, London.

Oberoi, H. (1994), *The Construction of Religious Boundaries: Culture, Identity and Diversity in the Sikh Tradition*, University of Chicago Press.

O'Hanlon, R. (1985), *Caste, Conflict, and Ideology: Mahatma Jotirao Phule and Low Caste Protest in Nineteenth Century Western India*, Cambridge University Press, New York.

Omvedt, G. (1976), *Cultural Revolt in a Colonial Society: The Non-Brahman Movement in Western India, 1873 to 1930*, Scientific Socialist Education Trust, Bombay.

Pandey, G. (1978), *The Ascendancy of the Congress in Uttar Pradesh, 1926–34: A Study in Imperfect Mobilization*, Oxford University Press.

——— (1990), *The Construction of Communalism in Colonial North India*, Oxford University Press, Delhi.

Parekh, B. (1989), *Colonialism, Tradition and Reform: An Analysis of Gandhi's Political Discourse*, Sage, New Delhi.

Ramanujan, A. K. (1991), *Folk-Tales from India: A Selection of Oral Tales from Twenty-Two Languages*, Pantheon Books, New York.

Richman, P. (1991), *Many Ramayanas: The Diversity of a Narrative Tradition in South Asia*, University of California Press.

Rudolph, L. I. and S. H. (1967), *The Modernity of Tradition: Political Development in India*, University of Chicago Press.

Sarkar, S. (1983), *Modern India: 1885 to 1947*, Macmillan, Delhi.

Sarkar, T. (1993), 'Women's Agency Within Authoritarian Communalism: Rashtrasevika Samiti and Ram Janmabhoomi', in G. Pandey (ed.), *Hindus and Others: The Question of Identity in India Today*, Viking, New Delhi.

Sengupta, B. (1972), *Communism in Indian Politics*, Columbia University Press.

——— (1980), *The Communist Party of India (Marxist)*, Calcutta.

Sharma, P. K. (1969), *Political Aspects of States Reorganization in India*, Mohini Publications, New Delhi.

Silverberg, J. (ed.) (1968), *Social Mobility in the Caste System in India: An Interdisciplinary Symposium*, Comparative Studies in Society and History Supplement III, Mouton, The Hague.

Smith, D. E. (1963), *India as a Secular State*, Princeton University Press.

Srinivas, M. N. (1962), *Caste in Modern India and Other Essays*, Asia Publishing House, New York.

Stein, B. (ed.) (1978), *South Indian Temples: An Analytical Reconsideration*, Vikas, New Delhi.

Subramaniam, C. (1978), *Speech on Language Policy*, Bharatiya Vidya Bhavan, Bombay.

Thapar, R. (1987), *Cultural Transaction in Early India: Tradition and Patronage*, Oxford University Press, Delhi.

——— (1989), 'Imagined Religious Communities? Ancient History and the Modern Search for a Hindu Identity', *Modern Asian Studies*, vol. 23, no. 2, pp 209–31.

Thomas, R. G. C. (ed.) (1992), *Perspectives on Kashmir: The Roots of Conflict in South Asia*, Westview, Boulder, Colorado.

Van Der Veer, P. (1991), *Religious Nationalism: Hindus and Muslims in India Today*, University of California Press.

Walch, J. C. (1976), *Faction and Front: Party Systems in South India*, Young Asia Publications, New Delhi.

Washbrook, D. A. (1981), 'Law, State and Agrarian Society in Colonial India', *Modern Asian Studies*, vol. 15, no. 3, pp 649–721.

Weiner, M. (1962), *The Politics of Scarcity: Public Pressure and Political Response in India*, University of Chicago Press.

———— (1967), *Party Building in a New Nation: The Indian National Congress*, University of Chicago Press.

Weiner, M. and J. O. Field (eds) (1975), *Electoral Politics in the Indian States*, Manohar, Delhi.

Weiner, M. (1989), *The Indian Paradox: Essays in Indian Politics*, Sage, Delhi.

Zachariah, M. and R. Sooryamoorthy (1994), *Science for Social Revolution? Achievements and Dilemmas of a Development Movement: The Kerala Sastra Sahitya Parishad*, Vistaar Publications, New Delhi.

THEORETICAL AND COMPARATIVE LITERATURE

Abercrombie, N., S. Hill and B. Turner (1980), *The Dominant Ideology Thesis*, Allen & Unwin, London.

Allcock, J. C. (1971), 'Populism: A Brief Biography', *Sociology*, vol. 5 (September), pp 371–87.

Anderson, B. (1983), *Imagined Communities: Reflections on the Origins and Spread of Nationality*, Verso, London.

Banks, M. (1996), *Ethnicity: Anthropological Constructions*, Routledge, New York.

Banton, M. (1983), *Racial and Ethnic Competition*, Cambridge University Press.

Barnes, S. (1977), *Representation in Italy: Institutionalized Tradition and Electoral Choice*, University of Chicago Press.

Barth, F. (ed.) (1969), *Ethnic Groups and Boundaries: The Social Organization of Culture Difference*, Little Brown, Boston.

———— (1981), *Process and Form in Social Life: Selected Essays of Frederik Barth*, vol. I, Routledge & Kegan Paul, London.

Basurto (1982), 'A Case of Late Populism: Mexico Under Echeverria', in M. Conniff (ed.), *Latin American Populism in Comparative Perspective*, University of New Mexico Press, Albuquerque.

Bell, J. D. (1977), *Peasants in Power: Alexander Stamboliiski and the Bulgarian Agrarian National Union, 1899–1923*, Princeton University Press.

Berger, S. (1987), 'Religion and the Transformation of Politics', in C. Maier (ed.), *The Changing Boundaries of the Political: Essays on the Evolving Balance Between the State and Society, Public and Private in Europe*, Cambridge University Press.

Billig, M. (1976), *Social Psychology and Intergroup Relations*, Academic Press, London.

Blackmer, D. L. M. and S. Tarrow (eds) (1975), *Communism in Italy and France*, Princeton University Press.

Borges, J. L. (1981), *Borges: A Reader*, Emir Rodriguez Monegal and Alastair Reed (ed.), Dutton, New York.

Brass, P. (1991), *Ethnicity and Nationalism: Theory and Comparison*, Sage, New Delhi.

Bratton, M. (1994), 'Peasant-State Relations in Postcolonial Africa: Patterns of Engagement and Disengagement', in J. S. Migdal, A. Kohli and V. Shue (eds), *State Power and Social Forces*, Cambridge University Press.

Brecht, B. (1964), *Brecht on Theatre: The Development of an Aesthetic*, Eyre Metheun, London.

Buchheit, L. C. (1978), *Secession: The Legitimacy of Self-Determination*, Yale University Press.

Chang-Rodriguez, E. and R. G. Hellman (eds) (1988), *APRA and the Democratic Challenge in Peru*, Bildner Center for Western Hemisphere Studies, New York.

Chubb, J. (1982), *Patronage, Power and Poverty in Southern Italy: A Tale of Two Cities*, Cambridge University Press.

Collier, R. B. and D. (1991), *Shaping the Political Arena: Critical Junctures, the Labor Movement, and Regime Dynamics in Latin America*, Princeton University Press.

Coniff, M. (ed.) (1982), *Latin American Populism in Comparative Perspective*, University of New Mexico Press, Albuqurque.

Connor, W. (1984), *The National Question in Marxist-Leninist Theory and Strategy*, Princeton University Press.

Dahl, R. (1982), *Dilemmas of Pluralist Democracy: Autonomy Versus Control*, Yale University Press.

Deats, R. L. (1968), *Nationalism and Christianity in the Philippines*, Southern Methodist University Press, Dallas.

de la Torre, C. (1992), 'The Ambiguous Meanings of Latin American Populisms', *Social Research*, 59, no. 2 (summer), pp 385–414.

di Tella, T. S. (1990), 'Menem's Argentina', *Government and Opposition*, vol. 25 (Winter), pp 85–97.

Dirks, N. B. (ed.) (1992), *Colonialism and Culture*, The Comparative Studies in Society & History Book Series, University of Michigan Press.

Eisenstadt, S. N. and R. Lemarchand (eds) (1981), *Political Clientelism, Patronage and Development*, Sage, Beverly Hills.

Esping-Andersen, G. (1990), *The Three Worlds of Welfare Capitalism*, Princeton University Press.

Fishman, J. A. (1988), 'Nationality-Nationalism and Nation-Nationalism', in Fishman et al. (eds), *Language Problems of Developing Nations*, John Wiley, New York.

Fox, J. (1994), 'The Difficult Transition from Clientelism to Citizenship: Lessons from Mexico', *World Politics*, 46, no. 2 (January), pp 151–84.

Germani, G. (1978), *Authoritarianism, Fascism and National Populism*, Transaction Books, New Brunswick, New Jersey.

Goodwyn, L. (1976), *Democratic Promise: The Populist Moment in America*, Oxford University Press, New York.

Gramsci, A. (1985), *Selections from Cultural Writings*, Lawrence & Wishart, London.

———— (1992), *Prison Notebooks*, Columbia University Press.

Harbeson, J. W., D. Rothchild and N. Chazan (eds) (1994), *Civil Society and the State in Africa*, Lynne Riener, Boulder, Colorado.

Hobsbawm, E. J. and T. Ranger (eds) (1983), *The Invention of Tradition*, Cambridge University Press.

Hofstadter, R. (1955), *The Age of Reform: From Bryan to F. D. R.*, Vintage Books, New York.

Horowitz, D. L. (1985), *Ethic Groups in Conflict*, University of California Press.

Jackson, R. H. and C. G. Rosberg (1982), *Personal Rule in Black Africa: Prince, Autocrat, Prophet, Tyrant*, University of California Press.

James, D. (1988), *Resistance and Integration: Peronism and the Argentine Working Class, 1946–76*, Cambridge University Press.

Kenworthy, E. (1973), 'The Function of the Little-Known Case in Theory Formation or What Peronism Wasn't', *Comparative Politics* (October), pp 17–45.

Key, V. O. (1949), *Southern Politics in State and Nation*, Alfred A. Knopf, New York.

Kornhauser, W. (1959), *The Politics of Mass Society*, Free Press, New York.

Juergensmeyer, M. (1993), *The New Cold War?: Religious Nationalism Confronts the Secular State*, University of California Press.

Laclau, E. (1977), *Politics and Ideology in Marxist Theory: Capitalism, Fascism and Populism*, New Left Books, London.

Laitin, D. (1986), *Hegemony and Culture: Politics and Religious Change Among the Yoruba*, University of Chicago Press.

———— (1992), *Language Repertoires and State Construction in Africa*, Cambridge University Press.

Levine, D. (ed.) (1986), *Religion and Political Conflict in Latin America*, University of North Carolina Press.

Lijphart, A. (1977), *Democracy in Plural Societies: A Comparative Exploration*, Yale University Press.

———— (1996), 'The Puzzle of Indian Democracy: A Consociational Interpretation', *American Political Science Review*, vol. 90 (June), pp 258–68.

Lipset, S. M. and S. Rokkan (eds) (1967), *Party Systems and Voter Alignments: Cross-National Perspectives*, Free Press, New York.

Lyrintzis, C. (1983), *Between Socialism and Populism: The Rise of the Panhellenic Socialist Movement (PASOK)*, Ph. D. dissertation, London School of Economics.

———— (1987), 'The Power of Populism: The Greek Case', *European Journal of Political Research*, vol. 15, pp 667–86.

Madsen, D. and P. G. Snow (1991), *The Charismatic Bond: Political Behavior in Time of Crisis*, Harvard University Press.

Martin, D. A. (1979), *A General Theory of Secularization*, Harper & Row, New York.

Marty, M. and S. Appleby (eds) (1991), *Fundamentalisms Observed*, University of Chicago Press.

Marx, K. (1977), *The Eighteenth Brumaire of Louis Bonaparte*, International Publishing, New York.

McClintock, C. (1989), 'Peru: Precarious Regimes, Authoritarian and Democratic', in L. Diamond, J. Linz and S. M. Lipset (eds), *Democracy in Developing Countries*, vol. IV, Lynne Rienner, Boulder, Colorado.

Meinecke, F. (1970), *Cosmopolitanism and the National State*, Princeton University Press.

Migdal, J. (1974), *Peasants, Politics, and Revolution: Pressures Toward Political and Social Change in the Third World*, Princeton University Press.

Mouzelis, N. (1986), *Politics in the Semi-Periphery: Early Parliamentarism and Late Industrialization in the Balkans and Latin America*, Macmillan, London.

Paige, J. (1975), *Agrarian Revolution: Social Movements and Export Agriculture in the Underdeveloped World*, Free Press, New York.

Perry, E. (1980), *Rebels and Revolutionaries in North China, 1845–1945*, Stanford University Press.

Pike, F. B. (1986), *The Politics of the Miraculous in Peru: Haya de la Torre and the Spiritualist Tradition*, University of Nebraska Press.

Putnam, R. (1993), *Making Democracies Work: Civic Traditions in Modern Italy*, Princeton University Press.

Roberts, K. M. (1995), 'NeoLiberalism and the Transformation of Populism in Latin America: The Peruvian Case', *World Politics*, vol. 48 (October), pp 82–116.

Rueschemeyer, D., P. Evans and T. Skocpol (eds) (1985), *Bringing the State Back In*, Cambridge University Press.

Schmidt, S. W., L. Guasti, C. H. Lande and J. C. Scott (eds) (1977), *Friends, Followers and Factions: A Reader in Political Clientelism*, University of California Press.

Schmitter, P. C. and T. L. Karl (1991), 'What Democracy is...And is Not', *Journal of Democracy*, vol. 2, no. 3 (Summer), pp 75–88.

Schmitter, P. C. (1992), 'The Consolidation of Democracy and Representation of Social Groups', *American Behavioral Scientist*, vol. 35, nos 4/5 (March–June), pp 422–49.

Schoultz, L. (1983), *The Populist Challenge: Argentine Electoral Behavior in the Post War Era*, University of North Carolina Press, Chapel Hill.

Scott, J. C. (1976), *The Moral Economy of the Peasant: Rebellion and Subsistence in Southeast Asia*, Yale University Press.

Sen, A. K. (1984), *Resources, Values and Development*, Harvard University Press.

Shils, E. (1972), *The Intellectuals and the Powers and Other Essays*, University of Chicago Press.

Smelser, N. (1962), *Theory of Collective Behavior*, Free Press, New York.

Sontag, S. (1980), *Under the Sign of Saturn*, Farrar, Straus & Giroux, New York.

Sowell, T. (1990), *Preferential Policies: An International Perspective*, William Morrow & Co., New York.

Stein, S. (1980), *Populism in Peru: The Emergence of the Masses and the Politics of Social Control*, University of Wisconsin Press.

Tajfel, H. (ed.) (1982), *Social Identity and Intergroup Relations*, Cambridge University Press.

Tambiah, S. J. (1986), *Sri Lanka: Ethnic Fratricide and the Dismantling of Democracy*, University of Chicago Press.

————— (1992), *Buddhism Betrayed? Religion Politics and Violence in Sri Lanka*, University of Chicago Press.

Tilly, C. (1978), *From Mobilization to Revolution*, Addison-Wesley, Reading, Massachusetts.

Turner, V. (1969), *The Ritual Process: Structure and Anti-Structure*, Aldine Publishing Co., Chicago.

Weber, M. (1958), *The Religion of India: The Sociology of Hinduism and Buddhism*, Glencoe, New York.

————— (1978), *Economy and Society: An Outline of Interpretive Sociology*, University of California Press.

Wolf, E. (1969), *Peasant Wars in the Twentieth Century*, Harper & Row, New York.

Zald, M. and J. McCarthy (1987), *Social Movements in an Organizational Society: Collected Essays*, Transaction Books, New Brunswick, New Jersey.

INTERVIEWS

The list of interviews is arranged accoding to the case to which the interview pertained and the party affiliation, if any, of the interviewee. Interviewees who were in different parties are listed under the party(ies) about whose experience they provided much information.

General

These interviews were conducted in Madras unless otherwise stated.

DK and Its Precursors

Ki. A. Pe. Viswanatham (Tiruchi); Lakshmikantha Bharathi; K. Veeramani; 'Tiruvarur' Thangarasu; 'Nagai' Kaliappan (Madras, Madukkur); 'Nagai' K. Murugesan; 'Naathikam' Ramaswami; A. S. Venu; 'Kuruvikkarambai' Velu; N. D. Sundaravadivelu; Ka. Ma. Kuppuswami (Vallam); Devasagayam (Lalgudi).

DMK

V. R. Nedunchezhian; Sathyavani Muthu; K. Anbazhagan; 'Murasoli' Maran; K. A. Krishnaswamy; Era. Sezhiyan; M. P. Subramaniam; R. M. Veerappan; S. D. Somasundaram; L. Ganesan; 'Senji' N. Ramachandran; 'Veerapandi' S. Arumugam; 'Pulavar' K. Govindan; O. P. Raman; 'Panruti' S. Ramachandran; C. V. M. Annamalai; K. Appadurai; Alamelu Appadurai; Durai Murugan; K. Kalimuthu; Raja Mohammad; Rahman Khan; Ko. Si. Mani (Kumbakonam); Vai. Gopalswami; S. Madhavan; K. Rajaram; K. Raghavanadam; P. U. Shanmugam; Rama. Arangannal; 'Kovai' Sezhiyan; T. K. Ponnuvelu; Vallimuthu (Kovilpatti); Aladi Aruna; S. S. Thennarasu; Sulochana Sampath; Kuppuswami; Sa. Ganesan; Viduthalaivirumbi; Tirunavukkarasu; Velur Narayanan; N. V. N. Somu; P. A. K. Palaniswami; 'Kavignar' Kudi Arasu; S. V. Sargunam; G. R. Edmund; K. Arivazhagan; Rama. Subbiah.

ADMK

R. M. Veerappan; V. R. Nedunchezhian; Sathyavani Muthu; K. A. Krishnaswamy; K. Raghavanandam; S. Madhavan; S. D. Somasundaram; K. Rajaram; P. U. Shanmugam; G. Viswanathan; 'Panruti' S. Ramachandran; J. C. D. Prabhakaran; Velur Narayanan; K. Kalimuthu; H. V. Hande; Raja Mohammad; Azhagu Tirunavukkarasu (Idamelayur); V. P. Balasubramaniam (Dindigul); P. H. Pandian; Aladi Aruna; G. R. Edmund; Vallimuthu (Kovilpatti); Kuzha. Chelliah; Madhusoodhanan; L. Perumal; N. V. N. Selvam; B. Valarmathi; R. D. Seethapathi; Sulochana Sampath; Alamelu Appadurai.

Congress

C. Subramaniam; G. Karuppiah Moopanar; M. P. Subramaniam; 'Vazhappadi' K. Ramamurthi; A. Chellapandian; A. Chengalvorayan; N. Somayajulu; Ilayaperumal; P. Nedumaran; A. R. Marimuthu; A. N. Sivaraman; M. K. T. Subramaniam; N. M. Mani Varma; 'Naathikam' Ramaswami; 'Sivaji' Ganesan; Ma. Po. Sivagnanam; Dr. Sowrirajan.

CPI

P. Manickam; A. Srinivasan; K. Murugaiyan (Thanjavur); R. V. Ananthakrishnan (Vikramasingapuram); C. S. Subrahmanyam.

CPI-M

A. Nallasivan; G. Veerayyan; K. Ramani (Coimbatore).

Socialists

S. C. C. Anthony Pillai; A. R. Marimuthu.

Muslim League

Abdul Latheef; 'Chengam' Jabbar.

Tamil Arasu Kazhagam

Ma. Po. Sivagnanam.

Republican Parties

Moorthy; Tirunavukkarasu; Seppan; Bhim Rao.

Caste and Farmers' Associations, Independent Trade Unions

K. Nagaimugan; K. Ramadas; Subramaniam; 'Kathadi' Kuppuswami; V. Ramanibai; 'Kovai' Sezhiyan; Sivaswamy (Thondamuthur); Renu (Tiruvannamalai); Kuchelar.

General

K. S. Ramanjam; Rama. Subramaniam (Thanjavur); Vridhachalam (Karanthattankudi).

Interviews Pertaining to Case Studies

Mannargudi

DK

R. P. Sarangan, K. Nallathambi (Mannargudi); Aa. Subramaniam, Venkatesan (Nidamangalam); Balasubramaniam (Madukkur); Narayana Asari (Kottur).

DMK

'Mannai' P. Narayanaswami, 'Ullikottai' Arunachalam, Ku. Balakrishnan, Pazha. Balasubramaniam, K. Ramachandran (Mannargudi); 'Sithamalli' N. Somasundaram, S. S. Nathan, Krishnan (Nidamangalam); 'Mundasu' Natarajan (Kumbakonam); Samad (Kuthanallur); A. K. Subbiah (Sithamalli).

ADMK

M. Manimaran, S. Gnanasekaran, Gnanasundaram (Mannargudi); Mahalingam (Nemmeli—Adichapuram); Azhagu Tirunavukkarasu (Idamelayur); Aa. Subramaniam (Nidamangalam).

Congress

Siva. Rajamanickam, Kakkaji, Singaravelu Udayar (Mannargudi); Swaminatha Udayar (Kumbakonam); 'Kombur' Venkatesan (Kombur); Sivanandan Saluvar (Idamelayur); K. S. Ramaswamy (son of Kunniyur Sambasiva Iyer—Madras).

CPI

P. Venkatesa Solagar, Amirthalingam Pillai, P. Thangavelu, M. Selvaraj, 'Vakkottai' S. Murugayyan, Duraiarasan, Ambikapathi (Mannargudi); A. K. Subbiah (Perugavazhndan—Sithamalli); V. Rangaraj (Kottur).

CPI-M

N. Govindarajan, K. Natarajan (Mannargudi); Soma. Tamilarvan, A. Thangavelu (Nidamangalam).

General

Nadanam (journalist), K. S. Rajagopala Mudaliar, K. R. Santhankrishnan (Mannargudi); Sigamani Vaniar (Adichapuram: Paddy Producers' Association & Farmers' Association); Velu Nair (Nidamangalam: retired journalist).

THANJAVUR DISTRICT (BACKDROP TO MANNARGUDI)

DK

'Tiruvarur' Thangarasu (Madras); Nagai Kaliappan (Madras, Madukkur); Tirumangalakkudi Ku. Govindarajan (Kumbakonam); P. Sivasankaran, Rangaraj, 'Kavalakkudi' Marimuthu, Thangaraj, V. Subramaniam, Neikuppai Ganesan, S. S. Maniam, Kamaraj, Malliam Kannayyan (Tiruvarur); Ka. Ma. Kuppusamy (Vallam); Thangarasu (Rajagiri); S. S. Batcha (Nagaipattinam); G. N. Sami (Darasuram); Pulavanjiyar (Madukkur); Tiriloki Govindarajan (Tiruppanandal); R. Rathnagiri (Thanjavur).

DMK

L. Ganesan (Madras); Manikkavasagam, T. S. Ramalingam, Pazhani Manickam, A. V. Pathi (Thanjavur); Ko. Si. Mani, S. Padmanabhan, Ku. Si. Krishnamurthi, Durai (Kumbakonam).

ADMK

S. D. Somasundaram, Kuzha. Chelliah (Madras); Ko. Vi. Narayanaswami (Kumbakonam); S. S. Mani (Thanjavur).

Congress

G. Karuppiah Moopanar, A. R. Marimuthu (Madras); Ramamirtha Tondaman (Tattuvancheri); S. Singaravadivelu (Thanjavur).

CPI

K. Murugayyan (Thanjavur).

CPI-M

G. Veerayyan (Madras); A. Natarajan (Kumbakonam).

General

Pirai. Arivazhagan, Saravana Tamizhan (Tiruvarur); K. Karuppannan (Kumbakonam); Rama. Sundaram, Rathnam (Thanjavur); Vridhachalam (Karanthattankudi).

SERMADEVI

DK

T. M. Peer Mohammad, Ilango (Kallidaikurichi); Panneerselvam (Tirunelveli).

DMK

Vai. Gopalswami (Madras); M. S. Sivaswani (Tuticorin); 'Pathamadai' Paramasivam (Pathamadai); Dr. R. V. Chockalingam, 'Nellai' Buhari, A. L. Subramaniam, Majeed (Tirunelveli); K. S. Subramaniam, Thara Nagore Mohideen (Kallidaikurichi); Shanmugam Pillai, Isaki Pandian (Ambasamudram); D. S. A. Sivaprakasam, Ma. Su. Muthu Kutty (Mukkoodal); P. Azhagiya Nambi (Palayamcottai); K. V. Thevan, Ku. Ve. Lakshmanan (Veeravanallur).

ADMK

P. H. Pandian, Aladi Aruna, G. R. Edmund, 'Nellai' Veerabahu (Madras); Vallimuthu (Kovilpatti); V. Karuppuswami Pandian, P. Ilamathi, M. M. Mohideen (Tirunelveli); T. P. S. H. Amarnath Prabhakar (Mukkoodal); 'Kooniyur' Madasami, Sivan Pandian (Sermadevi); S. Sethuramasubramaniam (Pappakudi); Radha (Veeravanallur).

Congress

A. N. Sivaraman, 'Kumari' Anandan, C. Hariharasubramania Iyer (Madras); Chellapandian, N. Somayajulu, K. S. Rajagopal, M. S. T. Muthiah (Tirunelveli); Dhanushkodi Adityan, S. Swaminathan (Palayamcottai); M. S. Selvaraj (Arumuganeri); S. Thangam Pillai, S. Ananthanarayanan (Kallidaikurichi); A. P. C. V. Chockalingam (Tuticorin); S. S. Rajalinga Raja, Sangamuthu Thevar (Ambasamudram); Ma. Subramaniam, Sankaralinga Adaviyar, Subbiah Adaviyar (Veeravanallur); Krishnaswami Bharathi (Nainaragaram); Gajendra Thevar (Rajakuttralaperi); Rathnasabapathi (Koyiloothu).

Socialists

C. Hariharasubramania Iyer (Madras); M. S. T. Muthiah (Tirunelveli); Subbiah Adaviyar (Veeravanallur).

CPI

V. P. Nayakam (Ambasamudram); R. V. Ananthakrishnan (Vikramasingapuram).

CPI-M

A. Nallasivan (Madras); Sornam/Easwaramoorthy (Sivanthipuram); S. K. Palaniswami (Veeravanallur); Pandian (Tirunelveli).

General

Aa. Sivasubramanian (Tuticorin); M. C. Sankaralingam (Tirunelveli).

DINDIGUL

DK

Jagannathan, Govindammal (widow of M. R. Mathiran Chettiar).

DMK

P. T. R. Palanivel Rajan; S. Kaverimaniam (Madurai); Abdul Samad, Samadharmam, K. Angusami, Oomer Shah, V. S. Lakshmanan, Maya Thevar, Manimaran, O. N. Sivagnanam, M. Basheer Ahmed, G. Lakshmanan, Kepparar, Abdul Razack, Noorjehan Begum, Karuppiah, R. Sanjeevi Rajan, N. Dayanidhi, N. N. Alagar, K. Subban, N. Palanisami, K. Pichai, Mohideen, K. Ramamurthi, R. Alagiriswami, Rathna Kumar, V. Subramaniam, A. Subramaniam (Dindigul).

ADMK

Qadir Shah (Madras); Samadharmam, K. Angusami, V. P. Balasubramaniam, C. Srinivasan, Gopalakrishnan, Sivanath Babu, Jeyaseelan (Dindigul); Rayappan, Sesu, Arokiam (Vellodu); Thulasi (Narasingapuram); Selvaraj (Nallamanayakkanpatti); Raja (Kallipatti).

Congress

K. A. Vasimalai, Raju Naidu, P. V. Das, C. K. C. M. Dulkarnine, Rangasami Reddiar, Dhanasami, Bacha, Subbiah, Rangasami Pillai (Dindigul); Velliah Pillai (Thadicombu).

Janata Dal

Chandran, Hariharan, Johnson (Dindigul).

CPI-M

Charles, S. A. Thangarajan, Kumaravelu, A. Narayanan (Dindigul).

CPI

Madanagopal, Ramasami, A. Chinnasami (Dindigul).

Tamil Arasu Kazhagam

Muthulakkayyan (Dindigul).

TIRUVANNAMALAI

DK

A. M. Muthuswami, B. Neelakantan, B. Vaiyapuri, Tirumalai, Uthirandam Arunachalam (Tiruvannamalai); Dhanakoti Gounder (Tanipadi); Ganapathi, Ramachandran (Tandrambattu); Venkatrama Naidu (Bondai); Balakrishanan (Narayanakuppam).

DMK

S. Murugaiyan, 'Avur' Ramalingam, Azizullah, J. Malik, Murugan, N. Venkatachalam, Qutubuddin, L. Periasami, V. Kumarasamy, D. Venugopal Gounder (Tiruvannamalai); V. A. Krishnan (Vettavalam); C. Kannan (Kilpennathur); Dhanakoti Gounder (Tanipadi); C. Jayaraman, Ramdas (Tandrambattu); K. Manickam (Konalur); Nainar (Somasipadi).

ADMK

P. U. Shanmugam (Madras); V. Pavan Kumar, Pandurangam, E. Va. Velu, Khaleel Pasha, A. P. Kuppuswamy, K. R. Venkatesan (Tiruvannamalai); K. P. Kannan (Kilpennathur); Vijayakumar, Janardhanam, K. Srinivasan (Vettavalam); Dhananjayan (Tandrambattu); Rajamani (Endal); Ramu (Konalur).

Congress

Sivarama Reddiar, T. S. Thirunavukkarasu, K. V. Ghaffar, S. Ramanuja Mudaliar, A. S. Ravindran, Mani Varma, Narayanasami Reddiar, Narayanasami Mudaliar, Natesa Mudaliar, Veeraraghavan, T. N. Kuppusami, S. V. Warisjaan, P. Thandavarayan (Tiruvannamalai); N. C. Ramaswami Gounder (Tandrambattu); Sahadeva Gounder (Edathanoor); D. Pattusami (Madras); Dhanakoti Chettiar (Vettavalam); Venkatachalapathi Chettiar (Tanipadi); R. Devarajan (Vengikal); Kannan (Olappadi).

Janata Dal

S. Govindarajan (Tiruvannamalai).

CPI

T. N. Kuppusami (Tiruvannamalai).

Muslim League

M. B. Chotte Sahib, Basheer (Tiruvannamalai).

Farmers' Association

R. Renu (Tiruvannamalai).

NORTH ARCOT DISTRICT (BACKGROUND TO TIRUVANNAMALAI)

DMK

G. Sami Naidu, Annamalai Gounder, Marappan, N. Sundaram, Muni Chetty, T. S. Kittayyar, Shankar, Dr. M. Krishnan (Tirupattur)

ROYAPURAM

The interviews in this section were conducted in Madras.

DK

Anbukkarazu, 'Lotus' Ramasami.

DMK

V. S. Anandan, P. Ponnurangam, Era. Manoharan, 'Kavignar' Kudi Arasu, P. A. K. Palanisami, S. V. Sargunam, Kapada Raje, Ganesan, 'Kathadi' Kuppusami, N. Vedachalam, Balasubramaniam, Radhakrishanan, Mari, Veeranathan, Mathivanan, M. Pavadaisami, G. Pavadaisami, K. V. Raman, Dayalan, Sethu.

ADMK

Sathyavani Muthu, R. D. Seethapathi, Velur Narayanan, 'Vannai' Mu. Pandian, Madhusoodhanan, N. Vedachalam, Margabanthu, Das.

Congress

Chengalvorayan, Dr. T. Kannan, V. Ramanibai, Aru. Shankar, D. Chandran, Thangaraj, Ananthakrishanan, Ganesan, Munusami Chettiar, D. Arumugam, K. Vaikuntam Chettiar, Chinnavelu Chettiar, Selvam, Gopal, Gregory, K. Ramdas.

Janata Dal

Arumugasami, Mayakrishnan, Thangarajan.

CPI

'Nagai' K. Murugesan, A. Srinivasan, Tha. Pandian, Manickam, 'Russia' Manickam.

CPI-M

S. Veeramani.

Tamil Nadu Toilers' Party

Kulasekaran.

Vanniar Sangam

Durairaj.

NEWSPAPERS AND JOURNALS CONSULTED

English

The Hindu (TH), *The Indian Express* (and Sunday Standard) (IE), *Hindustan Times* (HT), *National Herald* (NH), *The Times of India* (TI), *Frontier Times* (FT), *Bharat Jyoti* (BJ), *The Searchlight* (TS), *Free Press Journal* (FPJ), *Assam Tribune* (AT), *Northern Indian Patrika* (NIP), *Amrita Bazaar Patrika* (ABP), *Hindustan Standard* (HS), *The Madras Mail* (MM), *The Illustrated Weekly of India* (IWI), *India Today* (IT), *The Statesman* (Statesman), *Patriot, Dawn, Motherland, Tribune, Frontline, Aside.*

Tamil

Dinamani (DM), *Nam Nadu* (NN), *Dravida Nadu* (DN), *Kudi Arasu* (KA), *Tamil Arasu* (TA), *Viduthalai, Murasoli, Kilarchchi, Janasakthi, Manram, Kanchi, Kumudham, Ananda Vikatan.*

Name Index

Subject Index